EXAMINATION COPY

Scholarly Resources is pleased to send you this book at no charge for your examination. When you have reached an adoption decision, we request that you complete this brief form and return it to us at the address given below.

Book Title: ____________________

Name: ____________________

Institution: ____________________

Department: ____________________

I am adopting this book for use in:

Course title: ____________________

Term: ____________________ Enrollment: ____________________

_______As a Primary Text _______As a Supplementary Text

_______As Recommended Reading

_______I am not adopting this book for the following reason(s):

Scholarly Resources Inc.
104 Greenhill Avenue • Wilmington, DE 19805-1897
800-772-8937 • 302-654-7713
E-mail: market@scholarly.com • www.scholarly.com
Contact: Toni Moyer, Marketing Manager

The Human Tradition in America

CHARLES W. CALHOUN
Series Editor
Department of History, East Carolina University

The nineteenth-century English author Thomas Carlyle once remarked that "the history of the world is but the biography of great men." This approach to the study of the human past had existed for centuries before Carlyle wrote, and it continued to hold sway among many scholars well into the twentieth century. In more recent times, however, historians have recognized and examined the impact of large, seemingly impersonal forces in the evolution of human history—social and economic developments such as industrialization and urbanization as well as political movements such as nationalism, militarism, and socialism. Yet even as modern scholars seek to explain these wider currents, they have come more and more to realize that such phenomena represent the composite result of countless actions and decisions by untold numbers of individual actors. On another occasion, Carlyle said that "history is the essence of innumerable biographies." In this conception of the past, Carlyle came closer to modern notions that see the lives of all kinds of people, high and low, powerful and weak, known and unknown, as part of the mosaic of human history, each contributing in a large or small way to the unfolding of the human tradition.

This latter idea forms the foundation for this series of books on the human tradition in America. Each volume is devoted to a particular period or topic in American history and each consists of minibiographies of persons whose lives shed light on that period or topic. Well-known figures are not altogether absent, but more often the chapters explore a variety of individuals who may be less conspicuous but whose stories, nonetheless, offer us a window on some aspect of the nation's past.

By bringing the study of history down to the level of the individual, these sketches reveal not only the diversity of the American people and the complexity of their interaction but also some of the commonalities of sentiment and experience that Americans have shared in the evolution of their culture. Our hope is that these explorations of the lives of "real people" will give readers a deeper understanding of the human tradition in America.

Volumes in the Human Tradition in America series:

Ian K. Steele and Nancy L. Rhoden, eds., *The Human Tradition in Colonial America* (1999). Cloth ISBN 0-8420-2697-5 Paper ISBN 0-8420-2700-9

Nancy L. Rhoden and Ian K. Steele, eds., *The Human Tradition in the American Revolution* (2000). Cloth ISBN 0-8420-2747-5 Paper ISBN 0-8420-2748-3

Ballard C. Campbell, ed., *The Human Tradition in the Gilded Age and Progressive Era* (2000). Cloth ISBN 0-8420-2734-3 Paper ISBN 0-8420-2735-1

Steven E. Woodworth, ed., *The Human Tradition in the Civil War and Reconstruction* (2000). Cloth ISBN 0-8420-2726-2 Paper ISBN 0-8420-2727-0

David L. Anderson, ed., *The Human Tradition in the Vietnam Era* (2000). Cloth ISBN 0-8420-2762-9 Paper ISBN 0-8420-2763-7

The Human Tradition in
THE AMERICAN REVOLUTION

Phillis Wheatley, *Poems on Various Subjects: Religious and Moral* (London, 1773). Engraving. *Courtesy of the American Antiquarian Society*

The Human Tradition in
THE AMERICAN REVOLUTION

No. 2
The Human Tradition in America

Edited by

Nancy L. Rhoden
and
Ian K. Steele

A Scholarly Resources Inc. Imprint
Wilmington, Delaware

First published 2000
Printed and bound in the United States of America

Scholarly Resources Inc.
104 Greenhill Avenue
Wilmington, DE 19805-1897
www.scholarly.com

Library of Congress Cataloging-in-Publication Data

The human tradition in the American Revolution / edited by
Nancy L. Rhoden and Ian K. Steele.
p. cm. — (The human tradition in America ; no. 2)
Includes bibliographical references and index.
ISBN 0-8420-2747-5 (alk. paper). — ISBN 0-8420-2748-3
(pbk. : alk. paper)
1. United States—History—Revolution, 1775–1783
Biography. I. Rhoden, Nancy L. (Nancy Lee), 1965– .
II. Steele, Ian Kenneth.
E206.H88 2000
973.3'092'2—dc21 99-29787
[B] CIP

∞ The paper used in this publication meets the minimum requirements of the American National Standard for permanence of paper for printed library materials, Z39.48, 1984.

For our families,

who continue to teach us

the wonders of life and the limits of history

About the Editors

Nancy L. Rhoden, whose Ph.D. is from Princeton University, teaches early American and English history at the University of Southern Indiana. She is the author of *Revolutionary Anglicanism: The Colonial Church of England Clergy during the American Revolution* (1999) and coeditor of *The Human Tradition in Colonial America* (1999).

Ian K. Steele, whose Ph.D. is from the University of London, teaches British Atlantic and American colonial history at the University of Western Ontario. His best-known books are *The English Atlantic, 1675–1740: An Exploration of Communication and Community* (1986), *Betrayals: Fort William Henry and the "Massacre"* (1993), and *Warpaths: Invasions of North America* (1994). He is coeditor of *The Human Tradition in Colonial America* (1999).

I believe in aristocracy, though—if that is the right word, and if a democrat may use it. Not an aristocracy of power, based upon rank and influence, but an aristocracy of the sensitive, the considerate and the plucky. Its members are to be found in all nations and classes, and all through the ages, and there is a secret understanding between them when they meet. They represent the true human tradition, the one permanent victory of our queer race over cruelty and chaos. Thousands of them perish in obscurity, a few are great names. They are sensitive for others as well as for themselves, they are considerate without being fussy, their pluck is not swankiness but the power to endure, and they can take a joke.

—E. M. Forster, *Two Cheers for Democracy* (1951)

Contents

Introduction

The Revolutionary Players

Nancy L. Rhoden

The American Revolution has no shortage of famous players. Historical accounts routinely feature successful generals, politicians, and activists, but the Revolution involved thousands of players, and perhaps hundreds of distinct stages and plays. As a civil war, the Revolution profoundly affected not only the makers of history but also the survivors, those who endured the tumultuous events and whose lives were altered by the accompanying political, social, or economic changes. To demonstrate the variety of individual perspectives on the Revolution, this volume allows nineteen diverse characters to walk across the stage and linger for a few moments. Our historical actors will tell their own stories, in quoted passages or soliloquies, but they will also be interviewed by expert narrators. Each account, arranged by order of birth into seventeen chapters, presents an intriguing individual tale, but collectively these experiences also offer insights on the meaning and the impact of the Revolution, especially for those "real people" who did not find themselves in leadership roles at the center of the political or military contest.

The players whose lives fill these pages are a diverse and disparate group from northern, middle, and southern colonies, or the frontier. Some were elite members of society, others lacked political or social influence, and a few barely scraped together a living. The politician and diplomat Arthur Lee was a maker of history, but lesser known characters also contributed to the war effort. Benjamin Gilbert and Jacob Nagle both served in the American military. All witnessed the chaos of war as it disrupted their own lives or presented new opportunities. Baroness Friederike von Riedesel followed her husband, a Hessian general fighting with the British, in his North American travels. A few characters, or their loved ones, spent time as prisoners of war, including the legendary frontiersman Daniel Boone, but most accounts reveal the situation of the home front. Elizabeth Drinker and her servant Jane Boon witnessed Philadelphia changing hands from the Americans to the British and then back again. Some were idealists such as antislavery advocate Anthony Benezet; others were concerned with the practical matters of simple survival. Their allegiance in the Revolution ranged from American patriotism to loyalty to Britain. Changing views or sides was a definite option, which some of our actors exercised, and others tried to avoid taking a position. An early patriot, Simon Girty, became a loyalist, Ashley Bowen preferred neutrality, and William Smith presented himself as a moderate but was a committed patriot by the end of the contest. Among the loyalists were Mohawk leader Mary Brant and Cherokee warrior Dragging Canoe, who were fighting more for their own people's sovereignty than for the rights of a distant English king. African-American subjects include the Boston slave and poet Phillis Wheatley and the free black minister Absalom Jones. Although most of the figures featured here were born in North America, Benezet, Lachlan McGillivray, Eliza Lucas Pinckney, Smith, and William Prendergast were immigrants, Wheatley had arrived on board a slave ship, and Riedesel was a sojourner. Ethnically and nationally, these figures depict America's diversity during the revolutionary era.

Most of our historical actors left written accounts that have survived to the present. In the letterbook of Eliza Lucas Pinckney, the journals of Ashley Bowen, Elizabeth Drinker, and Friederike von Riedesel, or in Benjamin Gilbert's diary and Jacob Nagle's memoir, we find descriptions of the authors' lives and commentaries on the world around them. Others left published texts that express their diverse interests and opinions; Anthony Benezet, William Smith, Judith Sargent Murray, and Phillis Wheatley were all published authors. Such accounts offer a window to understanding how people lived in the past, what they experienced, and what values they held. For those who did not leave many written texts, such as Jane Boon, Dragging Canoe, Absalom Jones, or rural rioter William Prendergast, their lives must be reconstructed painstakingly through the accounts and correspondence of contemporaries or through public documents, including court records. From these sources, expert historians have assembled their biographies.

As an historical genre, biography allows a reciprocal evaluation of the impact of one person on public events and the significance of those same public events to individual lives. In the case of both famous and little-known personalities, the pattern of their lives demonstrates human actions and initiatives in the face of the social forces and circumstances in which they lived. Biographies of history's lesser-known figures show how ordinary people reacted to events and problems; as case studies, they reveal how the larger narrative played out in individual lives. As a result, the so-called common people are less common and far more adaptive and innovative than one might imagine. Their tales also allow modern readers to take an intellectual journey to another time and place, to put themselves in the place of these historical actors, and to get a glimpse of the world in which they lived. At times, their lives appear remarkably understandable; on other occasions, very distant and uncertain.

The question of typicality once led most professional historians to dismiss biography as a method that emphasized the particular or the peculiar and exaggerated the roles of individual actors, including the legendary great men of history. The characters assembled in this volume cannot represent the "average" experiences of people in America during the revolutionary era. Most have left too many records to be considered typical, but they do demonstrate the great range of experiences and responses. In the attempt to make sense out of chaos and to understand complex events, historians regularly discern patterns in their reading of the past. Yet for most of our protagonists, the revolutionary era was a confusing time, which seemed to defy simple explanation. From their perspective, might modern historians' clear answers be distortions? Could history generalize from biography, or could biography reveal the flaws of sweeping generalizations? Those historians bent on celebrating the American Revolution as a unifying, iconic event, still of great consequence to American "civil religion," are impatient with the variety of voices, but did our historical characters recognize that they lived in a multicultural America?

After visiting with these historical actors, we would like to pose our own questions. Did they understand and agree with the constitutional arguments behind colonial protest? Did they follow the decisions of the Continental Congress, the campaigns of the Continental and British forces, or the actions of celebrities such as George Washington? Undoubtedly these are intriguing questions, but they are ours. By listening thoughtfully we might discern more clearly what issues were most important to the participants. National goals seemed far less clear or significant, for they merited less attention in their written accounts than the modern reader might expect. By contrast, matters of family preservation and local interests attracted a good deal of their attention. Often the pivotal moments in the burgeoning nation's history went unnoticed—or at least unrecorded. Textbooks on the American Revolution take note of such events as the Stamp Act protest in 1765, the Boston Tea Party, the beginning of the armed conflict at Lexington and Concord, and the landmark decision of the Continental Congress to declare independence in July 1776. Understanding those public events remains crucial to evaluating the causes of the revolutionary crisis, but otherwise careful commentators, such as Ashley Bowen or Elizabeth Drinker, made little or no mention at all of them. Had they failed to see the importance of these national events, or might we be better advised to pay closer attention to the local allegiances of contemporaries?

While the American Revolution may be portrayed quite accurately as a series of political, military, and constitutional struggles between British officials and disgruntled American colonists, an examination of individual biographies allows the modern reader to personalize those traditional accounts and humanize what might otherwise appear to be a mass of arguments and actions. Biography renders seemingly impersonal events more tangible, while it also forces us to realize that individual tales frequently can challenge the very categories of historical analysis. Categories such as loyalist and patriot appear firm and fixed, but discerning the political affiliation of people in the past is not always so straightforward as the historical labels may imply. Political concepts and military goals, such as independence after 1776, became personalized, as young men who were transformed into soldiers experienced their own rites of passage into manhood, just as the nation achieved political independence. While the United States separated politically from Britain, individuals often redefined, or internalized, the meaning of those grand international events in their own lives: Arthur Lee, Eliza Lucas Pinckney, and William Smith all struggled with what it meant to be a member of the British Empire and what it meant to be an American. The wartime experiences of Judith Sargent Murray and Elizabeth Drinker aptly depict contemporaneous women's fear of enemy attack and marauding soldiers, whether friends or foes. The spirit and resilience of these struggling characters are impressive, in success and in failure. Such personalities, "the sensitive, the considerate, and the plucky" who reveal "the true human tradition" in the American Revolution, are worth meeting; E. M. Forster, who supplies the title for this series and this volume, might have been pleased to make the introductions.

In these diverse biographies, modern readers can find the opinions of contemporaries on the causes of the American Revolution, its meaning, and its legacies. Particularly evident are dramatically different views on many revolutionary values, including liberty, independence, and freedom. By examining these biographies, can we discern the "ideological origins" of the American Revolution, those central ideas that launched and sustained the Revolutionary War? What impact did revolutionary ideas have on these players?

American patriots first defined liberty as simply the rights of Englishmen, but when Anglo-American grievances were not resolved in the 1760s and early 1770s, American revolutionaries waged a war for political independence from Britain. Arthur Lee understood the constitutional arguments of his fellow patriots, and soldiers such as Benjamin Gilbert and Jacob Nagle joined the revolutionary army. As a principle and a natural right, liberty could justify opposition to British authority, and freedom was the goal. From the floor of the Continental Congress, or at the local Liberty Tree, revolutionaries mobilized the masses and forged a democratic revolution based on popular sovereignty. The revolutionaries would have to defeat an impressive military and naval power; consequently, Ashley Bowen thought that they were likely to be defeated; Eliza Lucas Pinckney and Judith Sargent Murray both warned of the necessity for virtue, and William Smith, at first, promoted reconciliation.

For many loyalists, such as Lachlan McGillivray or Elizabeth Drinker, the Revolution marked the unfortunate end of America's membership in an empire that already ensured personal liberty and freedom, an empire they respected at least more than they trusted the American revolutionaries. Several loyalists are featured in this volume, because they comprised a significant portion of Americans whose perspectives have been overlooked, and because their struggles illuminate the general problems of loyalty and allegiance that every resident of the rebelling British colonies faced. In choosing to return to Scotland, McGillivray represents the thousands of loyalists who left the thirteen colonies during or after the Revolution to seek refuge in the British Empire. As Quakers, Anthony Benezet and Elizabeth Drinker were obliged to follow the pacifist teachings of their faith, but Drinker appeared to favor the British, especially after revolutionary authorities imprisoned her husband. For many loyalists, tyranny resided not in the actions of British authorities, but in the hands of revolutionary committees.

Native American allies of Britain were fighting their own war of independence, one that predated the Revolutionary War and persisted beyond its 1783 conclusion. Indeed, it is difficult to regard the American Revolution for Mary Brant or Dragging Canoe as a subplot of a single play. The lives of frontiersmen Daniel Boone and Simon Girty, as well as the tales of Indian loyalists, demonstrate that the Revolution had a serious impact on Indian country. It unleashed a flood of American settlers onto interior lands, which directly challenged Indian sovereignty. Western migrants such as William Prendergast and Daniel Boone associated personal liberty with individual landownership, and Americans collectively claimed the national right to expand beyond the Appalachian limit previously set by British authorities.

Other contemporaries defined liberty and independence, not in terms of territorial expansion, but in those of extending and fulfilling the Revolution's language of universal rights and its promise of equality. Phillis Wheatley's revolutionary poetry reminded readers that the stirring message of "all men are created equal" had yet to be applied to African-American slaves, while the accomplishments of this enslaved poet questioned established ideas about the innate inferiority of African Americans. With the formation of independent African-American churches in Philadelphia, Absalom Jones promoted the liberty of black self-determination. Anthony Benezet must have hoped that revolutionary ideals of freedom and equality would encourage Americans to end slavery decisively throughout the new nation. Although northern states adopted immediate and gradual emancipation laws during and after the Revolution and some slaves had been manumitted voluntarily by their owners, slavery's national demise became a hope deferred. Yet, in a post-revolutionary world where no one wanted to be dependent upon anyone else, all sorts of relationships of dependency came into question, including slavery. White servants like Jane Boon, as well as African-American slaves, may well have wondered whether the Revolution's promise of equality would result in new opportunities for personal freedom or social mobility.

Women's experiences in the Revolution varied tremendously; the ethnically diverse female subjects in this volume span loyalists and patriots, the elite and the impoverished, the enriched and the enslaved. All but Jane Boon enjoyed a privileged educational background. Even the Mohawk Mary Brant had been educated as an Englishwoman, although she and Boon did not leave an extensive paper trail as the other female actors did. The Revolution's legacy for women was mixed: it provided a language of equality that could be applied to gender issues, but little impetus to do so, and most male revolutionaries had no desire to destroy the existing dependent relationships within the family. Judith Sargent Murray's views on gender and the need for improved, equal educational opportunities for women had been shaped, in part, by her understanding of the meaning of the American Revolution. For Elizabeth Drinker, Eliza Lucas Pinckney, and Baroness Friederike von Riedesel, their forced wartime separation from their husbands allowed a measure of female autonomy, which would have been rare and often unwelcome in peacetime. In widowhood, Eliza Pinckney found the freedom to resume her management of plantation affairs, a task she apparently relished, but she too must have spent much of the war worrying about the fate of male family members.

As the panoramic stage fills with these historical players, the modern audience may well be struck by the diversity of both their revolutionary experiences and their interpretations of the American Revolution. For some, the Revolution offered opportunities for adventure, travel, and prosperity, which broadened their worldviews; for others, it challenged that measure of familial harmony, social authority, or economic stability that they had achieved in the years before the outbreak of war. There were winners and losers, but also survivors. At war's end and for several decades to follow, some of these contemporaries rejoiced that the American Revolution had accomplished so much; others lamented that so many promises remained unfulfilled. The engraved portrait of Phillis Wheatley, published in her *Poems on Various Subjects: Religious and Moral* (1773) (see frontispiece), captured her creative, refined spirit, but also the real contradictions of her status both as a published poet and the chattel property of John Wheatley. While seated at her writing desk composing her famous poetry, Wheatley must have wondered if the egalitarian sentiments of the revolutionary era could possibly herald a new era of political, social, economic, and racial equality. In America, the new bastion of liberty and peace, would "Heavenly Freedom spread her golden Ray"?*

*Phillis Wheatley, "Liberty and Peace" (1784), as quoted in *The Collected Works of Phillis Wheatley*, ed. John Shields (New York: Oxford University Press, 1988), 239.

1

Anthony Benezet
America's Finest Eighteenth-Century Antislavery Advocate

Maurice Jackson

Philadelphia schoolmaster and social critic Anthony Benezet (1713–1784) challenged racial conventions of his day by asserting the equality of blacks and by urging Quakers of Pennsylvania to renounce slavery. Born in France, young Benezet and his family migrated to Holland and England before coming to America. He became a teacher, writer, Quaker humanitarian, and social activist. His experiences at the African Free School, including his instruction of Absalom Jones, contributed to his opinions on racial equality. Although Benezet rejected the life of a merchant, his arguments about slavery demonstrated his thorough understanding of eighteenth-century consumer society. He blamed slave owners, as well as traders, for creating a climate of opinion that sanctioned slavery. American revolutionaries later protested against British taxes with economic boycotts; Benezet had refused to buy or use the products of enslaved Africans.

By renouncing slavery in 1772, the Philadelphia Yearly Meeting set a new pattern for the Quaker community, and antislavery sentiment spread in Pennsylvania and other northern states during and after the American Revolution. How was Benezet able to persuade fellow Quakers to abandon slaveholding, a labor and racial system that was firmly established throughout the English colonies? As Maurice Jackson argues, Benezet's publications demonstrated African accomplishments and humanity, while they confronted European and American stereotypes about Africans' suitability for slavery. Given his strenuous objections to slavery, why did Benezet not support an armed slave rebellion? Why did this activist not assume a prominent and partisan role in the American Revolution? Benezet understood that the concepts of freedom and independence could be applied to enslaved Africans when Thomas Jefferson or Patrick Henry would not, or could not, publicly make that connection. To what extent did the Revolution allow more people to share Benezet's opinions, or at least wonder if political equality might inspire racial equality? What accounts for Benezet's popularity at his death and his continued legacy in the nineteenth century?

Maurice Jackson, a historian at Georgetown University, is working on a book-length study of Anthony Benezet.

Anthony Benezet was born to Huguenot (Protestant) parents in Saint-Quentin, Picardy, France, on January 31, 1713. His parents had braved a generation of intensifying religious persecution, during which they were forced to join the Roman Catholic Church, into which Anthony was baptized a day after birth. Anthony's father, Jean Etienne Benezet, still belonged to a nonviolent Huguenot resistance group called Inspirés de la Vaunage, but in 1715 he finally fled with his young family to Holland and then to England. Anthony would later write to a friend of his family's oppression by French persecutors: "One of my uncles was hung by those intolerants, my aunt was put in a convent, two of my cousins died in the galleys, and my fugitive father was hung in effigy for explaining the gospel differently from the priests, and the family was ruined by the confiscation of his property."[1] Such a family history might have led Anthony in various directions; whether for this reason or not, he came to have a deep sympathy for other oppressed and exiled people, particularly African slaves.

Although moderately successful during sixteen years in England, Jean Benezet moved his family once more in 1731, to Philadelphia, the "City of Brotherly Love." Quakers, members of the Society of Friends, associated with the family during their first years in Philadelphia, although the Benezets were not Quakers; Anthony's father and several of his sisters soon joined the Moravian Brethren. Jean Benezet also allied himself with George Whitefield, an itinerant English leader of the Christian revival known as the Great Awakening, and revealed his own sympathy for blacks by contributing to Whitefield's unsuccessful attempt to start a Nazareth training school for blacks on five thousand acres of land near the Delaware River.

Anthony had been apprenticed to a Quaker merchant in London. As a merchant in training, he had not been a success, but he seems to have been attracted to his master's religion. Anthony became a Quaker soon after arriving in Pennsylvania and held to that faith for the rest of his life. Five years later, Anthony married Joyce Marriot, granddaughter of prominent Quaker physician and "ministering Friend," Griffith Owen. Both the children born to them died in infancy. Joyce, like her grandfather, became a "ministering Friend," a public spiritual figure in a religious community that allowed women to address religious meetings and did not believe in a "hireling ministry."

Although he was the eldest son of a versatile father who had become a successful Philadelphia dry goods importer, Anthony Benezet had no desire to join his brothers among the "buyers and sellers" of Philadelphia. Anthony always refused to have his portrait painted, but it is known that he had a small frame and a "frail constitution." As an adult, he would study medical journals in search of ways to improve his health and, at some point, he became a vegetarian against the advice of his good friend, Dr. Benjamin Rush. Perhaps because of his weak frame and dislike for commerce, Anthony sought what he thought would be a less strenuous vocation. But more likely it was his love of books, his mastery of several languages, his love of children, and his passion for the truth that led him to become an innovative teacher in a Quaker day school in 1742 as well as a prolific writer. Unhappy with the education of girls, he founded a girls' school in 1755. He developed a new way to teach students to read, and he wrote *An Essay on Grammar* (1778) and *The Pennsylvania Spelling Book* (1778). From about 1750 he tutored black students, free and slave, in his home in the evenings.

Perhaps what most distinguished Benezet from his Quaker contemporaries in Philadelphia was his association with blacks in other than a slave-owning capacity. After two decades of tutoring blacks privately, he went on to establish and teach in the Friends School for Black People, later called the African Free School, which opened its doors in a Quaker building in the summer of 1770. Among Benezet's many black students were Absalom Jones and Richard Allen, who became prominent ministers, Methodist and Episcopalian respectively; together they founded the Free African Society. Another of his students was James Forten. These three free blacks later petitioned Congress to repeal the Fugitive Slave Act of 1793. Forten also led the opposition to the American Colonization Society and was joined in that struggle by Benezet, who was also against sending blacks back to uncertain lives in an unfamiliar Africa. In describing his thoughts about his black students, in the epilogue of his *Short Observations on Slavery*, Benezet uncharacteristically reverted to the third person:

> A. Benezet teacher in a school established by the private subscription, in Philadelphia, for the instruction of the Black children and others of that people, has for years, had the opportunity of knowing the temper and genius of the Africans; particularly of those under his tuition, who had many, of different ages; and he can say with truth and sincerity . . . and he is bold to assert, that the notion entertained by some, that the Blacks are inferior to the Whites in their capacities, is a vulgar prejudice, founded on the Pride of Ignorance of their lordly masters who have kept their

> slaves at such a distance, as to be unable to form a right judgement of them.[2]

Although Quakers had not yet officially denounced slavery, their community included a substantial minority who spoke out against this injustice to their black fellow human beings. There were several intellectual, religious, and social links between Quakerism and abolitionism that became evident in Benezet's works. The first was "that all people were equal in the sight of God"[3] and carried an "inner light" within them. Quakers did not think of blacks as equal socially, but regarded involuntary servitude of any person as wrong. Second was the Quaker doctrine of nonviolence, which Benezet would use most effectively in attacking slavery, citing travelers' journals to show how Africans were captured violently, starved during the "middle passage," and then beaten on their masters' plantations. A third Quaker rule was that "Friends should avoid ostentation and sloth in their daily lives" as that "made both masters and children lazy."[4] Benezet believed that greed, luxury, and vanity corrupted human beings and that the quest for wealth was the root of the evils of his time, including the burgeoning Atlantic slave trade.

The Pennsylvania Quakers included three prominent early antislavery activists and writers, Anthony Benezet and his friends Benjamin Lay (1677–1759) and John Woolman (1720–1772). Quite naturally they made Quaker slave traders and slave owners their first targets. Linking his Quaker beliefs with his growing hatred of slavery, Benezet began a career as a teacher, writer, and activist with the purpose of freeing enslaved Africans and educating them. One of his early antislavery tracts argued: "Thus an unsatiable desire for gain hath become the principal and moving cause of the most abominable and dreadful scene that was perhaps ever acted upon the face of the earth."[5] He dismissed the claims of those who tried to make a distinction between the slave owners, some of whom had inherited their slaves, and slave traders who were in the business for profit. He believed that anyone "who is not blinded by the Desire of Gain" should recognize that "the right by which these Men hold the Negro in Bondage is no other than what is derived by those who stole them."[6] Linking the slave trade to a worldwide drive for profits, Benezet wrote his friend Samuel Fothergill that "it is frequent to see even Friends, toiling year after year, enriching themselves, and thus gathering fuel for our children's vanity and corruption."[7]

Benezet crusaded for the freeing of the slaves, though he never traveled as John Woolman did in order to spread the message, and was never as dramatic as Benjamin Lay, who became notorious for his radical departures from the quiet Quaker way. Once he kidnapped a Quaker child to show whites the grief felt by Africans when they or their children were stolen from their African homeland. At the 1738 Philadelphia Yearly Meeting, Lay arrived dressed in a military uniform with a sword hidden under his coat and a bible fitted with a bladder of blood-colored juice. During debate, Lay denounced Quaker slavemasters: "It would be as justifiable in the sight of the Almighty . . . if you should thrust a sword through their hearts as I do this book!"[8] The blood-colored juice then splattered over the gathering. Benezet never employed such antics, but did follow Lay in refusing to eat food or wear clothing that he believed was produced by the labor of enslaved Africans.

Benezet had seen Benjamin Lay scorned by the Quakers for antislavery activities, but he saw no one shunned for owning slaves. He decided that a different course was needed to convert the Society of Friends to antislavery. Half a century after the Quaker debate began, and thirty-four years after Lay's "bloody" outburst, the 1772 Philadelphia Yearly Meeting still seemed poised to defeat yet another motion requiring Quakers to disavow slavery and free their slaves. Benezet, who had been silent throughout the meeting, solemnly rose. Weeping profusely, he walked to the front of the meeting and recited from the Book of Psalms: "Ethiopia shall soon stretch out her hands unto God."[9] His message was that the children of Africa were God-fearing, God-loving, and worthy of God's grace. Benezet's message, backed by his life of service, carried the day. The Quakers became the first white community to raise a collective voice against slavery in the Americas. Many Quaker slaveholders had, over the decades of debate, manumitted their slaves, and others had not replaced slaves who died in captivity. Many Quakers simply had no further need for the institution; there had been a large influx of German and other European immigrants who provided cheap labor.

Although the Quakers had finally taken their stand on religious grounds, slavery continued to flourish among a much larger group of people who could not be converted by religious arguments alone. In his unending campaign against the slave trade and slavery, Benezet incorporated secular arguments from an impressive array of reading. His library was full of current scientific studies, and he read from the libraries of prominent Philadelphia gentlemen including James Logan, Benjamin Rush, and Benjamin Franklin. Benezet used every available source to add rational support for his religious, moral, and ethical arguments against slavery.

Benezet found rational endorsement for his crusade in the writings of Enlightenment philosophers and jurists. Charles Louis de Secondat, baron de Montesquieu, clearly denounced slavery in his *The Spirit of Laws* (1748), and Scottish philosopher Francis Hutcheson insisted that slaves who were sold into faraway countries had never legally forfeited their freedom. In his *A System of Moral Philosophy* of 1755, Hutcheson argued for universal liberty, happiness, and benevolence and proclaimed that "no endowments, natural or acquired, can give a perfect right to assume power over others, without their consent."[10] Benezet generally agreed with Hutcheson, except on the right of the enslaved to use violence in resistance. As a Quaker who believed strictly in nonviolence, Benezet hoped to avoid violence through the education of blacks and the renunciation of slavery by whites. Benezet was also fond of Scottish jurist George Wallace's *A System of the Principles of the Law of Scotland* (1760), especially the idea that there could never be any legal title for the possession of one human being by another, and thus all transactions for human flesh were legally void. With such support from rationalists, Benezet could write to Abbé Raynal that "men are noble, only in exact proportion with their being rational."[11] Benezet could embrace natural-law theory and insist that every human was born free by a right based in the law of nature. Nevertheless, the political remained religious for Benezet. Government was an "ordinance of God" and, "no legislature on earth can alter the nature of things, so as to make that to be right which is contrary to the law of God."[12]

History can be a powerful aid to revolution, and Benezet studied African history with a clear purpose that did not prevent him from studying his sources with remarkable care. In seeking to understand African folkways and customs, he read all the available English, French, and Dutch sources, using an impressive number of the narratives of adventurers, factors and accountants of the Royal African Company, and surgeons and crewmen of the slave ships. Although Benezet was using such historical sources as early as his 1759 *Observations on the Inslaving, Importing and Purchasing of Negroes*, his most substantial and influential historical study was *Some Historical Account of Guinea*, first published in Philadelphia in 1771. This ambitious study was divided into twenty-one chapters, in which "some account will be given of the different parts of Africa, from which the Negro is brought to America."[13] He laid out several premises that directly contradicted prevailing European notions of Africa. He insisted that "scarce a country in the whole world is better calculated for affording the necessary comforts of life to its inhabitants" and that they "still retain a great deal of innocent simplicity: and when not stirred up to revenge from the frequent abuses they have received from the Europeans in general, manifest themselves to be a human, sociable people, whose faculties are as capable of improvement as those of other men." Finally, he asserted that their economy and government were in many ways commendable, and "it appears that they might have lived happy, if not disturbed by the Europeans."[14]

Benezet's ranging study included a description of southernmost Africa, a country "settled by Caffers and Hottentots: Who have never been concerned in the making or selling of slaves."[15] He explored in detail what was known of the Kongo and Old Benin, in present-day Nigeria. Later in the work he described the lives of the Jalofs, Fulani, and Mandingos of West Africa. He directly confronted the myth of the natural inferiority of Africans and the superiority of the Europeans who had come to save the supposedly "feeble race." He described an abundant Africa, although it was inhabited by people who produced only what they needed. Rare for his time, Benezet distinguished between those Africans who collaborated with slave traders and those who were their victims. His understanding of the societies, tribal structures, and social geography of eighteenth-century Africa was remarkably accurate for a writer of his era, and *Some Historical Account of Guinea* became one of the first school texts on African history.

Benezet's use of his sources can be evaluated by considering Jean Barbot's works. Benezet had long been familiar with *Barbot on Guinea: The Writings of Jean Barbot on West Africa 1678–1712*, which consisted of a travel journal, plus all the letters written while he was in West Africa. As early as 1758, Benezet was quoting Barbot to prove that the slaves sold by the Africans themselves were mostly prisoners of war, a point that would touch Quaker consciences. In *Some Historical Account of Guinea*, Benezet echoed Barbot's belief that the townsmen of Benin, "are very honest and just in their dealings: and they have such an aversion for theft, that by the law of the country it is punishable by death."[16] Benezet was being somewhat selective, for in this same letter Barbot also noted that Guineans were not so scrupulous in dealing with slave traders. Barbot wrote that "few or none of the Blacks are to be trusted, as being crafty and deceitful, and who will never let slip an opportunity of cheating an European."[17] Benezet seldom quoted negative descriptions of Africans from Barbot or others. This was not because he had a utopian notion of African perfection, but because he knew that negative descriptions already abounded. Benezet refused to write anything that would give support to advocates of slavery.

Benezet used these travel accounts to link the evils of the Atlantic slave trade, African wars, and human greed, and to describe the consequences of the spread of British and French commercial slave trading deep into the heart of Africa. One passage he cited from a former slave trader's journal showed how the whites came loaded with goods with which to purchase slaves from local tribesmen. A native king, having no slaves at hand, soon launched forays into neighboring tribal territory, inciting a war to justify his capture of slaves. Upon victory and the capture of villagers, the conquerors would "usually carry the Infants in Sacks, and gag the Men and Women for fear they should alarm . . . Villages near the factories [European trading forts], which is the King's Interest not to ruin."[18]

To demonstrate African accomplishments, Benezet studied ancient African dynasties and kingdoms from the work of Leo Africanus, a Moroccan historian of Africa who wrote in the first half of the sixteenth century. Benezet learned of peoples living well communally, without private property or overlords. He wrote that "ambition and avarice never drove them into foreign countries to subdue or cheat their neighbors."[19]

Benezet also entered the debate over the number of blacks forcibly taken from Africa, the number perishing during the "middle passage," and the number reaching the "new world." Benezet started by extracting, from the printed *Liverpool Memorandum-book*, a list of that port's slave trade, which he estimated carried thirty thousand Africans a year into American slavery. Adding an estimate for the London and Bristol trades, he concluded that "at least One Hundred Thousand Negroes [are] purchased and brought on board our ships yearly from the coast of Africa."[20] Benezet also knew that millions of enslaved Africans did not live to reach western shores due to disease, maltreatment, and resistance, which was expressed mainly by their leaping overboard to their deaths during the Atlantic crossing.

Benezet was primarily addressing English-speaking audiences, and he paid special attention to the English colonies of Jamaica and Barbados. He described the white indentured servants of Barbados and argued that Europeans were as suitable as Africans for labor in the tropics. He quoted the rector of St. Lucy Parish in Barbados, who believed that if there were any inadequacies among blacks in the arts or in the "common affairs" of life, it was attributable to lack of education and the "depression of their spirits by slavery"[21] rather than to any lack of natural ability. Benezet's evaluation of the situation for the blacks in the West Indies was confirmed by the unnamed author of *An Account of the European Settlements in America*, who wrote that "the Negroes in our colonies endure a slavery more complete, and attended with far worse circumstances, than what any people in their condition suffer in any other place in the world, or have suffered in any other period of time."[22] In *A Short Account*, Benezet had already documented the treatment of the slaves in Barbados. Using the account of Sir

Hans Sloane, the well-known English author of the *History of Jamaica*, Benezet detailed the atrocities against the blacks. As he made note of the disproportionate number of blacks to whites in South Carolina, Benezet used Sloane to describe Jamaica as having three times as many blacks as whites and, because the slaves made frequent attempts to revolt, blacks were never trusted or left idle. Benezet believed that once the enslaved Africans realized their own strength they would try to "get their Liberty, or to deliver themselves out of the miserable slavery they are in."[23]

It is difficult to estimate the direct readership of *Some Historical Account of Guinea*, or of Benezet's dozens of other works. Although this particular study was apparently not republished in London, Paris, or Dublin, as some of his other works had been, it certainly had its impact on the British abolitionist movement. Formerly enslaved Ottabah Cugoano, whose account was published in London in 1787, referred his readers to "the worthy and judicious" Benezet as giving "some very striking estimations of the exceeding evil occasioned by that wicked diabolical traffic of the African slave trade."[24] *Some Historical Observations* was also praised two years later by Olaudah Equiano, another former slave writing in England as part of the developing antislavery movement there. Kidnapped as a child, Equiano relied upon Benezet when describing his native Nigeria. Equiano's dramatic kidnapping scene in his *Interesting Narrative of the Life of Olaudah Equiano or Gustavus Vasa, the African* is remarkably similar to a description printed by Benezet eighteen years earlier. John Wesley read, appreciated, and copied from Benezet's works. Even William Wilberforce, the leading English abolitionist in Parliament, quoted Benezet in debate. Thomas Clarkson, another prominent British crusader against the slave trade, referred to *Some Historical Account of Guinea* as "this precious book," in which "I found almost all I wanted. I obtained by means of it a knowledge of, and gained great access to, the great authorities of Adanson, Moore, Barbot, Smith, Bosman, and others."[25]

As the American Revolution approached, Benezet readily exploited the obvious irony in the rhetoric of revolutionaries railing against tyranny and the threat of their own "enslavement" while holding slaves themselves. In the wake of the Stamp Act crisis, he had already asked "how many of those who distinguish themselves as the Advocates of Liberty, remain insensible and inattentive to the treatment of thousands and tens of thousands of our fellow man," the enslaved Africans.[26] Benezet refused to accept the hypocrisy of many of his peers, such as Benjamin Franklin and Patrick Henry, who claimed that they opposed slavery, yet owned slaves. Upon receiving Benezet's *Some Historical Account of Guinea* from the leading anti-slave-trade advocate in Virginia, Henry admitted in his letter of thanks: "I take this Opportunity to acknowledge ye receipt of Anthony Benezet's book against the slave trade. I thank you for it. Would anyone believe that I am a Master of Slaves of my own purchase? I am drawn along by ye general Inconvenience of living without them; I will not, I cannot justify it."[27] Yet Henry refused to release his slaves.

Benezet used the political troubles in titling *The Potent Enemies of America Laid Open*, published in 1774, but readers soon learned that the two enemies were slavery and alcohol. Throughout the Revolutionary War, Benezet sought to extend to the blacks the rights that the American revolutionaries had won for themselves. He wrote in *Notes on the Slave Trade*: "It cannot be, that either war, or contract, can give any man such a property in another as he has in his sheep or oxen. Much less is it possible, that any child of man, should ever be born a Slave. Liberty is the right of every human creature, as soon as he breathes the vital air. And no human law can deprive him of that right, which he derives from the right of nature."[28]

As a pacifist, Benezet had not believed in the American revolutionaries' right to use violence in resisting George III's government; surprisingly, Benezet was able to publish antiwar pamphlets in Philadelphia repeatedly during the American Revolution. He was also most concerned, throughout his writings, with the risk that slavery would provoke violent uprisings among those suffering it. In a letter to his friend John Phipps, Benezet wrote what he would never have put in a pamphlet:

> With respect to the Danger of the Southern Colonies are exposed to from the vast disproportion there is between the number of Negroes, and the whites, but it was too tender a point to expose to ye view of such of the blacks, as can read. In the treatise, the Proportion in South Carolina is said to be fifteen Blacks to a white, but by their own account, the difference is rather twenty to one. In Georgia and South Carolina the Negroes are not hemmed in by the some hundreds of miles, as they are in the Islands, but have a back Country uninhibited for some hundreds of miles, where the Negroes might not only retire, but who expect to be supported & assisted by the Indians.[29]

Benezet realized that in places such as South Carolina, where blacks outnumbered whites so significantly, the potential for violent revolution existed. No doubt he knew of the 1739 Stono Rebellion, which put fear in the hearts and minds of the slave owners, who clamped down harder on the blacks in the aftermath. Benezet realized the potential of African and Native American unity in the face of white rule.

Benezet was much more tolerant of the propensity of the Africans, in the words of the old Negro spiritual, to "Steal Away." Running away seemed to be legitimate resistance to the passivist Benezet; in numerous publications he denounced laws that encouraged the murder of runaways. In his letter to Phipps he had referred approvingly to the Maroons, escaped slaves who established their own runaway communities. In South Carolina this occurred near the Sea Islands off the Atlantic Coast, but maroonage was much more common in the mountainous areas of the West Indies, in Latin America, and especially in Brazil.

Benezet also alluded to the necessity to make plans for the "freedom of those amongst us, after a reasonable period of time."[30] He later called for some reparations to the freed blacks in the form of communally shared land. This land-sharing plan was amazingly similar to African forms of communalism, or primitive communism, which existed before European conquest and which Benezet knew of from his reading. His idea of allotting lands to freed blacks preceded, by almost a century, the Reconstruction dream of "forty acres and a mule."

Like other opponents of slavery in the 1780s, Benezet came to focus on the abolition of the slave trade as the practical first target in the abolition of the institution. In 1783, Benezet wrote to Britain's Queen Charlotte, urging her to help end the British slave trade. Two years earlier his brief *Notes on the Slave Trade* had proclaimed the "inconsistence of slavery with every right of mankind, with every feeling of humanity, and every precept of Christianity; not to point out its inconsistency with the welfare, peace and prosperity of every country, in proportion as it prevails."[31] He described the sufferings the trade brought upon blacks and then confronted whites directly. First, he addressed the "Captains employed in the trade." He described the kindness of the African people whom the slavers separated from their loved ones, then: "[You] forced them into your ships, like a herd of swine. . . . You have stowed [them] together as close as they ever could lie, without any regard to decency. . . . Such slavery . . . is not found among the Turks at Algiers, no, nor among the heathens in America."[32] Benezet begged the slave-trading captains to quit their horrid trade immediately.

Benezet then turned his attention to the slave merchant, telling him that "it is your money, that is the spring of all." He challenged the morality of the slave sellers and urged them to promise hypothetically that "I will never buy a slave more while I live." Moving in on the conscience of the reformed merchant and his readers, Benezet asserted, "Oh let his resolution be yours! Have no more any part in this detestable business."[33]

Benezet also appealed to the plantation owner who might claim "I pay honestly for my goods, and am not concerned to know how they are come by." The goods referred to were, of course, his chattel slaves, whom the plantation owner viewed merely as part of his property. Benezet accused the planter of not being as honest as a pickpocket, housebreaker, or highwayman. He indicted him for fraud, robbery, and murder, and told him that it was his "money that pays the merchant, and through him the captain and the African butchers," before concluding that he was "the spring that puts all the rest in motion."[34] Thus no one who had any part in slavery, from the "man-stealer" to the ship captain, to the merchant to the plantation owner, to the men or women who proclaimed their innocence because they inherited the homeless slaves, was truly innocent.

Benezet had repeatedly confronted those who claimed "that if the English were to drop this Trade entirely, it would be immediately thereupon carried on by other Nations, to a much greater Degree than it is now."[35] He also challenged those who asserted that an end to slavery "would lessen if not ruin, some other considerable branches of our commerce, especially the Sugar and Tobacco Trades, because of the Difficulty in getting Hands enough, in the room of the Blacks, to work and labor in those plantations."[36] Characteristically, Benezet answered these questions in moral terms, reinforced with facts about the ability of white labor to perform adequately in the tropics. He ended by alerting whites to the "impending catastrophe" of slave revolt if the slave trade were to continue.

Anthony Benezet described himself in his Last Will and Testament with these words: "Be it remembered that I, Anthony Benezet, a teacher of the Free School for the Black People of Philadelphia." Before his death he helped found the Society for the Relief of Free Negroes Unlawfully Held in Bondage, which later grew into the Pennsylvania Society for the Abolition of Slavery. He made arrangements that, after his wife was provided for, the remainder of his savings would go to the African Free School and the newly formed Abolitionist Committee. He may not have been as radical in his views as the nineteenth-century abolitionist martyrs John Brown or Nat Turner, or as well remembered as Frederick Douglass or William Lloyd Garrison, but Benezet's influence upon his contemporaries was unmatched. Great social reformers, both men and women, use every possible means to achieve goals of equality and justice. Benezet was no different. But what set him apart from others of his era was his great imagination in using every available resource and in developing new weapons in the arsenal of antislavery politics. At the very root of his thinking was the belief that black men, women, and children were indeed human beings equal to all others.

Of his funeral, Benezet's first biographer wrote: "Never had the city on such an occasion seen a demonstration in which persons of all classes participated. There were the officials of the city, men of all trades and professions, various sects and denominations, and hundreds of Negroes testifying by their attendance, and by their tears, the grateful sense they entertained of his pious efforts on their behalf."[37] The *Pennsylvania Gazette*, as well as *Watson's Annual Journal*, noted Benezet's death on May 13, 1784, paid tribute to his legacy, and noted that hundreds of blacks followed his coffin in the streets. Although Benezet had said upon his deathbed, "I am dying and feel ashamed to meet the face of my maker, I have done so little in his cause,"[38] the blacks who followed or wept at his funeral procession felt otherwise. Two years later, Jean Pierre Brissot, an acquaintance who later became prominent in the French Revolution, wrote eloquently of Benezet:

> What author, what great man, will ever be followed to his grave by four hundred Negroes, snatched by his own assiduity, his own generosity, from ignorance, wretchedness, and slavery? Who then has a right to speak haughtily of this benefactor of men? . . . Where is the man in all of Europe, of whatever rank or birth, who is equal to Benezet? Who is not obliged to respect him? How long will authors suffer themselves to be shackled by the prejudices of society? Will they never perceive that nature has created all men equal, that wisdom and virtue are the only criteria of superiority? Who was more virtuous than Benezet? Who was more useful to society, to mankind?"[39]

Long after Benezet's death, antislavery advocates continued to invoke his name. Antislavery newspapers and periodicals of the early nineteenth century, time and again, resurrected the legacy of Benezet. African-American leaders continued to pay homage to the gentle Quaker decades after his death. A half-century after he died, James Forten Jr., the eldest son of the famed black abolitionist and former Benezet student, spoke before a Philadelphia Female Anti-Slavery Society meeting in April 1836. He told the gathering not to be upset at being called fanatics and to be proud to be in the company of people like Anthony Benezet. That the descendant of a slave invoked the name of Benezet first among those in the antislavery crusade showed the depth of black admiration for the man who dedicated his life to their cause.

There were many facets to Anthony Benezet. As a Quaker educator he had developed new ways to teach students to read, published *An Essay on Grammar* (1778) and *The Pennsylvania Spelling*

Book (1778), and showed special concern for the education of girls and blacks. He wrote religious and pacifist pamphlets, tracts against alcoholism, and a brief history of the Quakers. He led Quaker relief efforts to aid French-speaking Acadian refugees expelled from their Canadian homeland by British-American forces in 1755. To refute arguments about the innate inequality of blacks, he had read everything available about African civilizations. His command of languages allowed him to study travelers' journals in French, English, German, and Dutch and to visualize the African continent before European intrusion. He became a self-taught anthropologist, learning about the evolution of the human species as well as the economic and social systems that accompanied differing modes of production. Near the end of his life he began a comparable study of Native Americans, some findings of which were published the year he died as *Observations on the Situation, Disposition and Character of the Indian Natives of this Continent*. In this fifty-nine-page pamphlet he, predictably, quoted early travelers, insisted upon the rationality and human potential of the victims, and denounced their oppression and enslavement. Benezet lived as a humanitarian, empathizing and sympathizing with those who were suffering, especially the enslaved blacks.

In death, as in life, Benezet served as a symbol to those who fought against slavery. He usually led by quiet example and devout work. Some tried to ignore him, others scorned him. He lived modestly and plainly, preferring to use his meager salary as a teacher to help defray the cost of his publications and to run Quaker schools. He need not have uttered his deathbed regret that he had not done enough. The enslaved African men, women, and children whom he fought to free viewed him as a saint among sinners, a healer amid the wounded, and a godsend among infidels, which is why the largest gathering of blacks in Philadelphia up until that time, and a comparable number of whites, followed his casket along the streets of the city to the burial ground of the Society of Friends.

Notes

1. George S. Brookes, *Friend Anthony Benezet* (London, 1937), 5.

2. Anthony Benezet, *Short Observations on Slavery, Introductory to Some Extracts from the Writing of the Abbé Raynal on that Important Subject* (Philadelphia, 1781), 11–12.

3. Jean R. Soderlund, *Quakers and Slavery: A Divided Spirit* (Princeton, NJ, 1985), 17.

4. Ibid., 18.

5. Anthony Benezet, *A Caution and Warning to Great Britain and Her Colonies in a Short Representation of the Calamitous State of the*

Enslaved Negroes in the British Dominions. Collected from Various Authors, and Submitted to the Serious Consideration of All, and More Especially of Those in Power (Philadelphia, 1766), 16.

6. Anthony Benezet, *A Short Account of That Part of Africa Inhabited by the Negroes . . . and the Manner by which the Slave-Trade is Carried on*, 2d ed. (Philadelphia, 1762), 64.

7. Benezet to Samuel Fothergill, November 27, 1758, Quaker Collection, Haverford College, Haverford, Pennsylvania. Hereafter cited as Quaker Collection.

8. Roberts Vaux, *Memoirs of the Lives of Benjamin Lay and Ralph Sandiford: Two of the Earliest Advocates of the Emancipation of the Enslaved Africans* (Philadelphia, 1815), 17, 25–28; Soderlund, *Quakers and Slavery*, 16–17.

9. Roberts Vaux, *Memoirs of the Life of Anthony Benezet* (Philadelphia, 1817), 108–9.

10. Francis Hutcheson, *A System of Moral Philosophy*, 2 vols. (London, 1755), chap. 5, sec. ii, 2:301.

11. Benezet to Abbé Raynal, July 16, 1781, Quaker Collection.

12. Anthony Benezet, *The Plainness and Innocent Simplicity of the Christian Religion* (Philadelphia, 1782), 14; idem, *Some Historical Account of Guinea, its Situation, Produce, and General Disposition of its Inhabitants, With an Inquiry into the Rise and Progress of the Slave Trade, Its Nature and Lamentable Effects* (Philadelphia, 1771), 31.

13. Benezet, *Some Historical Account of Guinea*, ii.

14. Ibid., 2–3.

15. Ibid., 7.

16. Ibid., 38.

17. Jean Barbot, *Barbot on Guinea: The Writings of Jean Barbot on West Africa, 1678–1712*, 2 vols. (London, 1992), 1:334.

18. Benezet, citing Andrew Brue, in *Observations on the Inslaving, Importing and Purchasing of Negroes, with Some Advice thereon, Extracted form* [sic] *the Yearly Meeting Epistle of London for the Present Year* (Germantown, PA, 1759, 1760), 7.

19. Benezet, *Some Historical Account of Guinea*, 37.

20. Benezet, *A Caution and Warning*, 30.

21. Benezet, *Some Historical Account of Guinea*, 86.

22. Ibid., 73.

23. Benezet, *A Short Account of That Part of Africa*, 57.

24. Ottabah Cugoano, *Thoughts and Sentiments on the Evil and Wicked Traffic of Slavery and Commerce of the Human Species* (London, 1787); reprinted in *Three Black Writers in Eighteenth Century England*, ed. Francis D. Adams and Barry Sanders (Belmont, CA, 1971), 89.

25. Thomas Clarkson, *The History of the Rise, Progress and Accomplishments of the Abolition of the African-Slave Trade by the British Parliament*, 2 vols. (London, 1808), 1:208–9.

26. Benezet, *A Caution and Warning*, 3.

27. Patrick Henry to Robert Pleasants, January 18, 1773, Quaker Collection.

28. Anthony Benezet, *Notes on the Slave Trade* (Philadelphia, 1783), 8.

29. Benezet to John Phipps, May 28, 1763, Quaker Collection.

30. Ibid.

31. Benezet, *Notes on the Slave Trade*, 1.

32. Ibid., 3.

33. Ibid., 6–7.

34. Ibid., 7.

35. Benezet, *A Short Account of That Part of Africa*, 59.

36. Ibid., 80.

37. Vaux, *Memoirs of the Life of Anthony Benezet*, 135.

38. Ibid., 134.

39. Jean Pierre Brissot, extracts from *A Critical Examination of the Marquis De Chastellux's Travels in North America In a Letter Addressed to The Marquis*, dated July 1, 1786, Watkinson Library, Trinity College, Hartford, Connecticut.

Suggested Readings

Fuller titles of the key antislavery writings of Anthony Benezet include, in order of publication:

Observations on the Inslaving, Importing and Purchasing of Negroes, with some Advice thereon, Extracted form [sic] *the Yearly Meeting Epistle of London for the Present Year* (Germantown, PA, 1759, 1760).

A Short Account of That Part of Africa Inhabited by the Negroes . . . and the Manner by which the Slave-Trade is Carried on, 2d ed. (Philadelphia, 1762, 1763, 1768; Paris, 1767, 1768; London, 1768; Dublin, 1768).

A Caution and Warning to Great Britain and Her Colonies in a Short Representation of the Calamitous State of the Enslaved Negroes in the British Dominions. Collected from Various Authors, and Submitted to the Serious Consideration of All, and More Especially of Those in Power (Philadelphia, 1766, 1767, 1784, 1785, 1858; London, 1767, 1768, 1785, 1788).

Some Historical Account of Guinea, its Situation, Produce, and General Disposition of its Inhabitants, With an Inquiry into the Rise and Progress of the Slave Trade, Its Nature and Lamentable Effects (Philadelphia, 1771, 1784, 1788, 1815).

Serious Considerations on Several Important Subjects, viz., on War and Its Inconsistency with the Gospel; Observations on Slavery, and Remarks on the Nature and Bad Effects of Spirituous Liquors (Philadelphia, 1778).

Observations on Slavery, treatise bound with Serious Considerations on Several Important Subjects viz., On War and Its Inconsistency with the Gospel and the Bad Effects of Spirituous Liquors, 2d ed. (Philadelphia, 1778).

Short Observations on Slavery, Introductory to Some Extracts from the Writing of the Abbé Raynal on that Important Subject (Philadelphia, 1781, 1782).

Notes on the Slave Trade (Philadelphia, 1783).

The Case of Our Fellow Creatures the Oppressed Africans (London, 1783, 1784; Philadelphia, 1784).

For further reading on Anthony Benezet, see: Wilson Armistead, *Anthony Benezet* (London, 1859); George S. Brookes, *Friend Anthony Benezet* (London, 1937); Roger Bruns, "Anthony Benezet's Assertion of Negro Equality," *Journal of Negro History* 56 (1971): 230–38; Nancy Slacom Hornick, "Anthony Benezet and the African School: Toward a Theory of Full Equality," *Pennsylvania Magazine of History and Biography* 99 (1975): 399–421; Jean R. Soderlund, *Quakers and Slavery: A Divided Spirit* (Princeton, NJ, 1985); and Roberts Vaux, *Memoirs of the Life of Anthony Benezet* (Philadelphia, 1817).

2

Lachlan McGillivray
Indian Trader on the Southern Colonial Frontier

Edward J. Cashin

Before the American Revolution, the Scottish-born Indian trader Lachlan McGillivray (1719–1799) lived between worlds. Professionally and personally, he valued both his links to Scotland and the McGillivray clan and to those Indian cultures with which he traded, especially to the Creek Nation into which he had married. He also served the colonial governments of Carolina and Georgia as a British spy, interpreter, and adviser. In the 1750s, McGillivray proved an especially skillful diplomat on the southern frontier, contested terrain among the Creeks, the Cherokees, and rival European countries, but in the next decade he assumed the life of a Georgia planter, politician, and imperial merchant as well as Indian expert.

McGillivray's story, ably told by Edward Cashin, offers clues as to why a Scottish trader, once considered a hero of the Georgia Legislature, became a loyalist whom the revolutionaries banished from Georgia. Early in the conflict, he was a visible moderate, and his rice ship was burned in an attempt to disrupt British naval action. Although he returned temporarily to Georgia while it was under British occupation, McGillivray later moved back to Scotland. Had McGillivray defined himself as a loyalist, or did rivals do it for him? Did his closeness to the governor make the label inevitable? Was loyalism his choice or his fate? In his short life, Lachlan's son Alexander chose a different path; he tried to strike a new balance between his Indian family and the new republican state. Why did Lachlan choose Scotland and his clan rather than living among the Creeks, the people of his wife and son? Why did many Scots, whose well-remembered forebears were slaughtered at Culloden, choose to remain loyal to the British dynasty that had crushed those ancestors rather than rebel again in the name of liberty?

Edward J. Cashin is director of the Center for the Study of Georgia History at Augusta State University and author of *The King's Ranger: Thomas Brown and the American Revolution on the Southern Frontier* (1989) and *Lachlan McGillivray, Indian Trader: The Shaping of the Southern Colonial Frontier (1992)*.

The southern frontier in the eighteenth century seems a confusion of obscure names, places, and events to most students of history. One way of grasping the essentials of the period is to follow the career of one colonial who lived there through these years. If that individual happens to epitomize in his own life the development of frontier society, so much the better. By these criteria, Lachlan McGillivray is an ideal subject for a walk through the last half-century of colonial frontier history. Fortunately, his life is not only illustrative but also exciting.

The McGillivrays' ancestral seat was Dunmaglass in the Valley of the Nairn in Inverness-shire, Scotland. Since Gillivray, the first chief of the clan to reside in Dunmaglass, had pledged fealty to Farquhar McIntosh in 1268, the McGillivrays constituted a sept of the larger Clan Chattan, the clan of the McIntoshes. Georgia's founder, the Englishman James Edward Oglethorpe, sent his recruiters to Inverness, looking for fighting men such as the McIntoshes to hold Georgia's vulnerable southern borderlands against an attack from Florida by the Spanish and their Indian allies. The chief of Clan Chattan, Mackintosh of Mackintosh, agreed to the departure of his kinsmen, partly because his brother Aeneas had served Oglethorpe as a captain in the corps of rangers, and partly because the migration of some of these gentry would free Mackintosh lands for the more profitable business of sheep raising. Seventeen gentlemen paid their own passage from Inverness to Georgia, and the Georgia Trustees paid for 146 others, most of them Gaelic-speaking tenants of the gentlemen. Sixteen-year-old Lachlan McGillivray accompanied his uncle, John McIntosh of Holme. A veteran of the 1715 Rebellion, John McIntosh, called Mohr because of his great size in this company of tall men, led the contingent.

After a three-month voyage the *Prince of Wales* arrived at the mouth of the Savannah River in January 1736. Small boats took the Scots through the intercoastal waterway to the bluff on the Altamaha River, which they named Darien, after a failed Scots colony in Panama. John Mohr set his people to work at clearing fields and planting crops. A welcome diversion during the early days was the frequent appearance of Indians, as curious about the Scots as the Scots were about them. Men from different cultures found that they shared many of the same values. They competed in athletic contests, feats of strength, and footraces. Young Lachlan McIntosh, later a general in the American Revolution, won accolades for his speed afoot. His brother William learned to speak the language of the Creek Indians; so did Lachlan McGillivray. The Indians had a clan system, like the Scots; the spirit world was real to both cultures, and a cult of honor prevailed among both. On the southern frontier the Scots easily assimilated with the Indians because they had so much in common.

The Spanish War proved not to be the lark the Scots expected. Sixty-three men of Darien died in Oglethorpe's failed attempt to capture St. Augustine, and twenty were taken prisoner, including Darien's leader, John Mohr McIntosh. In the failure of Oglethorpe's siege, Darien received a mortal blow from which it never recovered. Although new recruits joined the survivors of the Florida invasion and helped Oglethorpe repel the Spanish counterattack on Frederica in 1742, many Highlanders, including Lachlan McGillivray, went to Charlestown to seek their fortune. With John Mohr McIntosh languishing in prison, there was no strong hand preventing their leaving Darien, and a community of Scots was already well established in Charlestown. They had organized a St. Andrew's Society in 1729, and the "Scotch" Presbyterian Church dated from 1731.

Some thought the Scottish governor, James Glen (1743–1757), gave preferential treatment to his fellow countrymen. Lachlan McGillivray happened to be particularly well favored. His kinsman Archibald McGillivray headed the largest Indian trading company, and Lachlan could speak the Creek language. Lachlan began his professional career on June 12, 1741, as an interpreter for a Carolina emissary to the Creeks. Archibald McGillivray, grown gray and wealthy, intended to retire from the Indian business in 1740 and return to Scotland. Fortunately for his young kinsman, he delayed his departure during Lachlan's apprenticeship to the company. After Archibald McGillivray returned to Inverness-shire in 1744, his company continued to engross the lion's share of the Indian trade under the name Brown, Rae, and Company. Patrick Brown retired to his indigo plantation on the Savannah River, and John Rae took Lachlan McGillivray and George Galphin into partnership. The company had warehouses in Augusta and exported their deerskins through Charlestown; Savannah lacked port facilities until 1751, and even then too few ships called there.

The secret of the success of Brown, Rae, and Company, which allowed them to monopolize the Creek trade, was their traders living in the Indian country and marrying Indian women and fathering their children. During their best years, prior to the Great War for Empire, the traders dealt reasonably with the Indian clients; that is to say, both sides indulged in only mild chicanery. Traders cheated on the lengths of the rich red cloth called "strouds" for their English town of manufacture, and the Creeks swapped "green" or poorly skinned hides when they could. In short, it was a happy time for a young Scot and a good time for the Creek Nation with Britain and France vying for preference.

Lachlan McGillivray held an exclusive license to trade in several Upper Creek towns and quickly became the most influential trader among those people, just as George Galphin in Coweta town increased his importance among the Lower Creeks. McGillivray built his house outside the village of Little Tallassee near the Coosa River. Little Tallassee was only nine miles from Fort Toulouse of the Alabamas, the outpost of the vast French territory. McGillivray's house marked the outermost British frontier, flaunting the British flag in the face of the French. By virtue of its location, McGillivray's post imposed upon him the important task of intelligence gathering. The spy services of British traders have not been fully appreciated by historians, partly because of the degeneration of the trade after 1763.

When he became chief trader to his towns in 1744, McGillivray was twenty-five, tall, fair of complexion, and vigorous. The *micos*, or chiefs, of any of his towns would have provided him with young women as an ordinary act of courtesy. An Indian maiden could take several lovers without harming her reputation, but after marriage, she was no longer free. Adultery brought swift punishment from the clan of the offended party, usually in the form of cropping the ears and a sound beating.

The Creek custom of allowing mothers final say in the management of the children presented a problem to the patriarchal Scots. A trader was a good catch for an Indian woman, giving her access to his supply of goods. The advantage for the trader was that he gained entry into the woman's clan and thereby acquired an extended family of allies. Lachlan McGillivray was unusual among his kind for two reasons. He considered the Creek woman he married, Sehoy Marchand (her father was French), his lawful wife and never took another. He defied Creek custom, undoubtedly with her consent, and sent their only son to Charlestown to be educated.

His marriage to Sehoy gained him access to her clan, the Wind Clan, the most prestigious among all the Creek families. Their union produced three children: Alexander, Sophia, and Jeannet. It is not clear which was oldest, but most likely Sophia was the firstborn. Alexander's birth has been mistakenly chronicled by several historians. Lachlan's will settled the question by stating that his son was born on December 15, 1750. Lachlan's younger brother Alexander lived in Charlestown; when Lachlan's son was old enough, he went to live with his uncle and studied writing under George Sheed and Latin under William Henderson at the free school.

Lachlan McGillivray scored his first diplomatic coup in 1744, when a delegation of eight Choctaws called on him and asked him to send goods to their towns. McGillivray sent a letter to South

Carolina's governor, James Glen, asking for instructions. Glen referred the letter to the Commons House. A special committee recommended that McGillivray be commissioned to negotiate a treaty with the Choctaw Nation. In return, McGillivray would be allowed a one-year monopoly of Choctaw trade.

Instead of acting on that recommendation, Governor Glen decided, in view of the Choctaw defection from the French camp, that this might be a good opportunity to attack Fort Toulouse. He directed McGillivray to invite the Upper Creek chiefs to Charlestown and asked McGillivray what he thought about the idea of an attack on the French post. McGillivray's letter has been lost with other Indian records of this period, but it so displeased the governor that he tried to prevent the renewal of McGillivray's license. McGillivray probably told the governor that it was a terrible idea: that the Creeks would oppose any British invasion of their country. The chiefs who visited Governor Glen in Charlestown expressed displeasure at another of his proposals, that a British fort be built among the Upper Creeks.

Impatient for British goods, Red Shoes, an important Choctaw chief, sent his brother to Charlestown to get supplies. With great fanfare, Glen arranged a treaty by which the Choctaws pledged to destroy the French fort in return for trade goods. Then Glen licensed a company other than McGillivray's to deliver the supplies. After two enormous shipments, that company went bankrupt. Brown, Rae, and Company quietly supplied the Choctaws after that, fueling the Choctaw revolt against the French, probably the most important military activity on the southern frontier during King George's War. In the process, the partners of Brown, Rae, and Company made a great deal of money.

By 1749 a Cherokee trader complained to Governor Glen that Brown, Rae, and Company, now generally referred to as "the Gentlemen of Augusta," controlled the Creek, Chickasaw, and Choctaw trade and were cutting into the Carolina trade with the Cherokees. With the dissolution of Oglethorpe's regiment in 1749 and the departure of the garrison at Fort Augusta, the gentlemen of the company assumed responsibility for governing Augusta. Early in 1750 the company leased a 500-acre tract at the junction of the Creek and Cherokee trails to the west of Augusta. McGillivray later moved his family to that site. The company built St. Paul's Church in 1750 and asked the Society for the Propagation of the Gospel to send over a minister. The Georgia Trustees, about to surrender the colony to the control of Parliament, were happy to oblige. Unfortunately, the first minister was terrified of the Indians who frequented the town and asked to be removed to Charlestown.

Governor Glen had to get over his pique with McGillivray, because some of the most influential Creek headmen lived in McGillivray's towns. The Wolf of Okchoy, better known as the Mortar, liked neither the English nor the French, but he considered the English the more dangerous and so flirted with the French. Enochtonachee, also of Okchoy, known by the traders as the Gun Merchant, was the best friend of the British during the decade before the outbreak of the Great War for Empire. The young warrior destined to become the greatest man in the Upper Creek town and spokesman for the Nation lived in McGillivray's town. He was Emistisiguo of Little Tallassee, and the traders paid him the compliment of calling him by that name.

McGillivray's information about French activities at Fort Toulouse was another reason for Governor Glen to forgive him for his good but unwelcome advice as to a British attack on Fort Toulouse. In fact, McGillivray became Glen's favorite interpreter. In 1749, Glen invited the Creek headmen to Charlestown to urge them to stop fighting the Cherokees, with McGillivray as interpreter. When Malatchi, of the Lower Creek town of Coweta, and the spokesmen for the Creek Nation finally agreed, Glen invited everyone back to Charlestown to celebrate. Glen received the sixty-nine Upper Creeks and twenty-four Lower Creeks with all the considerable pomp and pageantry he could muster. Members of his council and the most distinguished residents of Charlestown sat down on May 28, 1753, to draw up the treaty. Five interpreters stood by in case they were needed, but their services were not required. Lachlan McGillivray did all the translating so clearly and completely that the talks were reported verbatim in the South Carolina *Gazette*.

The official beginning of the Great War for Empire in 1756 coincided with the arrival of a new governor in Carolina, William Henry Lyttelton. McGillivray went to Charlestown in July 1756 to pay his respects to the governor and to brief him on the situation in the Indian country. His Creek friends resented the unlawful encroachment of settlers on the Ogeechee River. The Creeks claimed the Savannah River as their boundary and permitted the settlement of Augusta, but nothing more. Neither Lyttelton nor Georgia's governor, John Reynolds, could find a way to deal with the lawless folk on the Ogeechee. When these intruders shot and killed two Indians, creating a crisis that could have provoked a general war, the Augusta traders took matters into their own hands. They sent out a posse to arrest the guilty parties and dispatched a message to the Creek towns that the evildoers would be punished. McGillivray sent word to Lyttelton that the crisis had passed. Reynolds then fretted that McGillivray had not told him. In truth,

John Reynolds proved to be the wrong administrator for a colony still struggling into existence. In 1757, Georgia's first able governor arrived in the person of Henry Ellis, explorer, scientist, and member of the prestigious Royal Society. Ellis quickly quieted factionalism and taught Georgians the basics of self-government. Perhaps Ellis's greatest achievement was in Indian diplomacy. He maintained friendly relations with the Creek Nation when most of the Indians joined the French. Wisely, he worked through veteran traders such as Lachlan McGillivray and George Galphin.

Ellis named McGillivray a justice of the peace in Augusta in 1757, a sign that McGillivray had taken up permanent residence on the 500-acre tract previously leased by the company. McGillivray's role shifted with his Augusta residency. In Little Tallassee he had acted as intelligence agent for colonial governors; now he played host to Indian visitors to Augusta. In both places he acted as a link between two cultures. Reynolds had allowed Glen to preempt leadership in Indian affairs, but Governor Ellis challenged Lyttelton's continued claim to preeminence and gained McGillivray's respect and support.

Governor James Glen's notion of attacking Fort Toulouse gained a powerful proponent in William Pitt, when King George II reluctantly turned the war effort over to him. Pitt wrote a letter marked "Secret" to Lyttelton, asking the governor to start planning an invasion of Louisiana from the land side in conjunction with a naval attack on Mobile or New Orleans. Lyttelton knew practically nothing about Louisiana, Fort Toulouse, or the Creek Nation. Therefore, he made an unheralded visit to Fort Moore in June 1758 and quietly sought out McGillivray to ask his opinion on this urgent matter. The veteran trader James Adair happened to be in Augusta and added his advice to McGillivray's. They emphasized the extreme difficulty of transporting an army across so many rivers and warned that the British would have to fight the entire Creek Nation and probably the Choctaws and Chickasaws as well. They suggested that the expedition would face the same problems as General Braddock's ill-fated invasion of the Ohio country.

Although Lyttelton did not like their advice, he forwarded the traders' opinions to Pitt along with his own arguments in favor of a land invasion. He would win over the Creeks, he said, by sending them a message that he came as a friend. If they chose to oppose him, however, he would burn down their villages and put their women and children to the sword. Fortunately, the invasion never happened. Pitt postponed the operation in favor of a campaign against the rich French sugar islands of the West Indies. Pitt may have been swayed by the sober advice of McGillivray rather than the braggadocio of his governor.

The arrival in Carolina of the first British superintendent of Indian Affairs in the Southern Department in 1758 was of immediate interest to the gentlemen of Augusta and in particular to Lachlan McGillivray. Edmond Atkin, a Carolina trader and a bitter critic of Governor Glen, had written a long critique of the prevailing Indian administration in 1755, which led the ministry to entrust the Indian management in the south to him. The capable Sir William Johnson acted as superintendent in the Northern Department. Atkin's main complaint was that traders could not be trusted to act as intermediaries with the tribes. The position required an objective, altruistic person such as himself. Atkin harbored a particular dislike for Glen's favorite interpreter, McGillivray. He accused McGillivray's company of profiteering in the Choctaw war and illicit trading with the French.

Atkin never received the respect he felt he deserved. Insisting on protocol, he achieved burlesque. He required a thirteen-gun salute at Fort Moore; the garrison then had to hurry across the river to repeat the ceremony at Fort Augusta. Atkin published a proclamation forbidding traders to send goods into the Creek country until he had visited the main villages and distributed presents. It took him two months to recruit an escort of twelve men while traders chafed at his inaction. James Adair thought that Lachlan McGillivray would have been a more expeditious agent.

Atkin's imperious manner alienated the Indians he visited. Some of the greatest chiefs including the Mortar, Gun Merchant, and Togulki, son of Malatchi, went to Savannah to complain to Henry Ellis about Superintendent Atkin. They missed their winter hunt, they said, while Atkin loitered in the woods. Atkin insulted them, calling them Frenchmen, and refused them the courtesy of a handclasp. Ellis wrote to the ministry that Atkin caused problems where there were none. Atkin should have visited the Cherokee country. While Atkin scolded the Creeks for imaginary failings, the Cherokees launched a war on the Carolina and Georgia frontier.

When Atkin returned to Augusta on December 23, 1759, he found that the war had started without him. Governor Lyttelton, who aspired to lead an invasion of Louisiana, barely managed a march to Fort Prince George at Keowee in the Cherokee lower towns, with sickness and desertion weakening his army. When the Cherokees agreed to expel French agents from their country, he claimed success. He had barely returned to Charlestown when the Cherokees launched an offensive, driving frightened settlers before them to Forts Augusta and Moore. On February 5, 1760, Lachlan McGillivray learned that Cherokees had threatened settlers on the Little River northwest of Augusta. Without waiting for orders, he sent riders to the Creeks asking for help and set out from Augusta with fifty men. He found one hundred people huddled at James Germany's house. He furnished them with spades and axes and set them to building earthworks. Creeks under Escochabey, the Young Lieutenant of the Cowetas, and Talhichico, head warrior of the Cussetas, joined McGillivray. This was their land, and they meant to defend it against the Cherokees. The Indians brought with them to Germany's house a group of settlers who had become lost in a swamp as they fled the Cherokees. McGillivray returned with them to Augusta and entertained his Indian friends at his house.

On February 11 the leading citizens of Augusta met with their Creek rescuers and the neighboring Chickasaws. Lachlan McGillivray addressed the Indians and thanked them for their assistance. The Chickasaws said they were willing to live and die for the English. The Cherokee war parties reached Augusta and Fort Moore the next day. Three men who ventured out of Augusta were attacked; one was tomahawked and scalped. Sixty warriors assaulted fifteen settlers outside Augusta the following day. The Creeks slipped out of Augusta and rescued some stragglers, including three children the Cherokees had captured. Across the river, a group of militiamen riding out from Fort Moore were ambushed by Cherokees. Captain Ulrich Tobler was killed. The hatchet left in his head carried notches for other victims. Edmond Atkin, in fear for his life at Fort Moore, reported that the people were all running like sheep before wolves.

In spite of the danger, McGillivray and his Indian friends crossed to the Carolina side to recover grain he had stored. He was fired upon while crossing the river with the corn. He then roused a party of settlers and Indians, recrossed the river and chased the enemy away. The Cherokees fled in such haste that they left blankets and other belongings behind.

The crisis at Augusta passed, as the Cherokees returned to their country and to the siege of Fort Loudoun. That ill-placed symbol of British hegemony capitulated to the Indians. Even so, the garrison was massacred. Attakullakulla, the Little Carpenter, managed to save the life of John Stuart, who would replace Edmond Atkin as Indian superintendent in 1762. In 1760, the Georgia Assembly paid Lachlan McGillivray a unique honor by passing a resolution recognizing his heroism during the height of the crisis.

Governor Henry Ellis asked to be relieved for reasons of health. By the time his successor, James Wright, arrived on October 11, 1760, the greatest danger was over. Before the war ended two British expeditions marched into the Cherokee middle settlements, one in 1760 and the other in 1761, and destroyed all the villages within their reach.

After the Cherokee war crisis Lachlan McGillivray retired from the Indian trade, bought Vale Royal plantation outside Savannah, and adopted the lifestyle of a planter. With the profits from Indian trade, his good Inverness education, and his connections with the influential Scots of coastal Georgia and Charlestown, McGillivray was readily recognized as a member of that emerging social class sometimes termed the "elite" by social scientists. In McGillivray's day, one would have used the term "polite society." We do not know whether Sehoy and the girls lived with Lachlan at Vale Royal, but we know that his son Alexander did. As a planter could never have too much land, McGillivray increased his holdings to include a rice plantation on Hutchinson Island in the Savannah River and several other scattered holdings, more than ten thousand acres in all.

When Governor James Wright went to Augusta in October 1763 to draw up a treaty with nine hundred Indians representing five southern Indian nations, Captain Lachlan McGillivray led the Savannah escort. More important, McGillivray at his house in Augusta and George Galphin at Silver Bluff entertained the Indian headmen while waiting the arrival of the distinguished governors of Virginia, North Carolina, and South Carolina and their retinues. McGillivray and Galphin worked out an agreement before the formal conference began. John Stuart, the new superintendent, as well as the governors, had come to celebrate the end of the war and to exchange pleasantries. So they were surprised and pleased when the Creek leaders began the meeting with an offer to cede the land between the Savannah and Ogeechee Rivers, opening a fifty-mile strip of land for settlement.

Two actions on the part of government in 1763 had profound effects on the social fabric of the southern frontier. Locally, the Treaty of Augusta permitted the influx of hundreds of new settlers during the ensuing decade. Most of these newcomers did not know Indians and did not want to know them. Rather, they wanted to roll back the boundary to the next river west, the Oconee, even if it meant war with the Indians. More broadly, the Royal Proclamation of 1763 established a line down the Appalachians and prohibited settlement west of that line. Even though the prohibition was not well enforced, the decree funneled pioneer families down the mountain valleys into the Georgia backcountry. Unfortunately, the proclamation contained a phrase throwing the Indian trade open to all comers. The purpose was well intentioned, to prevent one company from monopolizing the trade, but the result was a chaotic, unregulated trading fiasco.

Old traders McGillivray, Galphin, and John Rae turned to new endeavors. In 1766, McGillivray, now an elected member of the Georgia legislature, obtained passage of a law providing funding to encourage new settlers. John Rae advertised for them in Ireland, and Galphin offered free transportation from Charlestown on his river boats. The resulting stream of Irish newcomers received grants of land in the new township of Queensborough on the Ogeechee River.

The Queensborough settlers took out proper titles to land, as did people in the Quaker-led community of Wrightsborough on the Little River. Wandering squatters called "crackers" by older Georgians caused trouble by trespassing on other people's property. They ignored the 1763 boundary line and crossed into Indian territory. Superintendent John Stuart met with Creek delegates at Augusta in May 1767 and told them that he wanted the line clearly marked so that no one could mistake it. He asked George Galphin to lead the survey of the upper line and Lachlan McGillivray to do the more difficult marking of the line behind the coastal parishes. Galphin and McGillivray knew where the line was supposed to run because they had worked it out with their Indian friends in 1763 at Augusta. McGillivray considered the marking of the line one of the most physically demanding tasks of his life. In his youth he had thought nothing of wading through swamps and swimming flooded rivers, but in 1768 he was almost fifty years old and unwell when he started out. The most difficult section crossed a twelve-mile stretch of the fabled Okefenokee Swamp. Some of the white members of the party suspected that their Indian companions were deliberately luring them into a death trap. The Indians were perhaps more frightened, for they believed that a race of invisible people inhabited the swamp and that at any moment some terrible thing could happen to them. It took thirty-one days to mark the line from the Canoochee River to the St. Marys. The *Georgia Gazette* sang McGillivray's praises, and the Commons House of Georgia passed another resolution recognizing his contribution.

McGillivray's exploits in running the line enhanced his celebrity status in Savannah. Honors followed: reelection to the Commons House and to a captaincy in the militia and an appointment as justice of the peace. Charlestown served as the exemplar for Georgia's new gentry, and McGillivray adopted the Charlestown fashions: his carriages and horses, his town house and range of lots in Savannah, his stable of race horses, and his plantations, Vale Royal, Springfield, and Sabine Fields. He gave land and slaves as gestures of friendship. And, in the best Charlestown fashion, he entered the import-export business in partnership with one of Georgia's wealthiest citizens, John Graham, a fellow Scot. The company assumed a trade earlier confined to Charlestown mercantile houses, the importation of slaves. Georgia merchants risked little or no capital of their own, because they bought slaves for planters on a commission of 5 percent. The advantage to a firm like McGillivray's was that the same planters were likely to purchase other commodities at their stores. Governor James Wright employed McGillivray's company for the export of his huge rice crop and for the purchase of goods he needed in London. To cut the middlemen's costs of his trade, Lachlan joined John McGillivray in purchasing a half-interest in the *Inverness* and hired his kinsman Daniel McGillivray to captain it.

Lachlan's son Alexander grew into young manhood at Vale Royal. He was six when McGillivray left Little Tallassee for Augusta, twelve when his father moved to Savannah. It must have been during those years that Alexander stayed with relatives in Charlestown and received a good education. By 1767, Alexander lived with his father and worked at the mercantile house of Inglis and Hall. In that year, Alexander's name appeared on a number of his father's legal documents as a witness.

Lachlan continued to act as an expert on Indian affairs. In 1770, Governor Wright asked McGillivray to call upon Lord Hillsborough, the American secretary, with suggestions on Indian policy. After his conference with Hillsborough in London, McGillivray went to Dunmaglass to see his ailing mother, Janet McIntosh McGillivray. She died before his arrival, and he mourned with his many relatives. He visited the grave of his cousin, Colonel Alexander McGillivray, who died bravely at Culloden. He persuaded his cousin William, chief of the McGillivrays, to move to Georgia, and he reminded William of his duty to marry and to perpetuate the chiefdom in Georgia. A few months after Lachlan's return to Savannah, William McGillivray followed him. Lachlan transferred his Hutchinson Island rice fields to William and took great pleasure in introducing his cousin to Savannah's gentry.

Governor Wright, made a baronet in 1773, arranged a second Indian congress in Augusta to obtain more land. The Cherokees had become heavily indebted to Augusta merchants and, prompted by the traders, they offered to exchange land for debts. Lord Hillsborough gave his permission, providing that the Creek Nation agreed, because that tribe also claimed the land above Georgia's Little River. The Creeks displayed great reluctance to yield more land or even to come to Augusta to discuss the matter. McGillivray added his powers of persuasion to George Galphin's, with the result that Creek delegates took their places at the Augusta Congress in June 1773. The Creeks stoutly refused to give up the land between the Ogeechee and Oconee and very grudgingly yielded the land east of the Ogeechee and above the Little River.

Governor Wright's hopes of selling the desirable lands and reimbursing the merchants were quashed by a sudden outbreak by a party of disgruntled Lower Creeks. Their attacks on the Georgia frontier in December 1773 and January 1774 created a panic throughout the southern frontier from Carolina to West Florida. Wright secured the consent of the governors of South Carolina, East Florida, and West Florida to impose an unprecedented trade embargo upon the Creek Nation until the leaders punished the guilty people.

With renewed fear of the Indians uppermost in their minds, most Georgians declined to join with those Savannah merchants who protested the British Coercive Acts on July 4, 1774. Lachlan McGillivray's name was prominent on a resolution of loyalty to the royal government. When Emistisiguo and other chiefs, speaking for the Nation, agreed to Wright's terms, the expansionist Georgians hoped that the governor would extract additional land from the humbled Creeks. However, the Indian traders and the merchants who supplied the traders argued against pushing the boundary farther west because Georgia would lose the trade to Mobile and Pensacola. Caught between competing pressures, Wright sided with the traders and reopened the trade, demanding only the deaths of five culprits. As it happened, the two greatest offenders were never caught. The previously loyal backcountry parishes joined the revolutionary movement after Governor Wright's October treaty. Lachlan McGillivray's role in the governor's decision is not clear, but the disappointed Georgians blamed him along with others who did business with the Indians.

During the critical year of 1775, opposition to Parliament's claim to absolute authority over the colonists increased in Georgia. Savannah's leading citizens gathered at the Liberty Pole on June 26, 1775. Future patriots and loyalists united for the moment in a common cause, a resolution protesting Parliament's efforts to raise revenue in America and stipulating that Georgians would take every constitutional means of redressing their grievances. The distinguished assemblage paid Lachlan McGillivray their highest compliment by electing him to chair the meeting. The gesture indicated that his fellows respected his judgment, his character, and his integrity.

After Georgia adopted the Continental Association, an agreement that barred trade with Britain, McGillivray could no longer support the movement. He could defend American rights, but he would not take sides against the king and against his people in Scotland. Once elected, McGillivray declined to take the chair in the extralegal Provincial Congress. Governor Wright showed his gratitude by nominating him to membership in the Council House of the Assembly.

Both Lachlan and William McGillivray had to pay the price for their loyalty early in 1776. A British fleet put in at the Savannah River for provisioning. The Georgia Provincial Congress called out the militia to resist what it regarded as a British invasion. Representatives of the revolutionary government put Governor Wright under house arrest, but he escaped by night to take refuge on the warship *Scarborough*.

Having failed to get provisions by negotiation, the British decided to seize the twenty merchant ships, loaded with rice and deerskins, which had been long detained at Savannah because of the trade embargo. Revolutionary Georgians decided to burn the rice boats to prevent the British from taking them. The ship selected to be set afire and set adrift among the merchant vessels was McGillivray's *Inverness*, loaded with McGillivray's rice and George Galphin's deerskins. The flaming *Inverness* caught on a sandbar and burned to a hulk, but did not carry the fire to the other ships. The British made off with sixteen vessels and three hostages.

The Georgians retaliated by arresting six of the most prominent loyalists, including Lachlan and William McGillivray, and holding them pending the release of the three Georgian hostages aboard the British warship. When the three were released, the McGillivrays were banished from Georgia. Twenty-five-year-old Alexander returned to Little Tallassee and his mother's clan. Superintendent John Stuart appointed him one of his deputies.

The exile of Georgia's royal government lasted three years. Late in 1778, Lieutenant Colonel Archibald Campbell led an invasion of Georgia. Savannah and the low country quickly surrendered, and Campbell occupied Augusta for two weeks until patriot reinforcement forced him to retreat. The British defeated the pursuing Americans at Briar Creek, and royal government was restored in the area of British occupation. Georgia had the unique distinction of being the only rebellious colony that was reunited with the mother country, if only for the duration of the war. Lachlan McGillivray returned with Governor Wright and was promptly elected to the royal Commons House of Assembly.

Father and son were reunited by the fortunes of war. John Stuart in Pensacola ordered his deputies David Taitt and Alexander McGillivray to lead a party of Creek Indians to cooperate with Lieutenant Colonel Campbell, whose army Stuart believed to be in Augusta still. Many of the Indians turned back when they discovered that Augusta had been abandoned by Campbell, but Taitt,

McGillivray, and a few others fought their way through enemy territory to Savannah. Surprisingly enough, they lingered at Vale Royal for almost a year. A family tradition, recorded by nineteenth-century Alabama historian Thomas Woodward, is that Sehoy and her daughters attempted to join Lachlan and Alexander at Vale Royal but could not get through enemy lines.

If she had tried to reach Savannah in September or October 1779, she would have found a combined French and American army barring the way. On September 3 a massive French fleet appeared off Tybee Island. Admiral Charles Hector, comte d'Estaing intended to oblige General George Washington by capturing Savannah on his way back to France. On September 12, he began the ponderous process of landing some forty-five hundred troops. General Benjamin Lincoln crossed over from Carolina with an estimated twenty-five hundred Americans to complete the siege of Savannah. The French scorned their inexperienced American allies for not knowing how to conduct a proper siege. They consumed three weeks with digging entrenchments around the town at a distance of two hundred yards from the contracted British works with their little more than two thousand defenders. On October 3, 1779, the French began an artillery bombardment that had little effect on the British regulars, as the shells passed over their lines and crashed into the town. Lachlan McGillivray's Vale Royal lay outside the British lines but was protected by a British warship anchored nearby. The McGillivray barn on Hutchinson Island housed a number of refugees, but mortars from a French ship behind Hutchinson Island made it unsafe. Lieutenant Colonel Thomas Brown's King's Rangers with his Indian allies defended the extreme right of the British lines. His friends David Taitt and Alexander McGillivray undoubtedly were there with their Indian escort. After a particularly severe bombardment on October 7 and 8, 1779, the allied grand assault occurred on October 9. Fighting was heaviest at Lachlan McGillivray's Springfield plantation on the Augusta Road. Count Casimir Pulaski, a Polish volunteer with the Americans, was killed in the attack. The British lines held; the attackers fell back. D'Estaing buried his dead, collected his wounded, and sailed away with his ships. London celebrated the victory with cannon salutes and fireworks.

Some of Alexander's Indian friends lingered in Savannah until June 1780, according to Lachlan McGillivray's expense accounts. By then, Charleston had fallen to the British (on May 12, 1780). Lieutenant Colonel Brown of the King's Rangers had been appointed to the post of Indian superintendent, succeeding John Stuart, who had died in Pensacola. Brown renewed Alexander's commission as deputy, and on April 11, 1780, Brown informed his supervisors that Alexander McGillivray and eight hundred Creeks were going to Pensacola to help defend it against the Spanish.

During the last days of British occupation, Lachlan McGillivray made up his mind to return to Scotland. He turned over his extensive holdings to his cousin John McGillivray in return for a pension of £500 per year. The formal surrender of Savannah took place on July 11, 1782. Lachlan had already left Georgia for London that May. John McGillivray was among the last to depart. He sailed with Governor James Wright on April 8, 1783. All the McGillivray holdings in Georgia were confiscated by the State of Georgia.

William McGillivray, the chief, enticed to Georgia before the Revolution, did not return to Georgia during the restoration of British rule because of an injury. In 1780 he married Barbara Mackenzie of Fairburn, Scotland. By 1783 the couple had two children, Barbara Jean and John Lachlan. Lachlan and John McGillivray joined William and his family in London where they applied for compensation for their losses. William became ill, probably from pneumonia, and the McGillivrays moved to sunny Cornwall for his health. He grew worse in Cornwall; his wife took him to Portugal, where he died. Young John Lachlan, an infant, inherited William's properties in Scotland, and John McGillivray, William's brother, managed them. In 1786, John received compensation from the government for the land he had obtained from Lachlan. He made out a will leaving everything to his nephew and future chief John Lachlan. John never intended to return to Scotland. He established a plantation in Jamaica and died there in 1788. His Jamaican holdings became part of John Lachlan's legacy.

In 1784, Lachlan returned to Dunmaglass and took up residence with Anne, sister of William and John, and his cousin. When she died in 1790, Lachlan was named "cautioner" or trustee of the estate of seven-year-old John Lachlan. In fact, Lachlan had seven properties in the Valley of the Nairn to manage, and he did so with his usual energy and efficiency. He put a stop to the cutting of trees and began a massive reforestation project. One order of his on November 11, 1791, was for twenty thousand trees. In addition, in 1778 he had founded, with twelve other gentlemen, the Northern Meeting, a yearly celebration of the Highland games, music, and dancing that has continued to this day.

By 1790 the children's closest relatives, including their mother, had died, so it fell to Lachlan "Lia" as he was called, Lachlan the Gray, to care for Barbara Jean and John Lachlan. He called John Lachlan "my Johnny," and sent him off to be tutored in Inverness, worried about his childhood ailments, and in general acted like a doting parent. Barbara Jean, growing into a handsome young lady, presided at Dunmaglass.

Lachlan did not lose touch with his family in America. He carefully followed the career of his son, Alexander. With the death of Emistisiguo in 1782, the Creek Nation looked to Alexander as their spokesman. He owed his ascendency to his participation, through his mother Sehoy, in the prestigious Wind Clan, his role as deputy superintendent under John Stuart and Thomas Brown, his Charlestown education, and his natural talents. The peace treaty in 1783 returned Florida to Spain, and Alexander regarded the Spanish in Florida as less aggressively threatening than the restless Georgians flushed with victory, but their expansion was still limited by the line of 1763, marked by his father. The nearly bankrupt State of Georgia needed land to pay its debts and signed treaties with a few unauthorized chiefs to obtain the long-sought-after Oconee strip. Alexander McGillivray refused to recognize those treaties, and a desultory war kept the frontier in ferment. One reason that Georgia ratified the U.S. Constitution so readily is that the state hoped the stronger federal government would help extend Georgia's Indian boundary. In this hope they were gratified when President George Washington invited McGillivray and a delegation of Creek chiefs to New York to sign a new treaty. McGillivray on horseback and the thirty headmen with their retainers in a caravan of wagons made an impressive procession as they made their way to New York. A Scot named Colin Douglass entertained McGillivray in Baltimore. The evening ended with the singing of nostalgic Scottish ballads, in which McGillivray joined. Alexander later wrote to thank his host, remarking that the strains of "Sweet Jim of Aberdeen" still vibrated in his ear. The New York reception amounted to a triumph for McGillivray. He and his authentic Indians were welcomed by New Yorkers in Indian garb, the Sons of Saint Tammany, forerunners of the New York political machine. Secretary of War Henry Knox escorted them to President Washington's residence for a more intimate reception. Alexander felt at ease in salons and at soirees and could hold his own in polite conversation. Abigail Adams, who did not brook fools lightly, commented that McGillivray dressed in fashion, spoke English like a native, and acted the part of a gentleman.

McGillivray and his chiefs signed the Treaty of New York, agreeing to move the Georgia boundary from the Ogeechee to the Oconee River. Some of McGillivray's people were disappointed that he gave up any land at all. However, their annoyance paled in comparison with that of the expansionist Georgians who had hoped for a great deal more.

We get a glimpse of Alexander McGillivray at home through the eyes of John Pope, a traveler through the frontier country in 1791. Pope met "the General," as his people called Alexander, at his upper plantation, Lachlan's house, where Alexander had been born and which he was rebuilding. McGillivray received his visitor graciously. Pope commented on McGillivray's wit and humor, the beauty of his wife, and the decorous behavior of the two children, Alexander (Aleck) and Elizabeth, who spoke English impeccably. Alexander owned several plantations cultivated by more than fifty slaves and kept a gentleman's table and a wine cellar. He showed Pope a set of gilt-edged books given him by President Washington as well as an epaulet that Washington had worn during the war. Alexander told Pope that he received presents from Scotland, too, remarking that he had had gifts from both his political father, Washington, and his natural father, Lachlan.

In April 1793, Alexander was taken ill on a journey to Pensacola. William Panton, trader to the Creek Nation, gave him all the care he could, but Alexander died after eight days of suffering, probably from pneumonia. A large number of people attended his funeral. Panton informed the Spanish governor that McGillivray had no papers on him, only a letter from his father and one or two others. Panton carried out Alexander's wish that Aleck be sent to Scotland to be brought up by Lachlan. Aleck and John Lachlan were nearly the same age, and we can imagine that they brightened Lachlan's life at Dunmaglass. Until his death at Dunmaglass on November 16, 1799, in his eightieth year, rich in the love and respect of his friends and relatives, Lachlan would be responsible for the education of John Lachlan, chief of the clan, and of Aleck, regarded as the next paramount chief of the Creek Nation. It was well that Lachlan was spared the sorrow he would have felt a few months later at the death of nineteen-year-old Barbara Jean. His grandson Aleck was never to return to his people, for only two years later he died of pneumonia. A happier future awaited John Lachlan. Thanks to Lachlan, John Lachlan's holdings were larger and more productive than any previous tenant of Dunmaglass. He married well and lived until 1852, leaving a fortune to the tenants of his estates. He was the last of his line to live at Dunmaglass. After his death the chiefdom passed to the Canadian branch of the clan.

Lachlan McGillivray did not cause the changes that occurred on the southern frontier, or in his native Inverness-shire. He exemplified them. There were villains enough among the Indian traders, but the best of them, such as McGillivray and Galphin, acted as intermediaries between the great chiefs and the governors, facilitating economic, political, and cultural interaction. They influenced the diplomatic and military history of the colonial era through the American Revolution. The children of traders and Indians have continued to exercise those links between cultures, from Lachlan McGillivray's day to our own.

Suggested Readings

Primary sources include Allan D. Candler et al., *The Colonial Records of the State of Georgia*, 26 vols. (Atlanta, 1904–1916), which are in typescript at the Georgia Department of Archives and History, Atlanta. Essential to a study of the early Indian trade is William R. McDowell Jr., ed., *Colonial Records of South Carolina: Documents Relating to Indian Affairs, May 21, 1750–August 7, 1754* (Columbia, 1958); and Samuel Cole Williams, ed., *Adairs History of the American Indians, 1930* (reprinted, New York, 1974). Secondary sources include John R. Alden, *John Stuart and the Southern Colonial Frontier: A Study of Indian Relations, War, Trade and Land Problems in the Southern Wilderness, 1754–1775* (New York, 1966). Russell Snapp takes issue with some of Alden's conclusions in *John Stuart and the Struggle for Empire on the Southern Frontier* (Baton Rouge, LA, 1996). The best study of the Indian trade is Kathryn E. Holland Braund, *Deerskins and Duffels: Creek Indian Trade with Anglo-America, 1685–1815* (Lincoln, NE, 1993). Basic to a study of the Revolution in Georgia is Kenneth Coleman, *The American Revolution in Georgia, 1763–1789* (Athens, 1958). See also Edward J. Cashin, *The King's Ranger: Thomas Brown and the American Revolution on the Southern Frontier* (Athens, 1989). For the McGillivrays, see John Walton Caughey, *McGillivray of the Creeks* (Norman, OK, 1938); and Edward J. Cashin, *Lachlan McGillivray, Indian Trader: The Shaping of the Colonial Frontier* (Athens, 1992).

3

Eliza Lucas Pinckney

Vegetables and Virtue

Gary L. Hewitt

Best known for her successful indigo experiments in Carolina, Eliza Lucas Pinckney (1722–1793) managed both her absentee father's plantations and later, in her widowhood, her husband Charles Pinckney's properties. Plantations thrived under her direction, although married women did not own land by law in her time and typically did not manage family businesses. Elite, but not exactly leisured, Eliza once presented the Princess of Wales with a dress of silk made from Eliza's own silkworms. In choosing to remain in Carolina after her husband's death, rather than return to England and rejoin her family, was Eliza fulfilling the duties of a deputy husband by preserving her children's inheritance, or did she also relish the opportunity to manage plantation affairs again?

As the daughter of a royal governor, Eliza Lucas had many English acquaintances. Her sons were educated in England, but they returned to Carolina and distinguished themselves as officers in the Continental Army. Why would members of the Pinckney family, who had long maintained ties throughout the empire, embrace the revolutionaries' cause? How influential was Eliza's example? As Gary Hewitt explains, she cultivated virtue and patriotism in her sons and grandsons with the same care she had applied to her garden. Pinckney family patriotism did not ensure economic prosperity throughout the Revolutionary War. Her sons remained prominent leaders, but middle-aged Eliza lost much of her own economic independence. In the aftermath of the Revolution, as a grandmother, Eliza wrote to her daughter's son, Daniel Huger Horry, in England and tried to interest him in American affairs by enclosing a copy of America's new federal Constitution. Horry settled in France, but he did change his name to Charles Lucas Pinckney Horry. Admired by George Washington, who later requested to be a pallbearer at her funeral, Eliza embodied the values of a republican mother even before there was a republic.

Gary L. Hewitt, an American historian at Grinnell College, Iowa, has completed a book-length study of the political economies and plantation systems of South Carolina and Georgia in the early eighteenth century.

Eliza Lucas Pinckney's young son Tom once observed that "Mama loves long letters."[1] Despite her earlier fears that she might not have enough "matter to support an Epistolary Intercourse," Eliza's surviving letters span nearly half a century.[2] Her extensive correspondence has proved a blessing for modern historians, who have found in those long letters a tantalizing window into the world of a woman of striking intelligence, vivacity, and charm. While Eliza did not quite write her "waking and sleeping dream,"[3] as she threatened one friend, her letters touched on topics as diverse as the prices of agricultural products, local politics, neighborhood romance and marriage, and the latest novels. Her mail was directed around the globe to friends, relations, and business associates from London to New England to the West Indies, and it was accompanied by gifts to cement these cosmopolitan friendships. Eliza Lucas Pinckney's world was as far-flung as the sprawling British Empire of the eighteenth century, and she tied it together with her letters.

Eliza was from the very circumstances of her life an extraordinary woman. Her education, wealth, and status all made her decidedly atypical for Carolinians of the mid-eighteenth century. Eliza read voraciously in literature and philosophy and wrote numerous long letters during an age when a minority of Carolinians, whether male or female, free or enslaved, was literate. She was born in the West Indies, educated in England as a girl, and returned for an extended stay there after her marriage. Although most Carolinians during this era, like Eliza, had been born outside the colony, most had not experienced her wide travels. She enjoyed the leisure and comforts that came with being a member of one of the wealthiest families in the colony: not only a library filled with books but also gardens, music lessons, and a constant round of visits and entertaining. Her father was a colonel in the British army and lieutenant governor of the wealthy colony of Antigua, her husband was a prominent South Carolina politician, and her two sons were leaders of the patriot cause during the American Revolution in South Carolina—both as generals in the state militia, and one as the state's delegate to the Constitutional Convention in 1787.

Eliza Lucas Pinckney's story is noteworthy but not simply because she was a wealthy and privileged lady. Her accomplishments were unusual for a woman of her wealth and status, or perhaps for any woman in the eighteenth-century Anglo-American world. Eliza directed important family business as she managed the Lucas family's three plantations from 1739 to 1745. She possessed a keen interest in the life of the mind, as her wide-ranging and frequent letters attest. She was also an amateur, though talented, scientist. Eliza was, as she put it once, "fond of the vegetable world," and for several years she was engaged in horticultural experiments that eventually led to the successful commercial cultivation of indigo in South Carolina—a crop that quickly became a major contributor to the wealth of the colony's plantation economy.[4]

Despite Eliza Lucas Pinckney's unusual level of activity and wealth, she helps to illuminate some of the central themes of revolutionary-era American life. Her education and thinking reflect the intellectual currents of the eighteenth century. Her travels from colony to colony and two sojourns in England illustrate the interlocking sinews of the British Empire. Her management of the family plantations and agricultural innovation depict a desire for success and profit among the planters of South Carolina. As a whole, Eliza Lucas Pinckney's life helps demonstrate how fluid women's roles could be in the eighteenth century. Her opportunities were tremendous, and she took good advantage of them to participate in the world of business and of the mind. Yet, Eliza was constrained by her sex as well. She was conscious that, as "a girl," her ideas were valued differently from those of her brothers. More profoundly, Eliza's horizons shrank after her marriage and the birth of her three children. Eliza moved easily into a new role of wife and mother and left some of the intellectual vivacity of her youth behind in favor of a more sober didactic sensibility, in which the education—especially moral—of her children was most important. Her desire to instill "virtue" into her sons' breasts stands out in her numerous letters—virtue that served both Eliza and her sons well when the Revolution came to South Carolina.

Eliza Lucas had lived a cosmopolitan life before she was out of her teens. Born on the British island colony of Antigua in December 1722, Eliza spent a few years in an English girls' school and briefly returned to her birthplace before moving to South Carolina in 1738 with her father and mother, George and Anne Lucas, and her younger sister Mary (her younger brothers, George and Thomas, remained in England at school). Her far-reaching travels were the consequence of her family's wide-ranging set of transatlantic connections. Her father was an important man on Antigua: he was heir to a large sugar estate and son of an assemblyman, and by 1733 he sat on that colony's Royal Council. George Lucas also had a promising military career. Beginning as a captain of a local militia in 1722, he had purchased a major's commission in the British army by the time the family moved to South Carolina.

The Lucas family was no less important in their new home. Here, too, the Lucases were closely connected to the wealthy and powerful planters and merchants who ran South Carolina by the

1730s. These connections were hardly accidental, since Carolina had a long-standing relationship with the Caribbean. From South Carolina's beginnings in the late seventeenth century, West Indian planters had invested heavily in its colonization. The islands had gotten crowded after a half-century-long sugar boom, and opportunities for planters' sons were declining. Sugar plantations needed food, too, and Carolina was close enough to provide a reliable and cheap supply of grain and meat that many West Indian planters, in pursuit of sugar profits, refused to grow for themselves. The Lucases followed this pattern. As early as 1713, Eliza's grandfather John Lucas had acquired substantial amounts of land in South Carolina, and his holdings had grown over the years. When the Lucases arrived in South Carolina in 1738, the family owned three thriving plantations on the Wappoo, Combahee, and Waccamaw Rivers, as well as several lots in the thriving provincial capital and port city of Charles Town (now called Charleston).

Major Lucas's status within the British Empire called him to the king's service when war broke out between England and Spain, only a year after his family's arrival in South Carolina. He was promoted to the rank of colonel and appointed lieutenant governor of his native island colony of Antigua, and so was forced to leave his wife and daughters behind in the comparative health and safety of the mainland. His departure, combined with Anne Lucas's chronic illness, left his family and affairs largely in the hands of his sixteen-year-old daughter Eliza, who made the most of this opportunity to exercise her considerable talents.

The most striking aspects of Eliza's life in South Carolina was her restless activity, both mental and physical. Many days she spent on the plantation, busy from before dawn to after dark. Perhaps the best illustration of her level of activity is her description of the course of a typical day to her friend, Miss Bartlett, niece of Eliza's close friends Elizabeth and Charles Pinckney. "In general," Eliza wrote, "I rise at five o'Clock in the morning, read till Seven, then take a walk in the garden or field." After breakfast, she spent an hour practicing music, then an hour reviewing French or shorthand. Then two hours were devoted to teaching her younger sister and the two slave girls who, she hoped, would teach the rest of the family's slaves. More music followed lunch, with needlework until dark, after which time she would "read or write." Yet her life was not all fancywork and modern languages. Thursdays were reserved entirely for "the necessary affairs of the family"—which meant writing letters, either on the "business of the plantation" or to her friends. Mixed into this schedule were variations: music lessons, entertaining visitors from neighboring plantations, and on Fridays going "abroad" to visit neighbors.[5]

Although Eliza chose to live "in the Country" after her father's departure, she was by no means socially isolated on their Wappoo River plantation. In her own neighborhood, she reported, there were six "agreeable families" with whom she socialized, and she frequently visited Charles Town, just seven miles away by water. Almost all political and business affairs were settled in the provincial capital, so most prominent families had houses in town, and Charles Town became the center of social life in the colony. By the time of Eliza's arrival, it was a bustling town of almost seven thousand inhabitants and boasted a literary society, a theater, and a weekly newspaper, as well as horse races, balls, and an endless round of informal visits among the elite. Eliza, as a single, wealthy, and attractive young woman, found herself at home in Charles Town society, where she developed intimate friendships with several families with whom she stayed while enjoying "all the pleasures Charles Town affords."[6]

Charles Town was not the limit of Eliza's social circle. She maintained a broad set of correspondents far beyond South Carolina. Her letters were directed across the empire in a sort of female counterpart to her father's imperial web of connections. She could not boast a commission in the army or a governorship, but Eliza still maintained in her letters the cosmopolitan flair of her youth, corresponding with her hostess during her youthful sojourn in England, a cousin in Boston who had been a companion in both Antigua and South Carolina, and a friend from school in England, who was the daughter of the governor of Pennsylvania. Even in South Carolina, Eliza's connections had a transatlantic feel: one of her closest friends, Miss Bartlett, was a visitor from England. Many early letters described the Carolina countryside and local news to her curious correspondents. Since Eliza's family was separated across the globe—her brothers were in England, her father in Antigua, and her mother and sister with her in South Carolina—much time was spent soliciting and passing along family news.

Eliza accompanied her letters with gifts. The variety of these gifts displays not merely a generous spirit made possible by great wealth; it also helps to illustrate aspects of colonial life as diverse as young ladies' activities and the commercial needs of the British Empire. To Miss Thomas in Philadelphia, she sent a tea chest that she had lacquered; to her father she sent one of her lacquered butler's trays. Ornamental work was one employment that occupied the time of many well-to-do young ladies in London and South Carolina and, not surprisingly, Eliza participated. Eliza's other gifts reveal more. Often she sent food across the sea: "a kegg of sweetmeats"[7] and turtle meat (for turtle soup, a delicacy) to England, or potatoes to New England. She also sent larger quantities of beef, rice, and even pickled eggs to her father in Antigua. Unlike her gifts of turtle or sweetmeats, these were profitable commodities in the Atlantic world. She even hoped to establish a lucrative market in eggs in Antigua. Thus, Eliza's correspondence reflected more than young ladies' crafts: she was a messenger on the outposts of a vibrant and dynamic English commercial empire. With the public world of imperial life largely closed to her sex, Eliza Lucas created around herself a different kind of personal empire—a social circle of family and female friends, brought together with friendly moral advice and gifts of turtle meat and japanned boxes, yet also tied together by the practical sinews of commerce and business.

The most striking aspect of Eliza's letters is her constant intellectual energy. Her two hours of reading a day were spent on books as diverse as John Locke's *Essay Concerning Human Understanding*, Samuel Richardson's novel *Pamela*, and Latin pastoral poems—all of which served as the basis for a lively commentary. Eliza's thoughts, so far as her letters reveal them, appear at first glance to have traveled along fairly conventional eighteenth-century paths. Alongside the everyday sociability of her letters is a fairly commonplace concern for duty to parents, adherence to moral principles, and following the principles and observances of the established church. Yet behind this conventionality lurked Eliza's realization that her attention to the life of the mind was unusual for one her age, especially unusual for a young woman. Shadowy figures of older women appear in her letters, chiding her for getting up too early, for working too hard, for reading too much (one woman threw Eliza's book into the fire), and perhaps even for thinking too much. Since women's roles were not so confined in eighteenth-century South Carolina as they would become a century later, Eliza did not self-consciously transgress beyond women's "proper" sphere. She was not a rebel, but she lived on the fuzzy boundaries between the world of women and the world of men.

Another characteristic of Eliza's thinking was a concern for self-discipline and self-reflection, concepts that infused eighteenth-century standards of virtue and manliness. Several times she commented on the propriety of the amusements that Charles Town had to offer: card games, promenades, balls, and the theater. She believed it was acceptable to indulge, at least in moderation, in these pleasures, but still feared the consequences that overindulgence would have on her own character. When she returned from lively Charles Town to the slow-paced life of her plantation and found it "gloomy and lonesome," she gazed inward, and wondered why her isolation could no longer "sooth my . . . pensive humour."

Had home changed, or had she changed? She "was forced to consult Mr. Locke" on the question of "personal Identity." Evidently, Eliza was pleased when her reading helped return her to her former "love of solitude."[8]

Yet underneath this self-reflection ran a current of lightness and self-effacement, not ponderous philosophizing and self-aggrandizement. She hoped that her correspondent (her Charles Town friend, Elizabeth Pinckney) would not "conclude me out of my Witts" or "religiously mad" because she was "not always gay."[9] Her thoughtfulness would turn neither to morbid self-reflection nor to a religious enthusiasm that led to events such as the suicide of Mrs. Le Brasures, who had killed herself to get to Heaven sooner. In addition, Eliza's moral comments were also part of the more important process of tying her social world together. This lighter side was most evident when one of Eliza's friends designed a cap for her, and named this new pattern a "whim." Eliza feared that the cap was ill-named, since she already had "so many whims before, more than I could well manage." "Perhaps," Eliza punned, the designer "thought the head should be all of a peice [*sic*], the furniture within and the adorning without the same"—that is, a whim on the head to match the whims within.[10] Nevertheless, Eliza sent the pattern along with her comment to her friend Miss Bartlett, who, Eliza thought, had not so many whims.

Eliza was as happy to give advice as patterns for caps, at least to those younger than herself. Miss Bartlett received a few moral and religious lectures, which Eliza usually turned in humorous directions. When a local planter had religious delusions, Eliza lectured on the importance of rationality in religious life, but finished her discourse with the jocular question of whether Miss Bartlett would "wish my preachment at an End."[11] Eliza changed the subject to the appearance of a comet in the Carolina sky, but quickly returned to the contemplation of whether this comet portended the end of the world, meditations on the "shortness of life," and finally the consolation regarding death that "the Christian religion affords the pious mind."[12] In general, Eliza's advice ran along less sober lines: the two exchanged poetry (and Eliza gave helpful criticism of Miss Bartlett's verses) and commentaries on the propriety of the heroine's behavior in the tremendously popular English novel *Pamela* (1741). Throughout Eliza's writings, a moral sensibility predominated; after Miss Bartlett returned to England, she asked Eliza to "write a poem on Virtue."[13] Eliza disclaimed any ability on that score—she was as likely to read ancient Greek, she said, as write a good poem on any subject—but Miss Bartlett's request says much of the relationship between the two young women and Eliza's character.

Eliza's two younger brothers, who had remained in England to complete their education, were the recipients of more sober moral lessons. The younger brother, Thomas, was gravely ill while Eliza was in South Carolina, a fact that elicited both cheerful encouragement and long meditations on mortality from his sister. George, on the other hand, was healthy and had entered the British army as an ensign at only fifteen years of age. Eliza feared the dangers her brother would encounter in the military, especially the violent passions provoked by the heat of battle and the company of soldiers. Instead, she counseled a "true fortitude," in which "rational principles" would provide him with the necessary courage to fight with honor, but not lead him to take unnecessary chances. A "composed state of mind" was what she recommended.[14] She understood that "Victory and conquest must fire your mind" as a soldier, but reminded George that "the greatest conquest is a Victory over your own irregular passions."[15] True virtue, for Eliza, allowed the rational mind to overcome desires for glory or revenge, while following the dictates of religion and conscience. While Eliza's image of man's virtue at war with his passions was by no means unusual for her era, she extended her concern for reason and virtue to both men and women. It seems, however, that she believed the stakes of male virtue were higher, even as the threats were stronger.

"But to cease moralizing and attend to business," Eliza punctuated one of her letters to her father (after describing her sisterly advice to George on the subject of virtue).[16] That Eliza would think of morality and business as separate pursuits indicates something about eighteenth-century political thought. Hers was an era before Adam Smith argued that an "invisible hand" could make individuals' pursuit of self-interest yield a public good. Rather, in her era, "irregular passions," including self-interest, threatened the virtue of Eliza's brother. For this reason, Eliza's business correspondence has a matter-of-fact quality quite distinct from her breezy social exchanges or her sober moral lessons. To be sure, Eliza paid close attention to the management of her family's South Carolina estates. She continually wrote to her father and her business associates in Charles Town about the day-to-day business of rice planting and international commerce. But Eliza usually did not make the effort to copy the text of these matters verbatim. She preferred simply to write memoranda into her letterbook noting the general subjects of her letters, or perhaps she copied them elsewhere or sent them to her father. In any event, the point remains that she considered business a separate realm, one of memoranda and ledger entries, not of personal relationships that merited word-for-word copies of letters. Of course, Eliza also had close personal attachments to most of the recipients of these letters: her father, the Pinckneys, and the other members of South Carolina's merchant elite who were also her friends. Thus Eliza might bring together these two worlds with her awkward transition from a moral concern for her brother to "attend to business."

That junction represented the outer limits of what Eliza could do as a woman in the British Empire. There were, however, times when Eliza carved a further breach in the masculine world of business, or at least exploited the blurry lines between women's and men's roles. From time to time, as she reported to her friend Miss Bartlett, she provided legal services for her "poor Neighbors" who could not afford the services of a lawyer. Eliza had a copy of an English legal handbook and used it to draw up wills for neighbors on their deathbeds. But Eliza knew when she was out of her depth—even when "teazed intolerable," she refused to draw up a marriage settlement (a sort of eighteenth-century prenuptial contract, intended to allow a bride to retain control of the property she brought to the marriage). She did finally serve as a trustee of the bride's property in that instance; this role was not an unheard-of one for a woman, but it was unusual for anyone as young as Eliza. The "weighty affairs" Eliza had on her hands led her to wonder whether she would become "an old woman before I am well a young one." Eliza understood that her attention to business and the world of "affairs," like her self-described "pensive humour" and her love of books, set her apart from most young women.[17] Perhaps for this reason, Eliza wanted Miss Bartlett to keep her lawyering a secret from her aunt and uncle, the Pinckneys.

Eliza Lucas's most famous activity during her first years in South Carolina was her agricultural experimentation on her father's plantations. "I love the vegitable world extremely," she told one friend, and her horticultural work was constant as long as she lived in South Carolina.[18] Within a year of her arrival in the colony in 1738, she began planting numerous crops in an effort to determine which ones might grow well in her new home. Many of them were common to her native West Indies: indigo, ginger, cotton, lucerne (a kind of alfalfa), and even cassava, a root crop originating in Brazil that became a staple for Caribbean slaves. None of these had been commercially successful in South Carolina, and Eliza did not always succeed. Her first crops of cotton and ginger were destroyed in a frost, and her lucerne, she reported, was "dwinderling."[19] She also experimented with Mediterranean crops and tried an orchard of fig trees. Not all of her horticultural efforts were directed toward commodities. While reading Virgil, she was struck by his descriptions of Roman gardens, which she thought might suit her own colony. So Eliza's busy mind immediately contemplated the "beauties of pure nature, unassisted by art" on her plantation.[20] She also considered how she might improve on nature, by planting a cedar grove as well as gardens of flowers and fruit trees.

Still, profit was never far from Eliza's active thoughts either. Her future husband, Charles Pinckney, accused her of having a "fertile brain at scheming," by which he meant schemes to make money.[21] Indeed, in most of her agricultural experiments, Eliza was interested in making them pay off, or at least hoped that they might "provid[e] for Posterity."[22] Her fig trees were planted "with design to dry and export them," and she carefully calculated the expenses and profits of that project.[23] She planted oaks in the hopes that they could be sold to shipbuilders. She even pickled eggs and sent them to the West Indies, hoping they might provide another source of income. In each venture, she looked for commodities that would serve as articles of trade in the dynamic commercial empire that Great Britain had created in the early eighteenth century. Just as Eliza's letters circulated around the empire, so too, did her produce.

In this context of searching for profitable export commodities, Eliza's most famous experiment developed. Indigo, a blue dye extracted from the *Indigofera anil* plant, was the object of Eliza's highest hopes and most diligent efforts. The dye had been produced in the first years of South Carolina's settlement in the late seventeenth century, but the production of rice and naval stores had quickly taken over the colony's economy. The drawbacks to these new staples had become evident by 1740. South Carolina's naval stores were of low quality and therefore price. Rice, which dominated the economy after 1730, was bulky in relation to its value, and many ships were needed to carry away the annual crop. With hostilities heating up after 1739, these ships were in danger from privateers, and insurance rates skyrocketed. War also cut off the colony's primary European markets for rice, and prices therefore dropped dramatically. By 1744, the colony was in deep recession from this squeeze on rice profits—something which, one imagines, went through Eliza's mind as she reviewed her plantation business each Thursday, or while she calculated the profits to be earned from her fig orchard. Indigo solved these problems: it was much more valuable per pound, and a year's product could be carried on a few well-armed ships. England's growing textile industry needed dyes, and so prices were high.

No wonder that Eliza, together with her father and her neighbors, invested so much time and effort in producing indigo. A great effort was necessary, since a number of logistical problems had to be overcome if indigo was to be produced profitably. South Carolina's climate was just barely suited to growing the plant, and

Eliza's first crop was destroyed by frost before the plants were mature, and the second by worms. Her father sent different strains of seeds repeatedly to restart the process. More problematic, however, was the high level of technical expertise required to oversee the production of the dye itself. Turning the gold leaves of the indigo bush into cakes of almost-black dyestuff required a series of stages of fermentation, stirring, and drying, all of which needed to be closely monitored in order to produce a high-quality dye. Colonel Lucas sent a series of indigo experts to help instruct the Carolina slaves in the processing of indigo, but these experts were more interested in keeping their secrets than in sharing their knowledge. One, Eliza thought, had deliberately ruined a batch of indigo by dumping too much lime into the vat of fermenting leaves. Eventually, however, the joint efforts of Eliza, her neighbors, and their slaves succeeded; in 1744 a small amount of dye was produced, along with a sufficient quantity of seed to sell to other Carolinians eager to find a secondary crop.

Indigo cultivation spread rapidly across South Carolina after 1745, a testament to the collective efforts of Eliza and her neighbors in developing the crop. Eliza's friend and neighbor (and future husband) Charles Pinckney helped promote indigo, publishing articles in the *South Carolina Gazette* that lauded it as the answer to South Carolina's economic problems. And indigo was not just a profitable export commodity; it was also well suited to the colony's existing economy. It complemented rice planting and slavery. By 1740 the colony's economy depended utterly on slaves to do the backbreaking work of planting rice. The production of indigo, especially, fit into this slave economy. Indigo cultivation and rice cultivation could coexist on the same plantation—they demanded different kinds of land and labor at different times of the year. Rice planters could easily move into the production of indigo, and they did so. One of Eliza Lucas's legacies to South Carolina was the revitalization of plantation slavery during a decade of hard times for the colony's key crop, rice. By the end of the 1740s the value of indigo exports approached that of rice exports, and the slaves who tended both found themselves busier than ever.

Slavery, it should be remembered, was an important part of Eliza Lucas's life in South Carolina. By 1739 about two-thirds of the colony's population was enslaved and of African descent, although this fact is nearly invisible in Eliza's letters, in which she rarely mentions her family's slaves. Slaves sometimes delivered her frequent messages to her friends in Charles Town, since she referred to "Mary Ann," "Togo," and "David" as conveyors of messages. Thus, slaves both produced Eliza's wealth and helped tie together her social world. Slavery drew Eliza's attention more often because of the possibilities of slave rebellion. This focus is not surprising: the Lucases arrived in South Carolina just before the Stono Rebellion erupted there in September 1739, the largest slave rebellion to occur in that colony or all of colonial North America. About one hundred slaves, crying "Liberty," rose up against their masters and fought their way toward Spanish St. Augustine, killing about twenty white Carolinians in the process. Although the rebellion was suppressed in a few days, and far more slaves were executed than whites had perished, white society was hardly calmed. The nearly simultaneous onset of war with Spain, and the Spanish offer of freedom to Carolina's slaves that had contributed to the rebellions, only made white Carolinians more nervous about the threat that their enormous numbers of slaves posed to their dominance and safety. Fears of slave rebellion echoed for the rest of the 1740s. Eliza Lucas noted several suspected slave conspiracies early in that decade, including one that implicated one of her family's slaves.

While the South Carolina Assembly responded to the Stono Rebellion by passing a strict slave code in 1740, restricting slaves' freedom of movement and ability to congregate, it does not appear that Eliza Lucas cracked down on her family's slaves. Indeed, Eliza may have had a more humanitarian notion of how to treat her slaves, although she could not have lived on her plantation without witnessing the daily brutality of slavery. In 1741, Eliza mentioned a "parcel of little Negroes whom I have undertaken to teach to read," and later she told her father of another one of her "schemes": she wished to teach two slave girls to read, so that they could in turn serve as "school mistres's [*sic*] for the rest of the Negroe children."[24] Her purpose in educating her slaves remains unclear. Perhaps teaching her slaves was yet another outlet for her seemingly boundless energy; perhaps she had some other plan. (Slave education would not be outlawed in South Carolina until a later rebellion in 1822.)

It seems possible that Eliza was less fearful of her slaves than many Carolinians, a feeling that her account of a strange event in 1742 helps illustrate. In March a wealthy planter, Hugh Bryan, in the religious enthusiasm of the Great Awakening, began to prophesy slave rebellions and cast himself in the role of Moses in leading slaves to freedom. His attempt to part the waters of a creek, however, failed—he nearly drowned—and Bryan quickly recanted his prophecies. Many white Carolinians feared the "consiquence [*sic*] of such a thing being put in to the head of the slaves," as Eliza put it, but, for her own part, Eliza seems to have appreciated the ridiculousness of the entire story more than its danger.[25]

The lesson she drew from it concerned the perils of religious enthusiasm and the importance of following natural reason even in contemplating religious matters. It is characteristic of Eliza Lucas that her mind turned quickly from the threat of slave rebellion to a didactic lesson, from fear to hope. It is also characteristic that Eliza opposed the Great Awakening's religious fervor and followed instead the mainstream Anglican theology of her friend Dr. Alexander Garden, commissary of the Church of England and opponent of religious revivalism.

In January 1744, Eliza Lucas's good friend, Mrs. Elizabeth Pinckney, died after a long illness. Four months later, Eliza Lucas married the widower, Colonel Charles Pinckney. Twenty-four years Eliza's senior, Charles Pinckney was an important man in South Carolina. In the 1730s he had served actively in the colony's Commons House of Assembly, and in 1736 he was elected speaker of the Commons House, a testament to his importance within the colony's political structure. The Pinckneys had been among Eliza's first friends in South Carolina. A close, even affectionate relationship between Eliza and Charles had emerged alongside the female friendship of Eliza, Elizabeth Pinckney, and the Pinckneys' niece, Miss Bartlett. It was Charles who lent Eliza books, assisted in her indigo experiments, and accused her of having a fertile mind for scheming. The two exchanged a continuous friendly correspondence, the breeziness and intimacy of which is striking between a single woman and a married man. Perhaps Charles was a father figure to Eliza, as he was about her father's age. Charles also may have substituted as a social companion for his increasingly ill wife —certainly, Eliza wrote far fewer letters to Elizabeth Pinckney than to Charles. In fact, Charles appears to have been the only man not a relative with whom Eliza cultivated a close correspondence.

Charles Pinckney was not the first man to fall for Eliza Lucas, although none of the earlier suitors gained her favor. When Eliza was only eighteen, two men conveyed their interest in Eliza to her father, who passed on these sentiments to the young lady. She refused them absolutely, and in characteristic form. As for the first, "the riches of Peru and Chili . . . could not purchase a sufficient Esteem for him"; the second she did not know well enough to consider.[26] She preferred to remain single. Indeed, she seemed to spend little thought on matters of the heart: "As to the other sex, I dont trouble my head about them. I take all they say to be words. . . ."[27] Matters had not changed the next year. Eliza reported a romantic "Conquest" of an "old Gentleman" to her friend Miss Bartlett several years later, but refused to provide details in her letter.

Indeed, Eliza promised that Miss Bartlett's uncle (Charles Pinckney himself!), who was "much pleased" with the entire affair, would provide a "full account."[28]

On the other hand, in 1741, Eliza signed her copy of one of her letters to Charles Pinckney oddly—"Eliza Pinckney"—which was three years later to be her married name.[29] Perhaps this was a slip of her pen when she copied her letter over in her letterbook, though one must speculate in that case as to whether her subconscious was busily at work. Regardless of Eliza's thoughts that day, it is clear that Eliza and her future husband had developed a close friendship before the death of Elizabeth Pinckney. There is something in the tone of these letters that betrays a high degree of affection and intimacy between the two. The rapidity of their marriage following Elizabeth Pinckney's death was hardly unusual in the eighteenth century, but it occurred soon enough that local gossips wondered whether Eliza had denied Mrs. Pinckney medical care as she was dying. Eliza was shocked by the implication that she would do away with her friend—but Eliza's marrying one of South Carolina's wealthiest and most important men probably made envious aspersions inevitable.

Marriage in May 1744 marked a basic transformation in Eliza's life. While she still looked after her father's plantations after moving to Belmont, the Pinckney plantation north of Charles Town, her activities on that score were necessarily reduced now that she had a husband (and her own household) to attend. This transformation was surely magnified when Eliza became pregnant within a month of their marriage, and gave birth to her first son, Charles Cotesworth, in February 1745. Three more births followed over the next six years: a son, George, in 1747 (who died two weeks after his birth); a daughter, Harriott, in 1748; and a son, Thomas, in 1750. In short order Eliza had become a wife and a mother, and her inclinations toward religious and moral instruction—already evident in her relationship with her brothers—quickly rose to the occasions. Charles apparently was of one mind with Eliza, and together they worked to educate their sons and daughter. Charles Cotesworth reputedly knew his letters before he could talk. The children memorized passages from the Bible and attended church regularly. Eliza's ample energies were now focused, it seems, on her children's education and her husband's happiness, "even in triffles."[30] Her energies were not limitless, on the other hand: with three living infants, and a bout of depression following the death of George, Eliza ceased writing in her letterbook for five years.

South Carolina, despite its wealth and vibrant social life, was still a province, and Charles Pinckney believed that his sons would be best educated at "home"—that is, in England. Eliza, of course, had herself been educated in England, and since the birth of Charles Cotesworth she had hoped that the family would be able to make an extended stay in the mother country. Charles Pinckney's hopes for appointment as chief justice in South Carolina put off the trip for several years, but the position eventually went to another, and Charles put his financial affairs in order for the long visit to England. He also was appointed by the South Carolina Commons House of Assembly as the colonial agent to the Board of Trade in London, providing the family with social and professional contacts in England, as well as more financial support. With these preparations done, in late April 1753 the family of five boarded ship for the voyage across the Atlantic and arrived twenty-five days later in England.

For Eliza, this move was both gratifying and unsettling. She very much desired to return to England. Although her brothers had since departed, she still had friends from her first stay there as a girl. Yet she also "gave a wistful look" at Charles Town as she left.[31] Eliza was now thirty-two years old, and had lived about half her life—all her adult life—in South Carolina. Soon after arrival the family settled near London, and Eliza set about the task of entering English society. Friendships from her earlier stay in London were quickly renewed, and the large community of Carolinians in London supplemented Eliza's lively social scene. At the same time, Eliza maintained her connections across the Atlantic and wrote long letters to women in South Carolina, full of the news from London. With her sons deposited in boarding school and her husband busy in London, Eliza entered the social world with all her energy—with winters at Bath, frequent attendance at the theater, and visits to and from her friends.

While London offered more social opportunities than South Carolina, the narrowing of Eliza's horizons that had begun with her marriage continued in England. Certainly, Eliza's letters ceased to show the kind of vivacity and energy that they had during her single life. Perhaps the variety of social connections in England available to Eliza allowed her to show her wit and charm in drawing rooms instead of in her letters. Yet this change in the tone of her letters also reflected a change in what she herself had to do. Her activities no longer included horticultural experiments, and her moralizing was restricted while her sons were at school. Although her sons' occasional illnesses demanded a mother's attention, socializing occupied most of Eliza's time.

Charles Pinckney became homesick soon after the family's arrival in London, but it is clear that Eliza did not share this feeling and, in fact, opposed returning to Carolina. Perhaps Eliza was less tied to the New World; the only sign that Eliza might have felt attached to America was her close attention to American affairs after the French and Indian War broke out in 1754. Her letters to South Carolina reveal no pining for that distant land. The outbreak of war, however, did dramatically change the Pinckney family's circumstances. Charles feared that South Carolina was in peril from French attack and desired to return to the colony so he could liquidate his plantations. The children would remain in the safety of English schools. Eliza was not enthusiastic about this plan. She feared the dangers of travel during wartime (her father had died in 1747 after being captured during the last war) and did not particularly want to return to South Carolina herself. Most important, she did not want to be separated from her children for the two or three years it would take for Charles to settle his Carolina affairs. Yet she submitted to her husband's wishes for the most part: Eliza and Charles left their sons in England and embarked for South Carolina in the early spring of 1758, but they took their ten-year-old daughter Harriott with them.

Separation from her sons was only the first of Eliza's trials that year. Less than a month after the couple's arrival in Charles Town, Charles Pinckney contracted malaria, lingered for three weeks, and died on July 12, 1758. Over the next month, Eliza buried her husband, began to arrange for the disposition of his estate, and went about the melancholy task of informing her sons and her family of Charles's death. In these letters, Eliza displayed her characteristic strength of character and moral sensibility, as well as her affection for her husband of fourteen years.

One can imagine how difficult it was to break this news by letter to her sons, only seven and thirteen years old. Not surprisingly, Eliza drew a potent moral and religious lesson from the untimely passing of Charles at fifty-nine years of age. His family more than ever had to depend on the strength of God, whose will was most clearly expressed in the unhappy event. She told her sons that their father's death was an exemplary one: "His sick bed and dying moments were the natural conclusion of such a life," and he "met the king of terrors without the least terror or affright," and "went like a Lamb into eternity." Eliza promised that she, as widow and mother to Charles Pinckney's children, would devote the rest of her life to honoring their father's memory by serving them. She concluded with an exhortation that her sons be "worthy [of] such a father as yours was."[32] To her mother, who had returned to Antigua after Eliza's marriage, Eliza repeatedly described the virtues (she used the word four times in her letter) of her husband and her hopes to meet Charles in eternity.

More pressing practical business included the settlement of Charles's estate and providing for the education of the children still in England. For Eliza, both were familiar territory. She had no problem assuming the management of Charles's affairs: paying debts, arranging for probate of the will, and maintaining the family plantations, which were run down after the Pinckneys' four-year absence. One imagines that Eliza's return to the world of business must have been unhappy at first, but that, with time, planting gardens and directing affairs were pleasant tasks. "I love a Garden and a book," Eliza wrote a friend in England five years after her husband's death, "and they are all my amusement" except for raising her daughter.[33] Eliza also renewed the vivacity and charm of her youth during these years, as she continued to build and maintain the friendships that she had made across the globe and sent more potatoes, limes, and beets around the world.

Yet managing these worldly matters demanded that Eliza remain separated from her sons; Charles Cotesworth did not return to South Carolina until 1768, and Thomas not until 1772. Eliza's direction of their education accordingly had to take place across the Atlantic. Here, too, Eliza gave the same counsel as she had to her brothers: she emphasized virtue, independence, and Christian morality to her sons. She gave advice on a wide variety of subjects, from proper treatment of servants to the importance of restraining one's passions. While Eliza feared that "the morals of Youth are taken little care of" at public schools and university and she knew that London offered "temptations with every youthful passion," she had faith in her sons' ability to maintain "moral Virtue, Religion, and learning."[34]

Her counsels were given to sons who followed a typical English gentleman's education—attendance at elite boarding schools, followed by a stint at, if not a degree from, Oxford or Cambridge University, and perhaps legal training at the Inns of Court in London. The next generation of planter-aristocrats received an English liberal education. It is ironic, then, that both Charles Cotesworth and Thomas Pinckney came of age in England and partook of an English gentleman's education just as the first stirrings of Anglo-American conflict appeared. Both sons identified with their native soil from the earliest phases of this conflict, with Thomas being known as the "Little Rebel" by his English friends and Charles Cotesworth in 1766 having a portrait painted of himself declaiming against the Stamp Act of 1765.

During the convulsions preceding American independence, Eliza saw her daughter Harriott married to Daniel Horry in 1768, and her two sons return to South Carolina, marry, and take their place on Pinckney family plantations. These domestic transformations did not leave Eliza alone or idle, since she still maintained the easy sociability of the South Carolina low country, and her new son- and daughters-in-law merely expanded her social circle. Eliza spent long periods with Harriott at Hampton, the Horry family estate. It must have gratified Eliza to see Harriott follow her mother's interest in gardening and to assist in the moral and intellectual training of her grandchildren, who were born with some regularity in the years following 1768. Eliza also appears to have become something of a medical practitioner in middle age; ailments and treatments played an increasing role in her correspondence with her South Carolina acquaintances.

Eliza Lucas Pinckney had spent her life enmeshed in a web of empire-wide connections. Her father was a colonial official, she had spent long periods of time in England, and her family had even at one point planned to settle in the mother country. Her friendships extended around the Atlantic, mostly among correspondents who were also connected with imperial administration. It is ironic, then, that her family would be so closely identified with the movement for American independence in South Carolina. While Eliza made few references in her letters to the crises leading to that independence, her sons, especially Charles Cotesworth, were intimately involved with the political storms that developed during the 1770s and usually favored a vigorous colonial response to the actions of the British ministry. Soon after the battles of Lexington and Concord in April 1775, Charles Cotesworth led a raid on the colony's armory that secured the government's weapons for the patriots, and later that year he was elected a captain in the South Carolina militia. Thomas soon followed his brother into the patriots' service, and both ended the war as high-ranking officers in the Continental army, with Charles Cotesworth becoming a brigadier general.

The Pinckney sons' deep support of the patriot cause is not altogether surprising, even considering their close connections with the British Empire. Their father had been central in the development of a distinctive political rhetoric in South Carolina in the 1730s, one that emphasized the necessity of virtue and independence in government. South Carolinians repeatedly decried attempts by royal governors to limit the prerogatives of the elected assembly, either by overt action or by insidious acts of "corruption": for instance, providing government offices to assemblymen friendly to the government. Charles Pinckney Sr. had experienced corruption firsthand just before the family's trip to England, when he was denied the office of chief justice of South Carolina in favor of a better-connected man. Even after their father's death, Eliza's consistent reminders to her sons to follow the paths of virtue and independence reinforced this basic understanding of politics. When the British ministry's acts began to look corrupt in the escalating crises following the Stamp Act, the Townshend Duties, and finally the Intolerable Acts, men such as the Pinckneys were willing to put aside their loyalty to the king and follow the path that they had been taught was virtuous.

During these crises, Eliza could not be virtuous in the same way as her sons. As a woman, her political role was restricted to the sidelines. When war came to South Carolina in 1778, however, women such as Eliza had to make choices about what to do, choices that indicated their loyalty and could also provoke reprisals from the partisan forces at war. With the British occupation of Charles Town and a bitter civil war raging over the countryside, there was no neutrality. Eliza, caught in the midst of these struggles on her son-in-law's plantation outside Charles Town, chose to support the patriot cause in her way. Much of the low country where Eliza's family lived was occupied alternately by British and American troops, leaving her subject to depredations from both sides, but mostly from the British. Since Eliza would not proclaim loyalty to the king, her houses in Charles Town were occupied by British troops who paid no rent, while her stock was carried off her plantations, and her slaves ran away or were captured, leaving her plantations to produce no income at all. In 1779, Eliza complained of her "losses" and the "almost ruined fortunes" of her sons, and two years later she found herself incapable of paying a debt of £60 sterling—an amount that would have been a trifle just five years earlier.

Eliza suffered more than economic losses. Both her sons were soldiers in the cause of independence, and she was daily concerned with their health and welfare. Thomas was injured and captured by the British in 1780, leaving her quite distraught with worry. Charles Cotesworth quickly offered to share his own estate with his brother and mother after these disasters, but both refused. For Eliza, what was most grievous was the loss of her independence, her ability to be free from obligation to others and to shower her own benevolence on her children and grandchildren. Here, Eliza shared in the ideas of virtue and independence that she had impressed upon her sons: she wanted to be dependent on no one, to provide for herself.

Following the war, times did not immediately improve. The War of Independence in South Carolina had become a bitter civil war among the colony's inhabitants, and this animosity persisted well beyond the coming of peace in 1783. Independence had thrust many poorer Carolinians into political activity, an unaccustomed phenomenon for the low-country planter oligarchy who had maintained the upper hand for so long. Sizable numbers of low-country planters had been loyal to the king or tepid in their patriotism, which made their property attractive targets for angry patriots, who pushed for bills confiscating loyalist estates and heavily taxing those whose support for the cause was less than fervent. Perhaps because Eliza Lucas Pinckney herself had no public political position—as a woman she had no formal political voice, and her husband's politics had been in the grave for nearly a quarter century—her estates (damaged as they were) could not be seized. In fact, the damage that Eliza's property received at the hands of the British probably helped demonstrate that the British did not consider her a friend. Finally, her two sons' conspicuous service in the patriot cause ensured that they would not be punished (Charles Cotesworth, indeed, sat in the state legislature). Eliza's son-in-law Daniel Horry was less lucky—his estate was punitively taxed, and a friend of the family believed that only the Pinckneys' "many Virtues" prevented it from being confiscated.[35]

Eliza spent most of the postwar years at the Horry plantation, where she continued her agricultural labors and helped oversee the education of her grandchildren. She even entertained President George Washington during his visit to South Carolina in 1791. A single letter to her grandson, Daniel Horry Jr., survives, in which she reprised for a third generation the moral and religious advice she had given her brothers and sons. A "liberal Education," a proper restraint of emotions and passions, and industriousness were the virtues she urged upon twelve-year-old Daniel, whom she saw as part of a "rising generation" whose "abilities and improved Talents" would raise the newly independent South Carolina in its "Second Infancy."[36] Eliza's basic message had not changed: virtue, restraint of passions, and self-control. To this, however, Eliza added a new message of service to one's nation. Historians have called this moral emphasis "Republican motherhood"—the notion that women, as mothers and grandmothers, could instill in their children the virtue needed to guide a nation. Eliza had been doing this job for three generations, but the political context of this work had changed in the meantime, from the world-spanning British Empire, to the independent State of South Carolina, and now to the new United States of America.

Eliza Lucas Pinckney was diagnosed with cancer in 1792, at seventy years of age. A year later she traveled to Philadelphia to consult with a famous physician, who failed to cure her. She died on May 26, 1793, and was buried the next day, with President George Washington serving as a pallbearer. (Washington had sought out Eliza during his visit to South Carolina two years earlier; he had wanted to meet the famous agriculturalist and the mother of two such conspicuous South Carolina patriots.) Eliza had lived a long and varied life. She had been the epitome of the cosmopolitan British Empire, and the mother of American patriots. She had been a society belle with extraordinary wit, charm, and manners, and had also been a devout Christian, a moralist, and an agricultural innovator. She was a vivacious single woman, a devoted wife and mother, and an industrious widow, but her life was never entirely defined by her connections to men. Her legacies lived long after her death—her descendants continued to experiment with new crops such as sugar and cotton, and the Pinckneys remained politically prominent in South Carolina. Eliza Pinckney is well remembered as the mother to this famous family; she should be remembered also in her own right.

Notes

1. Eliza Lucas Pinckney (hereafter, ELP) to Mrs. Evance, June 19, 1760, in Elise Pinckney, ed., *The Letterbook of Eliza Lucas Pinckney, 1739–1762* (Chapel Hill: University of North Carolina Press, 1972), 151. Hereafter cited as *Letterbook*. All dates before 1752 are Old Style, except that the year is taken to begin on January 1.

2. Eliza Lucas (hereafter, EL) to Miss Bartlett (hereafter, Miss B.), January 14, 1742, *Letterbook*, 26.

3. Ibid.

4. ELP to C. C. Pinckney, September 10, 1785, quoted in *Letterbook*, xxv.

5. EL to Miss B., ca. April 1742, *Letterbook*, 34–35.

6. EL to Mrs. Boddicott, May 2, 1740, *Letterbook*, 7–8.

7. EL to Mrs. Boddicott, June 29, 1742, *Letterbook*, 42.

8. EL to Mrs. Pinckney, ca. July 1741, *Letterbook*, 19.

9. Ibid.

10. EL to Miss B., ca. April 1742, *Letterbook*, 31.

11. EL to Miss B., ca. March 1742, *Letterbook*, 29.

12. Ibid., 29–30.

13. EL to Miss B., ca. May 1743, *Letterbook*, 62.

14. EL to George Lucas, June 1742, *Letterbook*, 45.

15. EL to dear Brother, July 1742, *Letterbook*, 52–53.

16. EL to Father, February 10, 1743, *Letterbook*, 59.

17. EL to Miss B., ca. June 1742, *Letterbook*, 41.

18. EL to Miss B., ca. April 1742, *Letterbook*, 35.

19. EL to Father, June 4, 1741, *Letterbook*, 15.

20. EL to Miss B., April 1742, *Letterbook*, 36.

21. Ibid., 35.

22. EL to Miss B., May 1742, *Letterbook*, 38.

23. EL to Miss B., April 1742, *Letterbook*, 35.

24. EL to Charles Pinckney, February 6, 1741, *Letterbook*, 12; EL to Miss B., April 1742, *Letterbook*, 34.

25. EL to Miss B., March 1742, *Letterbook*, 29–30.

26. EL to Colonel Lucas, ca. April 1740, *Letterbook*, 6.

27. EL to Miss B., January 1742, *Letterbook*, 27.

28. EL to Miss B., May 1743, *Letterbook*, 62.

29. EL to Charles Pinckney, February 6, 1741, *Letterbook*, 12.

30. ELP to Gov. George Lucas, ca. 1745, quoted in Marvin R. Zahniser, *Charles Cotesworth Pinckney: Founding Father* (Chapel Hill: University of North Carolina Press, 1967), 8.

31. ELP to Mary W. Wragg [?], May 20, 1753, *Letterbook*, 75.

32. ELP to Charles and Thomas Pinckney, August 1758, *Letterbook*, 94–95.

33. ELP to Mr. Keate, February 1762, *Letterbook*, 181.

34. ELP to Charles Pinckney, February 7, 1761, *Letterbook*, 158–59; ELP to Charles Pinckney, April 15, 1761, *Letterbook*, 167.

35. Edward Rutledge to Arthur Middleton, February 26, 1782, quoted in Zahniser, *Charles Cotesworth Pinckney*, 73.

36. ELP to Daniel Horry Jr., April 16, 1782, in Elise Pinckney, ed., "Letters of Eliza Lucas Pinckney, 1768–1782," *South Carolina Historical Magazine* 76 (1975): 167.

Suggested Readings

Baskett, Sam S. "Eliza Lucas Pinckney: Portrait of an Eighteenth Century American." *South Carolina Historical Magazine* 72 (1971): 207–19.

Chaplin, Joyce E. *An Anxious Pursuit: Agricultural Innovation and Modernity in the Lower South, 1730–1815*. Chapel Hill: University of North Carolina Press, 1993.

Coon, David L. "Eliza Lucas Pinckney and the Reintroduction of Indigo Cultivation in South Carolina." *Journal of Southern History* 42 (1976): 61–76.

Kerber, Linda. *Women of the Republic: Intellect and Ideology in Revolutionary America*. Chapel Hill: University of North Carolina Press, 1980.

Pinckney, Elise, ed. *The Letterbook of Eliza Lucas Pinckney, 1739–1762*. Chapel Hill: University of North Carolina Press, 1972.

———. "Letters of Eliza Lucas Pinckney, 1768–1782." *South Carolina Historical Magazine* 76 (1975): 143–70.

Ravenel, Harriott H. *Eliza Pinckney*. New York: Scribner's, 1896.

Woloch, Nancy. "Eliza Pinckney and Republican Motherhood." In *Women and the American Experience*, 51–64. New York: Alfred A. Knopf, 1984.

Zahniser, Marvin R. *Charles Cotesworth Pinckney: Founding Father*. Chapel Hill: University of North Carolina Press, 1967.

4

William Smith
Philadelphia Minister and Moderate

Nancy L. Rhoden

As an educator and minister, William Smith (1727–1803) of Philadelphia had the opportunity to influence his students and his Anglican parishioners. While he had shared his opinions on the Seven Years' War from the pulpit, the classroom, and in print, he became much quieter during the American Revolution. As an ordained clergyman of the Church of England, Smith had taken obligatory oaths to support the monarchy. Because such promises were serious legal and religious obligations, how could he even consider becoming an American revolutionary? A Scot, like Lachlan McGillivray, Smith had witnessed rebellion in Scotland in the 1740s, colonial warfare in the 1750s, and colonial protest against British authority in the 1760s, and he remained in America throughout the Revolutionary War. Still, McGillivray favored loyalism; why would Smith lean more toward the patriot cause? Smith served as a member of early revolutionary committees, preached patriotic sermons at the request of the Continental Congress, and even took an oath to the rebel government. While loyalist colleagues denounced him for his patriotism, patriots feared that he was a loyalist. Why were his contemporaries so uncertain about his political opinions, and how did their estimations of Smith's character affect his political reputation, public image, and professional opportunities?

Unlike many other subjects in this volume, Smith recorded his opinions on important events of the 1760s and early 1770s that led to revolution, including the Stamp Act riots and the closing of Boston's port after the Tea Party. Having understood the constitutional grievances of the rebelling colonists, why did he not embrace independence in a public and committed fashion? Smith professed moderate opinions, which he probably hoped would allow him to fulfill his career ambitions or preserve his church's usefulness in the new republic, but how possible was it to remain neutral, or moderate, during the Revolutionary War?

Nancy L. Rhoden, who is coeditor of this volume, teaches early American history at the University of Southern Indiana. She has written *Revolutionary Anglicanism: The Colonial Church of England Clergy during the American Revolution* (1999).

When the Reverend William Smith looked out from the pulpit of Christ Church on June 23, 1775, he noticed that most of the pews were filled with colonial elite, including members of the Continental Congress and officers of the Third Battalion of Philadelphia. Other congregants probably included members of the lower social orders, perhaps even the seamstress Betsy Ross, a member of this parish. As Smith described the body, it was "a great and mixt assembly of his fellow-citizens, and a number of the first characters in America, now met in consultation, at a most alarming crisis."[1] Smith had prepared his text with his patriot audience in mind, but he also must have considered how unusual it would be for a minister of the king's church, the Church of England, to sanction colonial resistance to British authority. How much should he say about the political disputes with England, which a couple of months earlier had erupted with the exchange of gunfire in distant New England? How little would be acceptable to his waiting audience?

William Smith, best known as the first provost of the College of Philadelphia (now the University of Pennsylvania), was an educator, clergyman, and author. As a political and social commentator, Smith wrote about colonial Pennsylvania politics, French-Indian interaction on the frontier and in the Seven Years' War, education's role in creating informed citizens, and the beginnings of the American Revolution. While he characterized himself as belonging to "that despised Class call'd *Moderate Men*," modern historians have depicted him most often as controversial, since he regularly became embroiled in political contests.[2] In hindsight, Smith could be labeled a moderate, or a quiet American patriot, but that decision was not an easy or an obvious one in the turmoil of the 1770s. Many contemporaries found it difficult to define his political opinions or determine whether he was a defender of the American Revolution or a loyal supporter of the Crown, and some believed he was too opinionated to be truly "moderate." Such diverse acquaintances as John Adams, Ezra Stiles, or Dr. Benjamin Rush claimed that Smith's character defects included haughtiness, slovenliness, irritability, and habitual drunkenness. His professions of moderation may have been sincere, but his temperament and reputation caused many contemporaries to wonder whether Smith's moderation was inspired by ambition or other disguised motives.

Born in Aberdeenshire, Scotland, on April 20, 1727, William Smith was the son of Elizabeth Duncan, who traced her lineage through an old Scots family, and Thomas Smith, a minor landholder. If his subsequent writings provide any clues, Smith likely proved a capable student after entering King's College, Aberdeen, in 1743. He attended the college for four years, although he may not have been granted a degree. There Smith must have witnessed the 1745 rebellion, which began as an uprising of several of the Highland clans; the rebels came to his city, which remained loyal to the Hanoverian monarchy of England and Scotland. Many Highlanders remembered this rebellion well enough to become loyalists in the American Revolution, but the memories of eighteen-year-old Smith did not dissuade him later from leaning more toward the American rebels.

By 1750, Smith was petitioning the English Parliament for a salary increase on the behalf of Scots schoolmasters. While in London he learned of an opportunity to serve in America as a tutor to two young boys, sons of Colonel Josiah Martin of Long Island, New York. Smith and the boys departed England in early March 1751 and arrived in New York on the first of May. Smith must have made an impression on some prominent English churchmen during his visit to England, since he carried with him a recommendation from the archbishop of Canterbury. For two years, Smith resided with the Martin family on their estate.

His early career in New York and Pennsylvania demonstrates Smith's involvement in the political and social affairs of the colonies. Long before the goal of creating an educated citizenry to sustain a republican government arose after the Revolution, Smith had articulated his beliefs about education's role in shaping citizens. In publications of the 1750s and 1760s, Smith had advocated missionary schools to train promising Indian scholars as educators among their own people; he expected Indian-white relations on the frontier to improve as a result. With similar objectives, Smith looked to improving the education of non-English settlers in the backcountry, especially the German immigrants. In his proposals to the Society for the Propagation of the Gospel in Foreign Parts (SPG), Smith presented his uncharitable descriptions of Pennsylvania Germans, whom he feared were potential allies of the French: "For as the generality of these Germans place all happiness in a large farm, they will greedily accept the easy settlements which the French will be enabled to offer them. . . . Whenever we can teach them to distinguish between French and English governments, especially if they are also united to us by a common language, it is to be hoped that no efforts of our enemies will ever be able to draw them from us."[3] Smith displayed the ethnic and national prejudices of his society, but also his belief in using education to improve political unity among culturally diverse peoples.

Smith's most significant educational treatise, *A General Idea of the College of Mirania* (1753), presented a hypothetical college as a model for the intended college in New York. King's College (now Columbia University), which was chartered the following year, did not follow this plan, but influential friends were impressed, including Samuel Johnson, Anglican minister and supporter of the college, who encouraged Smith to take holy orders. The treatise led ultimately to his appointment as head of the Academy of Philadelphia, and when this academy became the College of Philadelphia, fictitious Mirania served as a model. In his day, college served primarily elite gentlemen and prospective ministers, but Smith planned to include a mechanics' school as well as a traditional school for the study of the classics and the learned professions. His stated objective of education was particularly noteworthy—the training of good citizens, whether they be mechanics or gentlemen.

In the summer of 1753, Smith sailed to England to take holy orders in the Church of England. His action followed that of dozens of Anglican ministers who had worked as private educators in the colonies before seeking ordination. Because the Church of England had no bishops in the colonies, candidates for orders had to make the long and expensive journey to England. In London, Smith renewed his acquaintance with the archbishop of Canterbury and met Thomas Penn, Proprietor of Pennsylvania, to discuss a position. On December 21, 1753, Smith was ordained deacon and two days later ordained priest in the chapel at Fulham Palace and licensed to preach in Pennsylvania. As was customary, Smith swore an oath of allegiance to the king twice, once before each ordination, and promised to maintain the liturgy of the Church of England unaltered. Later events in the Revolution would cause Anglican ministers to recall these oaths and wonder whether American patriotism contradicted these previous promises before God.

Upon his return to America in May 1754, in part through Benjamin Franklin's influence, Smith joined the Academy of Philadelphia as a teacher of logic, rhetoric, ethics, and natural and moral philosophy. When the institution later received permission to grant degrees, Smith became the provost of the College, Academy, and Charitable School of Philadelphia. From the beginning of his forty-year career as an educator, he excelled as a teacher, an educational theorist, and a public orator. Ranking among the city's leading intellectuals, Smith later published an address before the American Philosophical Society and other works that encouraged scientific investigation, including an essay on the transit of Venus. He also pursued his diverse interests through publication of *The American Magazine, or Monthly Chronicle for the British Colonies* in 1757–58. This magazine reprinted European news, communicated the latest scientific discoveries or inventions, and offered an account of the ongoing French and Indian War, as well as publishing original prose essays and poetry. Smith had found an outlet for his own religious-philosophical writings and social commentaries as well as a place to publish the literary work of his most promising pupils.

In the eventful year of 1757, Smith's *American Magazine* began publication and the College of Philadelphia held its first commencement, while the French and Indian War raged. At commencement exercises Smith urged all recent graduates to continue to learn throughout life and to serve their country in the present war against France and her Native American allies. In addition to student activism, Smith urged clerical involvement in public affairs, particularly "in Times of public Calamity and Danger."[4] A couple of years earlier, in response to Thomas Barton, a fellow Anglican minister on the Pennsylvania frontier, Smith had supplied his views on the duties of Protestant ministers. First, he articulated what he believed to be a prevailing public opinion, "you will hear it said–A Minister professing the Doctrine of the meek and blessed Jesus, should confine himself to Subjects spiritual and eternal. What have the Clergy to do with civil and temporal Concerns?"[5] The rest of the letter attempted to counter these opinions. Smith was disputing Quakers in the province about the necessity of defending the frontier against Indian or French attack. As pacifists, Quakers opposed taking up arms; as men of the gospel, Anglican ministers wanted to promote harmony, but they endorsed a "just war" ideology. Contrary to "those Quietest & non-resisting Principles which at present sway the Government of this Province," Smith argued that war was sometimes necessary, particularly in the defense of religious and civil liberties, and in such cases ministers should inspire their parishioners.[6] He warned, however, that ministers should not interfere in civil matters any further than absolutely necessary "for such a Conduct might engage us in Broils, ruffle our Tempers, and unfit us for the more solemn Part of our Duty."[7] This cautionary statement closely resembled official SPG instructions that their missionaries avoid meddling in civil affairs, a reasonable precaution given that such colonial missionaries usually labored where Anglicanism was a minority religion. No doubt glad to use Smith's endorsement to support his own work, Barton published *Unanimity and Public Spirit* (1755), a sermon that he may well have plagiarized, with Smith's original letter serving as a preface.

In advising distant, rural ministers like Barton, William Smith provided informal leadership to the scattered Anglican clergy of Pennsylvania and he regularly conveyed information to or from England, even though his relationship with the SPG differed from that of his rural colleagues. When he became provost of the college, the trustees supplied Smith with a healthy salary of £200 annually (later augmented), which was much more generous than the £50 or £60 stipend granted to SPG missionaries. Such missionaries also received salaries, when possible, from their parishioners, but frontier poverty made SPG assistance crucial. Smith received a small SPG stipend of £25 in the 1760s for serving the vacant parish of Oxford, Pennsylvania, but he was not financially dependent upon such a sum. Nonetheless, he observed the SPG requirement of a biannual report. Despite Smith's influence, his fellow ministers did not universally regard him as their leader; in the late 1750s, colleagues from Christ Church wrote to England denouncing his political involvement.

Smith not only corresponded regularly with English ecclesiastical officials but he also linked himself to the Penn family, Pennsylvania's Proprietary leaders; consequently, he antagonized members of the Pennsylvania Assembly, which regularly contested Proprietary interests. Smith's earlier collaboration with Benjamin Franklin at the College of Philadelphia also ended, and their relationship became a well-known public quarrel. Franklin increasingly sided with the assembly, rather than the Penns, and cooperated with those Quaker politicians Smith criticized. The Franklin-Smith quarrel also became personal: Smith wrote against the granting of an honorary degree to Franklin; Franklin tried to sabotage Smith's fundraising for the college by depicting it as a narrowly sectarian institution; and Smith may have spread the word in England that Franklin's son William was illegitimate. Although Smith and Franklin both agreed that Quaker pacifism should be rejected in the face of the French-Indian attacks, Franklin did not use the opportunity to attack Quaker officeholding. Smith's 1755 publication, *A Brief State of the Province of Pennsylvania*, and the 1756 sequel urged that Quakers and German allies should not be allowed to hold office or vote, specifically because, he charged, their religious pacifism made them unfit for political office and incapable of discharging the duties of government. For his partisan role in the controversy, Smith's critics accused him of opportunism and of trying to win additional favor with the Penns to secure himself a possible bishopric in the colonial church.

Fascinated by the frontier, Smith published his opinions on the Indians of western Pennsylvania and encouraged the spread of the gospel there as part of what he saw as a worldwide shift of civilization from east to west. His impressive publication, *An Historical Account of Colonel Bouquet's Expedition Against the Ohio Indians in the Year 1764* (1765), considered why England's General Edward Braddock had been defeated and offered practical advice on the Indian "advantages over European troops in the woods."[8] Smith urged that the English reject the principles of European wars and adjust to fighting in the forest by using lighter troops who were thoroughly trained to walk and run over logs and ditches and to load and fire their guns from different positions. He expressed unusually progressive views on the Indian character, which supported his belief that Indians were "fit subjects of cultivation." Though treacherous enemies in battle, Smith wrote, Indians exhibited "tenderness and humanity" in their treatment of prisoners, as well as other "virtues which Christians need not blush to imitate."[9] In the late 1750s, Smith had purchased land at the Falls of the Schuylkill, and in the early 1760s he began to acquire his first tracts of land in western Pennsylvania, a practice he continued for thirty years. Such land speculation was exceedingly common, but it may explain, at least in part, his commitment to expansionism and provide some rationale for his favorable depiction of interior Indian tribes.

After years of criticizing provincial politicians, especially about defense of the frontier, Smith had made some influential enemies, and by 1758 his long-standing disputes with the lower house led to his imprisonment. His legal problems were linked with those of William Moore, justice of the peace in Chester County, Pennsylvania, who had angered members of the colonial assembly and was charged in 1757 with improper conduct of his office, but who was declared innocent by the provincial governor. After the assembly had dissolved, Moore published critical remarks against it in the *Pennsylvania Gazette* and in a German-language paper of which Smith was a trustee. When the new assembly met in 1758, it charged both Moore and Smith with libel and ordered their arrest. On January 6, 1758, Smith was taken into custody and convicted of libel eighteen days later. From jail, he claimed he was the victim of both Quaker persecution and an abuse of power by the assembly. In publishing the controversial remarks, Smith had only republished what had already appeared in the English-language papers, and so he felt his prosecution had more to do with a 1756 accusation of libel that had been dropped. Furthermore, the assembly had decided that Smith could not question whether a legislature could legally accuse someone of libel against a previous assembly. It also refused to accept Smith's appeal to the king and ordered the sheriff to disregard any writ of habeas corpus or any other writ that might free Smith from jail. Smith refused to apologize to the assembly, and was committed to jail, but he prepared his appeal directly to the king in council.

From inside his jail cell, Smith made new friends. Since he could not attend class, his students came to the jail for instruction in moral philosophy. Romance bloomed too, when Smith fell in love with William Moore's daughter, Rebecca, who visited her father in jail, and Smith began to write poetry about "Amanda" in her honor. He was freed in April when the assembly adjourned, and he and Rebecca were married in June 1758. Despite these new beginnings, Smith's legal problems persisted: he was taken into custody again for a couple of days in September, and his appeal in England was stalled. To pursue the appeal in person, Smith sailed for London at the end of the year. This must have been a difficult decision, since Rebecca was expecting their first child. (A son, William Moore Smith, was born in June 1759.) Smith's departure also posed problems for his *American Magazine*, which suspended publication. He did find justice in London, for the Privy Council vindicated Smith and denounced the assembly's actions as contradicting English statutes. Benjamin Franklin was in London at the same time as an agent of the Pennsylvania Assembly, and in that capacity he opposed Smith's appeal. Smith resented the persistence of Franklin and the assembly attorneys, and this conflict further soured their personal relationship.

Having resolved his legal problems and returned to Philadelphia, Smith witnessed the escalation of tensions between England and her colonies. As an Anglican minister, Smith probably was predisposed toward loyalism during the early days of revolution. After all, the Church of England was the official, established church in England, and its members were supposed to support the royal government. The relationship between religion and government differed appreciably in Pennsylvania, which did not have an established church. Nonetheless, colonial Anglican ministers in all regions recognized the intimate connections between the English church and the empire and had sworn oaths to support the king. By virtue of living in America, ministering to colonists who often supplied their salaries, purchasing colonial land, and marrying and raising a family, ministers like Smith, though they were not born in the colonies, had established strong economic and emotional ties to their new home. Since the jurisdiction of the bishop of London was both loose and distant, ministers did not have an immediate chain of command to which they could appeal for answers about their conduct during the Revolution. Where possible, ministers gathered informally to discuss their situation, but ultimately they made individual choices.

Colonial Anglican clergy divided into loyalists or patriots as the Revolutionary War continued, but most favored neutrality, a position which revolutionaries often refused to recognize or interpreted as disguised loyalism. SPG ministers in New England, who faced a Congregationalist establishment, were predominantly loyalists. Farther south, greater proportions were either neutral or patriot. In southern colonies, such as Virginia, where the Anglican church was legally established, patriotism flourished among its clergy. In Pennsylvania, many of the rural SPG clergy were loyalists, but Philadelphia ministers divided on the question of political affiliation. At first, Smith acted as a moderate by urging reconciliation and, like all ministers of the gospel, proclaiming his role as peacemaker, but when efforts at political reconciliation failed, Smith supported colonial liberties. Though he was not an ardent revolutionary, he took an oath to the revolutionary Congress and continued to preach. Since he had not shied away from controversy earlier in his life, one might wonder whether his claims of moderation reflected more mature beliefs or a personal and professional strategy designed to weather the storm.

In the mid-1760s, Smith had opposed the Stamp Act as an inappropriate parliamentary act, which took money from the colonists without the approbation of their colonial legislatures. In a letter to Josiah Tucker, a noted political economist and dean of Gloucester, Smith expressed such opinions in his characteristically moderate manner. He feared the negative consequences of what he considered a short-sighted or mistaken policy, although he believed Parliament had not intentionally designed the act to be oppressive. On the other hand, he concurred in colonial arguments against the stamp tax and considered it insulting to the colonists, for it denied them the rights of Englishmen and perhaps even their "affinity and Brotherhood to Englishmen." Smith acknowledged that English officials could force their will on the issue, but not without losing the affections of the colonists and their trade. The solution, he urged, was "Moderation of Conduct."[10]

Rumors also circulated in the 1760s that the Church of England might appoint a colonial bishop. Fearful that such an official could serve as the iron hand of the imperial state, religious dissenters in the colonies and in England and some colonial Anglicans opposed the efforts of northern and middle colony clergy to secure an episcopate. Smith's moderate views may reflect a conciliatory position on this controversial issue, but they are also consistent with professional ambition. Smith had sent colonial petitions proclaiming the need for a bishop, but he disapproved of the episcopate campaign of the 1760s, the methods of New Jersey clergyman Thomas Bradbury Chandler, and the "two [*sic*] great zeal of our late Jersey conventions, for which they thought me too cold."[11] He apparently agreed with many of Chandler's arguments in *Appeal to the Public* (1767), but he wished it had not been published because of the subsequent attacks in the press against

Anglicanism. As an alternative to a bishop, Smith proposed to revive commissaries, a colonial supervisory position in the church, which had operated earlier in the century with only limited powers. This solution combined his political astuteness with his career ambitions: Smith recognized how unlikely it was that the English government would send a bishop, and in turn suggested that he himself might be named commissary of Pennsylvania and New Jersey. Smith joined others to deny that episcopal advocates wanted bishops with political powers, and he denied, too, that the movement for a bishop could be considered another effort, like the Stamp Act, aimed at destroying colonial liberties. In the fall of 1768 he began publishing a series of eighteen articles in the *Philadelphia Gazette* under the pseudonym "The Anatomist." Then Smith and Chandler split, as Chandler continued to fan the flames of contention with the publication of *The Appeal Defended*, *Appeal Farther Defended*, and *What Think Ye of Congress Now*. Chandler's outspokenness led to his forced exile to England in 1775, but Smith avoided the episcopacy issue and most other controversial matters after the conclusion of his "Anatomist" series in January 1769.

Smith's apparent neutrality faced a clear challenge in 1774 with the formation of a Committee of Correspondence in Philadelphia. According to Smith's own manuscript on the commencement of the American Revolution, he joined with a number of other respectable Philadelphia citizens in May 1774 to respond to Boston's difficulties, namely, the Port Bill, which would close Boston harbor, effective June 1, 1774. This Philadelphia committee quickly composed a letter dated May 21, 1774, to the people of Boston, which empathized with their situation, but recommended reconciliation; it even suggested that repaying the East India Company for the tea destroyed at the Boston Tea Party might be an appropriate way to end the dispute and yet preserve constitutional liberty. They noted that the value of the tea tax was not the central issue, but "*the indefeasible right of giving and granting our own money* (A RIGHT FROM WHICH WE CAN NEVER RECEDE)."[12] Bostonian rebels would have agreed with that last judgment (if not the issue of repayment), but the Philadelphia commentators disagreed with their northern associates on the question of tactics. Instead of Boston's proposed nonimportation and nonexportation agreements, these Philadelphians urged that, as a first step, a congress of delegates from various colonies should petition the king. Radicals objected to the lukewarm tone of this committee, but Smith and other moderates managed to continue as delegates to the provincial convention that wrote instructions for the Continental Congress delegates.

In serving on such revolutionary committees, Smith did not wholeheartedly endorse the radical trajectory of the Revolution so much as he publicly tried to advance the cause of reconciliation for both America and England. In describing his committee service a year later, Smith noted, "God knows that my Endeavors to promote conciliatory measures were so strong during the meeting of our provincial Convention last Summer whereof I was a member that I was considered as one willing to sacrifice essential liberty for temporary safety and even as an advocate for the measures of the Administration respecting this country. I persevered however to recommend moderation."[13] As the radicals gained power, Smith left the political limelight; in November 1774 a Philadelphia Committee of Inspection was elected to enforce the boycott, but Smith had not run for election. Since revolutionaries increasingly argued that those who did not actively support the Revolution were against them, Smith's efforts at restoring peace could easily be misinterpreted.

Critics were not exactly paranoid in fearing that Smith could be a mouthpiece for the English establishment. Smith had actually written both the secretary of the SPG and the bishop of London about his appointments and apparently solicited their advice about his conduct on revolutionary committees. Daniel Hind of the SPG supported Smith's participation, which he considered "a Fortunate Omen" that could bring about a mutually acceptable plan of accommodation.[14] Likewise, the bishop of London seemed pleased with Smith's appointment; he remarked with pleasure that the Church of England clergy had displayed "Temper and Moderation" and had not beaten the war drum like the ministers of other denominations.[15] Like Hind, the bishop charged Smith with the important duty of helping to restore peace between England and her colonies.

Smith's position on pre-revolutionary committees suggests his respected status in Philadelphia. In fact, he usually found himself in great demand on public occasions in the city. Perhaps his listeners appreciated his literary flair, his descriptive prose, or his imagination. The Anglo-American disputes of the 1760s and 1770s provided additional opportunities for political commentary, and ministers such as William Smith likely felt flattered by invitations to speak at important events. He claimed that he wished the pulpit could have been reserved entirely for the gospel, "yet when unavoidably called to speak from thence I could not appear cold to the interests of this or the Parent Country which appear to me inseparably connected." Indeed, the provost considered seriously the utility of such appearances. Ministerial silence, he warned, would convey the erroneous impression that "the Church Clergy are tools of power, slavish in their tenets and secret enemies to the principles of the Revolution . . . [and] give a deadly wound to the Church in America."[16]

For a variety of reasons, many Anglican ministers accepted invitations to speak before patriot audiences, including the one assembled in Christ Church on June 23, 1775. In that particular sermon, Smith drew an analogy between the present Anglo-American disputes and a disagreement between the tribes of Israel who first settled the Holy Land. Whereas that ancient controversy had been resolved peacefully with the intervention of a mediator, Phineas, no such person had emerged in England or the colonies. Additionally, Smith made an indirect reference to the English Glorious Revolution of 1688 as a legitimate precedent for opposing a corrupt government. Echoing a text he had written two decades earlier, he noted that "the doctrine of absolute NON-RESISTANCE has been fully exploded among every virtuous people. The free-born soul revolts against it." Resistance against government was sometimes justified, as in the 1688 revolution, but Smith did not wish to encourage "Pulpit-casuistry." He acknowledged the democratic impulses of the revolutionaries, and noted that the American people, not its ministers, would have to determine whether resistance was warranted. "But to draw the line, and say where submission ends and resistance begins, is not the province of the ministers of Christ, who has given no rule in this matter, but left it to the feelings and consciences of the injured."[17] Generally well received by American revolutionaries, this sermon was also distributed in England.

In their promotion of patriotism, American revolutionaries extended a common New England practice, the fast-day sermon, throughout the rebelling colonies on June 1, 1774, and July 20, 1775. Fast days, which were government-sponsored days of public prayer, afforded ministers of all denominations a key role in American protest, a chance to urge their formula of repentance and regeneration. Some ministers undoubtedly relished such opportunities, glad for the chance to be relevant to current issues. Others noted that the events served as litmus tests to distinguish patriot clergy from the neutral or loyalist ministers. As the Anglican clergy of Philadelphia jointly explained in a long letter to the bishop of London on June 30, 1775, they had attempted to promote reconciliation privately, "But as to public advice we have hitherto thought it our Duty to keep our Pulpits wholly clear from every thing bordering on this contest, and to pursue that line of Reason and Moderation which became our Characters." Further, they explained,

> But the Time is now come, my Lord, when even our silence would be misconstrued, and when we are called upon to take a more public part. The Continental Congress have recommended the 20th of next Month as a day of Fasting, Prayer & Humiliation, thro' all the Colonies. . . . Under these Circumstances, our People call upon us, and think they have a right to our advice in the most public manner from the Pulpit. Should we refuse, our Principles would be misrepresented, and even our religious usefulness destroyed among our People. And our complying may perhaps be interpreted to our disadvantage in the Parent Country.[18]

Refusing to speak could label them as loyalists, but participation could alienate church officials, including their bishop. Although this letter employed their usual deferential style of writing, Smith and his colleagues did not deliberately limit their discussion to what they thought the bishop wanted to hear. They acknowledged the power of rising popular sovereignty by suggesting that people would decide matters concerning their "own civil happiness." If the ministers appeared to urge any contrary position, their usefulness would be destroyed and, the clergy claimed, "our Consciences would not permit us to injure the Rights of this Country. We are to leave our families in it, and cannot but consider its Inhabitants intitled, as well as their Brethren in England, to the Right of *granting their own money*; and that every Attempt to deprive them of this Right, will either be found abortive in the end, or attended with Evils which would infinitely outweigh all the Benefit to be obtained by it."[19] Buried within this letter emphasizing reconciliation, the clergy had championed the rights of their fellow colonists. Carried by Richard Penn, then former governor of Pennsylvania, who did not set sail until July 8, 1775, this letter could not have reached England until long after the fast day had occurred.

By the end of August, Smith believed that all but two ministers of the Church of England in four neighboring colonies had preached on the July 20 fast, and several of these sermons were printed (including those of Smith, Jacob Duché, and Thomas Coombe), in contrast to the June 1 fast day, which the Philadelphia clergy had not widely observed. By preaching on July 20, Smith and his colleagues identified themselves with the revolutionary cause, while ostensibly aiming to preserve the church. Rejecting exile even for others, Smith felt that too many clergy had fled the colonies unnecessarily, including Chandler. Fearful of the long-term consequences for the church, Smith argued, "If our Clergy were generally to quit their people at this time I say we should not have the appearance of a Church or people left."[20]

Determining Smith's views throughout the rest of the Revolution is made more difficult by the relative scarcity of documents written during the war and by his continued professions of moderation. After the exchange of gunfire, he persisted in his public belief that reconciliation was possible, although it was becoming more remote. In August 1775 he wrote to the SPG, "Would to God that a suspension of hostilities & a negociation could take Place, before either side have proceeded too far in measures so ruinous to both. For this I pray & for this I labor daily & in such a way perhaps as may subject me to the blame of the violent of both sides. . . . But God knows my love is strong & my zeal ardent for the prosperity of both Countries."[21] Due in part to such expressions of devotion to both countries, Smith faced persecution by both loyalists and patriots. Extreme patriots presumed his moderation to be disguised loyalism. No doubt this phenomenon contributed to earlier historians' attribution to Smith's pen of a pamphlet entitled *Plain Truth* (now usually attributed to James Chalmers), which attacked Thomas Paine's *Common Sense*. Likewise, some of his loyalist colleagues in the church, including Thomas Bradbury Chandler, had found him too unsupportive in the campaign for colonial episcopacy, and therefore presumed him too warm toward the American patriots. So had Jonathan Boucher, a loyalist minister in Maryland who, legend has it, had so antagonized his patriot parishioners that he preached with loaded pistols on a nearby pillow. By May 1775, Boucher had apparently considered writing and publishing an attack on Smith for his support of the Revolution, but instead he asked Smith to employ his "cold & cautious worldly Wisdom" to prevent civil war.[22] Other Anglican ministers thought Smith was too supportive of the rebel cause. At the end of December 1776, fellow clergyman Samuel Seabury Jr., a loyalist from New York, described quite favorably the conduct of missionaries north of the Delaware River, but railed against the Philadelphia clergy who had promoted rebellion, both in the press and from the pulpit, and thereby inflamed popular passions. Seabury mentioned Smith specifically, since the former had been asked many times why he had not joined the rebels as Dr. Smith had.

According to American revolutionaries, Smith's patriotism was not so certain. In January 1776 the Philadelphia Committee of Safety investigated allegations that Smith had spoken of the Continental Congress disrespectfully, but it did not find sufficient evidence to prosecute. He was also suspected of writing a series of newspaper articles, under the pseudonym "Cato," which argued that the English constitution was the best form of government and which urged more efforts for reconciliation in the spring of 1776, when revolutionaries were turning toward more radical goals, including independence. The authorship of these articles, Smith's early biographer claimed, can be "established by the fact that the letters were later listed in the prospectus for Smith's collected works."[23] Nonetheless, in public acts Smith seemed to be identifying with the revolutionary cause and supporting colonial grievances. Perhaps as a test or as a sign of confidence in him, he was asked in February to deliver a funeral oration in memory of General Richard Montgomery, in the course of which Smith argued that the Revolution was a spontaneous act of self-preservation that had resulted from the injustice of parliamentary claims to supersede colonial legislatures. He noted firmly that Parliament aimed to mark the colonies "with such a badge of servitude as no freemen can consent to wear," but at the end of the text he again included his desire for the restoration of their "former harmony."[24] Smith did not urge reconciliation at all costs; he concluded that if grievances could not be redressed, the sounds of war should be preferred to the bonds of slavery. Nonetheless, American patriots did not receive this speech as well as his June 23, 1775 sermon; John Adams "described the oration as an 'insolent performance.' "[25]

Smith's political sentiments had not changed sufficiently to keep pace with the increasing radicalization of the Revolution, and this only became more evident with the passing of the Declaration of Independence. Unlike his friend Jacob Duché of Christ Church, Smith never became a loyalist. Unlike another ministerial colleague, William White, whose patriotism led to an appointment as chaplain of the Continental Congress, Smith's revolutionary inclinations were far less evident. Independence proved a difficult step for many colonists, particularly for Anglican ministers who had personally pledged their loyalty to the king. Prayers for the king and the royal family, which were mandatory parts of the Anglican liturgy, had become offensive to revolutionaries by 1776; consequently ministers were urged to drop the prayers. When Pennsylvania required officeholders to take an oath of allegiance to the new government, many rural clergy refused and closed their church doors, but Smith complied, and it does not appear that he did anything against the revolutionary cause throughout the war.

No doubt the community continued to suspect Smith of loyalism, because of his association with the king's church, his early professions of moderation, and the loyalism of his former colleagues. In late August 1777, Smith, Thomas Coombe, and many others were detained as General William Howe's army advanced toward Philadelphia, but the Supreme Executive Council permitted Smith to return to his property on the Schuylkill River, outside Philadelphia and not far from Valley Forge. To secure this parole, Smith likely had promised to do nothing to assist the invading British forces. Coombe, who had refused the oath to the new government, departed for England. Meanwhile, the British occupied Philadelphia from late 1777 until the early summer of 1778, and the city's Anglican churches, including Christ Church, became places of worship for the British military and their chaplains, who reinstated prayers for the king. No longer a resident of Philadelphia, Smith was not pressured to assume the pulpit during British occupation, but he did return to the city after the British evacuated.

Despite his reasonable fear that his letters could be scrutinized for incriminating information, Smith continued correspondence with the Penn family in England, including Lady Juliana Penn. Smith's letter of June 7, 1778, addressed to Lady Penn, expressed his concern over the imminent evacuation of the British and the return of the radical revolutionaries, who had been expelled from the city nine months earlier. Although Smith claimed these returnees would not have any legitimate grounds for charging him with behavior inimical to the American Revolution, he still worried about the fate of his wife Rebecca, their seven children, and himself. Nonetheless, Smith's moderate opinions allowed some revolutionaries to befriend him. On December 8, 1778, he preached in Christ Church at a Masonic gathering, in the presence of George Washington.

Smith had not been an alarmist in fearing the return of the radical revolutionaries to Philadelphia, though he could not have foreseen what would happen to his own career and his college. He probably had hoped that the college would resume classes with the evacuation of the British; while in the city, the British had used college buildings as a military hospital. Indeed, many colonial colleges experienced similar wartime disruptions, including occupation by either the British or the Americans. The college reopened, but by November 1779, the Presbyterian-controlled state legislature abrogated the charter of the College of Philadelphia (or at least ended the tenure of the trustees and the faculty) and in its place formed the University of the State of Pennsylvania. The private charter of the college was dissolved (it would be restored in 1789), a new board of trustees created, and Smith lost his provostship. The stubborn Smith, clearly annoyed by his dismissal from the college, did not relinquish the provost's house easily; nearly a year elapsed before he surrendered the keys.

In 1780, Smith and his family settled in Chestertown, Kent County, Maryland, where he served as the rector of the parish church and received the comfortable salary of six hundred bushels of wheat annually. He also was put in charge of the local free school, which soon thereafter was granted a charter as Washington College. The Revolution had reinforced many of Smith's pedagogical values, including religious toleration, and provided new reasons for educating the nation's sons. In stirring prose, he articulated not only the mandate of this college but also the goals of post-revolutionary America. Optimistically he predicted that Providence would bless America, but he warned too that Americans needed to cultivate their own virtue and avoid luxury and corruption. "In short, lasting provisions must be made, by GOOD EDUCATION, for training up a succession of *Patriots, Lawgivers, Sages* and *Divines*; for LIBERTY will not deign to dwell, but where her fair companion KNOWLEDGE flourishes by her side."[26] These were suitable words for a college, named in honor of George Washington, which would produce educated republican citizens.

Once the Revolution had concluded, American success reshaped Smith's political opinions and encouraged him to offer stronger statements of patriotism. In so doing he depicted himself clearly on the winning side, a useful and politic announcement for one who had seemed to wobble in his loyalties. Smith's public image was certainly enhanced by delivering patriotic eulogies at the death of revolutionaries, including one in 1789 for the Reverend David Griffith, bishop-elect of Virginia and a Revolutionary War hero, and old animosities melted away when Smith spoke on the occasion of Benjamin Franklin's demise. During the sermon for Griffith, Smith commented that divine Providence had caused the colonial Church of England in the states to organize as a new church, independent of all foreign authority, civil and ecclesiastical. The transformation from the king's church to an independent American Episcopal one was not so simple as Smith portrayed it, but by associating himself with the new church and by serving regularly at Episcopal Church conventions, Smith constructed for himself a public identity as a revolutionary patriot, after the fact. At war's end, Smith seemed convinced that independence was the right decision, although at the time he undoubtedly feared the move was too radical. In his authorship of parts of a new prayer book, Smith seemed to embrace revolutionary change. Likewise, the events of the Revolution had strengthened Smith's love of America and his long-standing confidence in America's destiny. Before a Maryland Episcopal Church convention in 1784, Smith proclaimed that "this American land shall become a great and glorious empire!"[27] As he saw it, national independence heralded a new age in American progress.

The journey from empire to republic had not been an easy one for Smith, and his own career seemed to falter along the road. His efforts at reconciliation during the Revolution had not secured peace, but had only rendered him suspect to both loyalists and patriots. Revolutionary politics in Pennsylvania deprived him of his cherished provostship, although he was restored temporarily to the post from 1789 until 1791—only to be dismissed again when the college became the University of Pennsylvania. He had long aspired to a higher post in the Anglican Church and he appeared to have been so rewarded when the Maryland Episcopal Church Convention of 1783 elected him bishop. The General Convention, however, did not confirm his election, owing mostly to various reports of Smith's public intoxication at the New York Episcopal Convention in October 1784. When Smith died in 1803, he was preparing his writings for publication in five volumes, only two of which were published that year. Smith had observed and commented on many events in the history of colonial Pennsylvania and the emerging nation, and yet he was frequently misunderstood, for he claimed to be a moderate man living in radical times.

Notes

1. William Smith, *A Sermon on the Present Situation of American Affairs. Preached in Christ-Church, June 23, 1775* (Philadelphia, 1775), i.

2. William Smith to Lady Juliana Penn, April 21, 1778, in Society Collection, William Smith folder, Historical Society of Pennsylvania, Philadelphia, Pennsylvania. Hereafter cited as HSP.

3. Smith to SPG Secretary, May 30, 1754, as quoted in Horace Wemyss Smith, *Life and Correspondence of the Rev. William Smith, D.D.*, 2 vols. (Philadelphia, 1879), 1:46.

4. Thomas Barton, *Unanimity and Public Spirit, A Sermon Preached at Carlisle, And some other Episcopal Churches, in the Counties of York and Cumberland, soon after General Braddock's Defeat . . . To which is Prefixed, a Letter from the Reverend Mr. Smith, Provost of the College of Philadelphia, Concerning the Office and Duties of a Protestant Ministry, especially in Times of public Calamity and Danger* (Philadelphia, 1755). Quotation from title.

5. William Smith, "The Preface," in Barton, *Unanimity and Public Spirit*, vi.

6. William Smith to the archbishop of Canterbury, October 22, 1775, as quoted in James P. Myers Jr., "Thomas Barton's *Unanimity and Public Spirit* (1755): Controversy and Plagiarism on the Pennsylvania Frontier," *Pennsylvania Magazine of History and Biography* 119 (1995): 233.

7. Smith, "The Preface," xii, xvii.

8. William Smith, *An Historical Account of Colonel Bouquet's Expedition, Against the Ohio Indians in the Year 1764* (Philadelphia, 1765), 37.

9. Ibid., 27, 28.

10. William Smith to Dr. Tucker, Dean of Gloucester, December 18, 1765, in William Smith, "Notes and Papers on the American Revolution," HSP, Am.159, 36–37; or quoted in part in Deborah Mathias Gough, *Christ Church, Philadelphia: The Nation's Church in a Changing City* (Philadelphia, 1995), 128.

11. Smith to SPG Secretary, May 6, 1768, in William S. Perry, ed., *Historical Collections Relating to the American Colonial Church* (Hartford, CT, 1871) 2:427. Hereafter cited as *HC*.

12. As quoted in Albert Frank Gegenheimer, *William Smith: Educator and Churchman, 1727–1803* (Philadelphia, 1943), 160. Full text in Smith, "Notes and Papers on the American Revolution," HSP, Am.159, 6.

13. William Smith to the bishop of London, July 8, 1775, *HC* 2:473–74.

14. Daniel Hind, SPG Secretary, to William Smith, August 29, 1774, Hawks Collection, Series C (William Smith Manuscripts), Archives of the Episcopal Church of the U.S.A., Austin, Texas, S, II, 4-7-18. Hereafter cited as Hawks Collection.

15. Richard Terrick, Bishop of London, to Smith, September 3, 1774, Hawks Collection, II, 5-7-19.

16. Smith to SPG Secretary, July 10, 1775, *HC*, 2:477–78.

17. Smith, *A Sermon on the Present Situation*, 21–23.

18. Philadelphia Clergy (Richard Peters, William Smith, Jacob Duché, Thomas Coombe, William Stringer, and William White) to the bishop of London, June 30, 1775, *HC*, 2:470.

19. Philadelphia Clergy to the bishop of London, June 30, 1775, ibid., 472.

20. Smith to SPG, July 10, 1775, *HC*, 2:476.

21. Smith to SPG, August 28, 1775, ibid., 479.

22. Jonathan Boucher to Smith, May 4, 1775, Hawks Collection, S, II, 7-7-21.

23. Gegenheimer, *William Smith*, 178.

24. William Smith, *An Oration, in Memory of General Montgomery, and of the Officers and Soldiers who fell with him, December 31, 1775, before Quebec; Drawn up (and delivered February 19th, 1776) at the Desire of the Honorable Continental Congress* (Philadelphia, 1776), 24–25.

25. Gough, *Christ Church, Philadelphia*, 137.

26. William Smith, *An Account of Washington College in the State of Maryland* (Philadelphia, 1784), 4.

27. William Smith, "A Sermon Preached Before A Convention of the Episcopal Church" (1784), in Ellis Sandoz, ed., *Political Sermons of the American Founding Era, 1730–1805* (Indianapolis, IN, 1991), 833.

Suggested Readings

For biographies of William Smith, see Albert Frank Gegenheimer, *William Smith: Educator and Churchman, 1727–1803*

(Philadelphia, 1943); Thomas Firth Jones, *A Pair of Lawn Sleeves: A Biography of William Smith (1727–1803)* (Philadelphia, 1972); and Horace Wemyss Smith, *Life and Correspondence of the Rev. William Smith, D.D.*, 2 vols. (1879; New York, 1972). Useful articles on Smith and the colonial Church of England clergy include: Edgar Legare Pennington, "The Anglican Clergy of Pennsylvania in the American Revolution," *Pennsylvania Magazine of History and Biography* 63 (1939): 401–31; James Warnock, "Thomas Bradbury Chandler and William Smith: Diversity within Colonial Anglicanism," *Anglican and Episcopal History* 57 (1988): 272–97; Ralph L. Ketcham, "Benjamin Franklin and William Smith: New Light on an Old Philadelphia Quarrel," *Pennsylvania Magazine of History and Biography* 88 (1964): 142–63; James H. Hutson, "Benjamin Franklin and William Smith: More Light on an Old Philadelphia Quarrel," *Pennsylvania Magazine of History and Biography* 93 (1969): 109–13; and James P. Myers Jr., "Thomas Barton's *Unanimity and Public Spirit* (1755): Controversy and Plagiarism on the Pennsylvania Frontier," *Pennsylvania Magazine of History and Biography* 119 (1995): 225–48. Related books include: John Calam, *Parsons and Pedagogues: The S.P.G. Adventure in American Education* (New York, 1971); Deborah Mathias Gough, *Christ Church, Philadelphia: The Nation's Church in a Changing City* (Philadelphia, 1995); and John F. Woolverton, *Colonial Anglicanism* (Detroit, 1984). See many of Smith's publications, available in microform, as part of the "National Index of American Imprints Through 1800" (Charles Evans Collection); and his letters in William S. Perry, ed., *Historical Collections Relating to the American Colonial Church*, vol. 2, *Pennsylvania* (Hartford, CT, 1871). Important manuscript sources on Smith include collections at the Historical Society of Pennsylvania, Philadelphia, the University of Pennsylvania, and the Archives of the Episcopal Church of the United States in Austin, Texas.

5

William Prendergast and the Revolution in the Hudson River Valley

"Poor Men Were Always Oppressed by the Rich"

Thomas J. Humphrey

A leader in New York anti-rent riots of the 1760s, William Prendergast (1727–1811) aimed for freedom from onerous or unstable leases and liberty from chronic debt and unending tenancy. Instead of emphasizing intercolonial protests against British authority, Prendergast found the local situation more critical. He sought justice, as he saw it: the eviction of new tenants and their replacement with rebels. Prendergast and his followers did not advocate a social revolution; they did not aim to take landlords' property, but rather they defended the traditional system. Once captured by the British, Prendergast faced trial for treason against the king. He had burned out farmers, assaulted people in the presence of many witnesses, and ridiculed the court system and the head of state. Why then did a royal governor pardon him?

Prendergast's fascinating story, as told by Thomas Humphrey, demonstrates the importance of the rural population in the Revolution. How did rural rioters differ from the more famous Sons of Liberty, whose activities usually centered on the major seaports? For many tenants, the Revolution offered an opportunity to side with the British against their patriot landlords in the hopes of obtaining land rights. Prendergast's son joined the British army, but was William's wartime moderation consistent with his earlier goals? How had he come to possess in 1771 the lands that he had previously rented? After the war, the extended Prendergast family, including seventy-eight-year-old William and sixty-eight-year-old Mehetibal, moved west. While loyalist landlords of New York had lost their estates, the patriots had not. Government confiscation of property aimed to punish loyalism, not to offer economic equality to the landless. Would Prendergast or his children have been disappointed by that reality, or did the promise of expansion into the frontier offer sufficient hope for his brand of independence?

Thomas J. Humphrey, a historian at Cleveland State University, has completed a book-length study of eighteenth-century agrarian rioting in the Hudson Valley, New York.

William Prendergast was born in Ireland in 1727 and died in western New York State in 1811, and he provides a vital link between the colonial world in which he lived and the post-revolutionary world his children inherited. In colonial New York, rural people such as Prendergast rioted for land almost continually against New York landlords who owned most of the arable land in the Hudson Valley and who constituted the colonial social and political elite. Like hundreds of rural people who lived during the revolutionary period, Prendergast did not participate in Stamp Act protests, join boycotts of British goods in the early 1770s, support the patriot movement against the British during the Revolutionary War, or take part in the debate over the Constitution of 1787. Prendergast, however, resembled his neighbors who worried more about getting, or keeping, land and supporting their households than they did about the political struggles of the Revolution. In the face of advancing armies that jeopardized their welfare and stability on the land, these farmers refused to join either side in the war and sometimes joined both sides to protect their interests in the land. Prendergast also moved west in the early nineteenth century, again like thousands of rural people, preferring to farm new land on the frontier to staying in the increasingly crowded rural communities in the east. Through Prendergast and his family, we may glimpse their rural way of life, their choices during the American Revolution, and their struggles to own land and attain stability in eighteenth-century New York.

According to his gravestone, William Prendergast was born in the port of Waterford, in County Kilkenny, Ireland, in 1727. He worked as a shipwright while he lived in Waterford, but emigrated to the Hudson Valley sometime before 1754, settling in Dutchess County on the east side of the Hudson River. He could not have bought land in the region, because the Philipse family claimed the land on which he wanted to live and refused to sell any to settlers or to tenants already living on the land. Landlords such as the Cortlandts, Livingstons, Beekmans, Van Rensselaers, and the Philipses owned much of the arable land in the Hudson Valley, especially on the east side of the river, and they refused to sell. They all preferred prospective settlers to become tenants who paid rent, and they usually required tenants to pay rent with agricultural products, such as wheat, which they could sell in Albany, Poughkeepsie, and New York City. These men and their families derived great wealth from the rent and other fees their tenants paid. Frederick Philipse, who held the land Prendergast farmed, claimed two hundred thousand acres and owned two mansion houses, one of which was a full three stories high, and at least thirty slaves. New York landlords such as Frederick Philipse easily translated their economic power into political power and dominated New York colonial politics. Prendergast became a tenant farmer on Frederick Philipse's estate.

Although tenants in the Hudson Valley often signed written and sometimes printed leases with their landlords for land, tenants on Frederick Philipse's estate agreed to verbal leases. Prendergast became a tenant who lived on his leasehold at the will of the landlord. In the early 1750s, Prendergast agreed to a developmental lease for approximately 120 acres of unimproved land without rent for five years. The Philipses outlined the style of leases they used when they applied for compensation for the property they lost during the Revolutionary War. The lease stipulated that Prendergast begin paying his annual rent, £4 12s. New York currency, or the equivalent in winter wheat, five years after he first settled on the land. Developmental leases enabled new tenants to spend the first five years of the lease clearing land, building a house and barn, planting crops, and making the farm reasonably productive before they began paying rent. During the developmental period, tenants needed food and money, or at least credit, to buy necessities such as seed, candles, and perhaps clothes. Tenants usually bought these goods at stores operated by the landlords. When the developmental period ended, tenants ostensibly began paying rent. Most tenants paid rent yearly, but most also failed to pay rent at some point, because of poor crops, bad weather, or simply choosing not to pay. On the eve of the Revolution, all but two of the tenants who lived on Philipse's Highland Patent with Prendergast owed at least two years' back rent, and all of them owed the Philipses money. Such a system of credit made the tenants economically, socially, and politically beholden to their landlords, who used their economic power both to force tenants to vote in particular ways and to ostracize their political opponents. If a tenant fell too far in debt, the landlord could evict him, sell the improvements made to the leasehold, and keep that money to eradicate the debt.

In 1755, as Prendergast was clearing his land as a tenant, he met Mehetibal Wing and married her. Mehetibal was a Quaker who lived in Quaker Hill, New York, near Pawling. She and her sister, Abigail, were the daughters of Jediah and Elizabeth Wing, and both had been born in Rhode Island. Abigail Wing married Nathan Hiller, who lived on a farm neighboring William Prendergast's on Philipse's Highland Patent. Mehetibal began having children when she was eighteen, in 1756, and bore a child approximately every two years after that until 1781, when she was forty-five. She and William Prendergast had thirteen children, at least eleven of whom survived into adulthood. Of that eleven, all but Elizabeth and Martha married, and all but two lived into the 1820s and 1830s.

Prendergast and his family probably followed the general agricultural production patterns of his neighbors. Most farmers in the region spent the developmental period of their leases clearing the land and preparing it for planting. Although Prendergast may have tried to clear the land by himself, his wife and neighbors, including Nathan Hiller, probably helped. In the early stages of his tenancy, Prendergast used the lumber harvested from the leasehold to build a house, a barn, fences, and pens for animals. When he cleared new land, Prendergast used the lumber to pay rent or to trade at local markets. After they had cleared enough land to build a shelter, Prendergast and his wife began clearing for crops, diversifying production as much as possible. If they relied too heavily on one crop and that crop failed, they would go hungry. As a result, farmers in the region grew wheat, oats, barley, corn, and potatoes. Both Prendergast and his wife worked hard to provide food for the household. Mehetibal, for instance, kept a small fruit and vegetable garden near the house, in which she grew lettuce, pumpkins, tomatoes, and peas, and nurtured a small orchard of apple and pear trees. She also sewed clothes, mended torn or worn clothes, spun yarn, churned butter, kept chickens, and cooked all the family's meals. She and the children also joined William Prendergast in the fields, particularly during periods of intense labor such as plantings and harvests. Mehetibal helped on a more regular basis with weeding crops and with other more mundane chores in the fields and on the farm. Prendergast, for his part, would have planted winter wheat, a valuable crop, oats, corn, pumpkins, and potatoes. He also probably acquired some chickens, milk cows, pigs, cattle, and sheep. Such a variety of crops ensured food for the household if one crop or another failed and enabled them to pay rent with those goods they produced in abundance. Furthermore, like his rural neighbors, Prendergast probably traded his surplus, such as extra wheat or butter, at local markets for those goods he and his family could not produce on their farm or that they could buy cheaply. They lived according to the agricultural cycles of the crops they planted and the rhythms of their farm animals.

Prendergast and his tenant neighbors could not always trade freely at local markets. The Philipses, like other New York landlords, restricted the market activities of their tenants. They required their tenants to grind their grains, such as winter wheat and corn, at their gristmills, and tenants paid approximately 10 percent of what they had ground for the service. The Philipses also demanded that tenants saw their logs at the manor lord's sawmills, again for a fee. Although some tenants might have traveled beyond the manor for these services, the distances they would have had to travel prevented many from doing so, and the fees the Philipses charged were not exorbitant. In addition, the Philipses required tenants to give them first chance to buy surplus agricultural goods, and they tried to force tenants to buy and sell their goods at stores operated by the manor lord. For the tenants who needed their grain ground, logs cut, and available markets, manor services proved convenient. Landlords, for their part, provided their tenants with important services, and their mills and stores provided them with another source of revenue.

Prendergast and other dissatisfied rural people in the area disliked some aspects of their tenancy. They found landlords oppressive and their leases onerous. Prendergast, for instance, leased his land at the will of the landlord, Frederick Philipse. Under such an arrangement, the landlord could evict a tenant whenever he chose without cause. Although the Philipses rarely did so, the threat undermined tenants' stability on the land. When Beverly Robinson, who operated the Philipse Highland Patent, claimed nearby land concurrently claimed by the Wappinger Indians and demanded that tenant farmers in the region agree to new, shorter leases, disgruntled rural people fought to keep their land. Many of them had already signed 999-year leases with the Wappinger Indians, and tenants on Philipse's Highland Patent also thought they held long-term agreements with the Philipses. The one- to three-year leases Robinson wanted them to sign jeopardized their continuity on the land and thus threatened the stability of their households. The Wappingers responded by seeking legal counsel and taking the Philipses to court over legal ownership of the land. Not surprisingly, the Wappingers did not fare well in a court dominated by New York landlords who empathized with the Philipses. Anglo-European colonists, however, had other reasons for not giving the land to the Wappingers. John Morin Scott, one of the attorneys who represented the Philipses, argued that favoring Indian claims over colonists "will be a Dangerous Tendency," because " 'Twill open a door to the greatest Mischiefs inasmuch as a great part of the Lands in this Province are supposed to lie under much of the same Scitiuation."[1] The court did not decide against the Indians until 1767, but Beverly Robinson began forcing tenants to sign shorter leases in the early 1760s. In the summer of 1765, Robinson and the Dutchess County sheriff, James Livingston, started evicting tenants who refused to sign the new leases. They sometimes burned rebellious tenants out of their houses to make way for new tenants who would agree to the new leases. The tenants wanted to own the land on which some of them had been living and working for thirty years, and to have the Philipses and Beverly Robinson jeopardize their landholding was more than many of them could bear.

In the fall of 1765 disgruntled rural people met at Samuel Towner's tavern approximately three miles south of Pawling, to discuss their response to Robinson's new leases. During the meeting, Prendergast stepped forward to lead the rural rioters in raids to "turn out all the People who had taken the short leases" and to evict those new tenants placed on the farms of rebellious tenants. Prendergast vowed to lead the rural rioters in their fight to restore "Justice" and to "relieve the oppressed," and he announced that it "was high Time the great Men such as the Atty Gen: & the Lawyers, should be pulled down."[2] The rioters wanted to own the land on which they lived and worked, and the leases they desired amounted to fee-simple landholding, in which they possessed the land without restrictions. On November 21, 1765, Samuel Munro Jr., whose father sat in jail for helping the Wappinger Indians against the Philipses, followed Prendergast's orders and led about forty men to James Covey Jr.'s house. When Munro banged on the door, Covey refused to answer, but the rioters broke the door down and threw Covey and his wife onto the ground in front of the house. They told them to leave and never return to their farm. For the rest of that day, hundreds of rioters marched throughout the countryside and similarly evicted other tenants and their families who had signed new leases with the Philipses. After they evicted these tenants, the rioters usually selected rebels to take over the farms, and mediators chosen from among the rebels adjudicated conflicting claims to individual leaseholds.

In March 1766 colonial authorities mounted an effort to stop the rioting, and they managed to capture a few rioters and take them to jail in New York City. When William Prendergast learned of these arrests, he proposed to go to New York City to gain the prisoners' release "by Force" if necessary.[3] Prendergast led approximately two hundred men to the edge of New York City and threatened to burn down parts or all of the city unless the rioters were released. His threat to burn the city could scarcely be dismissed as an idle one, given that the incidence of arson among slaves and other disgruntled people in the city was high and that a fire could completely destroy an eighteenth-century town. Prendergast also used the opportunity to voice the rioters' demands more publicly. He insisted that the landlords give the rioters perpetual leases for the land on which they already lived and worked. Moreover, according to Prendergast, the rioters did not want to pay more in rent than the quitrent due the king for the land. Some of the landlords in New York paid the king a fixed fee, or quitrent, for the proprietary use of the land instead of providing services. The Philipses paid the quitrent, because the king ultimately owned the land in the colony and had granted them permission to use it, to derive income from it, and to will it to their heirs. Many tenants, particularly Prendergast, became especially angry when they learned that the Philipses paid only £4 12s. in quitrent yearly for their 200,000-acre estate, the same annual rent he paid for his 120-acre leasehold. Nor did Prendergast's rent differ much from other tenants' in the region, who paid, on average, £3 15s. New York currency per 100 acres. Simply put, Prendergast and his fellow rural rioters, like contemporaneous rural rioters in other parts of the Hudson Valley, hated and rebelled against tenancy because it inhibited their permanence on the land. The rioters set a few small fires around the city, but pulled away and moved back into the countryside. Once there, again they harassed the tenants who had signed shorter leases.

In late May 1766, Prendergast led a group of about sixty rioters to Robert Hughson's house either to evict Hughson or compel him to join the rioters. Hughson was not at home, but his wife was. Although she refused to open the door, Prendergast pushed it open and told Hughson's wife that if they did not leave the house and farm immediately, the rioters would burn down their house with them inside. Robert Hughson had rightly feared the mob, but he could not move because his wife was close to delivering their baby. The rioters attacked Hughson's home because he had accepted a shorter lease, and because his father George had also helped local officials to deliver eviction notices to dissident tenants and to gather evidence against the rioters for the local justice of the peace. When Robert Hughson complained to his father of the ill-treatment his wife had received from the rioters, George Hughson complained to the local justice of the peace, Samuel Peters. Peters obtained writs for the arrest and eviction of the rioters. While delivering the writs, he and the elder Hughson ran into a formidable crowd of rioters who chased and caught them. After binding Hughson and Peters, the rioters carried their prisoners to Samuel Towner's house, held them prisoner overnight, and beat them for securing evidence against the rioters. Prendergast also tried to coerce Hughson and Peters into swearing to give evidence in favor of the rioters in any future court proceedings, or at least not to give any testimony against them. Both men refused, and Prendergast decided to compel the men to swear the oaths.

The next day the rioters constructed a country courtroom in a nearby field where they took their enemies to stand trial for their crimes against the rioters and against the rural people who lived in the region. In this "courtroom" the rioters, and not New York landlords, held power, and the agents of the landlords bowed their heads and spoke softly to their riotous superiors. The courtroom was twelve feet by twelve feet, marked off by a wooden-railed fence. Inside that square, the rioters had constructed a smaller, similar square that served as the dock in which the prisoners stood. Approximately two hundred rural rebels gathered around the "courtroom" as Prendergast marched around, brandishing a large sword and warning Peters and Hughson of their punishment if they refused to destroy any evidence they might have collected against the rioters or to give evidence in support of the rioters in future court proceedings. Prendergast declared that the rioters would ride Peters and Hughson on a rail "to the first convenient Place of mud and water, and there duck them as long as we think proper, and from thence we would take them to a White Oak Tree, and there whip them as long as we think proper, and thence take them out of the country and there kick their Asses as long as we think fit."[4] In refusing to take the oath, Peters remarked that Prendergast had an "Odd way of treating Men." Then Prendergast exploded, yelling out "*that if the King was there he would serve him so for Kings had been bro't to by Mobs before now*."[5] Suitably cowed, Peters and Hughson destroyed the writs of eviction they carried and the written evidence they held against the rioters. Regardless of their compliance, the crowd of rioters refused to be denied the chance to inflict their brand of justice on men who had so openly threatened their welfare. They first grabbed Peters, dragged him through the mud, and beat him, stopping only when Peters promised not to "take advantage of them for keeping him in Custody."[6] After the crowd similarly beat Hughson and extracted the same promise from him, they released their prisoners.

The country courtroom set up by Prendergast and the rioters, and their activities in it, offer some insights into the members of this crowd. Primarily, they held their own court because they knew that they could not receive equitable treatment inside an official court, with New York landlords so completely dominating these institutions. That Beverly Robinson could evict tenants from the land before a court decision on the dispute between his father-in-law and the Wappinger Indians, and that he could do so with the apparent backing of the law, suggests that landlords controlled the courts and legal system in colonial New York. Prendergast and his fellow rioters were aware of these inequities. By constructing their own court, these rural rebels tried to gain power in a world in which they felt powerless. They wanted to turn their world upside down.

Once inside the courtroom, with the power to mete out his brand of justice, Prendergast offered various clues to the cultural heritage he carried with him from Ireland to New York, and to those traditions of his fellow rioters. Prendergast parceled out traditional forms of discipline publicly so everyone in the community could join in the activities, and he condemned his enemies with historically loaded language that the crowd understood. When he threatened to have Peters and Hughson tied to a "White Oak" tree and whipped, for instance, Prendergast may have been alluding only to a stout tree against which the rioters might whip their antagonists, but references to a "White Oak" tree offer other potentially rebellious meanings. In the 1760s, Philadelphia ship carpenters called themselves White Oaks and marched in parades under the insignia of the White Oak, often affixing green sprigs of the tree to their coats. During the Stamp Act riots in that city, these White Oaks protected Benjamin Franklin's house from the rioters because he had organized mechanics, including ship carpenters, into military organizations in the 1740s and 1750s. The link between Prendergast and Philadelphia ship carpenters is tenuous, but the White Oaks in Philadelphia were loosely arranged as an ethnic organization and were related to the Whiteboys in Ireland and the Hearts of Oak in Ulster. In 1793, Arthur Young, an English agricultural writer who toured and wrote about France in the late 1780s, described the Whiteboys as rural rioters from Kilkenny who reached their height of popularity and power in the late 1750s through the 1770s. The Whiteboys were Irish tenants who rioted against absentee English landlords. In the 1790s, Young noted that these Irish rebels were apparently first "known by the name of *levellers*."[7] The ethnic connection between the Irish Whiteboys, Irish ship carpenters, and Prendergast's references to a "White Oak" tree is more plausible because Prendergast grew up in County Kilkenny, where the Whiteboys enjoyed particular popularity, and was a ship carpenter before he immigrated to the Hudson Valley.

Prendergast also invoked menacing references to the English Civil War, suggesting that knowledge of that event remained in the cultural heritage of colonial New Yorkers and that colonists of distinct social groups perceived the references differently. Figures from the English Civil War, such as Oliver Cromwell, resurfaced as important characters for eighteenth-century American colonists. Prompted by a revival of religious evangelicalism in the 1740s, the poorer and less-educated people rekindled in their folklore a favorable image of Oliver Cromwell as the leader of the New Model

Army and as the defeater of tyranny. On the other hand, wealthy and politically powerful colonists detested Cromwell as the man responsible for the perils of standing armies. Similarly, other American colonists remembered favorably the men responsible for the Civil War and, especially, for the execution of the king; the inhabitants of Saybrook, Connecticut, had reserved house lots for these regicides. When, in 1766, William Prendergast declared that mobs had overcome kings before, he called up images of these various attacks on people in authority, and by doing so he emphasized the rioters' collective contempt for men who abused their social and political power.

Beverly Robinson and Frederick Philipse did not long endure the rioters' insurgency. In July 1766, they called on the British army for help in defeating the rioters. The British troops encountered and skirmished with a small band of rural rioters that Prendergast commanded near a bridge in Patterson, New York. Two British soldiers were wounded, and one died later, but the regulars routed the crudely armed rioters. Mehetibal and the wives of many of the rioters feared that their husbands would be killed by the British troops, and they persuaded them to surrender to the British and plead for the governor's mercy. So many rioters surrendered that the British housed them in a nearby log church. Prendergast would not surrender, but he was captured a short time later. Under heavy guard, Prendergast was taken from Patterson to Poughkeepsie, where he stood trial for capital treason against the king, because he had led an armed rebellion and because he had waged war against the king's troops. If convicted, he faced a gruesome death. Prendergast's arrest and removal to Poughkeepsie apparently excited rural people throughout the eastern part of the southern Hudson Valley, and they threatened a more general insurrection against New York landlords. A large number of rural rioters positioned themselves near Quaker Hill, New York, vowing to fight for their land to the last man. Again, New York landlords called on the British army to defeat the rioters, and approximately two hundred troops marched out and put down the rebellion.

Once in irons, Prendergast never stood a chance. New York landlords ruled colonial politics, and their power extended to the courts. Furthermore, they wanted desperately to make an example of Prendergast, the known leader of the rioters. Rioters and obedient tenants alike knew Prendergast's fate was sealed: tenants could not be "defended in a Course of law because they were poor." They knew "there was no Law for poor Men."[8] Prendergast was tried in a specially convened Court of Oyer and Terminer, which was a commissioned court consisting of several judges that presided over cases of treason and felonies. Once in front of that court, Prendergast met few allies. All the justices were powerful and prosperous New Yorkers. Most owned land and rented some of it to tenants or were related to those New York landlords who had watched in horror as hundreds of rural people rioted for their land in the Hudson Valley in the 1760s. Judge Robert R. Livingston was a cousin of Robert Livingston Jr., the lord of Livingston Manor, and he operated the lower part of his family's estate. Justice William Smith Jr. had married into the Livingston family. Another justice, John Morin Scott, was also acting as the Philipses' attorney in their ongoing struggle against the Wappinger Indians over the very land on which the rioters began their protests in the fall of 1765. In addition, Scott was a leading member of the New York City Sons of Liberty who, when Prendergast traveled to the city to ask for help from that group, refused to assist the rural rioters. Other Sons of Liberty also sat on the court, too, a point not missed by Prendergast, who ruefully noted that if "opposition to Government was deemed Rebellion, no member of that Court were entitled to set upon his Tryal."[9]

Prendergast did not have a lawyer at the trial. Instead, he defended himself with the help of his wife. While Prendergast tried to refute the arguments presented by Attorney-General John Tabor Kempe, Mehetibal's behavior during the trial "attracted the Notice of the Audience," because she "never failed to make every Remark that might tend to extenuate the Offence, and put [her husband's] Conduct in the most favourable Point of View." Her attention to the details of the prosecution's case, her ability to stall their opponent's arguments with convincing rebuttals, and her "affectionate Assiduity fill'd every Observer with a tender Concern." Her skill at contradicting the prosecution's case prompted one of the king's attorneys to "make a Motion to move her out of Court, lest she might too much influence the Jury," but the justices denied the request.[10] Despite Mehetibal's powerful presence in court, Kempe's case proved too strong. The testimony lasted three days, the jury returned a guilty verdict one day later, and the justices rendered their sentence twenty-four hours later.

The court gave Prendergast what it described as the "usual severe sentence for Treason." The justices determined that Prendergast should be taken back "whence he came and from thence shall be drawn on a Hurdle to the Place of Execution, and then shall be hanged by the Neck, and then shall be cut down alive, and his Entrails and Privy members shall be cut from his Body, and shall be burned in his sight, and his Head shall be cut off." The court further ordered that Prendergast's body be quartered and disposed of at the "King's Pleasure."[11] Although the members of the Court of Oyer and Terminer had fulfilled their roles as administrators of justice, they meant only to show rural rebels what might happen if they rioted again. When they delivered their sentence, they also recommended that the king mercifully review the prisoner's fate. Nonetheless, after the court read how it wanted Prendergast to pay for his crimes, he "fell like a slaughtered ox," uttering a cry that melted to tears "even those lease susceptival [*sic*] of Compassion."[12]

When Mehetibal heard the sentence, she ran out of the courtroom, borrowed her sister's prettiest dress, and dashed the seventy miles on horseback to New York City to appeal for the life of her condemned husband. Governor Henry Moore knew that the court had recommended that the king review Prendergast's sentence, and thus agreed to Mehetibal's plea for a temporary stay of execution so the king could examine the case. Although the governor generally was not an ally of New York landlords, neither he nor the landlords wished to provoke an all-out rural rebellion by executing a man who had become such a popular leader. By leading the riots, Prendergast had become so well liked that Sheriff James Livingston, who was charged with carrying out the sentence, could not find anyone willing to help execute the leader of the riots. Those rebels who rioted after Prendergast was arrested did so in his name. Others attempted to break Prendergast out of the jail in Poughkeepsie, but he convinced his liberators that more harm would fall on them if he ran, and so he remained in jail. His popularity extended so far into the community that the sheriff had to offer double and then triple the usual pay for executioners, and he had to promise them anonymity so they could avoid harassment by Prendergast's supporters. Still, no one stepped forward. Men who had not participated in the riots, and who might otherwise have volunteered to help the sheriff, probably were afraid of reprisals from their neighbors if they helped put to death such a popular leader. Thus, the sentence and the recommendation for the king's mercy restored order in the region and reestablished the landlords' power in the community. In December 1766, King George III granted Prendergast an official pardon, and he returned to his farm in the Philipse Highland Patent, gaining ownership of his land in 1771, when the Philipses decided to sell off land in the Highland Patent to raise money for other business ventures.

Prendergast stood out among rural people in the region, and among rural rioters, because he led the riots against Robinson and the Philipses. Otherwise, he and other rural rioters in the second half of the eighteenth century shared similar goals. They wanted to own the land on which they lived and worked and to provide some kind of landed inheritance to their children. Land ownership provided them with the kind of stability tenants could not achieve. Most people who had become tenants, like Prendergast, either could not afford to buy land or they could find no land to buy because New York landlords owned most of the available arable land. Once these people began farming their lands, many of them fared well and some prospered. Nevertheless, they were still tenants, and tenancy meant long-term and short-term instability on the land, which proved debilitating. Thus, rural rioters rejected short leases and wanted to eliminate the Philipses' claims to the land and pay the quitrent to the king themselves. The Philipses, like other New York landlords who faced rural rebellions on their estates during the period, battled just as hard to keep their land because land ownership provided the basis for political and economic power. Prendergast, for his part, achieved his goal of land ownership before the Revolution.

Between 1771, when he took ownership, and 1777, Prendergast apparently sold his farm in Dutchess County to his first son Matthew and moved north into Rensselaer County. Although he had moved, he could not escape his past, and he remained a potentially dangerous enemy in the eyes of those New York landlords who became patriots. Patriot landlords in the region feared that their tenants might join the British army during the war in the hopes that the king might give them their leaseholds. The landlords' fears were well founded. Just as Ethan Allen in Vermont threatened to join the British to assure Vermont's independence from New York, in May 1777 hundreds of tenants on Livingston Manor rioted for land against their patriot landlords. They timed their riot to coincide with a rumored British invasion of the northern Hudson Valley and were more concerned with surviving the war and owning their land than fighting in the war. Leading patriots knew many rural people cared more about their material condition than the political battles of the Revolution. Robert R. Livingston noted that many rural people vowed to fight for the king primarily because if the king "succeeded they should have their Lands."[13] Still others became bandits who attacked patriots and loyalists alike who threatened to take their land. Patriot landlords such as the Livingstons and Van Rensselaers did not offer land to tenants to fight for the patriot cause. Tenants would have taken the offer. To landlords, Prendergast represented a likely candidate to lead rural insurgents against New York patriot landlords in future rebellions that might jeopardize the patriot cause.

Patriots primarily suspected Prendergast of loyalism because he refused to side with them against the British. Prendergast, however, did not join the British against the patriots either. In that respect, he resembled hundreds of rural people throughout the Hudson River Valley who refused to join either patriots or loyalists during the Revolutionary War, because British and patriot armies marched near and through the region. These armies attacked people who openly supported the other side and regularly stole their goods and property. To avoid such confrontations, many rural people did not join either side. Likewise, men feared for the welfare of their families. Rural men knew that "their families must want when they are killed."[14] For these rural people, familial bonds, material conditions, and permanent possession of the land proved stronger and more important than the political debates of the Revolution.

Patriots tried to dissuade people from joining the British. They often forced suspected Tories and people who would not openly join the patriot movement to sign bonds to ensure their proper behavior during the war. While these people did not necessarily have to put up the money when they signed the bond, patriots used the bonds to take the property of people who later acted for the British, or at least against the patriots. When persons refused to sign bonds, patriot leaders assumed those persons would act against them and sometimes forced them to leave the area. Prendergast had signed at least three of these bonds. On one occasion in the fall of 1777 and twice more a year later, the New York Committee for Detecting and Defeating Conspiracies and the New York Committee of Safety demanded that Prendergast sign bonds for £150 to £250 New York currency to ensure his good behavior during the course of the war. Sometimes patriots simply took goods from disaffected people to support their war effort and reimbursed them. In late 1778 the Albany Committee of Correspondence paid Prendergast an unknown amount for agricultural goods, probably cattle and crops, taken from his farm by a local patriot militia unit and by the Continental Army.

Patriots also persecuted William Prendergast because he had more direct links to loyalists and the British army. Prendergast's oldest son, Matthew (1756–1838), had joined the loyalists in the early years of the war. We may never know whether Matthew Prendergast stood in the courtroom, or just outside, during his father's trial and heard the subsequent sentence announced, but he certainly knew of the rural riots his father led. He also understood the inequities between his family and the families of the politically and economically powerful landlords, and he probably watched his mother ride away to New York to plead for his father's life. To Matthew Prendergast, the king deserved respect and loyalty because he had saved his father when New York landlords wanted him executed. At the beginning of the war, Matthew Prendergast, then in his early twenties, joined Abraham Cuyler's group of New York loyalists. In 1780 he led a group of loyalists who fought and captured some Connecticut patriots on Long Island. He moved to Nova Scotia after the war, but had moved back to his family's farm in Pawling, New York, by 1790. He moved to western New York with his family in 1805, where he served as a justice of the peace and as a supervisor for the town. Matthew Prendergast dutifully kept his British military uniform and wore his long hair tied in a queue in British military fashion for the rest of his life.

William Prendergast and his family remained on their farm in eastern New York from the end of the war until 1805, when he and his family migrated west. He appears in the first federal census of 1790 with eleven people living in the household—one white male under sixteen years, five white men over sixteen years, and five white women. Matthew evidently still lived on the farm in Pawling with his wife Anna. James had become a doctor and moved with his family to Steuben County, New York, by the end of the century. By 1800, Jedediah Prendergast and his wife Penelope Chase headed a household in Rensselaer County, as did Martin and his wife Martha Hunt. Presumably, they lived near their father. Thomas apparently lived with one of his relatives because he does not appear in the census records. Between 1800 and 1805, however, the Prendergasts decided to sell their lands in eastern New York, pool their resources, and move. The group of twenty-nine crowded into four covered wagons, crossed part of New York, headed east into Pennsylvania, floated on a flatboat to Louisville, Kentucky, drove the wagons to Nashville, and then headed slowly overland back through Pennsylvania and into New York. When the group ventured into Ripley, New York (now Quincy), William Prendergast's tired son Thomas exclaimed, "I have traveled far enough."[15] Matthew Prendergast, now acting as the head of the family, bought the land and hut of Josiah Farnsworth and stayed.

During the winter, most of the Prendergast party moved toward more settled regions of the state to find food. Two men stayed behind to find suitable land to settle. In early 1806, Matthew and James Prendergast bought approximately thirty-three hundred acres from the Holland Land Company on the western shore of Lake Chautauqua, built a log hut to live in, and began clearing land for planting. The rest of the family returned in the spring. William and Mehetibal Prendergast built a small farmhouse of their own on a slight hill overlooking a nearby creek, later named

Prendergast Creek, where they both died a few years later. He was eighty-four and she was seventy-four. They were buried in the family cemetery a few hundred yards up the hill from their house.

Why the Prendergasts decided to sell their land, migrate west, and start farming all over again remains unclear. Prendergast and his family probably moved for many of the same reasons other farmers left the relative safety and solid infrastructure of the east for the relative danger and unknown of the frontier. Migrants were often lured by cheap land in newly opened western territories, or felt constrained by the increasing size of New York's rural population. Prendergast probably knew that he could not provide a landed inheritance for all of his children in eastern New York, because so many people were moving into the northern Hudson Valley and settling on previously uninhabited land. By the early 1800s available land was becoming scarce. In western New York, still very much the frontier in 1805, Prendergast and his family could buy enough land to provide for themselves and for their children. His desire to own land, and enough land to be able to distribute it among his children, remained relatively consistent throughout his life. That Prendergast could give his children land meant that he could offer them some assurances of economic independence and political autonomy, because as landowners they would be socially and politically beholden to no one.

William Prendergast lived long enough to see his fellow colonists in North America rebel successfully against the British and establish their own country. Prendergast remains an important historical figure not because he participated in the Revolution on either side, but because he tried not to join either side. He and many other rural people in the Hudson Valley cared more about keeping their farms and providing for their families than they did about the political battles of the Revolution. To that end, he did not pledge his support for patriots or loyalists. Prendergast also represented those thousands of rural people in New York's Hudson Valley who increasingly believed that their labor on the land made that land valuable and entitled them to own it. Land ownership offered them economic and political independence. Such a perception of independence and liberty countered, and sometimes conflicted with, the notions of freedom espoused by many New York patriots. Although both groups of people lived in the new nation formed after the Revolution, their distinct notions of independence suggest that Americans thought differently about the Revolution they had waged so recently. Prendergast, like others who lived during the revolutionary period, spent his life searching for a place where he could provide security for his family and where he could furnish his children with the foundation for a stable life.

Notes

1. John Morin Scott, quoted in Oscar Handlin and Irving Mark, "Chief Daniel Nimham v. Robert Morris, Beverly Robinson, and Philip Philips—An Indian Case in Colonial New York, 1765–1767," *Ethnohistory* 2 (1964): 240.

2. Deposition of James Covey Jr., November 23, 1765, Unsorted Legal MSS., Box 1, John Tabor Kempe Papers, New-York Historical Society, New York. Hereafter cited as NYHS. In the same box, see the depositions of Ebenezer Weed and Felix Holdrige. See also David Akin's evidence for the trial of William Prendergast, no date, Lawsuits, C-F, John Tabor Kempe Papers, NYHS.

3. David Akin's evidence in Lawsuits, C-F, and Robert Hughson's Deposition, May 27, 1767, Unsorted Lawsuits, Box 4, both in John Tabor Kempe Papers, NYHS.

4. George Hughson and Samuel Peters both quoted Prendergast as passing this judgment on them, in Irving Mark and Oscar Handlin, eds., "Land Cases in Colonial New York, 1765–1767; *The King v. William Prendergast*," *New York University Law Quarterly Review* 19 (1942): 179–84, quote on 181.

5. Samuel Peters, quoted in Mark and Handlin, "*The King v. William Prendergast*," 184; emphasis in original.

6. Ibid., 185; and Samuel Peters's affidavit, June 7, 1766, Unsorted Lawsuits, P-U, Box 4, John Tabor Kempe Papers, NYHS.

7. Arthur Young, Esquire, "The Account of the WHITEBOYS in Ireland," *The American Minerva* (New York), December 30, 1793.

8. Moss Kent's testimony and Sheriff James Livingston quoting Prendergast, in Mark and Handlin, "*The King v. William Prendergast*," 175, 191.

9. William Smith, quoting Prendergast, in William Sabine, ed., *Historical Memoirs from 16 March 1763 to July 1778 of William Smith*, 2 vols. (New York: Arno Press, 1966), 1:30.

10. *The Boston Gazette*, September 15, 1766.

11. *New-York Gazette*, September 1, 1766.

12. William Smith, quoted in Staughton Lynd, *Anti-Federalism in Dutchess County, New York* (Chicago: Loyola University Press, 1962), 50.

13. Robert R. Livingston to John Jay, July 17, 1775, quoted in Staughton Lynd, "The Tenant Rising at Livingston Manor, May 1777," *New-York Historical Society Quarterly* 48 (1964): 167.

14. Robert R. Livingston to John Jay, July 17, 1775, quoted in ibid., 167.

15. A. W. Anderson, *The Story of a Pioneer Family* (Jamestown, NY: Jamestown Historical Society, 1936), 3.

Suggested Readings

As is often the case with the "lower sort" of people who lived during the eighteenth century, William Prendergast left few direct sources to help us tell his biography. As a result, I have relied on many sources to piece together his life, and the ordinary lives of farmers in the Hudson Valley. For the rhythms of farming, and of farm life, see Lambert Burghart's farm notebook at the Albany Institute of History and Art; and the papers of Elkannah Watson at the New York State Library, Manuscripts and Special Collections (NYSL), Albany. For my general comments on leases, tenancy, and rural production in the Hudson Valley, I drew on my reading of 3,338 leases and rent records for Rensselaerwyck at NYSL; Livingston Manor at NYSL and at the New-York Historical Society, New York; Philipsburg and the Philipse Highland Patent at the David Library in Washington's Crossing, Pennsylvania; and Cortlandt Manor at Sleepy Hollow Restorations in Westchester, New York. For Prendergast's trial as a rioter, see Irving Mark and Oscar Handlin, eds., "Land Cases in Colonial New York, 1765–1767; *The King v. William Prendergast*," *New York University Law Quarterly Review* 19 (1942): 165–94. For rural rioting in New York in the second half of the eighteenth century, see Irving Mark, *Agrarian Conflicts in Colonial New York, 1711–1775* (New York, 1940); and Sung Bok Kim, *Landlord and Tenant in Colonial New York: Manorial Society, 1644–1775* (Chapel Hill, NC, 1978). For William Prendergast's life after the Revolution, see A. W. Anderson, *The Story of a Pioneer Family* (Jamestown, NY, 1936); and the description of the Prendergasts in western New York in the Foote Papers at the Chautauqua County Historical Society, Chautauqua. The land transaction papers are held at the Mayville Court House in Mayville, New York. For New York during and after the American Revolution, see Edward Countryman, *A People in Revolution: The American Revolution and Political Society in New York* (New York, 1980); Alan Taylor, *William Cooper's Town: Power and Persuasion on the Frontier of the Early American Republic* (New York, 1995); and Alfred F. Young, *The Democratic Republicans of New York* (Chapel Hill, NC, 1967).

6

Ashley Bowen of Marblehead
Revolutionary Neutral

Daniel Vickers

Growing up in Marblehead, Massachusetts, Ashley Bowen (1728–1813) naturally looked to the sea for a livelihood, and his maritime orientation later influenced his attitudes on the American Revolution. He had his own rigging shop in 1772, but the war devastated the business and challenged his ability to provide for his large family. Bowen's life story is one of declining personal fortune, punctuated by his participation in the British assault on Quebec in 1759 and scarred by increasing poverty during the Revolutionary War. Although Bowen apparently did nothing contrary to the American cause, neither did he support it vocally. He was convinced that the Americans were no match for superior imperial forces. How much of Bowen's economic difficulties during the Revolution came from his neutrality, and how much from the impact of the Revolution on Marblehead? Since moderation had helped William Prendergast weather the war, why had success escaped Bowen's grasp?

Like Prendergast, Ashley Bowen seemed particularly centered on local affairs, especially riots concerning the inoculation hospital and the impact on Marblehead's economy of closing the port of Boston. What role did crowd action play in pre-revolutionary Marblehead, in comparison with the rural riots Prendergast had led? Why does Bowen's diary not contain more information about famous and important Boston events? For Bowen, the American Revolution threatened not only his economic independence as an artisan and provider for his family but also his personal liberty to worship in a church, which patriots often considered inimical to the American cause. Unlike William Smith, Bowen's attachment to the Church of England did not require solemn promises to defend the king. As Daniel Vickers demonstrates thoroughly, Bowen's story serves as a reminder that while American revolutionaries attempted to label contemporaries as loyalists or patriots, not everyone fit nicely into those categories.

Daniel Vickers teaches history at the University of California at San Diego. In addition to numerous articles on colonial maritime history, he is the author of *Farmers and Fishermen: Two Centuries of Work in Essex County, Massachusetts, 1630–1850* (1994).

On a "fair and pleasant" Wednesday, May 11, 1774, Ashley Bowen and the other residents of Marblehead, Massachusetts, learned that by way of punishment for the insolence of the Tea Party the previous autumn, the port of Boston was to be closed. "This day came to town an Act of Parliament," wrote Bowen in his journal, "Great to be done." The British wasted little time. On Friday, Bowen heard that General Thomas Gage, the new governor, had arrived in Boston with a sizable naval escort to help him enforce the closure; and the following Tuesday the thunder of formal cannon fire rolling across the bay from the provincial capital signaled that Gage had assumed the "helm of Government." Several weeks passed while the governor mustered his forces and the colonists considered their response, and then on June 1 the act took effect and the port of Boston was blocked up.[1]

Bowen could never have guessed that the closing of Boston harbor would mark the beginning of the end for Britain's colonial empire in North America. Nor could he have known that Marblehead had just passed the high-water mark of its own history, or that he himself would be financially ruined in the tumult to come. Yet a sense of foreboding ran through everything he wrote during the weeks surrounding these events. "Sad times . . . terrible times," he summarized on the day the act came into effect. Ever since Gage had moved the main provincial customs house to Marblehead, the streets had been "filled with tide waiters and other officers," all of them "strange faces," whose presence worried Bowen. Now there were guard boats in the harbor and British regulars stationed in the town—for the long haul it seemed, since many of them had brought their wives. For ordinary port dwellers, the influx of imperial authority could only be a source of anxiety. "Tis supposed there is not one black negro slave in this town," mused the diarist, "but many white are in town this day."[2]

Ashley Bowen kept his daily journal from the beginning of the revolutionary crisis through the summer of 1777 and then from the fall of 1778 to the late winter of 1780. In spare, unadorned entries, the journal described the progress of the political struggle and the military contest from a maritime perspective, that is, from the viewpoint of someone who had spent all of his fifty years on or near the ocean. A Marbleheader, an American, and a middle-aged man of the world, Bowen was at once disturbed by Parliament's program of imperial reform, suspicious of the patriot politicians' motives, and, above all, convinced that the colonists would never defeat the British navy. He was no patriot—no "jack tar in the streets"—but neither was he one of the "King's Friends."[3] Rather, he was an ordinary citizen of a seaport community, whose political ideas fit into nobody's scheme of what a patriot or loyalist should be.

Ashley Bowen was born in 1728, the son of a well-to-do notary and justice of the peace in the small but growing seaport of Marblehead on Massachusetts' North Shore, a few hours by water from Boston. At the age of eleven, like virtually every other boy in town, Ashley went to sea—although unlike most of them, he shipped out, not as a fisherman, but as a cabin boy apprenticed to Captain Peter Hall, who was to train him for a ship's command. Most ships' boys did well for themselves in colonial New England; roughly half of them at some point in their careers became shipmasters themselves. Unfortunately for Ashley, however, Captain Hall proved something of a fraud, and for several years the boy served him afloat and ashore, cooking his meals, cleaning his cabin, and even helping Hall and his wife run a general store in Majorca, without ever learning anything about running a vessel. The drudgery and the petty tyrannies the boy endured would have been supportable had he been taught anything about ship handling, navigation, or the customs of eighteenth-century commerce, but with each passing year, Bowen saw his chances dwindling to make something of himself.

Finally, at the age of seventeen, Bowen ran away and launched himself on a seafaring career of his own that lasted nearly twenty years. He tried his hand at all manner of trades: shipping himself on coastwise voyages to the West Indies, boating on the Delaware River, whaling off the Carolina coast, fishing on the Grand Banks, and sailing to Europe and the Mediterranean. To make up for his lost apprenticeship, he took lessons in navigation while ashore in Bristol, England, and badgered Marblehead merchants for the command of a trading schooner. He was soon a mate and served frequently in that capacity, and he even commanded a number of coasting voyages along the American shore. Still, he never recaptured the ground he had lost as a youth; the captaincy of a true oceangoing vessel, the goal of any colonial mariner, always eluded him.

His seafaring career did reach a peak of sorts during the Seven Years' War. In April 1759 he enlisted, along with several dozen of his neighbors, in the British assault on Quebec. After sailing to Halifax, he was assigned to HMS *Pembroke* and interviewed by its commander, Captain John Simcoe. The latter was probably amused when Ashley defined his country of origin as Marblehead, but he was impressed by the sailor's experience, especially "up the Mediterranean," and he assigned Bowen "to walk the quarterdeck as midshipman."[4] For the better part of the year, he played a small but active role in the expedition, transporting troops up the St. Lawrence, bombarding French positions around the city, ferrying soldiers around the siege, and assisting James Cook (sailing master of the *Pembroke* and future Pacific explorer) to chart the river. He was part of a diversionary attack below Quebec the night before the Battle of the Plains of Abraham, and a week later he "had the happiness of seeing Eng[lish] colors marched into the City" at the very crest of British military power in North America.[5] Although the expedition took Bowen away from New England for only seven months, it was the adventure of his lifetime. He returned to his journal again and again in later years to make editorial adjustments to the story, and he always loved to reminisce about it to any willing ear, especially to recount his dealings with the "immortal Cook."[6] As a friend later observed of Bowen: "All his views of Marine Greatness were from the omnipotence of the British Navy, and . . . he [never changed] in the slightest degree the form of thought which his mind had taken, when he left the St. Lawrence."[7]

For two years after his return, he skippered a transport schooner out of Boston, provisioning British troops along the St. Lawrence River, and then in 1763 he quit the sea for good and returned to Marblehead. The major reason for this decision was that he was now married. In 1758, after two decades of marine service and approaching his thirtieth birthday, he had met and wed a young woman from Boxford, Massachusetts, named Dorothy Chadwick. Like the great majority of sailors who had survived their years before the mast but never been promoted to the quarterdeck, Bowen was losing his enthusiasm for the hardships of incessant voyaging. Over a period of five years, he gradually wound down his seafaring career, while he decided to see "how it would suit to live on shore," and then finally, in 1763, he took up the rigging trade, and spent nearly all his remaining years—and there were fifty to come—at home in Marblehead.[8]

Through the later 1760s and early 1770s, Ashley Bowen rode the remarkable pre-revolutionary boom in Marblehead's fishing and shipping industries. Busy making suits of rigging, mending shrouds and straps, and fixing sails for the local fleet of trading schooners and brigs while Dorothy sewed flags and pendants for them, he soon attracted the business of Robert Hooper and Jeremiah Lee, two of the richest shipowners in New England. From the latter in particular, Ashley received "a great many favors . . . [and] the benefit of all his transients' rigging as well as his own."[9] By 1770, he could claim that the loft he shared with sailmaker William Courtis bore "the best character in this Province," and in October of 1772, he felt confident enough of his business to move into new quarters on his own, rented from Lee at £6 a month.[10] As the colonial period drew to a close, Ashley Bowen was acquiring the type of craft mastership that, under normal circumstances, would have ensured that his household, which now included several young children, could maintain itself in comfort and independence.

Bowen's career as a rigger ashore was neatly framed by the imperial crisis that led to the American Revolution, yet at no time during this period did imperial politics seem to hold any real importance for him. The diary he kept made no reference to any of the events that historians today believe were critical to the unfolding crisis, in spite of the fact that so many of them occurred in Boston, less than a few hours away by water. True, as a writer, he was never expansive, and the journal itself was always intended to be primarily a record of his own work. Yet, if such disturbances as the seizure of John Hancock's sloop *Liberty* in July 1768, the Boston Massacre of March 1770, or the Boston Tea Party of December 1773 had really seemed portentous to him, he could have mentioned them briefly.

During the Tea Party episode, Bowen was, indeed, absorbed in public affairs, though the issue at hand was not the defense of American liberty but rather the attempt by the Marblehead gentry—patriots in the main—to construct an inoculation hospital on Cat Island. In local terms, this was no small event. Inoculation was not a routine procedure in the eighteenth century, and the construction of the hospital was attended by many anxious town meetings and several brief riots. Bowen described the incident in comic-opera fashion, but his sympathies lay mostly with the fishing people of the town, who were suspicious of the project from the start and doubly so once some of the patients contracted the disease against which they had been inoculated. Tension reached a peak when a handful of residents stole a bundle of infected clothing from Cat Island and tried to sneak it back into town. When their neighbors spotted them approaching shore, the culprits threw most of the garments overboard but were apprehended and put under lock and key for the night. The next day, the outraged townspeople tarred and feathered these men, placed them in a cart, and, in a procession that numbered close to one thousand (including a fifer and several drummers), marched nine miles to Salem and back. It was the fear of smallpox and not taxes that prompted this—the greatest single demonstration in Marblehead during the prerevolutionary period.

A week later, another party of inhabitants, tired of the anxiety of dealing with the constant parade of sick and recovering patients, rowed out to the island after dark in disguise with tubs of tar in hand and burnt the hospital down. When two of them were arrested on suspicion of arson and placed in Salem jail, wrote Bowen, "our fishermen all rose in a body and went to Salem and brought them home again. . . . Finis for the Isle Cat."[11] The whole story took several months to evolve, and Bowen recorded it in greater detail than any other event in his life save the siege of Quebec. Not once did he interrupt it with news about the Tea Duty or American resistance to it. In the political context of the times, the hospital incident did nothing for the patriot cause save to throw several Marblehead radicals, including Elbridge Gerry and John Glover who had helped to found the hospital, into bad repute and to distract people like Ashley Bowen from the imperial cause brewing about them.

Only with the news in May 1774 of the Boston port closing did Bowen begin to suspect that some corners were now being turned—in his own affairs, the life of the town he lived in, and in the history of the empire. Once politics began to bear on basic rhythms of life in Marblehead, everyone had to take notice. For one thing, Bowen's rigging business slackened immediately. The previous summer, he had been busy in his loft six days in every week, usually with a man or two to help him. In July of 1774, however, he worked a mere fifteen days, and usually without help. The harbor was busy enough that summer but in unconventional ways. In order to redirect shipping traffic out of Boston, Governor Gage had moved the customs house to Marblehead, which became the port of call for most foreign ships with business in Massachusetts. Naval transports visited regularly now, fetching and delivering British troops. Sloops from the coast of Maine carrying firewood could only proceed to Boston after stopping at Marblehead and taking on a customs officer and a number of armed guards.

Over the next twelve months, as the political crisis deepened, the movements of trade gave way to the maneuvering of troops, and Bowen began to brood. "No news," he muttered, "is commonly good news."[12] Men-of-war were now cruising off the coast; transports from England were landing fresh troops in Boston every month; and redcoats were tramping the roads of eastern Massachusetts searching for weapons and ammunition. In Bowen's estimation, the Americans stood very little chance of resisting British arms. Whenever diplomatic or military intelligence arrived, he invariably put the gloomiest possible interpretation on it. In February 1775, Lt. Col. Alexander Leslie marched from Marblehead to search out rebel arms in the north end of Salem, and he was stopped at the Salem drawbridge by an angry crowd. The British never completed their mission, and the incident has gone down in patriot annals as "Leslie's Retreat." Although Bowen's version of events does not contradict this story, the lesson he drew from it was quite different. In his account, the redcoats marched with impunity up to the bridge, demanded that it be let down, and then "marched over as far as they pleased and returned back again."[13] Similarly, the Battle of Bunker Hill in June made it into Bowen's journal, not as an American victory, but as the burning of Charlestown followed by the driving of rebel troops out of their entrenchments. In December, Bowen was ready to believe a mistaken report that Newport, Rhode Island, was in ashes; and when rumors began to fly the following March that the British were about to abandon Boston, Bowen concluded that they would probably burn that city, too. Nothing of the sort happened, but when the troops departed, the Marblehead journalist was plainly more impressed by the fleet of "one hundred sail . . . [with] four fifty gun ships," that carried them away to Halifax than he was with the fact that Massachusetts was now effectively independent.[14] Not everything went the patriots' way that year—the "cold" news from Quebec that Benedict Arnold and his army had been defeated was one key setback—but to read Bowen's diary, one would think the revolutionary cause had already been lost.[15]

Bowen felt he had good reasons to be skeptical, for as an ex-mariner his attention was normally trained on the sea, and there the British navy reigned supreme. Marblehead juts into the Atlantic and affords an excellent prospect over most of Massachusetts Bay. All his life, Bowen had lived and worked on or beside the ocean, and maritime matters had always occupied a large part of his journal. Even after retiring from active seafaring, his rigging business had kept him in constant contact with the shipping and fishing industries of the port, and from his rigging loft by the waterfront, he generally noted the comings and goings of vessels around the harbor. After the outbreak of war in the spring of 1775, however, the port of Marblehead was shut down as Boston had been a year before, and the most prominent vessels to be seen off the coast now were those of the British navy. Two of them, HMS *Lively* and *Merlin*, patrolled the waters around Marblehead for most of the subsequent year. At different times they intercepted incoming ships, boarded vessels in the harbor, practiced their shipboard artillery, and on one occasion, set officers on shore to dine with prominent Tories in town. They even seized a few unfortunate local residents who ventured out on the water and impressed them into the British service. Bowen himself was captured and taken on board the *Lively* in April of that year, although "acquitted" in turn and returned to land.[16] Fifteen years earlier, Bowen had watched a British expeditionary force with naval support take Quebec, one of the great military citadels of the New World, and the thought that Marblehead's few coastal batteries manned by ill-trained local militia could have turned back any determined imperial assault struck him as ludicrous.

When the war began, Ashley Bowen's deepest fears were for the safety of his family and neighbors in Marblehead. Throughout the Revolution, his perspective on events remained that of a townsman, and his immediate reaction to any event was normally to consider its local impact. On the one hand, he celebrated when a local crowd forced the *Lively* to return six of the ten men that it pressed in February 1775. On the other hand, he complained in August 1775 that "Poor Marblehead is threatened by [Washington's] Headquarters of a visit from that quarter if we let any of the King's men land or supply them with even water." In his own language, "our people" always meant his neighbors, whether they were beating the bushes for spies, fleeing the seaport for fear of British attack, negotiating with imperial officers on board vessels in the harbor, or fighting in the trenches surrounding Boston.[17] In his view, the war's hardships bore less on the colonies as a whole, or even on New England, than on his own hometown, caught in the middle of a struggle from which there would emerge, he believed, no winners. That summer he concluded, "War's no dependence on anything; between two stools the ass comes to the ground. . . . Poor, poor, oh poor Marblehead!"[18]

Throughout the Revolutionary War, Bowen maintained a civil relationship with many patriot neighbors. While in Boston on unspecified business in November 1776, he dined with Captain Nicholson Broughton, a Marblehead shipmaster who had served as an officer in the Continental Army and helped Washington launch the American navy by commanding an armed schooner, the *Hannah*. On a shipping voyage that took him to Philadelphia in 1779, Bowen stopped by the Continental Hospital to pay a visit to a pair of wounded neighbors who had been serving on the American frigate *Deane*. The very next day, he sent some money home to his family "by Squire Dalton of Newbury," one of Massachusetts' most ardent revolutionaries.[19] Many of Bowen's acquaintances in Marblehead supported themselves and performed their patriotic duties by privateering, and the unemployed rigger remained on cordial terms with several of these privateers throughout the war. At Boothbay Harbor on the coast of Maine in 1777, he supped with Edward Fettyplace Jr., the son of the captain of the coastal guards at Marblehead and commander of the privateer *Dolphin*. Bowen's eldest son was willing enough to serve on Yankee privateers during the opening years of the war—and this never seemed to trouble his father either.

On balance, however, Ashley Bowen was profoundly unenthusiastic about the struggle for independence. While seldom hostile to the revolutionary cause, nearly everything he said about the patriots and their activities was veiled with sarcasm. In his eyes they were "the gentry"—or sometimes the "stern foremost gentry"—ambitious and self-interested troublemakers who had waded into water well over their heads and were now inducing their enthusiastic but innocent countrymen to accompany them.[20] In general, their efforts struck him as foolish or even comical. Their early recruiting efforts he termed "mob musters."[21] In 1777 he mocked their attempts to provide for coastal defense by arming single-masted sloops to do battle with the three-masted brigs of the British navy. On July 5, 1779, the town celebrated the anniversary of independence with a volley of cannon fire, but in Bowen's opinion this also smacked of stage play and was only another instance of "gentry" bravado.[22] Conservative to the core, Bowen considered the revolutionaries to be mainly poseurs, willing to shed others' blood for a cause that was ultimately only that of their own advancement.

One of the biggest obstacles to his adopting the patriot cause was his attachment to the Church of England. Bowen had been brought up Anglican, and although his wife Dorothy came from a Congregational family, he normally attended St. Michael's Church, and all of their children were baptized there. During their marriage, Bowen rarely mentioned religion in his diary, but after Dorothy's death in 1771, church matters began to enter his diary on a regular basis. His second wife, Mary Shaw, was Anglican, and on Sundays during the last years before the war, they would attend church together in the morning, and then Ashley would return by himself for Evening Prayer. After the outbreak of hostilities in the spring of 1775, however, services at St. Michael's were irregular. The Anglican minister, Joshua Wingate Weeks, was a staunch loyalist and had to flee Marblehead, leaving his pulpit empty, and although he returned briefly in 1776, he was eventually declared a person inimical to the American states, and in February 1777, St. Michael's was closed. Bowen was deeply disturbed by what he perceived as the patriots' attack on a long-standing personal tradition. "St. Michael's Church shut up by the laws of the land. . . . Poor poor times for the Episcopalians of America. The Whigs have the day."[23] When Good Friday came that spring, Bowen complained that with "the Church of St. Michael's being in bondage by the men of Liberty we had no prayers nor preaching."[24]

St. Michael's had come under scrutiny, of course, because it was a parish of the Church of England, whose head was George III, a foreign monarch with whom Americans were at war. The Reverend Weeks had refused to delete prayers for the king and royal family from his services, and he seems to have refused as well to take a required oath of loyalty to Congress. Consequently, the patriots decided that as a stronghold for loyalist sympathy, the church could not be tolerated. Yet, Bowen himself never connected his Anglican faith with any personal attachment to the British crown. For him, the Church of England meant prayers and preaching of the rich and formal nature that had always been its stock-in-trade and that were simply not available anywhere else in Marblehead. Indeed, after St. Michael's was closed, he began to refer to the town's two Congregational Meeting Houses as "Salt Peters" and "Dry Bones," since their Sabbath observances seemed to him barren and ineffectual. So worried was he that his preferred liturgy might vanish from the land that he began to employ his empty hours in transcribing by hand the Anglican Book of Common Prayer.

For this New Englander, therefore, the connection between religion and revolution was close and meaningful. In the summer of 1776, Bowen had enough time on his hands to explain in verse why this was so:

> As for opinions, I confess
> I never upon them laid stress
> Sometimes a Whig, sometimes a Tory
> But seldom steadfast in one story.
> The reason is, I'm not yet fixed
> So my religion is but mixed,
> Yet, most of all I do incline
> The Old Episcopalian line;
> Yet not so fixed on this head,
> But I can turn my coat for bread
> Yet don't mistake my meaning as
> If from the truth I meant to pass;
> The essential parts of my opinion
> Are not in any sect's dominion
> Nor will I e'er be tied to think
> That in one spring I ought to drink.[25]

The poem then veers off into a detailed list of religious faiths and sects—some, such as Papists, Quakers, and Anabaptists known to anyone, but others, such as Erskinites and Glasites quite obscure—the point of which was to explain why he rejected the claims of each to possess a monopoly on the truth. That Bowen's attempt to justify his political ambivalence could slide so quickly into a lengthy treatment of his spiritual antidogmatism is, indeed, a measure of how deeply he confounded the two. In his view, the Revolution had accomplished nothing for religious liberty, and he regarded as two-faced those who claimed it had.

When Bowen wrote that he could turn his "coat for bread," he was talking from experience, for in order to survive the Revolution in plain material terms, the diarist and his family were forced to make do as best they could. His rigging business slackened during the political crisis in the summer of 1774 and then collapsed outright with the rest of the local economy when war broke out in the spring of 1775. "Dull, dull, dull times," wrote Bowen after four idle days in a row in April 1775, "No business in hand."[26] Bowen recorded sixteen days of work in his loft in the month before the battles of Lexington and Concord, but only three in the month after, and very little if anything for several years after that. That summer, an ensign from Congress noted that in Marblehead, with the fishery "now at an end," many of the men had joined the army and the rest were out of work. "Their situation is miserable," the visitor continued, "the Streets & Roads are fill'd [with] the poor little Boys & Girls who are forc'd to beg of all they see. . . . I do not want ever to see such another Place."[27]

That Bowen should have found himself so utterly unemployed is, nonetheless, a little mysterious. Certainly the British naval blockade cut decisively into the local economy, but there still were American privateers about, and presumably they would have needed repair and refitting. Bowen mentions American cruisers and coasters, and they too required work from time to time. Yet, through every month of the war for which journal entries survive, Bowen's rigging loft was empty. Perhaps his lukewarm politics worked against him. Though there is little positive evidence of this, the fact that he sometimes was able to find employment in other communities where he was not well known suggests that this may have been an issue. In the fall of 1776 he spent three weeks in Lynn and another three in Boston working on the rigging of several vessels; and in 1779 he passed the better part of two months in Beverly doing the same. Indeed, these three trips account for almost all the rigging work Bowen was able to obtain during the Revolution. As a householder and father of five (a teenaged son, Ashley, two younger siblings, Hannah and Nathan, as well as a pair of infant girls, Mary and Sally), he had to cast about for other means to support the family. New Englanders had always been accustomed to cobbling together a living from several different sources, but the circumstances of war would test the Bowens' ingenuity to the limit.

In some ways Ashley was fortunate. The Bowen family owned a farm, once his father's but now under the management of his brother-in-law, John Prince, and Ashley had some claim on its produce, if he was prepared to work in its fields and gardens. Indeed, the first time that he admitted his household was running short, in September 1775, when he had "no sort of provisions at all," he turned to the farm and sold off some of his father's hay.[28] Later that fall he went to work on the farm and carried off twenty-two and one-half bushels of potatoes, some of which he kept for himself. Periodically throughout the next few years, he worked for his brother-in-law and for some of the other farmers in the area, occasionally for cash but also for meals or goods and favors in return. Thus, Bowen helped the loyalist merchant Robert Hooper harvest his hay in the summer of 1776 and received a half-cord of wood from him early the following spring. Marblehead, as the name suggests, was never well suited to agriculture, and the Bowen farm was not a very large one. Ashley knew that the casual employment and occasional gifts that he could obtain there would never see his family through the war.

During the summer of 1777, therefore, he returned to the sea after fifteen years' absence and joined a couple of wooding expeditions to the Maine coast in a schooner owned and commanded by another retired Marblehead mariner, John Twisden. On both occasions they toured the shoreline between Casco Bay and the mouth of the Penobscot River and completed their lading by purchasing firewood on land and rafting it out to the schooner. Judging from Bowen's diary, the New England shore was buzzing with marine activity. Up and down the coast he encountered privateers, prize ships, blockade runners, and other wooding sloops. On the second trip home, he left Falmouth "in company with 20 sail"—most of them local freighters like himself.[29] When Ashley returned to Marblehead, Twisden paid him off with a few cords of wood and perhaps some cash as well.

The following summer was also spent in wooding, but the patriots in Marblehead were bent on drafting Bowen into active duty. They hounded him so doggedly that in the fall of 1778, in order to avoid being posted to a guard ship, he decided to quit Marblehead entirely for a while and go to sea again. Fifty years old, he shipped out with a fellow Marbleheader, Thomas Boyles, as mate on the schooner *Sally*, bound for the West Indies. The precise nature of this voyage is a little obscure, but whatever their cargo and business, they had almost reached Barbados three weeks later when they were captured by a British privateer and carried into Antigua. The vessel was condemned, but the next afternoon, Bowen signed on with a stranger, Nathaniel Hayward, on the sloop *Eagle*, headed for Bermuda. What Hayward was up to Bowen never admitted, but several facets of this cruise were peculiar, to say the least. Not only did they call in at both British and American ports, from Antigua and the Bermudas to Baltimore and Philadelphia, but the name of the vessel changed halfway through the voyage from the

Eagle to the *Dolphin*. Captain Hayward may well have been sailing under whichever flag suited his purposes at the moment. In any event, Bowen remained mum on the subject, and when they arrived in Pennsylvania six months later, he took his discharge and pay and went ashore. After two weeks "adrift" in Philadelphia, he took passage with a schooner bound for Massachusetts, purchased a barrel of flour for his family, and sailed home.

What were his wife and children doing in his absence? On this issue Bowen's journal is almost mute. Cold and hunger must have attended them constantly during the Revolutionary War—witness Ashley's interest in the arrival of ships and cargo throughout these years. Vessels carrying flour from Baltimore or Philadelphia and sloops dodging the British navy to haul firewood from down east were subjects of serious interest. His second wife, Mary, may have shared in Ashley's enforced idleness, but given that the problem of making do with less was usually the mother's to solve, this would seem unlikely. Unfortunately, since Ashley, like most eighteenth-century male diarists, almost never described the activities of any women, we can only guess at what these activities may have been. But with four stepchildren and two infants of her own to feed, clothe, and nurse on next-to-no income, she must have found her energy and ingenuity taxed to the limit. Even at the best of times, maritime families had too many young members to support, and the Bowens were no exception. Like all seaports, Marblehead traded in infectious disease, and the mortality of local children was such that a great many of them never grew up. Visitors to Marblehead were always struck by the swarms of little children in the streets; what they had indirectly noticed, however, was the relative scarcity of older and more productive family members. In 1779, after twenty-one years of marriage, only four of the eight children born to Bowen and two wives were still alive, and the oldest of these was only fifteen. When the fishery had been a going concern, young sons could begin to contribute something toward family welfare in their early teens, and with money flowing into the household, their sisters could have made themselves useful by helping to sew clothes, spin wool, or provide room and board for transient mariners. During the Revolution, however, much of this scraping by was impossible.

One alternative that wartime always offered to young men in seaside communities was the chance to go privateering. All of Massachusetts' seaports were engaged in raiding commerce throughout the Revolution, and the landing and sale of prize ships was a source of constant activity and interest along the coast. This was almost the only brand of maritime service that Bowen had never tried, but he now lacked the youth or the patriotic ardor to begin. On one occasion, he earned a few days' work cleaning out a British transport ship that had been captured by three armed American schooners off Cape Ann, but that was the limit of his involvement. His eldest son, Ashley Jr., however, saw things differently. Born in 1761, this boy would in the normal course of events have been fishing on the Grand Banks or learning the ropes in the West India trades by the time the war broke out. Instead, his father had packed him off to live with his mother's family in the safety of their upland farm in Boxford. In the spring of 1776, Ashley Jr., however, aware of his own family's hardships and perhaps thirsty for adventure as well, decided to ship out on a privateer. On June 4, Bowen reported that his son had returned to Marblehead the previous night "and sat off again today a-roving."[30]

For the better part of a year Bowen heard or mentioned nothing of him, but then in the late winter of 1777, Ashley Jr. landed in Boston with enough prize money to buy his family a barrel of flour, a firkin of butter, some tea and sugar, two bottles of wine, three bottles of porter—and leave his father about £8 in change. After spending the next year ashore, the younger Ashley set off privateering again in the spring of 1778. He sent a few letters to his father, which were mentioned briefly in the diary, though their contents were never described, and then he disappeared. Bowen never discovered what had happened to his son; the diary only mentioned him one more time, on May 27, 1793, when Bowen noted that "this day my son Ashley hath been absent fifteen years."[31] This was not only a personal tragedy but an economic disaster as well. In a world without social security, parents depended on their older children's earnings, and with Ashley Jr. gone, the family's future seemed grim.

Bowen described one more wooding voyage in the summer of 1780, in the middle of which he was captured by a British schooner near Penobscot Bay and freed again, and then the journal stopped. Whether he kept a diary that has since been lost through the subsequent years, or whether he simply tired of describing his enforced idleness we cannot know. After the Revolution ended, he took up his record-keeping habits from time to time: first in June 1786, to record that St. Michael's was now formally reopened with a new resident minister. Although the journal is fairly informative for the years 1788 to 1795, his interest in it was plainly diminishing, and it is not hard to guess why this was so. Like most ordinary diarists of the eighteenth century, Bowen intended his writings to recount his work, and like most working people of the day who had passed beyond their fiftieth birthday, the Marblehead shiprigger was slipping gradually into retirement. In his case, the process was accelerated by the war, but it was probably coming anyway.

Ashley Bowen emerged from the American Revolution in circumstances far different from those in which he had entered it. The United States was now an independent nation, though national issues scarcely, if ever, attracted his attention. Marblehead itself had been leveled by the war, its fleet of schooners reduced from 150 to fewer than two dozen vessels, half the men in town left unemployed, and one-third of the women widowed. In time the town would recover, for fish markets remained healthy through the end of the Napoleonic Wars, and the port was more prosperous during the first decade of the nineteenth century than ever before. But the merchants, fishermen, and waterfront craftsmen who had together constructed the *colonial* fishery and fish trade—men like Ashley Bowen—were ruined; and many of the women who had borne and sustained their families while the men were off at sea or away at war were now single parents, middle-aged, and unlikely to find another spouse. For the society of this fishing port, the war amounted to an upheaval of tectonic dimensions.

Bowen lived on, "under bare poles" as he put it, until his death in 1813. Vigorous to the end, he outlasted his second wife, married yet again, to Hannah Graves, a woman half his age, and fathered six more children—the last when he was sixty-nine. His fondness for things British—the church, the navy, and the empire—never left him, and this loyalty must have irritated some of his neighbors, but his friends recognized that "his country was dear to him as well." At his funeral, the Congregational minister prayed at the house and the Episcopalian minister presided over the burial. He was interred, as his friend William Bentley reported, "at a spot chosen by himself in the New M[eeting] H[ouse] ground, with his kindred, but so as to rise & face St. Michael's Church."[32] Splitting the difference to the grave and beyond, Ashley Bowen chose to be remembered as a neutral.

His tale reminds us that the real people of the American Revolution seldom fit into tidy and predictable categories. Ashley Bowen was born in comfortable circumstances, but he died so poor he had to send his youngest child away to be raised by another family. He passed his life amid the contagion of epidemic disease, yet he survived to eighty-five and managed to outlive eight of his fourteen children. Though a sailor and a seaport artisan, he was not a political radical; though he believed in liberty, he mistrusted those who were willing to go to war for it; and though he followed the Anglican faith, he chose to be buried in a Puritan graveyard. Yet, for all his idiosyncrasies, Ashley Bowen was as American as Paul

Revere, and any attempt to read him out of the Revolution can only distort its history.

Notes

1. *The Journals of Ashley Bowen (1728–1813) of Marblehead*, ed. Philip Chadwick Foster Smith, Colonial Society of Massachusetts, *Publications*, 2 vols. (44 and 45), (Boston, 1973), 45:394–96. Hereafter cited as *Diary*.

2. Ibid., 395–99.

3. Jesse Lemisch, "Jack Tar in the Streets: Merchant Seamen in the Politics of Revolutionary America," *William and Mary Quarterly*, 3d ser., 25 (1968): 371–407; Wallace Brown, *The King's Friends: American Loyalist Claimants* (Providence, RI: Brown University Press, 1965).

4. *Diary*, 44: 57.

5. Ibid., 96–97.

6. William Bentley, *The Diary of William Bentley, D.D.*, 4 vols. (Salem, MA: Essex Institute, 1905–1914; reprint ed., Gloucester, MA, 1964), 3:124–25, 293, 331; 4:148–49.

7. *Essex [County] Register*, February 6, 1813.

8. *Diary*, 44:45.

9. Ibid., 170. By "transients" he meant those ships from abroad that were visiting Marblehead to do business with Lee.

10. *Diary*, 44:231.

11. *Diary*, 45:386–87.

12. Ibid., 402.

13. Ibid., 430.

14. Ibid., 480–81.

15. Ibid., 474.

16. Ibid., 436.

17. Ibid., 437, 442, 444, 445.

18. Ibid., 436, 453.

19. Ibid., 534.

20. Ibid., 426.

21. Ibid., 425.

22. Ibid., 537.

23. Ibid., 497, 511.

24. Ibid., 515.

25. Ibid., 522–23.

26. Ibid., 436.

27. "Ensign Williams' Visit to Essex County in 1776," *Essex Institute Historical Collections* 83 (1947): 144–45.

28. *Diary*, 45:454.

29. Ibid., 528.

30. Ibid., 489.

31. Ibid., 597.

32. Bentley, *Diary of William Bentley, D.D.*, 2:148; 3:124.

Suggested Readings

This chapter is based on *The Journals of Ashley Bowen (1728–1813) of Marblehead*, ed. Philip Chadwick Foster Smith, in Colonial Society of Massachusetts, *Publications* (Boston, 1973), vols. 44, 45. These volumes are superbly annotated and allow for many of the themes touched upon in this essay to be investigated in greater detail. Other aspects of Bowen's life, also reconstructed from these diaries, can be found in Daniel Vickers, "An Honest Tar: Ashley Bowen of Marblehead," *New England Quarterly* 69 (1996): 531–53. Readers interested in investigating the personal history of another sailor whose life spanned the years of the American Revolution should consult *The Nagle Journal: A Diary of the Life of Jacob Nagle, Sailor, From the Year 1775 to 1841*, ed. John C. Dann (New York: Weidenfeld & Nicolson, 1988); see also Chapter 17 of this volume. The wider context of maritime life in the late colonial, revolutionary, and early national periods is discussed in Samuel Eliot Morison, *The Maritime History of Massachusetts, 1783–1860* (Boston: Houghton Mifflin, 1921; reprint ed., Boston: Northeastern University Press, 1979); Jesse Lemisch, *Jack Tar vs. John Bull: The Role of New York's Seamen in Precipitating the Revolution* (New York: Garland, 1997); W. Jeffrey Bolster, *Black Jacks: African American Seamen in the Age of Sail* (Cambridge, MA: Harvard University Press, 1997); and Daniel Vickers, *Farmers and Fishermen: Two Centuries of Work in Essex County, Massachusetts, 1630–1850* (Chapel Hill: University of North Carolina Press, 1994). For more detail on the impact of the Revolutionary War on Marblehead and surrounding towns, see Ronald N. Tagney, *The World Turned Upside Down: Essex County during America's Turbulent Years, 1763–1790* (West Newbury, MA: Essex County History, 1989).

7

Dragging Canoe (Tsi'yu-gûnsi'ni)
Chickamauga Cherokee Patriot

Jon W. Parmenter

While the colonists waged war against Britain, a war for independence raged between interior tribes and white settlers. In the settlers' intercolonial struggle, young men who favored the Revolution found an avenue for political and social leadership. As a voice of Cherokee youth, Dragging Canoe (ca. 1732–1792) demonstrates another intergenerational struggle over the preservation of hunting territories and long-standing definitions of manhood. In opposition to his elders, including his own father, Dragging Canoe refused to give up hunting lands in exchange for peace with the American colonials. By leaving the Cherokee Nation and creating a new multiethnic community, the Chickamauga militants, patriots to their own cause, declared independence from the peace initiatives of Cherokee leadership.

Dragging Canoe and the Chickamaugas were fighting, as Jon Parmenter argues, for "life, liberty, and the pursuit of hunting," and using methods that American revolutionaries should have understood best: resistance. Why, then, did American raiders, who violated Cherokee-American treaties of 1777, often fail to distinguish between the peaceful eastern Cherokee and the Chickamauga? To unify the Cherokee Nation, Dragging Canoe had worked with Lachlan McGillivray's son, Alexander, to try to persuade the Chickasaw to join the Shawnee-Creek-Chickamauga confederacy. By 1783 the Cherokee had lost three-quarters of the territory it held before the Revolution, and many of its towns had been destroyed. Meanwhile, Britain ceded to the United States land upon which Indian allies resided. Was the Chickamauga strategy of raiding American settlers more successful in uniting the Cherokees than in resisting white encroachment? Why did the terms of the peace treaty of 1783 not signal the end of Dragging Canoe's militant efforts? When Dragging Canoe died, his forces were still intact, but a year and a half later the Chickamauga sued for peace. Given that Dragging Canoe had appealed originally to discontented young Cherokee warriors, how might he have maintained his authority among the Chickamauga until his death, perhaps in his sixtieth year?

Jon W. Parmenter is a historian at St. Lawrence University, Canton, New York. He has published "Pontiac's War: Forging New Links in the Anglo-Iroquois Covenant Chain, 1758–1766," *Ethnohistory* 44 (1997): 617–54. His research and published work focus on eighteenth-century Indian diplomacy.

In March 1775 a large delegation of Cherokee headmen and warriors traveled to Sycamore Shoals (near modern Elizabethton, Tennessee) on the Watauga River for a meeting with Richard Henderson, a North Carolina lawyer and organizer of the Transylvania Land Company. Ignoring the ban on Indian land sales to private individuals, established by the Royal Proclamation of 1763, Henderson sought to purchase from the Cherokees a huge tract of 27,000 square miles between the Cumberland and Kentucky Rivers, or most of the modern state of Kentucky. Upon learning of Henderson's intent, Tsi'yu-gûnsi'ni, a Cherokee war leader known to the settlers as "Dragging Canoe,"[1] delivered an impassioned speech against the proposed transaction. If the elder Cherokee leadership did not stop the ongoing cycle of land cessions, Dragging Canoe warned, the Cherokee Nation would soon be compelled

> to seek refuge in some distant wilderness. There they will be permitted to stay only a short while, until they again behold the banners of the same greedy host. Not being able to point out any further retreat for the miserable Cherokees, the extinction of the whole race will be proclaimed. Should we not therefore run all risks, and incur all consequences, rather than submit to the loss of our country? Such treaties may be all right for men who are too old to hunt or fight. As for me, I have my young warriors about me. We will have our lands.[2]

Despite Dragging Canoe's opposition, his own father Attakullakulla and two other prominent Cherokee "beloved men" (elder political leaders of Cherokee communities) signed Henderson's deed on March 17, 1775, and exchanged the Cherokees' best hunting grounds for a reported £10,000 in trade goods. Dragging Canoe, outraged over the sale and "stamping his foot on the ground" for emphasis, warned Henderson that "a black Cloud hung over the country they were selling" and promised that "it was the bloody Ground, and would be dark, and difficult to settle it."[3]

Although best known for this promise to transform Kentucky lands into the "dark and bloody ground," Dragging Canoe's career in the American revolutionary era holds much more significance than his ability to issue (and deliver on) colorful threats. Dragging Canoe's precise date of birth is unknown, but contemporary descriptions of his pock-scarred face suggest that he survived the devastating smallpox epidemics that ravaged the Cherokee in the late 1730s. Born into an "Overhills" Cherokee family (so called from their homelands in what is modern eastern Tennessee), he earned his name as a young boy by literally dragging a canoe across a portage in order to accompany his father's war party against the Shawnees (who, ironically, would later become his closest allies). By 1774, Dragging Canoe was identified by British Deputy Indian Superintendent Alexander Cameron as "the only Young Warrior of Note now over the Hills,"[4] and after 1775, his determined leadership and the widespread dissemination of his message of resistance drew a following that transcended traditional Native American patterns of loyalty to kin, village, or nation. Dragging Canoe recognized the need for solidarity among diverse Indian peoples in the face of an expanding settler population, and through his constant, spirited recruiting efforts, he forged a distinct, multiethnic community (eventually known as the Chickamauga Cherokee) dedicated to preserving the territorial integrity of the Cherokee Nation.

Dragging Canoe's speech at Sycamore Shoals represented a "declaration of independence" for himself and the followers he would attract both within the Cherokee Nation and from other neighboring Indian peoples. Eighteenth-century Cherokee society lacked coercive institutions, which meant that political decisions depended on the ability of recognized leaders to persuade others to accept their viewpoint. Achievement of consensus on matters of foreign policy often was contingent on the maintenance of harmony between the elder beloved men and the young warriors. In 1775, Dragging Canoe and the young warriors broke with the Cherokee leadership, which favored peace and accommodation with colonial settlers after the conclusion of the "Cherokee War" against the southern colonies in 1761. Dragging Canoe devoted the rest of his life to fighting his own "revolution," attempting to forge a new consensus among the Cherokee, one that would preserve Cherokee homelands and the way of life those lands made possible.

John Stuart, British superintendent of Indian Affairs for the Southern Department, learned in the autumn of 1774 of the growing dissatisfaction among Cherokee young men with the beloved men's policy of trading land for peace. With the young people "ripe for mischief," the chiefs and leading men "were falling into contempt."[5] Outside "pan-Indian" diplomatic influences from the Shawnees and Delawares of the Ohio Valley, and the growing internal threat to the established pattern of masculine roles in Cherokee society, complicated the traditional generational conflict inherent in the Cherokee political structure. As early as 1770,

Shawnee and Cherokee representatives began to discuss their mutual problems from settler encroachment on their homelands and the prospects for a cooperative response. By the time of the 1775 Henderson Purchase they were being pushed to extreme limits, but emboldened by an expanding range of contacts with militants from other Native groups. Dragging Canoe spoke for many young Cherokee warriors when he denounced the progressive surrender of their hunting grounds. The loss of the ability to hunt threatened the very identity of young Cherokee men, since only those with proven competence in providing for a family could marry, start their own families, and hope to achieve a place of prominence in village life. With the curtailment of opportunities for male social advancement through warfare after 1761 (owing to increased friendly contacts between the Cherokee and their Indian neighbors and to the resolve of the Cherokee leadership to avoid the indiscriminate retaliation of white colonists for transgressions committed by their warriors), hunting assumed still greater importance in the minds of Cherokee young men. By 1775, even the ample gifts obtained by the beloved men in exchange for land cessions could no longer satisfy the warriors.

The "anarchy and distraction"[6] prevalent in the Cherokee Nation after the Henderson Purchase became more pronounced after news of the April 1775 outbreak of hostilities between Britain and the American colonies reached the Cherokees. The Continental Congress organized its Indian Department in July 1775 and sent representatives into the field to urge the Indians to remain neutral in the war. Superintendent John Stuart also tried to keep the southern Indian nations at peace, while reminding the Cherokees that "there is a difference between the White People of England and the White People of America, this is a matter which does not concern you, they will decide it among themselves."[7] Yet Cherokee involvement in the Revolutionary War would come on their own terms and at their own time. Dragging Canoe and his warriors regarded the outbreak of hostilities as an opportunity to reassert their claim to lands lost in the preceding decades.

Dependent on the British for military supplies, Dragging Canoe traveled to Mobile in March 1776 to meet John Stuart's brother, Henry Stuart, who was then employed as an agent in the British Indian Department. Dragging Canoe complained bitterly of the shortages of ammunition among his people and enhanced his case by pointing out that the Cherokee "were almost surrounded by the white people, that they had but a small spot of ground left for them to stand upon, and that it seemed to be the intention of the white people to destroy them from being a people." When Henry Stuart told Dragging Canoe that the Cherokees only had themselves to blame for making so many private sales, Dragging Canoe disavowed any role in those transactions and "blamed some of their old men who he said were too old to hunt and who by their poverty had been induced to sell their land, but that for his part he had a great many young fellows that would support him and that they were determined to have their land."[8]

Stuart, accompanied by thirty horses loaded with ammunition, slowly made his way to the Cherokee town of Chota (near modern Loudon, Tennessee), arriving in late April 1776. Here he and Deputy Superintendent Cameron tried to encourage the Cherokee to use the ammunition for hunting, not against the nearby white settlements. Their efforts proved fruitless, however, after the arrival of a delegation of fourteen deputies from the Shawnees, Mohawks, Ottawas, Delawares, and Nanticokes in early May 1776. Painted black to symbolize their preparedness for war, the northern Indians described the great numbers of settlers they had seen on their seventy-day journey to Chota from Fort Pitt (modern Pittsburgh). A formal conference followed ten days after their arrival, at which the delegates offered belts of wampum to the Cherokees, containing messages that expressed the militants' desire "to drop all their former quarrels and join in one common cause," and stating their preference to "die like men [rather] than to dwindle away by inches." Dragging Canoe received these belts in public council, and then his followers joined in singing war songs with the northern deputies. The principal chiefs who opposed the militants' position, when confronted with this open display of defiance from their young men, could only sit down "dejected and silent."[9]

Dragging Canoe and his warriors made a dramatic statement for war by joining the representatives from the northern nations. They did so over the heads of their own elders and in opposition to the intentions of their British allies. Indeed, from the outset of the Revolutionary War, Cherokee and British purposes never meshed. Although Stuart received orders from General Thomas Gage in December 1775 to employ the Indians against the American "rebels," he refrained from encouraging the Cherokee to make indiscriminate attacks on the frontier settlements, concerned that through such tactics "the innocent might suffer and the guilty escape."[10] Throughout the Revolutionary War, as Stuart endeavored to restrain his Indian allies from all military involvement except that under the direct supervision of British army or Indian Department officers, it became increasingly clear to Dragging Canoe that he would be fighting his own fight.

Inspired by the visit of the northern deputies to Chota, Dragging Canoe sent off messages inviting Creek Indians to join his warriors, but Creek headman Emistisiguo rejected these overtures.

Somewhat chastened, Dragging Canoe and his followers "seemed to repent of their having been so precipitate, but they had gone too far to retreat."[11] Determined to strike first, Dragging Canoe led one of three parties of Cherokee warriors against the white settlements on the Holston River, within the bounds of the Henderson Purchase. Unfortunately for the Cherokee militants, Dragging Canoe's own cousin, Nancy Ward (a respected "beloved woman"), betrayed their plans to traders in the Cherokee Nation, and they rushed back to the settlements to give advance warning of the impending attack. Two hundred warriors under Dragging Canoe engaged a frontier militia force sent out from Eaton's Station at Long Island Flats (near modern Kingsport, Tennessee) on July 20, 1776, but the frontiersmen turned them back, and Dragging Canoe suffered gunshot wounds in both legs and lost thirteen men. Undeterred, Dragging Canoe's party continued to fight for another three weeks, driving off settlers and burning cabins as far north as modern Abingdon, Virginia. Returning to Chota with a few scalps and plunder probably saved Dragging Canoe's reputation as a warrior after his July 1776 defeat, but his initial campaign proved costly in two ways. The Americans learned the value of keeping informants in the Cherokee country, and subsequently Dragging Canoe and the militants experienced serious problems with "security leaks." Only rarely in subsequent years would they have the ability to launch large-scale attacks with the element of surprise. Also, by raiding settlements across the boundary line, Dragging Canoe forfeited any hopes, however slim, for reconciliation with the new United States.

With the southern seacoast free from the threat of British invasion in the summer of 1776, armies from Virginia, the Carolinas, and Georgia turned their attention to retaliating against the Cherokees. Some idea of the Americans' mindset may be gained from this July 1776 statement of William Henry Drayton, chief justice of South Carolina, urging the military commanders to "make smooth work as you go—that is you cut up every Indian corn field and burn every Indian town—and that every Indian taken shall be the slave and property of the taker; that the nation be extirpated, and the lands become the property of the public."[12]

Four American expeditionary forces swept through Cherokee country from August to October that year, destroying food, supplies, and entire towns as they went. Unable to mount effective resistance against such overwhelming odds, the ammunition-strapped Cherokees fled to the west and south. Colonel William Christian of Virginia reached the Big Island Town, home village of "a chief called the Dragon Canoe [*sic*] lately raised to Power . . . [who] was the principal agent in hastening the War" in late October. Here he found the Indians "had ran off hastily, some of them had shut their doors and some had not: they had carried off their cloathes and the best of their household goods," but left behind most of their provisions. Christian then destroyed what he estimated to be "between forty and fifty thousand Bushels of corn and ten or fifteen thousand bushels of potatoes."[13]

The extent of destruction created by wandering American armies drove many Cherokee to seek clemency. Meeting with Colonel Christian in November 1776, Overhills "beloved men" Attakullakulla and Oconostota sued for peace and dissociated themselves from the actions of the young warriors. Dissatisfied with the professions of the old men, and knowing that he would eventually need to deal with the young warriors, Christian demanded that the headmen surrender Dragging Canoe and Alexander Cameron (whom the Americans mistakenly believed had encouraged the Cherokee to take up arms). Threatened with further destruction, Oconostota agreed to try and bring in the two men.

Although he lacked the authority to deliver on his promise, Oconostota's pledge revealed the extent to which Dragging Canoe's actions divided the Cherokee Nation. The experiences of the summer of 1776 led many Cherokees to conclude that further hostilities against the United States were to be avoided at all costs. Not so for Dragging Canoe. Outraged by Oconostota's betrayal, and attempting to secure further supplies from the British at St. Augustine, Florida, Dragging Canoe dictated a letter to Cameron on November 14, 1776, in which he made a necessary and appropriate statement of loyalty to the crown, and warned Cameron of the price on both their heads: "They [the Americans] offered at last £100 for you, and £100 for me, to have us killed. Let them bid up and offer what they will, it will never disturb me. My ears will always be open to hear your Talks and our Father's [the King of England]. I will mind no other, let them come from where they will. My thoughts and my heart are for war as long as King George has one enemy in this country."[14]

Dragging Canoe also communicated his continued defiance to the Americans, dismissing an invitation to hear a message left for him by Colonel Christian with the statement that he "had already heard all the talks."[15] Unwilling to participate in the beloved men's diplomacy with the United States, Dragging Canoe led what historians have called a "secession" of his followers from the Overhill Cherokee towns of Big Island, Tellico, Toqua, and Chilhowie to Chickamauga Creek (north of modern Chattanooga, Tennessee), where they were joined by refugees from other parts of the Cherokee Nation. Chosen for its remoteness from American settlements, its location astride several major land and water communication routes, and its proximity to British commissary John McDonald (who had a supply line to St. Augustine), Chickamauga Creek became home for an estimated "4 or 5 hundred warriors, separated from the rest of their Nation with sentiments of determined Hostility to the United States" by March 1777.[16]

Known afterwards as "Chickamaugas," Dragging Canoe's faction of militant Cherokees continued the war on their own terms, disregarding efforts of peace-minded Cherokees to come to an understanding with the United States. By characterizing the Chickamauga migration as a "secession movement," however, historians have misunderstood Dragging Canoe's objectives and overemphasized the extent to which the initial movement of an estimated 20 to 30 percent of all Cherokee warriors compromised the position of the Cherokees in the Revolutionary War.

By the winter of 1776–77, relocating away from the accommodationists represented the only viable option for Dragging Canoe and his followers. Although viewed negatively from the perspective of state societies operating under monarchical or constitutional governments, factional politics and the subsequent "fissioning" or "segmentation" of individuals unable to abide by the decisions of the established leadership represented the very lifeblood of the Cherokee polity. Paradoxically, only by putting approximately two hundred miles between his own followers and those Cherokee willing to make peace with the United States could Dragging Canoe hope to set his own example of leadership and eventually reunite his Nation behind a consensual position of resistance. That winter circumstances still permitted Dragging Canoe to exploit the flexible and dynamic nature of the Cherokee political system for what he considered patriotic ends. The Chickamaugas' "secession" represented not a selfish movement of rash individuals determined to bring down the wrath of the United States upon their relatives, but a calculated risk undertaken by Dragging Canoe to preserve the territorial integrity of the entire Cherokee Nation.

We have only a limited understanding of Chickamauga demography, owing to the understandably keen interest of contemporary literate observers in the number of Chickamauga fighting men. Certainly, women, children, and the elderly were present in Chickamauga towns, as family and kin connections figured prominently in individual decisions to migrate. Women played an especially critical role among the Chickamauga by growing corn in great quantity to support their warrior husbands, brothers, cousins, and sons. A few noted beloved men, such as Ostenaco (a longtime rival of Attakullakulla), also joined the Chickamauga and lent credibility to the movement by their presence. Yet the admittedly imperfect sources indicate that Chickamauga towns contained a significantly greater proportion of young men than the usual 20 to 25 percent established by modern scholars for "normal" eastern Native American societies.

The radical choice made by Dragging Canoe and his followers did not come without bitter feelings and almost immediate consequences for the Cherokee Nation. Shortly after moving southward, the Chickamaugas referred to themselves as the *Ani-yunwiya* (real people) and labeled the accommodationist Cherokees "Virginians." Chickamauga raids on white settlements after 1777 often brought retaliation on peaceful eastern Cherokee communities by American armies unable or unwilling to distinguish between the two groups. On the other hand, the relocation of the Chickamauga dissidents enabled accommodationist Cherokee leaders to free themselves from responsibility for the militants' actions in their negotiations with the United States. More important, Dragging Canoe always welcomed new arrivals from the ranks of the accommodationists to his Chickamauga towns. His "open door" policy extended to warriors from other Indian nations, sympathetic white settlers and traders, and runaway slaves willing to share in his cause. While other Cherokees cast their hopes on the benevolence of the United States, Dragging Canoe and the Chickamaugas persisted in their struggle to eliminate "the amazing great settlements" in their hunting grounds.[17]

In late March 1777, American Colonel Nathaniel Gist (formerly a well-known trader among the Cherokee) sent a message to Dragging Canoe, ostensibly from the Shawnees, expressing hope that the Chickamaugas "would no more listen to the lying bad talks carried you by some of their foolish people"[18] and advising them to make peace with the United States at a treaty scheduled for that spring. Dragging Canoe turned down the invitation and issued a cryptic promise to Gist not to do "anything that will make you ashamed of me among your people."[19] In this way, Dragging Canoe communicated, through his words and his subsequent actions, what he believed the Americans understood and respected: ongoing violent resistance and an absolute refusal to surrender.

Dragging Canoe and the Chickamaugas stayed away from the two American peace treaties with the Cherokees in early 1777. Between these two treaties (DeWitt's Corner, negotiated with Georgia and South Carolina on May 20, 1777, and Long Island of the Holston, negotiated with Virginia and North Carolina on July 20, 1777), the accommodationist Cherokees ceded another five million acres of land to the United States. Yet news of these proceedings only stiffened Chickamauga resolve. Dragging Canoe led a bold raid in April 1777 within a few miles of the Virginia negotiators, killing two men and stealing horses to demonstrate his contempt for the proceedings. When word of the Virginians' intent to secure twenty Cherokee hostages (to ensure the Nation's compliance with the terms of the 1777 Long Island treaty) reached the Chickamauga towns, the militants declared "that all the hostages they can keep will not save them."[20]

Alarmed by the willingness of some Cherokees to make peace with the Americans, Superintendent Stuart ordered Cameron to supply food and ammunition only to those still engaged in hostilities, and to remind the Cherokees "that they themselves are Principals in this War, that the defense of them and their land is one of the great causes of it."[21] These strong words and the inability of the United States to deliver promised supplies to the distraught Cherokees swelled the ranks of the Chickamaugas to nearly one thousand warriors by 1778.

During the campaigns of 1777 and 1778, the Chickamaugas cooperated with the British war effort in the south, raiding the western settlements to prevent frontiersmen from joining the Continental Army, and disrupting American communications and supply routes in the lower Ohio Valley in tandem with the Shawnees. Food shortages after 1776 limited the size and geographic range of Chickamauga war parties, but their superior knowledge of the country, their effective use of advance scouts and field signals, and their ability to strike hard against their targets and then disappear before effective retaliation could occur rendered them a serious threat to the southwestern backcountry settlements. The very mention of the names of prominent Chickamauga warriors such as Dragging Canoe, Bloody Fellow, Doublehead, and John Watts intimidated frontier families for years to come.

Despite the potential advantages to be gained by utilizing the effective guerrilla tactics of the Chickamaugas, British generals never took full advantage of the potential services of their southern Indian allies. While the Indians grew impatient with repeated suggestions that they wait until their movements could be coordinated with regular troops, the British officers minimized their dependence on the warriors, partly to reduce the expense of outfitting the Indians and partly out of fears of alienating loyal and neutral white settlers if they were known to back Cherokee raids. Even after the British shifted their attention after 1779 to concentrate on winning the war in the south, Indian allies figured hardly at all in Secretary of State Lord George Germain's strategy to "Americanize"[22] the conflict by relying on loyalist forces to police and defend territory liberated by British regular troops.

Nevertheless, the Chickamaugas cooperated occasionally with British troops, if only to ensure a continued supply of military goods. After John Stuart sent up a pack train of three hundred horses with £20,000 worth of goods to John McDonald in the spring of 1779, three hundred Chickamauga warriors responded to a call from Lieutenant Walter Scott of Cameron's Loyal Refugees to attack the frontiers of Georgia and South Carolina. News of the departure of the Chickamauga warriors reached Joseph Martin, Virginia's agent to the Cherokee, who had married into the family of Nancy Ward and, under the terms of the 1777 Long Island treaty, resided at Chota. Martin sent word to Virginia governor Patrick Henry, who ordered Colonel Evan Shelby to march against the Chickamauga towns during the absence of so many of their warriors. Shelby's force of seven hundred men killed only six of the "seceding Cherokees of Chiccamagga," but he destroyed eleven towns and twenty thousand bushels of corn, and plundered the bulk of the goods at McDonald's storehouse.[23]

Chickamauga warriors rushed home after learning of Shelby's advance against their towns, but arrived too late to prevent the destruction. Alexander Cameron reported the Chickamaugas "in very great confusion"[24] after Shelby's attack, but it had occurred prior to their planting of spring crops, and the presence of the British at Savannah and Augusta gave hopes for replenishment of their supplies. Most important, the attack did not break the will of the Chickamaugas. Twenty years after the event, Dragging Canoe's brother, Turtle-at-Home, recalled in an interview the warriors' feelings of anger and disgust, not despair, on their return to the Chickamauga settlements, "to see our Nation, from the want of unanimity, insulted with impunity."[25]

The temporary devastation of the Chickamaugas' home base prompted Dragging Canoe to renew his efforts to secure outside Indian allies to help forge the elusive, but in his view critically necessary, unanimity of purpose within the Cherokee Nation. The convenient visit in July 1779 of the messenger from the British commander of Detroit, Kissingua, a "half Ottawa, half Miamis" man who "speaks most languages [and] is acute, resolute, and artfull,"[26] provided an opportunity for Dragging Canoe to notify the northern Indians of his resolution to continue fighting the war they began together in 1776:

> We cannot forget the Talks you brought us some years ago into this Nation, which was to take up the Hatchet against the Virginians—we heard and listened to it with attention, and before the time that was appointed to lift it we took it up & struck the Virginians, our Nation was alone and surrounded by them, they were Numerous and their Hatchets sharp, and after we lost some of our best Warriors we were forced to leave our Towns & corn to be burnt by them, and now we live in the Grass as you see. But

> we are not yet conquered, and to convince you that we have not thrown away your talk . . .we now give you beads from us to be delivered to all the red men of our way of thinking, that they must never let the Hatchet stand still.[27]

The Chickamaugas spent the next two years concentrating on their own objectives, partly because of their need to recover from Colonel Shelby's campaign, and partly owing to administrative chaos in the southern district of the British Indian Department after the death of John Stuart in March 1779. The continuing encroachments of white settlers into eastern and middle Tennessee in the wake of the 1776 and 1779 American attacks violated even the generous boundaries of the two Cherokee-American treaties of 1777. This unceasing movement of people initiated a cycle of conflict, which began with Chickamauga raids, followed by frontier militia forces retaliating against the peaceful eastern Cherokees, followed by more young warriors leaving the eastern towns to join the Chickamaugas for renewed raiding.

Even after the Chickamaugas learned of the British surrender to the United States at Yorktown in October 1781, they continued their hostilities and eluded American expeditionary armies by sending false messages of their own intention to come in for a peace treaty. By September 1782, North Carolina governor Alexander Martin had lost patience with the Chickamaugas and ordered an expedition against their towns. Assuming the success of the expedition, Martin wanted his state's Cherokee treaty commissioners (some of whom were officers leading the campaign) to dictate the following terms to the Chickamaugas: they were to return to the original Cherokee settlements "from whence they are emigrants"; to relinquish their claim to their current settlements; to surrender all their American prisoners, loyalist refugees, runaway slaves, and stolen property; and finally to make a cession of land, which would reduce them to a "harmless and inoffensive situation."[28]

With the prospect of peace on those terms, the Chickamaugas chose to resist, and they succeeded in rendering the North Carolinians' expedition a failure. Romanticized as the "last battle of the American Revolution," the engagement at Lookout Mountain on September 20, 1782, consisted of burning abandoned towns and vandalizing cornfields; the Chickamauga suffered no casualties. Forced to admit that the Chickamauga remained at large, the frustrated Governor Martin marveled at these obstreperous Indians who asked "no favours, being still determined to do all the injury they can."[29]

Dragging Canoe and the Chickamaugas relocated still farther down the Tennessee River in 1782, establishing the "Five Lower Towns" (near the intersection of modern Alabama, Georgia, and

Tennessee), in very defensible locations. Dragging Canoe made his home at Running Water Town (near modern Haleton, Tennessee), and these settlements would prove to be a thorn in the side of the United States for the next twelve years. Still determined to advance his objectives, Dragging Canoe's stubborn resistance earned the respect of Virginia governor Benjamin Harrison, who in November 1782 indicated his belief that the "Indians have their rights and our Justice is called upon to support them. Whilst we are so nobly contending for liberty, will it not be an eternal blot on our national character, if we deprive others of it who ought to be as free as ourselves?"[30]

All too few Americans of the revolutionary generation shared Harrison's opinion. Assuming that the "Indians who have assisted the British king, and waged war against the frontier inhabitants, are now in our power and at our mercy,"[31] congressional Indian policymakers believed that the Indians shared in the defeat of Great Britain, and that all former Indian lands within the territory ceded by King George III would become part of the new nation's domain. By 1783, the Cherokee Nation had lost 75 percent of the territory it had held prior to the Revolution, and over half of their towns lay in ashes. The Chickamaugas, far from being at anyone's mercy, continued to look far and wide for assistance in keeping up their struggle.

In January 1783 a large delegation of Chickamaugas traveled to St. Augustine accompanied by Shawnees, Delawares, Ottawas, and Iroquois, "to establish a firm league and confederacy amongst the different tribes of Indians in [the British] alliance for their mutual safety and defence."[32] Here the Indian speakers reminded Lieutenant Colonel Thomas Brown (one of Stuart's replacements in the reorganized southern Indian Department) of their expectation of continued support. Brown followed his orders and informed the Indians of the king's desire for them to end offensive operations, but advised that they should remain vigilant in defending their homelands against potential American incursions. With promises of traders with British goods coming to visit their nations, Brown sent the Indians home satisfied for the moment. Yet when he received orders on June 1, 1783, to withdraw all officials and traders from the Indian country (in advance of news of the Peace of Paris), Brown knew that he would be unable to help his former allies. He feared especially for the Cherokees, who, he believed, would be forced by the United States to relinquish some of their hunting grounds "for the temporary preservation of the rest."[33]

The 1783 Treaty of Paris ignored the Indians, and the Chickamaugas responded by paying it no attention. Dragging Canoe's brothers Badger and Little Owl journeyed to Detroit in March 1783 to request military supplies. Other Chickamaugas visited Esteban Miró, the new Spanish governor of Florida, in June 1783. Miró sought Indian allies as an insurance policy in the event of American aggression against Florida, and in 1784 he promised the Chickamaugas a supply of arms and ammunition. Above all, Dragging Canoe heeded the advice of the Shawnees, who advised him to "visit all your brothers the red people, and make everything straight and strong."[34]

Dragging Canoe renewed his raids on frontier settlements, fortified with a large supply of arms and ammunition given by Miró at Pensacola in June 1784. The Chickamaugas' resistance during the mid-1780s, however, relied more on the initiative of their leadership than on Spanish assistance. Although Virginia agent Joseph Martin considered Dragging Canoe "much attached to the Spanish interest,"[35] Miró never again gave supplies to the Chickamaugas, since he had come to the conclusion that the Chickamauga villages lay outside the jurisdiction of either Spanish Florida or Louisiana. Dragging Canoe continued to seek allies among the Creeks, Chickasaws, and Shawnees. He also continued to set a consistent example of resistance with guerrilla attacks on nearby settlements in eastern Tennessee and the Cumberland region (in the vicinity of modern Nashville, Tennessee) and by failing to attend the 1785 Hopewell Treaty meeting between the Cherokees and the United States.

Jurisdictional disputes between the United States, North Carolina, and the short-lived state of Franklin (carved out of western North Carolina) prevented anyone from observing the boundary line negotiated at Hopewell, and the flood of white settlers to the southwest continued unabated. The Americans who appropriated the Indians' lands only alienated potential friends in Indian councils, and the settlers' bellicosity only strengthened the position of militant Native leaders such as Dragging Canoe, who kept up resistance and bided their time.

Dragging Canoe found his quest for unanimity among the Cherokees very nearly fulfilled in 1788. After frontiersmen murdered neutralist Cherokee headman Old Tassel under a flag of truce in June 1788, many of the formerly peaceful Cherokees responded to the standing invitation of Dragging Canoe and joined the Chickamaugas in large numbers to avenge the brutal killing of their revered leader. Hanging Maw, Old Tassel's successor, could only watch as the Chickamaugas "led off many of his men to do mischief."[36]

The Chickamaugas repulsed Joseph Martin's invasion force at the second Battle of Lookout Mountain in mid-August 1788 and then pursued the retreating Americans into eastern Tennessee and Virginia, overrunning many settlements in their path. Chickamauga military strength peaked between 1788 and 1791, as Dragging Canoe's "confederacy" included 100 Shawnee warriors residing at Running Water, 350 Upper Creek warriors, and his own force of 700 Chickamauga fighting men.

The ongoing resistance of the Chickamaugas contributed to a shift in federal Indian policy in the south after 1790. Appointed governor of the territory south of the Ohio River in 1790, William Blount had a mandate from President George Washington and Secretary of War Henry Knox to secure peace with the southern Indians at almost any price. Fully half of the territory under Blount's jurisdiction remained in Indian possession, and Blount was charged with the impossible task of satisfying Indian complaints while simultaneously securing further land cessions and transportation rights for the United States. Furthermore, Blount's unyielding belief that the land losses of the Cherokee amounted to wartime conquests did little to satisfy the Indians who complained of encroachments beyond the 1785 Hopewell Treaty boundary line, and his well-known involvement in land speculation prior to his governorship earned him the nickname "Dirt Captain" among the southern Indians.

Dragging Canoe, predictably, would have nothing to do with Blount. Instead, he worked tirelessly during these years to promote unified Indian resistance to the United States. He forged ties with William Augustus Bowles, a former loyalist adventurer and self-appointed "Director-General of the Creek Nation," employing Bowles' associate George Welbank at Running Water to keep up a correspondence with Alexander McKee, the British Indian Agent at Detroit. Dragging Canoe sent sixty Chickamauga warriors to join the northern Indian confederate army under Miami headman Little Turtle that crushed General Arthur St. Clair at the Battle of Kekionga (near modern Fort Wayne, Indiana) on November 4, 1791. Inspired by the drubbing of St. Clair, Dragging Canoe began to work closely with mixed-blood Creek leader Alexander McGillivray (see Chapter 2 of this volume), who sent the Chickamauga headman to try to bring the Chickasaw Nation into the developing Shawnee-Creek-Chickamauga Indian confederacy during the winter of 1791–92.

The year of Dragging Canoe's greatest activity and success also proved to be his last. He died at Running Water Town on March 1, 1792, to the best of our knowledge, of natural causes. Blount characterized Dragging Canoe as a great warrior, who "stood second to none in the nation,"[37] and on June 28, 1792, Chickamauga headman Black Fox delivered a simple eulogy to the Cherokee National Council: "The Dragging Canoe has left the world. He was a man of consequence in his country."[38]

The Chickamaugas' resistance continued for two more years under the mixed-blood headman John Watts, eventually becoming so troublesome that congressional delegates considered a motion to grant the president (as opposed to Congress) the right to call out the army to defend the frontier against them. With assistance from Miró's successor, the Baron de Carondelet, Watts's Chickamaugas, fighting with the Creeks and Shawnees, made life miserable for settlers in the Southwest Territory until the summer of 1794, when an expeditionary force of 550 mounted men from Tennessee under Major James Ore attacked and burned the Chickamauga towns at Running Water and Nickajack, killing 50 Chickamauga. With their remote settlements at last breached, the Chickamaugas sued for peace at Tellico Blockhouse (near modern Lenoir City, Tennessee) on November 7–8, 1794. A relieved Blount granted them relatively lenient terms, asking only for an exchange of prisoners and promising that "the Lower Towns have only to keep peace on their part and it will be peace."[39]

Dragging Canoe left the world with his forces intact and ready to continue his struggle. In 1793, Governor Blount, who sent a brief historical account of the Chickamaugas to Secretary of War Knox, described the Five Lower Towns as home to "the young and active more or less from every town in the [Cherokee] nation," and he characterized the Chickamaugas as "the most formidable part" of the Cherokees, "not only from their disposition to commit injuries on the citizens of the United States, but from their ability to perform it."[40] More important for assessing Dragging Canoe's accomplishments is Turtle-at-Home's recollection of the Cherokee Nation on the eve of Dragging Canoe's death as "more unanimous than I had ever seen our people before."[41]

Critics of Dragging Canoe's "schism" point to the abandonment of traditional, town-based government by the Chickamaugas, as leadership became centralized under Dragging Canoe's charismatic authority. Detractors of the Chickamauga migration also note the subsequent loss of spirituality among the migrants, as the six major calendric rituals of Cherokee society telescoped into a single Green Corn festival at the Five Lower Towns during the 1780s. With the young men freed from the restraint of the old beloved men and perpetually at war, Chickamauga society, in the eyes of one observer, became one in which "the fearsome governed the fearful, and the strong ruled the weak. . . . Probably, the Chickamaugas experienced, as nearly as any human group has, the law of the jungle."[42] Dragging Canoe's "secession" undoubtedly came with a heavy price for the Cherokee Nation after 1776, as his incessant raids elicited punitive expeditions from the Americans that continued the war in Cherokee country and cost many Cherokee lives.

The divided nature of Cherokee politics and diplomacy after 1776 enabled the different factions to cultivate relations with different powers simultaneously, but this proved very dangerous on the revolutionary frontier. Finally, one could argue that Dragging Canoe's attempt to forge unanimity and consenus by separating from the main body of the Cherokee Nation ultimately failed to prevent extensive land losses during and after the Revolutionary War, which made their previous life-style of subsistence agriculture and long-range hunting untenable, and resulted in the rapid transition of the Cherokee to commercial agriculture in the nineteenth century.

To dismiss Dragging Canoe as a reckless incendiary, however, would be a mistake. In his refusal to barter Cherokee hunting grounds, Dragging Canoe was a "patriot" who fought for the integrity of the Cherokee Nation. He expressed his commitment to traditional Cherokee values through his rejection of policies that diminished the Cherokee resource base, through his continual warfare, and through his efforts to build consensus for this viewpoint throughout the Cherokee Nation. Dragging Canoe followed his chosen path with consistency and determination and fought for much longer than anyone expected. The loyalty of Dragging Canoe to the Cherokee people made agreements such as that at Tellico Blockhouse possible and helped to ensure the survival of Cherokee culture into the nineteenth century, when it flourished (albeit in new and unfamiliar ways) under the leadership of individuals from the Chickamauga faction.

Dragging Canoe's story, like that of so many Indians in American history, flits through the pages of governmental dispatches, lurid accounts of frontier atrocities, and popularized versions of his utterances. Yet from these scattered and frequently oblique passages, an image emerges of a patriot in his own right. Dragging Canoe's career helps remind us that the Indians were not helpless victims unable to resist their eventual subjugation and removal to the west by the United States. Even after the Revolution, Indians played a critical role in shaping their own destiny. Dragging Canoe's struggle for life, liberty, and the pursuit of hunting involved a relentless and bitter fight against American patriots. Nevertheless, his story deserves consideration if we are to remember all who strove for their own vision of freedom and justice in the American revolutionary era.

Notes

1. James Mooney, *Myths of the Cherokee*, Bureau of American Ethnology, *Nineteenth Annual Report, 1897–98* (Washington, DC, 1900), 538.

Other records render Dragging Canoe's name in Cherokee as "Chiucanacina," but Mooney's spelling is authoritative.

2. Quoted in Pat Alderman, *Nancy Ward and Dragging Canoe* (Johnson City, TN, 1978), 38. Cf. the version of the speech in Virginia I. Armstrong, *I Have Spoken: American History through the Voices of the Indians* (Chicago, 1971), 26.

3. The quotations are cited respectively from Deposition of Charles Robertson, October 8, 1777; Deposition of Nathaniel Henderson, October 27, 1778; Deposition of Samuel Wilson, April 15, 1777, in "Copies of Depositions Regarding the Henderson Purchase from the Cherokee Nation," Lyman C. Draper Collection, State Historical Society of Wisconsin, Madison (microfilm ed.), 1CC183, 1CC166, 1CC161.

4. Alexander Cameron to John Stuart, June 18, 1774, enclosed in Stuart to Thomas Gage, July 3, 1774, Thomas Gage Papers, William L. Clements Library, Ann Arbor, Michigan. Hereafter cited as WLCL. The traditions concerning the naming of Dragging Canoe may be found in J. L. Raulston and J. W. Livingood, *Sequatchie: A Story of the Southern Cumberlands* (Knoxville, TN, 1974), 33.

5. John Stuart to Earl of Dartmouth, December 15, 1774, in *Documents of the American Revolution, 1770–1783*, ed. Kenneth G. Davies, 21 vols. (Shannon, Ireland, 1972–1982), 8:244. Hereafter cited as *DAR*.

6. John Stuart to Thomas Gage, March 27, 1775, Gage Papers, WLCL.

7. Talk of John Stuart to the Cherokee Nation, August 30, 1775, Great Britain, Public Record Office, Colonial Office Papers, Class 5, vol. 76, f.179v. Hereafter cited as PRO CO5.

8. Henry Stuart to John Stuart, August 25, 1776, *DAR* 12:192.

9. Ibid., 202–3.

10. John Stuart to Alexander Cameron, December 16, 1775, *DAR*, 11:211.

11. John Stuart to Sir Henry Clinton, August 29, 1776, Sir Henry Clinton Papers, 18:11, WLCL.

12. Quoted in Tom Hatley, *The Dividing Paths: Cherokees and South Carolinians through the Revolutionary Era* (New York, 1995), 192.

13. Colonel William Christian to Patrick Henry, October 23, 1776, "Reports of Colonels Christian and Lewis during the Cherokee Campaign, 1776," *Virginia Magazine of History and Biography* 17 (1909): 61–63.

14. Quoted in John P. Brown, *Old Frontiers: The Story of the Cherokee Indians from Earliest Times to the Date of Their Removal to the West* (1938; reprint ed., Salem, NH, 1986), 161.

15. "Deposition of Robert Dews, taken at Fort Patrick Henry the 21st January 1777," in *The Colonial and State Records of North Carolina*, ed. W. L. Saunders and W. Clark, 30 vols. (Raleigh, 1886–1914), 22:996. Hereafter cited as *NCCR*.

16. Governor Patrick Henry to Governor Richard Caswell, March 14, 1777, *NCCR* 11:428. See also the population estimates for the Cherokee in Peter Wood, "The Changing Population of the Colonial South: An Overview by Race and Region, 1685–1790," in *Powhatan's Mantle: Indians in*

the Colonial Southeast, ed. P. Wood, G. Waselkov, and T. Hatley (Lincoln, NE, 1989), 61–66.

17. John Stuart to Lord George Germain, August 23, 1776, PRO CO5/77, f.126v.

18. "Copy of a Talk from Nathanael Gist to Oconostota, Raven, Dragging Canoe, and Tassel, dated Great Island Fort, 28 March 1777," enclosed in Stuart to Germain, June 14, 1777, PRO CO5/78, f.162.

19. "Reply of Dragging Canoe to Colonel Gist, April 1777," in *Early American Indian Documents: Treaties and Laws, 1607–1789*, vol. 18, *Revolution and Confederation*, ed. Colin G. Calloway (Bethesda, MD, 1994), 218.

20. Alexander Cameron to John Stuart, July 13, 1777, PRO CO5/78, f.199.

21. John Stuart to Alexander Cameron, July 11, 1777, Guy Carleton, Baron Dorchester Papers (microfilm ed. in David Library of the American Revolution, Washington Crossing, Pennsylvania), vol. 1, item 602. Hereafter cited as Carleton Papers.

22. John Shy, "British Strategy for Pacifying the Southern Colonies, 1778–1781," in *The Southern Experience in the American Revolution*, ed. Jeffrey J. Crow and Larry E. Tise (Chapel Hill, NC, 1978), 155–73.

23. Thomas Jefferson to President of Congress, June 19, 1779, Papers of the Continental Congress, 1774–1789, United States National Archives, Microfilm No. M247, reel 85, item 71, 1:242. Hereafter cited as PCC.

24. Alexander Cameron to Lord George Germain, December 18, 1779, *DAR* 17:268.

25. Carl F. Klinck and James J. Talman, eds., *The Journal of Major John Norton, 1816* (Toronto, 1970), 44.

26. Henry Hamilton to John Stuart, December 25, 1778, PRO CO5/80, f.165.

27. "A Talk from Some of the Cherokees to the Indians inhabiting the Wabache or Adjacent to it," July 12, 1779, Sir Frederick Haldimand Papers, British Library Additional Manuscripts 21777, ff.170–71. Cf. version of speech in E. Raymond Evans, "Notable Persons in Cherokee History: Dragging Canoe," *Journal of Cherokee Studies* 2 (Winter 1977): 184.

28. Governor Alexander Martin to Cherokee Treaty Commissioners, September 20, 1782, *NCCR* 16:710.

29. Governor Alexander Martin to Benjamin Hawkins, 1782, *NCCR* 19:938. See also E. Raymond Evans, "Was the Last Battle of the American Revolution Fought at Lookout Mountain?" *Journal of Cherokee Studies* 5 (Spring 1980): 30–40.

30. Harrison to Alexander Martin, November 15, 1782, *NCCR* 16:457–58.

31. Report of Committee on Southern Indian Affairs, March 4, 1785, in *Journals of the Continental Congress, 1774–1789*, ed. Worthington C. Ford, 34 vols. (Washington, DC, 1904–37) 28:119.

32. Lieutenant Colonel Thomas Brown to Sir Guy Carleton, January 12, 1783, Carleton Papers, vol. 3, item 6742.

33. Brown to Lord North, July 30, 1783, *DAR* 21:199.

34. Colonel Joseph Martin to Governor Alexander Martin, January 11, 1784, *NCCR* 16:924.

35. Joseph Martin to Governor Richard Caswell, May 11, 1786, *NCCR* 18:605.

36. Joseph Martin to General Henry Knox, August 23, 1788, PCC, reel 165, item 150, 3:363.

37. Governor William Blount to Secretary of War Henry Knox, March 20, 1792, in *American State Papers, Documents Legislative and Executive of the Congress of the United States, Class II: Indian Affairs*, ed. Walter Lowrie, Walter S. Franklin, and Matthew St. Clair Clarke, 2 vols. (Washington, DC, 1832–34), 1:263. Hereafter cited as *ASPIA*.

38. "Journal of the Grand Cherokee National Council," enclosed in William Blount to Henry Knox, July 4, 1792, *ASPIA* 1:271.

39. Proceedings at Tellico Blockhouse, November 7–8, 1794, *ASPIA* 1: 537.

40. William Blount to Henry Knox, January 14, 1793, in *The Territorial Papers of the United States*, ed. Clarence E. Carter, 26 vols. (Washington, DC, 1934–62), vol. 4, *The Territory South of the River Ohio, 1790–1796* (1936): 227–28.

41. Klinck and Talman, *Journal of Major Norton*, 44.

42. Fred Gearing, "Priests and Warriors: Social Structures for Cherokee Politics in the 18th Century," American Anthropological Association, *Memoir 93* (October 1962): 104.

Suggested Readings

The best general work on Indians in the American Revolution is Colin G. Calloway's *The American Revolution in Indian Country: Crisis and Diversity in Native American Communities* (Cambridge, Eng., 1995), but a chapter by James Merrell in *The American Revolution: Its Character and Limits*, ed. Jack P. Greene (New York, 1987), and an essay by Gary Nash in *The American Revolution: Changing Perspectives*, ed. W. M. Fowler and W. Coyle (Boston, 1979), are also valuable. James H. O'Donnell III's *Southern Indians in the American Revolution* (Knoxville, TN, 1979) remains the standard work on the subject, but should be supplemented by Gregory Dowd's *A Spirited Resistance: The North American Indian Struggle for Unity, 1745–1815* (Baltimore, 1992), which provides an excellent account of the "pan-Indian" confederacies that opposed the United States.

On the Cherokee specifically, see Tom Hatley's recent work, *The Dividing Paths: Cherokees and South Carolinians through the Revolutionary Era* (New York, 1995); Duane Champagne, *Social*

Order and Political Change: Constitutional Governments among the Cherokee, Choctaw, Chickasaw, and Creek (Stanford, CA, 1992); William G. McLoughlin, *Cherokee Renascence in the New Republic* (Princeton, 1986); and Ronald N. Satz, *Tennessee's Indian Peoples: From White Contact to Removal, 1540–1840* (Knoxville, TN, 1979). Useful biographical essays on several prominent eighteenth-century Cherokee and Chickamauga Cherokee individuals are scattered through the first three volumes of the *Journal of Cherokee Studies* (1976–1978). Additionally, Nathaniel J. Sheidley's groundbreaking essay, "Hunting and the Politics of Masculinity in Cherokee Treaty Making, 1763–1775," in *Empire and Others: British Encounters with Indigenous Peoples, 1600–1850*, ed. R. Halpern and M. Daunton (London, 1998), is of critical importance. Literature on the Chickamaugas is scarce, but in addition to the works cited in the notes, see James P. Pate, "The Chickamauga: A Forgotten Segment of Indian Resistance on the Southern Frontier" (Ph.D. dissertation, Mississippi State University, 1969), and Thomas L. Connelly, "Indian Warfare on the Tennessee Frontier, 1776–1794: Strategy and Tactics," *East Tennessee Historical Society's Publications* 36 (1964): 3–22.

8

Daniel Boone and the Struggle for Independence on the Revolutionary Frontier

Stephen Aron

Revered as an American folk hero, Daniel Boone (1734–1820) has been credited with blazing a trail through the wilderness and facilitating frontier settlement. Boone's contemporaries were less certain about his revolutionary patriotism; he faced a court-martial for the attack on Boonesborough, but was exonerated and then promoted. Boone's earliest bid for independence occurred as a hunter and trapper. Unlike Dragging Canoe, Boone killed for skins and, from the Indian perspective, wasted meat; his hunting reduced the supply of game and cleared the frontier of deer, bear, and their predators. Does that explain his conflict with Indians, who "robbed" him of his pelts? As a hunter, Boone left his family for long stretches of time, but by 1773 he had moved to Kentucky with his family.

Ultimately, Boone failed in his bid to become an independent landholder. After the American Revolution, Boone lost his Kentucky lands and traveled farther west into Spanish territory. At the time of their last migration, both William Prendergast and Boone were advanced in age. Did they migrate as the wards of their adult children, or did these barely literate and aging frontiersmen with large families consider themselves responsible for securing land for their sons? On the frontier such personal independence could not be achieved without dispossessing others, but Stephen Aron thoroughly explores Boone's attraction to Shawnee society as well as his activities as a trapper, surveyor, and would-be landowner. Did Boone choose among different versions of independence: frontier trapper, private landholder, or Shawnee hunter? Given his prolonged legal difficulties over land claims, Boone may have considered the wilderness a place of escape as well as a source of continued opportunity. More broadly, Boone's story also demonstrates how western antagonism toward eastern leadership fits in the imperial struggle. Whereas the colonists had achieved independence from Britain by 1783, Kentucky secured its independence from Virginia only in 1792.

Stephen Aron teaches American history at the University of California at Los Angeles. He is the author of *How the West Was Lost:*

The Transformation of Kentucky from Daniel Boone to Henry Clay (1996).

In the spring of 1778, the American Revolution entered its fourth year, and so did the settlement that Daniel Boone had founded in Kentucky. Although the establishment of Boonesborough nearly coincided with the outbreak of the American War of Independence, it was not revolutionary fervor that inspired Boone's move to Kentucky. Instead, the desire for a more personal independence, which required first and foremost the ownership of land, brought Boone and other white men across the Appalachians. That spring, however, neither the struggles of Americans for national independence nor the struggles of Kentuckians for personal independence were going well. For Daniel Boone, then a prisoner of the Shawnees at their village of Chillicothe, prospects for a landowner's independence appeared dim, indeed.

During Daniel Boone's lifetime, the ideal of personal independence blossomed. Earlier in the eighteenth century, such independence required a great deal of land and a great many slaves or tenants to work it. Only a gentleman freed from the toils of manual labor was considered truly independent. But by the era of the American Revolution, white men of lesser means were laying claim to that coveted status. These men still labored, but they did so for themselves, on land that they owned and could pass on to their children. Of course, these men also tended to have large families, and many children meant that more land had to be acquired to protect the independence of posterity. That search for additional lands had pushed the Boones and other pioneer families deeper into the "backcountry" of British America, in particular into the interior valleys of Pennsylvania, Virginia, and North Carolina. Extending that pursuit, Daniel Boone led independence-minded settlers across the Appalachians and into Kentucky in 1775.

Here the expansionist drive ran into especially determined opposition from still-independent Indian peoples. For the Indians whom Boone encountered in the Ohio Valley, independence did not depend on the individuated landholding that pioneers cherished. Yet during his months of captivity, the liberties that Indians did enjoy captivated Boone. Adopted by the Shawnees, Boone flirted with a different destiny, an independence based not on the private ownership of land, but on the freedom of an Indian hunter. Eventually, Boone chose the settlers' path, a decision that contributed to the loss of independence for the Indian peoples in the Ohio Valley.

But the achievement of American national independence did not secure for Boone the personal independence that he sought.

To the contrary, Boone's extensive land claims in Kentucky were all lost in the years after the American Revolution. In 1799, desperate for a fresh start, he left the United States, hoping to find in Spanish territory across the Mississippi the independence that had eluded him on American lands.

The sixth of eleven children of Squire and Sarah Morgan Boone, Daniel was born on October 22, 1734, Old Style (or November 2, 1734, New Style), near Oley Township, Pennsylvania. Like the founders of Pennsylvania, the Boones belonged to the Society of Friends, but the character of the colony was changing. An influx of German and Scots-Irish immigrants had challenged the dominance of the Quakers. The land hunger of the Scots-Irish especially threatened the established order and jeopardized, too, the peace that had generally prevailed between Quakers and Indians in Pennsylvania.

For their part, the Boones stayed on friendly terms with the Indian villagers who lived in and around the Schuylkill Valley. Indeed, when Daniel was a boy, an assortment of Indian hunters, primarily Shawnees and Delawares, visited the Boone family farmstead, where they always found a hospitable welcome. In the forests of southeastern Pennsylvania, young Daniel met and mingled with many of these same hunters, from whom he learned much about woodcraft.

Although Daniel and his family maintained harmonious relations with Pennsylvania's Indians, they shared with other colonists the quest for land ownership. When Squire Boone relocated from the south of England to southeastern Pennsylvania in 1713, the colony enjoyed a reputation as "the best poor man's country," a place where those of small means could obtain fertile yet cheap farmland. The flood of new settlers, however, diminished the availability of land and increased its price. With seven sons to whom he wished to bequeath farms, Squire Boone looked to acquire additional lands in less densely settled districts. To that end, he sold his Pennsylvania farm and joined thousands of other Pennsylvanians in the move south and west. The trek took the Boone family through the Shenandoah Valley of Virginia and to the Yadkin Valley of North Carolina, where they resettled in 1751.

Daniel accompanied his family to North Carolina, but the prospect of settling down and cultivating the soil did not excite him. He preferred to wander and he loved to hunt. Possessed of a sure shot and a strong knowledge of animal habits, Daniel resolved to make "the chase" his primary occupation. In the Carolina and Virginia backcountries, a number of men, mostly young and single, took up hunting, hoping that profits from the sale of deer- and bearskins would allow them to escape from the demands of farming. During the 1750s, Boone spent a good part of each year tracking game through the foothills of the southern Appalachians. In 1755 he interrupted his hunting to serve in General Edward Braddock's expedition against the French and Indians in the Upper Ohio Valley. The campaign was a military disaster, but it did enlarge Boone's knowledge of the "western country." The following year, twenty-one-year-old Daniel married sixteen-year-old Rebecca Bryan. Unlike many bachelor hunters who turned more diligently to husbandry once they married, Boone continued to pursue the chase in the fall and winter months when farm labors were lightest and animal skins heaviest.

In the 1760s, Boone extended the duration, the range, and the aim of his hunting trips. Early in the decade, backcountry men began to congregate along the headwaters of the Holston River in southwestern Virginia to hunt together for several months at a time in the western country that lay beyond the mountains. Boone did not enlist in these first "long hunts" across the Appalachians. Instead, he journeyed south to Florida in 1765. That venture proved disappointing, and in 1767, Boone went on a long fall and winter hunt to the north and west that took him as far as the Big Sandy River (whose course marks the present border between Kentucky and West Virginia). On May 1, 1769, in the company of five other men, Boone set off again for Kentucky. He did not return to his Yadkin home for two years, during which time he hunted game across much of southern and central Kentucky and scouted its soon-to-be-renowned Bluegrass plain.

Much about this venture was new and noteworthy. The timing of Boone's departure reversed the usual seasonal hunting calendar. Typically, backcountry men did not head out until after the harvest was in. By leaving in the spring, Boone abandoned entirely his role as a cultivator of the soil. That year and the next he did no farming. Those responsibilities and the well-being of his children—the Boones' sixth child arrived on December 23, 1769—were left in the hands of his very capable, if isolated and overburdened, wife. "A man needs only three things to be happy," as one of the Boones' grandsons remembered Daniel's creed, "a good gun, a good horse, and a good wife."[1] In his Pennsylvania-made rifle, Daniel had the first. In Rebecca, he clearly had the third as well—a woman whose family had also migrated from southeastern Pennsylvania to the thinly settled reaches of the Carolina upcountry and who knew how to make do in her husband's absence.

Although neighborhood gossips accused her of infidelity, no evidence has emerged to corroborate these rumors. But Daniel's activities in Kentucky would cost him the first of his keys to happiness, his treasured gun. For several months after leaving home, Boone and his companions enjoyed excellent hunting. They accumulated hundreds of skins that they expected to sell for considerable sums upon their return to the Yadkin Valley. But around sunset on December 22, 1769, while hunting near the Kentucky River, Daniel Boone and his partner John Stewart were surprised by a party of Shawnee Indians. Leading the Indian band was Will Emery or, as he referred to himself in pidgin English, "Captain Will." After confiscating the pair's peltry and equipment, including their cherished Pennsylvania rifles, Emery ordered Boone and Stewart to return to the other side of the mountains and warned that the "wasps and yellow jackets" would sting them severely should they return to Indian country.[2]

Years later, Boone allowed that Emery had treated him "in the most friendly manner."[3] Compared with English justice, under which convicted poachers sometimes received death sentences, Emery's confiscation of skins and rifles seemed truly lenient. At the time, however, Emery's actions, which deprived Boone of the profits of his hunt, stung plenty. He and Stewart resolved to regain their lost property—or at least to rebuild their stock of skins. Caught again, Stewart was killed for his second offense; Boone narrowly escaped with his life.

Boone stayed on the western side of the Appalachians through the next year. His hunting kept him well fed, but he failed to recoup his losses. On the way home in March 1771, Daniel and his brother Squire were robbed again by half a dozen Cherokees. Thus, he arrived home with nothing to show for his nearly-two-year excursion and nothing to pay off the debts he had accumulated. Upon his return to the Yadkin country, Boone was served with an arrest warrant for an unpaid debt to Richard Henderson.

Henderson, a prominent jurist on the North Carolina piedmont, was a leading target of self-styled "Regulators." These were backcountry men who had banded together in the late 1760s to intimidate profiteering merchants, deceitful lawyers, and corrupt colonial officials. Although Boone did not join the Regulators, he could not escape the turmoil that made the Yadkin a far less attractive home. With his property threatened by the claims of Henderson and other creditors, Boone looked to acquire new lands in the western country beyond the mountains.

Despite his run-ins with Indians, Kentucky still beckoned, and in the fall of 1773, Boone headed across the Appalachians once more. This time, however, he had more than skins on his mind, and he was accompanied by his and a number of other families. Indeed, this venture was a land hunt, not a long hunt, for Boone intended to settle his family in Kentucky. There, he hoped to acquire lands to guarantee his independence and to secure the future of his growing family, which by then included three sons and four daughters.

It was a daring and dangerous move. Circumventing colonial authorities, Boone and his fellow migrants had obtained no grant to the territory from the British crown or from the governors of Virginia or North Carolina. They planned instead to gain legal title simply on the basis of their occupying and improving the land. In this, they were following what backcountry folk referred to as the "ancient cultivation law." Although Boone and other backcountry men understood that this right of squatters had never been fully accepted by colonial lawmakers, they believed that legal title belonged to those who settled and farmed "vacant" lands—and they expected, or wished, that private ownership of Kentucky tracts awaited those bold enough to get "land for taking it up."[4]

In categorizing Kentucky lands as vacant, Boone, of course, erased the prior occupancy and improvements of Indians. True, no Indian villages were currently located in the Kentucky River region where Boone intended to settle. But Indians from adjacent territories, primarily from Cherokee towns to the south and from an assortment of multiethnic villages north of the Ohio River, actively hunted on these lands. That men like Boone competed for valuable animal skins posed a threat to the Indians' fur trade, and Ohio Valley Indians responded by expropriating pelts and warning white hunters away; far worse was the prospect of hundreds of families moving in and depriving Indians of any place in the woods of Kentucky. To prevent this, a group of Cherokees attacked the Kentucky-bound travelers. Boone's eldest son, James, who had ridden off to rendezvous with another man, was caught in an ambush. Shot through the hips, James and his companion suffered gruesome deaths. After the mutilated bodies were discovered the next day, Daniel still urged the expedition to push on. But the other would-be squatters refused, and the caravan turned back. Having lost their lands in North Carolina, Daniel, Rebecca, and their surviving children reluctantly accepted an invitation to winter in a cabin on the Clinch River.

Boone's next attempt to settle in Kentucky came in 1775. This time, however, Boone acted as the employee of his former nemesis, Richard Henderson. Several years earlier, Henderson and a number of other North Carolina lawyers and merchants had formed the Transylvania Company with designs on establishing a proprietary colony in the Kentucky country. Like the squatters in Boone's 1773 venture, Henderson and his partners decided to bypass British officials. But to avoid the trouble with Indians that the squatters had encountered, Henderson and his associates proposed to purchase the land from the Cherokees. In the fall of 1774, Henderson entered into negotiations with Cherokee headmen. Months before any agreement had been reached, he advertised in North Carolina and Virginia newspapers, announcing terms under which settlers might procure lands in the Transylvania Colony soon to be founded. On March 17, 1775, Henderson concluded the deal. A week prior to the treaty-signing ceremony, he had dispatched Boone and thirty men to cut a road from the Cumberland Gap to the Kentucky River, where they were to establish a base for the concern's operation. To thank Boone for his services, Henderson agreed to name the Transylvania Colony's first settlement Boonesborough. As a more tangible gift, he promised Boone a two-thousand-acre parcel.

Boone's dream of independence was now firmly tied to the fortunes of Henderson's company, but the fledgling colony faced challenges on a variety of fronts. The vast majority of Ohio Valley Indians remained unreconciled to the carving out of new farmsteads from their Kentucky hunting grounds. In making a deal with the Cherokees, Henderson pretended that no other Indian peoples had any claim to Kentucky. Many among the Shawnees and Delawares reacted angrily to the news of Henderson's purchase and demanded that the interlopers be driven from the Kentucky country. Among the Cherokees, too, a significant faction, primarily composed of young men, denounced the cession of land to Henderson and pledged to prevent any settlements. Barely a week after the deal with Henderson was made, a group of these angry young men ambushed Boone's company of road makers. The attack left two dead, another wounded, and the rest of Boone's party inclined to abandon their mission. But, remembered one pioneer, Boone's "firmness and fortitude" checked the panic and kept the Transylvania enterprise alive.[5]

In the ensuing months and years, Daniel Boone had many more opportunities to demonstrate his courage and enhance his standing. Intermittent Indian raids unsettled Boonesborough's settlers. Those who did not take quick refuge inside Boonesborough or another of Kentucky's forts were killed or captured. During one such foray in July 1776, a band of two Cherokees and three Shawnees kidnapped Boone's teenaged daughter Jemima and two of her peers, Elizabeth and Frances Callaway. Heading up a rescue party, Boone soon overtook his daughter's captors and freed the girls. But Boone was not able to save their livestock and cornfields from Indian raiders. With food supplies scarce and Indians lurking about, settlers relied on hunters to slip out from Boonesborough under cover of darkness and secure a store of meat. In these trying circumstances, Boone's skills and his valor earned him the respect and admiration of his neighbors. Thus, "by general consent" did the men at Boonesborough put themselves "under the management and control" of Boone.[6]

Boone's hunting and heroism helped to protect Boonesborough from Indian adversaries, but he was helpless to secure his Transylvania lands against other enemies. Word of Henderson's purchase alarmed rival land speculators and colonial officials. "There is something in that affair which I neither understand, nor like, and wish I may not have cause to dislike it worse as the mystery unfolds," wrote George Washington of the Transylvania Company's project.[7] With their own plans for engrossing Kentucky threatened, the colonial governors of Virginia and North Carolina issued proclamations condemning Henderson's stroke. Although the outbreak of the American Revolution removed these leaders from power, it did not diminish the outcry against the proprietors of the Transylvania Colony. Seeking to confirm the crown's control over the Ohio Valley and win Indian allies, British authorities declared that this and other private purchases from the Indians were illegal. At the same time, patriot leaders in the Virginia Assembly disputed the validity of the company's land claims. Increasing numbers of Kentucky pioneers also rejected the rule of the Transylvania partners, particularly after the proprietors doubled the price of lands within the colony in the fall of 1775. Internal and external opposition intensified the following year and led to the appointment of a commission by Virginia legislators to investigate the legality of the Transylvania Company's land claims. The appointment of the committee, oddly enough made on July 4, 1776, presaged the end of independence for the Transylvania Colony.

The demise of the Transylvania Colony once again deprived Boone of the independence he desired. The invalidation of the company's purchase cost him the two-thousand-acre grant that he had been promised. Moreover, it brought greater chaos to the land situation in Kentucky. If the Transylvania Company did not have the right to sell the land to private owners, who did? As yet, the government of Virginia, which seemed the likeliest successor, had established no system for transferring titles to individual freeholders. Nor was Virginia's authority uncontested. After all, that authority rested on the outcome of the American Revolution, which in 1776 and 1777 did not seem likely to lead to American independence.

Bolstered by British supplies, Ohio Valley Indians stepped up their attacks against Kentucky settlements in 1777. In March, two hundred Ohio Indians led by the Shawnee chief Blackfish began hit-and-run strikes that kept pioneers confined in their forts through planting season. By fall the short harvest and the greater danger caused seven stations to be abandoned; only four (including Boonesborough) remained occupied. Yet at Boonesborough, the situation at the beginning of 1778 was desperate. Not only were all land claims in jeopardy, but the settlers were also destitute of corn and livestock. Worse still, they had no salt to preserve the meat that hunters like Boone procured.

While captaining a salt-making expedition, Daniel Boone ran into Will Emery again. On January 8, 1778, Boone had led thirty men from Boonesborough to the lower salt spring at Blue Licks. There, they began to boil the saltwater into salt, while Boone hunted to keep the troop fed. But on the morning of February 7, Boone's hunt was interrupted. Surprised by four Shawnee men, he surrendered and was escorted to the Indians' main camp. Amid the scores of assembled warriors, Boone spotted Will Emery. It took Captain Will a moment to recall when and where the two had previously met; after some prompting from Boone, Emery remembered and exchanged hearty "howdydos" with his once and present captive. Boone was next introduced to Blackfish. So began an odyssey that nearly changed the course of Boone's life and the direction of his pursuit of independence.

What followed Boone's capture soon became the source of controversy and contradictory accounts—and so it has remained. Later Boone asserted that he had arranged the surrender of the remaining salt makers to save their lives and to distract the Indians from an immediate attack on the undermanned settlement at Boonesborough. At the time, he did not let the salt makers in on his plan. To persuade them to submit peacefully, he merely assured them that they would be well treated by the Indians and released to the British at Detroit. Imagine their surprise, then, when a few hours later they heard Boone promise to conduct his captors to Boonesborough in the spring "when the weather will be warm, and the women and children can travel . . . to the Indian towns." Then, we will "all live with you as one people," and "the young men," referring to the salt makers who had expected to be ransomed to the British, "will make you fine warriors, and excellent hunters to kill game for your squaws and children."[8]

During the next several months, Boone and the other salt makers were given the chance to live as one people with their captors. First, though, the prisoners endured a long trek through the snow and across the Ohio River to Chillicothe. Along the way, several of the salt makers scuffled with their captors, as if to demonstrate their unhappiness with the prospect of living as one people with them. Even Boone wrestled with one warrior who had ordered him to tote a kettle filled with salt. Arriving at the Shawnee village, Boone was forced to run the gauntlet, a ceremony intended to let grieving Indians vent their anger over the loss of loved ones. The blows of more than one hundred Indians staggered Boone, but he emerged unscathed. Indeed, he won cheers from captives and backslaps from captors after he ran over and laid flat his last assailant.

As well as a rite of mourning, running the gauntlet was the first step in the adoption of captives. Next, Boone and the others chosen for adoption into Indian families had their hair plucked in the Shawnee style and their skins scrubbed. "I never was washed so clean before or since," remembered one captive of his scouring by Shawnee women.[9] Symbolically purged of his whiteness, Boone was renamed Sheltowee, meaning Big Turtle, and he was welcomed into the family of Blackfish. One of Blackfish's sons had been killed during the rescue of Jemima Boone in 1776. The custom among the Shawnees and other Ohio Indians encouraged Blackfish to "cover the dead" by adopting a substitute for his slain child. Fittingly, the war chief chose Boone, the leader and hunter of the pioneer company, as a surrogate son.

Before he could settle into his new home, Boone, along with about half the salt makers, the ones who had been deemed unfit for adoption, were marched off to Detroit. The arrival of the Indians and their prisoners frustrated the British commander, Lieutenant Governor Henry Hamilton, who would have preferred that the attack on Boonesborough had not been delayed. But the interrogation of Boone lifted Hamilton's spirits. Faced with starvation, expecting no help from the Continental Congress, and impressed by the benevolence of the Indians, the settlers at Boonesborough, said Boone, would gladly surrender when he returned with the Shawnees. So pleased was Hamilton with this information that he presented Boone with a horse, a saddle, and some silver trinkets. Hamilton also attempted to ransom Boone, offering Blackfish £100, five times the bounty paid for the other prisoners. Blackfish refused; he would not sell his son.

Upon his return to Chillicothe, Sheltowee seemed to adapt to his new identity and his new situation. Although Blackfish was only a few years older than Boone, Sheltowee got along easily with his father and with the rest of his new kin. In a matter of weeks, he gained the affection of his relatives, the friendship of his neighbors, and the trust of his father, who soon allowed Boone to hunt at his liberty. Boone, no doubt, was delighted when Blackfish told him not to worry about planting and tending corn, for "you should not be required to do any drudgery."[10] Among Ohio Indians, women handled the cultivation of crops and the preparation of food. That had always been Boone's view of agricultural labor, though among backcountry settlers, it was not considered proper to leave farming to mothers, wives, and daughters. In fact, Boone appeared so comfortable with his new arrangements that suspicions arose among less adaptable adoptees. Typical was William Hancock, who had been adopted by Boone's old acquaintance Will Emery. Showing none of Sheltowee's flexibility, Hancock despised Emery and wondered how Boone could be content among "a parcel of dirty Indians."[11]

Boone's unexpected appearance on June 20, 1778, at the gates of Boonesborough did not eliminate such suspicions. Previously the people at Boonesborough had heard that he and the rest of the salt makers had been killed by the Indians. (Those reports prompted Rebecca to return to North Carolina.) Then escaped captives came back with even more disturbing news: Boone, they claimed, had consorted with the British and joined the Indians. Now Boone was back, exhausted and hungry after a four-day journey from Chillicothe to Boonesborough. Regaining his strength, he recounted the details of his escape and then vigorously denied the accusations against him. His surrender, he insisted, had saved lives and had delayed the assault on Boonesborough; his dealings with Hamilton and his apparent serenity among the Shawnees was all deception—while he waited the chance to flee.

Maybe so, but doubts persisted about Boone's leadership and his loyalties. To restore his tarnished reputation, Boone proposed and led a preemptive strike against Ohio Indian towns. The foray failed in all its objectives and deprived the fort of its most able defenders. This, at a time when the largest Ohio Indian force yet assembled, a mixed group including Shawnees, Wyandots, Miamis, Delawares, Mingoes, as well as a contingent of British militia, was on the march. Having killed few Indians and secured no plunder, Boone's company of about twenty men beat a hasty retreat, arriving at Boonesborough on September 6, one day ahead of Blackfish's 350-man army.

Mistrust of Boone grew after the Indians laid siege to Boonesborough. Before launching any assault against outnumbered pioneers, Blackfish and other war chiefs negotiated with Boone and other representatives from Boonesborough outside the station's walls. Blackfish reiterated his offer of good treatment if the men submitted peaceably and death if they did not (the women would still be adopted). To ease the journey of women and children, he brought forty horses; to entice the men, he conjured up a country teeming with game. The offer appealed to the hunter in Boone, who restated to Blackfish his preference for a peaceful surrender.

Back inside the fort, Boone urged fellow pioneers to accept the Indians' offer. Boone, however, was outvoted. Still, he pressed for more talks, hopeful that "they could make a good peace."[12]

At Boone's instigation, another parley was held outside the fort—with near disastrous results. According to accounts of Boonesborough settlers (we have no Indian testimony about this event), the meeting was a trick; at a prearranged signal, the Indian negotiators grabbed their Boonesborough counterparts and attempted to capture them. Fortunately, Boone and the other exposed pioneers were able to shake loose and dash back into the safety of the fort.

After ten days the Indians lifted their siege of Boonesborough. Unwilling to risk the high casualties of a frontal assault, the Ohio Indians unsuccessfully attempted to tunnel under the fort's walls. The campaign turned into a sniping contest, as Indians and pioneers exchanged verbal insults and long-distance shots. But a long siege was not congruent with the Indians' way of war. With the fall hunting season approaching, most of the warriors withdrew to attend to their other duties.

Boonesborough stood, but Boone's standing had slipped. Many at Boonesborough suspected him of selling out to the British. After all, alleged these accusers, his wife's family included a number of Tories, and he had been rewarded by Hamilton. Others raised questions about his excessively trusting and friendly relations with Blackfish. Most vehement in pressing these charges was Richard Callaway, whose efforts led to the convening of a court-martial at nearby Logan's Station.

The court-martial exonerated Boone, and his superiors in the Virginia militia affirmed the correctness of the verdict by promoting him from captain to major. With respect to the allegation that Boone was a Tory, the vindication was justified. The loyalism of his wife's family, the Bryans, did not make Boone a Tory. Nor did his admissions to Hamilton about the condition of Boonesborough amount to much. In truth, Boone was not a loyalist, but a *localist*. Like many other Kentucky pioneers, his attachments were to kin and neighbors, not to national or imperial causes.

Less easily dismissed were Boone's attachments to his Indian kin. Boone seemed so at home in Chillicothe, because he was at home there. Like many captives who chose to remain with their Indian adopters, Boone displayed considerable fondness for the Indians' way of life. True, white children generally adapted more easily than adults. As frontier violence escalated in the years before the American Revolution, racial animosity deepened, making it even less likely for adults to become "white Indians." With a casualty rate seven times the national average, Kentucky settlers suffered terribly during the Revolution. In this blood-stained atmosphere, most of Boone's fellow salt makers shared William Hancock's view of "dirty" Indians and looked for the first opportunity to flee from their adoptive families.

But before, during, and after the Revolution, Boone eschewed the Indian-hating sentiments that scarred the backcountry. The lessons of his youth stayed with him. In 1778 and for the rest of his life, he showed Indians trust, respect, and compassion. Whenever possible, he preferred to avoid shedding other men's blood. Near the end of his life, he vehemently contradicted those mythmakers who had exaggerated his exploits in warfare with Indians. "I never killed but three," he insisted, and these deaths did him no honor.[13]

Tempted though Boone may have been to stay with his Shawnee kin, he did give up his place in Blackfish's family. Galloping away, he remembered feeling very sorry. But ride away he did. Three months later, when he met Blackfish again outside of Boonesborough, Boone said he had run away because he wanted to see his wife and children. His attachments to blood relations, it seemed, were still stronger than those to his adopted kin; he had to escape from Chillicothe to protect his Kentucky family from an impending attack. He did not say that he had Kentucky land claims to protect as well.

The court-martial verdict officially closed the episode, but the whole experience humiliated Boone. Nor did Boone's vindication wipe the ill will away. Following the trial, Boone headed back to North Carolina to reunite with his wife. For her part, Rebecca resisted returning to Kentucky, and only reluctantly agreed to accompany her husband. For his part, Daniel did not wish to revisit the poisoned atmosphere at Boonesborough. The general consent that had earlier won Boone a position of leadership no longer existed there. Rather than keep the controversy alive, he decided to found a new settlement instead. At the age of forty-four, he made yet another start in his quest for landowning independence.

Daniel Boone lived another forty-two years, but the second half of his life did not resolve the tensions of the first. The establishment of national independence fired dreams of personal independence. Following the Revolution, hundreds of thousands of Americans moved west. Independence-minded men swarmed into Kentucky and soon displaced Indian peoples from their lands in the Ohio Valley. Boone participated avidly in this land-getting. But although he grabbed a great deal of land, he could not hold it. Repeatedly frustrated in his efforts to obtain and maintain a landowner's independence, he looked back longingly to the time in 1778 when he had had—and lost—his chance for another kind of life.

Having voided the claims of the Transylvania Company and created the County of Kentucky, the government of Virginia enacted its own land law in May of 1779, which appeared to resurrect Boone's fortunes. The act rescinded Boone's previous 2,000-acre grant, but it compensated him by offering "actual settlers" the right to purchase 400 acres at a special low price. Those who had made an "improvement" were eligible to "pre-empt" an additional 1,000 acres at a slightly higher, yet still discounted price. Taking advantage of these stipulations, Boone entered his claim for a 1,400-acre parcel situated "on the Waters of licking [River] including a small spring on the North East side of a small branch[,] a Camp & some Bushes Cut down at the same about 20 Miles East from Boonesborough." On December 24, 1779, he received a certificate for this tract, the first step on the road to legal title and, at long last, to independence.[14]

A complicated statute, the Land Act of 1779 threw up numerous roadblocks. More precise than most settlement and preemption warrants as to location, Boone's certificate still lacked any detail about the configuration of the tract in question. The actual boundaries of Boone's property awaited the official survey, which he and other certificate holders had three years to accomplish. Already, however, overlapping entries were proliferating, and Boone's rights were disputed. A court fight loomed.

With almost all claims entangled in expensive and time-consuming litigation, frustration in Kentucky with the rule of Virginia mounted. Many who had recently denounced the Transylvania proprietors now turned their anger on Virginia lawmakers. Adding to their fury were the preferences that the Land Act bestowed on monied men, who could purchase unlimited quantities of Kentucky land. Under Virginia's system of distribution, twenty-one individuals or partnerships received grants in excess of one hundred thousand acres each. Most of these engrossers, complained actual settlers, had not risked their lives by coming to Kentucky during the Revolution. Some had never even seen the lands they owned.

Boone took no part in these protests, for he made a business of locating lands for nonresident purchasers and for new settlers who poured into Kentucky during the 1780s. Unlike other employees who sued the Transylvania Company for lost lands, Boone remained loyal. He continued to scout land for some of the partners. On at least one occasion in 1785, he donated his locating services, for "reasons of past favors and good friendship."[15] For old friends,

Boone sometimes located vacant tracts and marked boundaries with no charge. From most clients, however, he exacted a hefty fee. Indeed, Boone and others in the business of locating "vacant" land sometimes took half of the identified tract as their cut. In 1782, Boone was appointed a deputy surveyor, enabling him to perform the official survey at the same time as he made the initial location. In his four years as an official surveyor, he executed close to 150 surveys. Surveying warrants varying from fifty to fifteen thousand acres, Boone struck side deals entitling him to thousands of acres. During the 1780s his landholdings mushroomed; on paper, at least, his Kentucky claims made under Virginia's land laws totaled over twenty thousand acres.

That figure suggested Boone had abandoned his quest for mere independence in favor of a more grandiose dream. From the time he signed on with the Transylvania partners, Boone traveled with monied gentlemen. Still, while Boone served great speculators and tried to emulate their acquisitiveness, he never mastered the imitation. In the world of hunters from which Boone hailed, courage and generosity were the measures of manhood and the basis of local authority. In the world of great speculators, however, accumulation of land established eminence. To maximize self-advantage, the "worthiest" land brokers bent rules. In Kentucky, concluded a transplanted Pennsylvanian, speculators must "much deceive others or lose very considerably."[16] Boone was ill equipped for the cutthroat practices of notable speculators. He was out of place in the courthouses and legislative halls where successful engrossers won their most important victories.

Indeed, the rules of law cost Daniel Boone all the lands he *thought* he owned. From the State of Kentucky, which gained its independence from Virginia in 1792, he procured grants to thousands of additional acres, but never managed to finish the acquisition process by gaining clear titles. Again and again, overlapping claimants contested Boone's claims. Ignorant of the intricate provisions of land laws, Boone lost one parcel after another.

Boone's deficiencies as a locator and surveyor cost him dearly. As more and more of his locations were found in conflict with other claims, Boone became enmeshed in countless lawsuits. Through the 1790s, he listened to litigants impugn his honesty and accuse him of performing "chimney corner" surveys, that is, making up boundaries instead of measuring them. Out of court, he also was threatened by those who had lost the lands that Boone had located for them. In some ways, the insinuations and intimidation must have reminded him of the humiliating court-martial of 1778.

Boone blamed his misfortune on complicated laws and insidious lawyers. As damage awards piled up against him, he became acidic about the injustices done him by judges and lawyers. Eventually he stopped appealing adverse judgments. Frequently he did not appear in court to defend himself. In the fall of 1798, when Daniel failed to respond to a plaintiff's complaint over six thousand acres of lost land, the judge ordered the sheriff of Mason County, where Boone resided, to take the absent defendant into custody. But the sheriff could not find Boone, who, having forfeited all his land claims, had decided to leave Kentucky forever. Ironically, that same year, the State of Kentucky named a county in his honor.

Once again, the dream of a landowner's independence lured Daniel Boone west. This time, his destination was the lower Missouri Valley, where the Spanish government had promised him a thousand arpents (about 850 acres), with additional grants to any sons and sons-in-law who accompanied him. Repeating the pattern of family migrations that had characterized the settlement of the southern backcountry and of Kentucky, son Daniel Morgan went first. Two years later, in 1799, father Daniel followed, joined by his wife Rebecca, his son Nathan, his daughters Susanna and Jemima, their respective spouses, and seventeen grandchildren. (Three of Boone's surviving children remained with their families in Kentucky.)

The following year, Spanish authorities appointed Boone as "syndic" of the district in which he lived. That position gave him a local authority that he had not enjoyed since 1778. It placed him in charge of criminal and civil matters, including land disputes. In contrast to the costly and complicated workings of American courts, Boone dispensed quick justice. He often faulted both parties and dictated his own compromises between overlapping claimants.

Two decades after he fled from Chillicothe, Boone was reunited with some of the Indians with whom he had lived briefly in Ohio. More than a thousand Shawnee and Delaware Indians had preceded Boone in the move from the Ohio to the Missouri Valley. Along the lower Missouri at the beginning of the nineteenth century, communities of refugee Indians were interspersed among clusters of Anglo-American farmsteads, and, for a few years at least, amity prevailed. Both sets of pioneers joined with nearby French villagers against the threats posed by Osage Indians and peacefully traded goods and services with one another. Both also mingled in more purely social gatherings. Even after the United States purchased the territory, hunting, horse races, and dances continued to bring peoples together. Marital unions occasionally extended these bonds. Neither Daniel nor any of his children crossed this line, but otherwise they associated freely with neighboring Shawnees and Delawares.

For his part, Daniel Boone frequently hunted with these Indians and entertained some of his former captors at his home. Many years later, one of his grandsons remembered a visit in which an aging Shawnee reminisced with Daniel about the time when he was their prisoner and their kinsman. The Indian recalled how Boone had agreed to surrender the settlers at Boonesborough, after which they would be taken to Chillicothe where "all [would] live like Brothers & Sisters." Then, concluded the Indian, "we were all glad."[17] For the moment, they were again.

These happy times along the lower Missouri did not last too long. What the American Revolution had done to Kentucky and the Ohio Valley frontier, the War of 1812 produced in the Missouri country; the floodgates of westward migration again opened. Between 1815 and 1820, the population of the Missouri Territory skyrocketed from twenty-five thousand to sixty-six thousand. These independence-seeking newcomers wanted land, which, of course, meant they wanted Indian lands. Very rapidly, the Missouri farms and hunting grounds of Shawnee and Delaware Indians became the private property of American pioneers.

Boone, too, endured another round of dispossession. Although the United States guaranteed to uphold existing land titles, Boone and others with Spanish-issued grants faced problems similar to the ones that had confronted Kentucky's early pioneers. Vague locations and unfiled papers hampered his efforts to establish clear title. In 1809 the American commissioners who were appointed to verify Spanish grants ruled that Boone's claim "ought not to be confirmed."[18]

Losing his land (again) embarrassed Boone, and it also spurred some influential friends into action. Boone, after all, had become an international celebrity following the 1784 publication of John Filson's widely circulated narrative of "The Adventures of Col. Daniel Boon." Subsequent editions and plagiarized accounts spread Boone's fame and amplified his heroic contributions to the founding of Kentucky and the fighting of Indians in the Ohio Valley. By the early nineteenth century, Boone had emerged as the foremost symbol of the independent American pioneer. To have this man who was credited with ushering civilization's triumph over savage wilderness left destitute and dependent seemed an unfit end. So Boone's champions managed to persuade Congress to restore his one thousand-arpent grant, as a gift for his services in the settlement of the western country—in particular, for his part in defending Kentucky during the Revolution.

Alas, when creditors from Kentucky heard of the grant, they rushed to Missouri to collect on old debts. A recent widower, Daniel had no spirit for more legal wrangling. In May 1815, he sold the tract that the United States had just bestowed upon him. He spent most of his remaining years at the home of his daughter Jemima and her husband Flanders Callaway. In his eighties, he still escaped to the woods to hunt. And then, in September 1820, Daniel fell sick while visiting the home of his son Nathan. He died after a brief illness. He was eighty-five years old and landless.

Notes

1. Lyman C. Draper interview with Joseph Scholl, Draper Manuscripts 24S217, State Historical Society of Wisconsin, Madison. Hereafter cited as Draper Mss.

2. Lyman Draper, "Life of Boone," Draper Mss. 3B53–54.

3. John D. Shane interview with Daniel Boone Bryan, Draper Mss. 22C14.

4. Joseph Doddridge, *Notes on the Settlement and Indian Wars of the Western Parts of Virginia and Pennsylvania from 1763 to 1783 inclusive* (1824; reprint ed., Pittsburgh, 1912), 85.

5. "Felix Walker's Narrative of His Trip with Boone from Long Island to Boonesborough in March, 1775," in *Boonesborough: Its Founding, Pioneer Struggles, Indian Experiences, Transylvania Days, and Revolutionary Annals*, ed. George W. Ranck (Louisville, KY, 1901), 163.

6. Ibid.

7. William Stewart Lester, *The Transylvania Colony* (Spencer, IN, 1935), 41.

8. Lyman C. Draper's interview with Joseph Jackson, Draper Mss. 11C62(8).

9. Orley E. Brown, ed., *The Captivity of Jonathan Alder and His Life with the Indians* (Alliance, OH, 1965), 14.

10. Lyman C. Draper interview with Delinda Boone Craig, 1866, Draper Mss. 30C53.

11. Draper, "Life of Boone," Draper Mss. 4B194.

12. Chester Raymond Young, ed., *Westward into Kentucky: The Narrative of Daniel Trabue* (Lexington, KY, 1981), 58.

13. John Mack Faragher, *Daniel Boone: The Life and Legend of an American Pioneer* (New York, 1992), 39.

14. "The Certificate Book of the Virginia Land Commission, 1779–1780," *Register of the Kentucky Historical Society* 21 (1923): 82.

15. Daniel Boone to Thomas Hart, August 11, 1785, Daniel Boone Papers, Special Collections, Margaret I. King Library, University of Kentucky, Lexington. Hereafter cited as Special Collections.

16. Extract from a letter from a gentleman living in Kentucky to his friend in Chester County, Pennsylvania, December 8, 1786, Wilson Collection, Special Collections.

17. Lyman C. Draper interview with Delinda Boone Craig, Draper Mss., 30C66–67.

18. Michael Lofaro, *The Life and Adventures of Daniel Boone* (Lexington, KY, 1978), 121.

Suggested Readings

The exploits of Daniel Boone were first publicized by John Filson in his *The Discovery, Settlement, and Present State of Kentucke* (1784), to which was appended a supposedly first-person account of "The Adventures of Col. Daniel Boon." Although this "autobiography" gave its frontier hero the voice of an Enlightenment philosopher, Boone did endorse the veracity of Filson's narrative. Among other early biographers, Timothy Flint, *Biographical Memoir of Daniel Boone* (Cincinnati, 1836), and John Mason Peck, "Life of Daniel Boone, the Pioneer of Kentucky," in Jared Sparks, ed., *The Library of American Biography* (New York, 1847), are notable, as both authors knew and interviewed Boone.

Biographers of Boone owe their greatest debt to Lyman C. Draper, who interviewed and corresponded with scores of Boone's contemporaries and descendants. The Draper Manuscript Collection, which includes Draper's unpublished biography of Boone, is housed at the State Historical Society of Wisconsin in Madison (and is available on microfilm). Numerous parts of the collection have also been published. The most valuable for tracing the life of Boone are Chester Raymond Young, ed., *Westward into Kentucky: The Narrative of Daniel Trabue* (Lexington, KY, 1981), and Ted Franklin Belue, ed., *A Sketch of the Life and Character of Daniel Boone: A Memoir by Peter Houston* (Mechanicsburg, PA, 1997). These and other sources are effectively used in John Bakeless, *Daniel Boone: Master of the Wilderness* (New York, 1939), and John Mack Faragher, *Daniel Boone: The Life and Legend of an American Pioneer* (New York, 1992), which currently stands as the definitive biography. For an interpretation of the world in which Daniel Boone lived and the quest for landowning independence, see Stephen Aron, *How the West Was Lost: The Transformation of Kentucky from Daniel Boone to Henry Clay* (Baltimore, 1996).

9

Philadelphia Quaker Elizabeth Drinker and Her Servant, Jane Boon

"Times Are Much Changed, and Maids Are Become Mistresses"

Alison Duncan Hirsch

Elizabeth Drinker (1735–1807) and her maidservant Jane Boon (ca. 1760–?) experienced many of the same events in Philadelphia during the Revolutionary War. Elizabeth's education, social position, and her servants' labor afforded her the ability and leisure to write a detailed diary, in which at first she rarely commented on public affairs. In comparison with fellow Philadelphian William Smith, why did so few public events of the Revolution touch Elizabeth's life sufficiently to merit recording? Beyond the localism (such as seafaring Ashley Bowen felt) that had also shaped Drinker's understanding of the conflict, she focused even more narrowly on her domestic situation. Given that Henry Drinker, Elizabeth's husband, was a merchant, patriot nonimportation campaigns affected his business and his political views. Quakerism also influenced both the Drinkers' interpretation of the Revolution and the community's definitions of their behavior. In petitioning with other women for the release of their husbands, Elizabeth likely drew upon egalitarian Quaker views on gender relations. As a Quaker, how effectively did Elizabeth defend her family's early ownership of slaves? Were the Drinkers loyalists, as their opponents contended, or pacifists, or both? Did Elizabeth finally reveal her political views by quartering a British officer in her home?

The Revolution distinctly challenged the elite Drinkers' fortunes and temporarily their social position, but how might Jane Boon's perspective on the Revolution have differed from that of her mistress? As Alison Duncan Hirsch demonstrates, the bustling household of the Drinkers reveals the dynamics of master-servant relations before the war, but also how the Revolution tested these relationships. In the American Revolution, Jane Boon discovered new opportunities; she married a German soldier and became the mistress of her own household. In contrast, Elizabeth Drinker noted a shortage of servants and their increasing insolence or independence. Had the political revolution unleashed a social revolution, or at least the promise of change, for Philadelphia's "lower orders"?

Alison Duncan Hirsch, who teaches colonial American history at Pennsylvania State University at Harrisburg, is the co-author of *Women, Family and Community in Colonial America: Two Perspectives* (1983).

On a clear Friday morning, September 19, 1777—as General William Howe's forces marched on Philadelphia and General Washington's army engaged in skirmishes to the west of the city—Jane Boon rose early, as usual, to do her morning chores. As one of two servant girls in the household of Henry and Elizabeth Drinker, she was probably responsible for stoking the fire, milking the cow, gathering eggs, and preparing breakfast for the family. But this was not a usual morning. At seven o'clock Jane ran to wake the family "with the News that the English were near."[1] Most of the neighbors had been up all night, with "horses galloping, women running, children crying, delegates flying, and altogether the greatest consternation, fright and terror that can be imagined."[2] By noon it became clear that the British arrival was not so imminent, but the Continental Congress and the Supreme Executive Council of Pennsylvania had already fled west to safety in Lancaster, Pennsylvania, and the town was "very much thin'd of its Inhabitance."[3] Among those who remained in the city were many well-to-do Quakers and their servants, women like Elizabeth Drinker and Jane Boon.

A week after Boon, Paul Revere-like, raised the alarm, the British forces actually arrived, marching into town just a block away from the Drinkers' three-story brick house on Front Street. "Well, here are the English in earnest," Elizabeth Drinker wrote in her diary, "about 2 or 3000 came in, through second street, without oppossition or interruption, no plundering on the one side or the other."[4] Drinker was pleased to see the British replace the Americans, who had imprisoned her husband, exiled him to Virginia, and seized family property. As a Quaker, Elizabeth opposed war and claimed to be neutral, but her bias toward the British was clear in September 1777. The American "Rebels," she wrote, were people "unacquainted" with "Humanity, justice and good Policy."[5] How her servants felt about the war is not so clear. Elizabeth Drinker and Jane Boon lived together through the Revolution, but they experienced the war in very different ways. For Elizabeth Drinker, the war brought fear and privation; for Jane Boon, it also brought excitement and opportunity. The Revolution separated Elizabeth from her husband for nearly eight months, but it brought Jane together with her future husband.

The main historical evidence for both women's experiences is Elizabeth Drinker's diary, which covers forty-nine years, supplemented by hundreds of family letters and her husband's business records and travel journals. Jane Boon, as far as we know, left no diary or papers. Historians have frequently used Elizabeth Drinker's diary as evidence of women's experience during the Revolutionary War, but the very nature of such sources has often meant that wealthy women's experiences stand for all women's. Elizabeth Drinker was just one woman, from a very select group, elite, well educated, with the leisure to keep a diary, as she did from 1758 to 1807. The household labor of her servants provided her the time to write and record the hardships war brought to the civilian population: the shortages of food, firewood, and hay for livestock; the plundering and displacement of civilians by both American and British forces; the terror of living in a time when every noise in the night seemed "alarming."[6] These nighttime noises must have held even greater terror for the servants, who were the ones sent to investigate their source. Servants bore the brunt of the extra work entailed when soldiers were quartered in their masters' and mistresses' houses and when shortages made foraging necessary. To understand women's experiences during the Revolution, we need to view them from the perspective not only of Elizabeth Drinker but also of her maidservants.

Jane Boon spent nearly four years in the Drinker house, including the most intense months of the Revolutionary War for Philadelphians, when the city was under strict military rule, first by the Americans, then by the British, and then by the Americans again. In normal times, the comings and goings of servants rarely seemed important enough to note on paper, but the war gave importance to mundane activities, and a maid's ordinary activities became noteworthy because they occurred in extraordinary times. Although Jane left no written records of her own, Elizabeth Drinker's diary mentions her frequently, and so that document can convey some sense of what the Revolution was like for both women.

Elizabeth Sandwith, the daughter of Philadelphia Quakers and granddaughter of Irish Quakers, began her diary, in 1758, at age twenty-three, two years after the death of both her parents within two months of one another. She continued her diary after her marriage to Henry Drinker in 1761. "I keep a little account of my daily proceedings, which I believe makes me less pertiqular in my letters,"[7] she wrote to her husband in summer 1771, when they were separated, as they were frequently over the years. Henry traveled often to attend Quaker meetings or Indian treaty conferences and to conduct business out of town; Elizabeth rarely accompanied him.

They were apart as well when she and the children went to the country to escape the summer's heat and epidemic disease, while Henry remained in the city to conduct business. Elizabeth's diary entries were short and sporadic for the early years of her marriage, but they grew lengthier, especially during the height of Revolutionary War activity in Philadelphia. By the time she died in 1807, her "little account" had grown to fill more than thirty volumes and to include not only her own "daily proceedings" but those of many others, particularly her family and servants.

Elizabeth Drinker was well educated for a woman of her time. Quakers believed in education for girls, though they still prescribed needlework for girls, mathematics and Latin for boys. She attended Anthony Benezet's school (see Chapter 1 of this volume), took French lessons, and learned to do needlework. After the death of their parents, she and her older sister, Mary (her only surviving sibling), auctioned off their father's estate, including the house, some furniture, "a servant girl's time, that has six years to serve, and a Negroe girl, about nine years of age."[8] The "servant girl" was the first of many Elizabeth would employ, in this case "owning" the young woman's labor for the number of years specified in her contract, or indenture. The black child, named Jude, was the last slave Elizabeth would own, and later, after Quakers adopted a policy prohibiting slaveholding, she came to be "very sorry we had sold the Child to be a slave for life," although, "when we sold her, there was nothing said against keeping or selling Negroes," and "we did not think we were doing wrong."[9] Jude's sale—the first of several until she was finally freed in her fifties—is testimony to the dangers slaves faced when their masters died or fell on hard times. The auction also illustrates the societal restrictions on even well-to-do white women. The standards of the time dictated that two unmarried sisters in their early twenties should not maintain their own household, and so Elizabeth and Mary sold their family home and boarded with other Philadelphia Quaker families until Elizabeth's marriage in 1761. Mary Sandwith never married and lived with the Drinkers all their lives. Elizabeth teased her husband about "how clever it was [of him] to have two wives,"[10] but she depended on Mary so much that one visitor referred to her as the family's "housekeeper,"[11] though of course Mary's status was much higher than that of a servant. She was, in effect, a surrogate parent who helped care for the children, and a household manager who supervised the servants.

Henry Drinker was a merchant descended from early English immigrants to the Quaker colony of Pennsylvania founded in 1681. At ten, he apprenticed himself, "with the Advice and Consent of his Father,"[12] to George James, a Quaker merchant in Philadelphia. He went on to enter a partnership with his master's son, Abel, to form the firm of James and Drinker. Henry was just slightly older than Elizabeth, who was his second wife. She had known him for some time before they married, since his first wife, Ann Swett, had been one of Elizabeth's closest friends. Henry and Ann had married in 1757, but Ann died a year later. At about the same time, Elizabeth began keeping her diary, and soon Henry began to make such regular visits that Elizabeth recorded them with the simple notation: "HD call'd."[13] After their marriage in 1761, Henry and Elizabeth remained close to Ann Swett's relatives. Both families were members of a tight network of elite Quakers whose prestige derived from their success in business as well as their reputation as upstanding members of the Society of Friends. Elizabeth participated in Quaker women's meetings, established in seventeenth-century England to give women a role in approving the marriages of members, disciplining those who went astray, and collecting and distributing charity to the poor, who were predominantly women and children. The Drinkers held firmly to Quaker principles against war and against swearing oaths, the so-called peace testimony and the testimony against oaths. They were also against ostentation and believed in the plain style of dark, undecorated clothing that Quakers in England and America had been wearing for more than a century. Like other elite Quaker women, though, Elizabeth Drinker's "plainness" did not mean inexpensive; she and her family wore fine fabrics and filled their city and country houses with fine furniture and linens. The Revolution would threaten their high standard of living both directly—as Americans and British alternately seized their property—and indirectly, as war cut off the Atlantic trade that brought over luxury goods and immigrant servants whose labor could be had cheaply.

Through both peacetime and time of war, the most important aspect of Elizabeth Drinker's life was her children. By 1774, when Jane Boon joined the family, Elizabeth had given birth to seven children, two of whom had died in infancy. She had also suffered two miscarriages. Her surviving children included three girls and two boys: Sarah, or "Sally" (b. 1761); Ann, or "Nancy" (b. 1764); William, called "Billy" (b. 1767); Henry Sandwith, called "little Henry" (b. 1770); and Mary, or "Molly" (b. 1774). She nursed all her children herself, the common practice among American women, even wealthy women who could have afforded to send their children to wetnurses. In England, wealthy women often hired a wetnurse to live with them or sent their infants to live in a nurse's home until weaning. Elizabeth Drinker employed wetnurses briefly for three of her children only after doctors advised her to stop breastfeeding for the sake of her health.

In addition to her role of caring for her home and children, Elizabeth saw herself as Henry's financial partner, and, indeed, she had brought substantial wealth into the marriage. She felt a keen sense of proprietorship in his business, and he reciprocated by involving her in real estate and business transactions. In 1774, when she took a ride with Henry to Kensington, on the Delaware River north of the city, she wrote that together they "climb'd up to the side of our new Ship which is building there."[14] Less than a year later, in March 1775, she recorded that the "New-Ship Chalkley, arriv'd here with servants—in Ballist."[15] James and Drinker imported manufactured textiles and other goods from England, but with the colony's perpetual labor shortage, an important part of the firm's business was indentured servants, who paid their passage to America by promising to serve a master for a number of years. After 1775, the trade in servants virtually ceased, as wartime hostilities limited the transatlantic trade.

In the years before the Revolution, the Drinkers had four or more servants living with them: a driver or coachman, a stableboy, a baby nurse, and one or more maids. Henry's apprentices also lodged with the family. The Drinkers hired household workers under several different arrangements. Some work was sent out to be done, such as laundry or sewing. Some women came as day workers, for specific tasks such as whitewashing or cleaning; others came to live in the house for a short time, in order to nurse a sick family member or to care for a mother lying in with a newborn. Drivers and maids were often wage workers, hired on a weekly or annual salary, and lived with the Drinkers, returning home only if they or their family members were ill. Other servants living with the family were bound, or indentured, as children or young adults, legally required to serve until the age specified by the contract, generally eighteen or older. Some came as servants to Pennsylvania from England, Ireland, or Scotland, and their labor served to pay off their ship passage to America. Others were American-born children of English, German, or Swedish ancestry, who received training and education in exchange for their labor. According to a 1700 Pennsylvania law, at the end of the indenture, masters had to give servants "freedom dues" of two complete suits of clothing, one of which had to be new.

Several young girls came to work for the Drinkers when their families fell on hard times, usually because of the death of their fathers. Sally Gardner, the daughter of Philadelphia Quakers, came to live with the Drinkers in 1766 when she was fourteen years old. Her father had died in 1764, leaving her mother to support three children, of whom Sally was the eldest. Her mother did not remarry until 1774, and sending the eldest daughter out to work was probably a financial necessity for this widowed mother. Perhaps in the spirit of charity to fellow Quakers, the Drinkers hired Sally at weekly wages of 2 s., 6 d. In 1770 she agreed to a yearly wage of £8, which meant a small raise, but she left before the year was up. "She was a girl of Spirit," Elizabeth Drinker recalled years later, after Sally's death, "but an affectionate and faithful little Nurse to my William when he was an infant."[16]

Sally Gardner was never bound, or indentured, to the Drinkers, but other girls were. Ann, or Nanny, Oat, the daughter of George and Sarah Oat, became bound to the Drinkers while she was still quite young. George Oat was a Quaker, but his wife apparently was not. Elizabeth first mentioned the family in July 1771, while the Drinkers were at the popular bath springs resort of Bristol, where the Oat family lived. When the doctor ordered Elizabeth to stop nursing her eight-month-old son Henry, the Drinkers decided to send him to Sarah Oat, who had agreed to nurse him. Elizabeth wrote that she felt "lost without my little dear" and visited him at Sarah's nearly every day for the next few weeks. Even after she returned to Philadelphia in mid-August, leaving her son behind, she returned frequently to visit. On one of those visits, Sarah expressed concern about her own children, and the Drinkers agreed to take Nanny home with them. The two families in effect exchanged children for a brief time: Henry stayed with the Oats for several more months; Nanny rode home with the Drinkers the same day, though their coach was so crowded that she had to ride sitting on the floor. Two months later, her brother Israel sailed for Bristol as a crew member on the *Chalkley*. Both children received an education as part of their agreements: Israel learned sailing, and Nanny learned household skills and briefly attended the Philadelphia Quaker school run by Hannah Catherall, where the Drinkers sent their own children.

Nanny remained with the Drinkers for five and one-half years, so she was part of the "family" Jane Boon joined in 1774. Quakers, as well as many other eighteenth-century Americans, used the word "family" to include everyone living under the same roof, servants as well as children and other relatives. In 1774 at least two young men were also living with the Drinkers, a clerk and a stableboy. George Baker, eighteen years old, had followed in the footsteps of his older brother Hilary as Henry Drinker's clerk; the brothers were the sons of a German schoolteacher in Germantown. The stableboy was Harry Catter, from the German state of Hesse. Like many German immigrants, he was probably a "redemptioner," granted free passage to Pennsylvania and then given a short time to procure the funds to repay the ship captain. The usual practice was for the new arrival to sell his labor for four or more years to an employer, who then paid the passage fee to the captain. Harry still spoke German, and so during the British occupation, he was able to interpret for the German mercenaries. The Drinkers sent Harry to school for a while, probably to learn to read and write English.

The hiring and supervision of servants was gender-specific. Henry Drinker and his partner hired the clerks, young men from well-to-do or aspiring families who wanted to serve apprenticeships with successful merchants. Henry also hired the male household workers—the drivers or coachmen and the stable hands—though Elizabeth probably had some influence, since the men were under her care while in the house. Elizabeth and her sister hired the female workers, though Henry was involved when an indenture was required: as head of the household, his signature made a document legally binding in an era when married women had no legal standing of their own. After the agreement, the day-to-day supervision of household servants was up to Elizabeth and Mary.

In December 1774 the Drinker family added a new servant. That month, Henry Drinker, Mary Sandwith, and Sally Drinker went to Wilmington, Delaware, because Benjamin Swett, the father of Henry's first wife, was near death. Elizabeth stayed behind in Philadelphia, as she nearly always did while her children were young. Henry and the others were gone for several days, and Elizabeth was beside herself at her family's prolonged absence, especially since baby Molly had a rash and four-year-old Henry had a sore throat, rash, and fever. Having already lost two children in infancy, Elizabeth considered any symptom cause for alarm. She was virtually alone in caring for the children, since she thought Nanny Oat unreliable. Perhaps Elizabeth was somewhat mollified when her family returned with a new addition to the "family." Jane Boon had family in Wilmington, and Henry's trip there coincides with the time she entered service in the Drinker household. Elizabeth's diary did not record Jane's arrival, yet later she could date it precisely: when Jane left in August 1778, Elizabeth noted that the girl had been with the family "3 years and near nine months."[17] So Jane probably rode back with the family to Philadelphia, as Nanny Oat had ridden from Bristol three years earlier.

Like many other young servants, Jane probably went out to work after the death of her father. Her mother remarried by 1777; Elizabeth had referred to her as "Deborah Elwell" when she paid a visit, the only one mentioned in the diary. Jane seems to have had few other close relatives: a cousin in Newport, Delaware, and an aunt in Wilmington. Some other young servants' families maintained more contact, through more visits and trips home. Jane may well have been unhappy in the first few months; in May 1775, she ran away or at least stayed out too late, for Elizabeth noted "I went out this afternoon to look for Jane."[18] This is Drinker's first mention of Jane Boon, although the girl had been with them for seven months. It is also one of the few instances—until years later—when Elizabeth called her by the formal name "Jane" rather than the diminutive "Jenny," like a parent reprimanding a naughty child. Servants did not ordinarily attract attention or merit mention in a diary unless they caused trouble. Elizabeth's concern was perhaps a selfish one—good servants were hard to find—but she also seems genuinely to have liked Jane. She felt quite differently about the other maidservants, "impertinent" Nanny Oat and "Saucy" Ann Kelly,[19] who joined the family in October 1775. Newly arrived from Ireland, where the depressed state of the linen industry and the high price of food led thousands to come to Pennsylvania in the early 1770s, Ann was probably indentured for at least four years. Unlike these other young servants, Jane Boon seems to have come close to becoming part of the Drinker family.

Jane was probably born about 1760. No birth record has been found, but her situation as Molly's nurse was similar to that of Sally Gardner, who had been fourteen when she became Billy's nurse. Jane was probably of Swedish ancestry, at least on her father's side. Anders Svenson Boon came to New Sweden (later Delaware) in 1640, and he and his wife Anna had six sons who became members of Pennsylvania's first volunteer militia, created in 1690. Jane may have been the daughter of Peter "Bom" and Deborah Monde, who were married at Wilmington's Swedish Lutheran church in 1747. Jane was almost certainly not a Quaker, since there is no evidence that she went to Quaker meetings with the Drinkers, as Sally Gardner had. Both her first and last names were common in the region—among Germans and English inhabitants as well as Swedes—so she is hard to pin down in the records. The difficulty in tracing Jane Boon is symptomatic of the problems in researching the history of women and the "lower sort," those who were not members of the wealthy, educated elite. Individuals who did not make a mark in politics, war, business, or religion simply were not recorded in public documents. Women's names generally found their way into the public record if they were wealthy and single or widowed, or if they committed some misdeed. Two earlier Jane Boons—who may or may not have been related to our Jane Boon—illustrate these biases of sources on women. In 1750 a Philadelphia innkeeper named Jane Boon wrote her will, and Edward Drinker, Henry's uncle, was one of the witnesses, perhaps indicating a prior relationship between the families. In 1763, another Jane Boon came to public notice for a very different reason. A mariner, John Boon, had placed a notice in the *Pennsylvania Gazette* announcing that he would no longer pay the debts of his wife, Jane Boon, since she had "run her said husband greatly in Debt and behaved, in other respects, very ill to him."[20]

Molly Drinker was eight months old when Jane was hired as her nurse. During Jane's first year with the family, Elizabeth continued to breastfeed Molly, so Jane's responsibilities for the baby were limited, but she also helped care for the other children, tending them when they were ill and walking them to school. The eldest child, Sally, was thirteen, slightly younger than Jane herself. Nancy was ten, Billy seven, and Henry four. Sally and Nancy had both left Hannah Catherall's school earlier in the year; later they went to "Mrs. Woods Kniting School"[21] and had private writing and French lessons. "Little Henry" started school in March 1774. A year later, his older brother, Billy, transferred to "A Mans School,"[22] where he began at age eight to learn skills needed in business. The Drinkers apparently did not send Jenny to school; she must have already had a basic education.

While Elizabeth was busy with household affairs in the spring of 1775, protest was becoming revolution in New England. In hindsight, Lexington and Concord were "the shot heard 'round the world," but at the time, many Pennsylvanians may have taken little notice of events in Massachusetts. Only when the Revolution hit home did Elizabeth Drinker write much about the war in her diary. One of the few hints of the start of hostilities is her notation in May 1775 that "Benjamin Franklin arrived here," home from London, where he had been unable to persuade Parliament to take a more moderate approach to colonial insubordination. This is Elizabeth Drinker's only notation of this most famous Philadelphian during his lifetime, although after his death she read his autobiography and found it "entertaining."[23]

Earlier in the century, Quakers had been active in politics, providing leadership in the Pennsylvania Assembly, but by the 1750s, when Henry Drinker came of age, Friends had largely withdrawn from the political arena, unable to reconcile their peace testimony with the need to vote funds for military defense during the Seven Years' War. Still, along with other leading Quaker merchants, Henry Drinker participated in the nonimportation movement that began with the Stamp Act crisis of 1765. The first mention of politics in Elizabeth's diary was on May 19, 1766, when "a Vessel from Pool brought the Account of the Repeal of the Stamp Act."[24] Later, as the protests became more radical, the Drinkers' Quaker pacifism led them to oppose revolutionary activity.

In December 1773, Elizabeth noted the news of the Boston Tea Party: "an account from Boston, of 342 Chests of Tea, being thrown into the Sea."[25] This bland statement belies the stake the Drinkers had in the tea shipments, since James and Drinker was one of four Philadelphia firms consigned to auction off the tea and could have expected to make a commission of nearly £600. Elizabeth nonetheless maintained her matter-of-fact tone when she remarked on the arrival of the "Tea Ship"[26] at Chester, south of Philadelphia, and its forced departure with cargo still unloaded, in an effort to prevent the sort of mob violence that occurred in Boston. Violence occurred anyway: Philadelphians made an effigy of Massachusetts governor Thomas Hutchinson, which was then "carted round the Town hang'd and burnt."[27]

Though symbolic, this sort of mob action represented a threat of physical violence and thus was not only an affront to Quakers' pacifism but also a danger to their business interests. A more serious threat was the formation of a committee to enforce the Continental Congress's resolution against trade with Britain, by imposing stiff penalties for imports and exports. John Drinker, Henry's older brother who was also a merchant, denounced the "new lords" who "made new laws, created new crimes and new punishments," and sought "vengeance against those who should dare to cross their measures."[28] Increasingly, as rising political passions forced individuals to take sides, Philadelphia's radical leaders suspected that Quaker merchants such as John and Henry Drinker were not the neutral pacifists they claimed to be, but rather were British partisans eager to protect the profits from their trade with England. Those who professed neutrality, as the Quakers did, were soon accused of being spies and traitors.

Even after Lexington and Concord, Elizabeth Drinker made few references to the unrest. Her relatively short diary entries, as well as occasional duplications and backdating of entries, hint that concerns about public affairs were beginning to have an effect on her. But the diary was not meant to record public events but simply "to help the memory,"[29] particularly in the areas of life that were Elizabeth's special province: the education of her children and the younger servants, the health of the entire family, including the servants, and the care of the house. On May 8, the day before George Washington arrived in Philadelphia to attend the Second Continental Congress, Elizabeth Drinker noted that coachman Bill Bolis went home to his lodgings to recover from the mild case of smallpox he suffered after being inoculated. Washington's arrival in Philadelphia, and his departure for New England a few weeks later, both went unremarked in the diary. Soon the war would impinge too directly on Elizabeth Drinker's world for her not to notice.

In January 1776 the Revolution came home to the Drinkers with a vengeance. John Drinker became the target of Philadelphia's Committee of Inspection and Observation, the group charged with enforcing the nonimportation policy voted by the Continental Congress. The committee accused him of refusing to accept Continental bills of credit (which Quakers saw as the currency financing the war effort) and had his store and warehouse locked up, with the windows and doors nailed shut. In June came the first intrusion into Elizabeth's own house, when inspectors from the city's Council of Safety arrived to collect lead window weights to be used for defense; Elizabeth noted with some satisfaction that her weights were iron, and the men went away empty-handed. On July 8, 1776, the Declaration of Independence was proclaimed in front of the State House, and many Philadelphians celebrated with "military parades, gunfire, and the ringing of bells day and night."[30] Elizabeth Drinker wrote nothing in her diary to indicate that she even noticed, but for years afterward she would be unable to ignore the Declaration's anniversary, celebrated on July 4. Quakers incurred the wrath of the radicals by refusing to join in lighting celebratory candles in their windows, which the mob then proceeded to break. On its first anniversary in 1777, Elizabeth wrote sardonically: "the Town Illuminated and a great number of Windows Broke on the Anniversary of Independence and Freedom."[31] A day that brought rejoicing for many brought fear and danger to Quaker homes.

In 1776 at least one member of the Drinker household took note of the Declaration; a few days after its publication, "George Baker left us, and went among the Soldiers."[32] Shortly afterward, American soldiers on their way north took over Philadelphia Friends' meetinghouses to use as quarters. By August the city's newspapers were filled with reports of British warships being sighted on their way to New York. Still, in spite of the presence of American soldiers and the proximity of British warships, Henry and Elizabeth were able to take a ten-day trip to New Jersey in October to visit a sick friend and attend Quaker meetings. Even after the authorities—"our present ruling Gentr'y," Elizabeth called them[33]—imposed martial law on the city in December 1776, Quakers still found ways to travel, as a pointed demonstration of their neutrality and disdain for war.

At the end of February 1777, Jane Boon went by boat to Wilmington to visit her aunt. Such a trip would soon be impossible, not just because of the dangers of traveling, but because Jenny had become indispensable in the Drinker household. As servants left, there were no replacements to be found, and the girl had taken on greater responsibilities. In May 1777, after five and one-half years with the Drinkers, Nanny Oat left to return home. Apparently, the Drinkers never gave her the clothing required by law, because four months later she called "to demand her freedom dues."[34] Elizabeth often was irritated when servants left her, and perhaps she had not been satisfied with Nanny's work, but the girl seems to have been justified in asking for her legal due. But Elizabeth was in no mood for "so much impudance"[35] from a former servant; Nanny could not have come at a worse time. In August, six-year-old Henry Drinker had become violently ill with intestinal worms and remained so sick that Jenny had to carry him up and down the stairs. Then, the revolutionary authorities had confiscated a valuable pair of andirons as part of a campaign to remove any metal items that could be melted down and used by the approaching British. In early September came the worst blow. Pennsylvania's radical authorities seized Henry Drinker and twenty other men, mostly Quakers, for being "disaffected to the American cause" and apt "to communicate intelligence to the enemy."[36] Henry claimed that the charges were disingenuous, that the real complaint was that the imprisoned men owned more than their fair share of wealth—"a Crime of a deep dye indeed!"[37] The prisoners were held at the Masonic Lodge until, a little over one week later, they were sent to Virginia. In the midst of all this turmoil, Nanny Oat and her father came demanding the clothes she was owed. After several such visits, and nine months after she had left, the Drinkers finally gave her some of her freedom dues.

Another servant was even more troublesome. When the British soldiers arrived in town, young girls such as Ann Kelly found them irresistable. "I have not been able to keep [her] from the Gate and Front-Door since the troops came in . . . she had so many of that sort after her," Elizabeth wrote to Henry. "We miss her much less than I could have expected."[38] Ann's departure was dramatic, indeed. One November evening, Jenny went into the yard and saw Ann with a young officer. Mary Sandwith accosted him, and he followed her into the house and threatened the family with his sword. The women locked themselves and the children in the parlor, and "our poor dear Children was never so frightend, to have An enrag'd, drunken Man, as I believe he was, with a Sword in his Hand, swareing about the House."[39] The incident was over within a matter of minutes, with the young man and Ann escaping over the fence. The next day, Elizabeth was still "in a flutter all day," but she had regained her nerve by the time she saw Ann's "Gallant" on the street two months later. She sternly told him, "If thee has no sense of Religion or Virtue, I should think that what you Soliders call Honor would have dictated to thee what was thy duty after thy behavour some time ago in this House."[40] When Ann came to offer to buy out the remainder of her time, Mary Sandwith threatened her with "puting her in the Work House,"[41] the city's prisonlike institution where the poor were forced to work for their maintenance. Elizabeth threatened to expose Ann's lover to his superior officers who were staying in the homes of her friends.

For some time, Elizabeth Drinker had successfully avoided taking a British officer into her own home. Unlike the Americans, who had ordered the Drinkers to quarter soldiers, the British at first politely requested housing. The first request came just ten days after their triumphant arrival in the city, and two days after the Battle of Germantown, northwest of the city. The sick and wounded, both British soldiers and American prisoners, were filling all the available public buildings, including churches, the theater, and the second floor of the State House (now Independence Hall). The initial request fulfilled Elizabeth's expectation of British gentility, a sharp contrast to the rough force imposed by the Americans: "An officer call'd this Afternoon to ask if we could take in a Sick or Wounded Captain; I put him off by saying that as my Husband was from me, I should be pleas'd if he could provide some other convenient place, he hop'd no offence, and departed."[42] Over the next few months, there were more requests. The British had already taken over many homes deserted by their owners when the American forces left Philadelphia, but the wealthy Quakers who remained owned some of the largest, most sought-after houses. Drinker continued to put them off, saying that she and her sister were "lone women" who could not quarter a strange man.[43] She had begun to hear horror stories from other women who had to put up with abuse from the British officers who lived with them: drunken and violent behavior, foul language, and no freedom of movement within their own homes. An officer turned away from Owen Jones's house swore at the family, drew his sword, and had his men hack the front door to pieces. Officers at Mary Eddy's house would not allow her to use her front door, but forced her and her family to use the back alley, which was ordinarily used only by servants.

At the same time, there were more and more frightening incidents at night. One night, Elizabeth thought she heard someone trying to open a window from the alley. Another night, when they saw two soldiers in the alley, Elizabeth and Mary went downstairs and loudly asked Harry Catter "if John and Tom were yet in Bed, Harry answered yes, Sister ordr'd him to untye the Dog and then come in."[44] There was no "John" or "Tom" in the house, but the "lone women" hoped to scare off would-be burglars by making them think men were there. From the window of Elizabeth's bedroom,

Jenny could see two men in the alley carrying a large bundle of clothing belonging to the baker's wife next door.

After several nighttime scares, Elizabeth began to see an advantage to having a British officer living in the house. She finally gave in to the persistent requests of Major Crammond, who convinced her that he was "a thoughtful sober young man, his Servant also sober and orderly."[45] He moved in at the end of December; immediately there were signs that things might not go smoothly. He came with "3 Horses 3 Cows 2 Sheep and 2 Turkeys with several Fowls, in our Stable," and "3 Servants 2 White Men and One Negro Boy" as well as "3 Hessians who take their turns to wate on him as Messengers or orderly men as they call'd em so that we have enough of such sort of Company."[46] The major sometimes stayed out late or had loud visitors. Yet, in spite of her complaints, Elizabeth seems to have liked the young man and frequently had him to tea. She wrote her husband in February to reassure him that the major and his entourage behaved as well as might be expected, that "we have neither Swareing or Gameing under our Roof, that we know of." The German orderlies were Anspachers, among the many mercenary soldiers hired by the British from the Prince of Anspach, southeast of Hesse, "great Creatures, who each day alternately set in our Kitchen or at Wells, to take orders." Elizabeth told her husband, "these 4 foreigners appear to be inofensive civel men, and behave with Decorum."[47]

By April 1778, Henry and the other suspected traitors had been in Virginia for seven months. Elizabeth and several other "destitute women"[48] decided to deliver a petition they had written to Congress and the Pennsylvania Assembly asking for the men's release. "[We] request you will take no offence at the freedom of women," they wrote, explaining that only the needs of their families had led them to take political action unusual for women. The right to petition, later enshrined in the First Amendment, was one of the few political rights women had. At Valley Forge, the women briefly visited George Washington, who granted them a pass to go through American lines to Lancaster. By the end of the month, the men were released, and Elizabeth was reunited with her husband, who was "much hartier than I expected, he look fat and well."[49] Perhaps as a prisoner in Virginia, Henry had fared better than his family at home, who were struggling with food shortages, although Elizabeth had assured him that, though firewood was scarce and food prices high, "we have wanted for nothing absolutely necessary."[50]

During Elizabeth's nearly month-long absence, Jenny must have had more work than ever. Wartime increased everyone's work, especially servants'. Shortages meant that some items ordinarily purchased were now made at home; in 1779, Elizabeth supervised candle making, although earlier she had been able to buy candles from a Quaker friend. She continued to pay tailors and dressmakers, who came as usual to fit her and the children at home. In peacetime, she sent her laundry out to be done by black or mulatto women who made their living as washerwomen, but wartime may have meant that laundry had to be done at home, or not done at all. Ironing was a frequently mentioned activity before and after the war, but now it may have gone by the wayside, as did housecleaning. Shopping became simpler in some ways, since shops were often closed, and on market days, when country farmers traditionally came to sell their goods, there was often "little to sell."[51] Food shortages meant that often there was not much of a variety of food to be cooked. On the other hand, shopping for necessities became more complicated because goods were so scarce and prices so high. At the height of the British occupation, Elizabeth noted the high prices of food: "Provisions are so scarce with us now, that Jenney gave 2/6p lb. for mutton this morning—The people round the Country dose not come near us with any thing, what little butter is brought is 7/6."[52] Farmers had to brave American sentinels in the countryside and British soldiers in town. Either side was likely to seize their goods coming into town or their profits going home. Generally the Drinkers did not suffer much because they could afford to pay inflated prices and they could send their servants out to do the shopping, made so much more time consuming by the war. Elizabeth continued to do charitable deeds as well, with the servants' help. Several times, she sent Jenny and Harry Catter to carry coffee and medicine to the wounded soldiers at the State House and other public buildings. Even charity brought additional work for servants.

In the midst of all this work, Jenny seems to have noticed one of the German orderlies, Philip Sibbal. Or perhaps he noticed her. The couple may have needed Harry Catter to interpret for them at first, which must have made the relationship all the more difficult to keep secret in such a full house, especially if Jenny slept in Elizabeth's bedroom, as maids often did. Elizabeth had other things on her mind: fear that the British were planning to leave Philadelphia mingled with her disillusionment with their behavior. On May 18, she was disgusted at the festivities honoring General William Howe with parades of coaches on the streets and decorated boats on the river, cannon salutes, and fireworks: "How insensible do these people appear, while our Land is so greatly desolated, and Death and sore destruction has overtaken and impends over so many."[53] Her political sympathies may have been with the British, but she had many personal friends on the American side who had been killed or injured. In June, Major Crammond and the two regiments of Anspachers received orders to embark. Harry Catter had finished his indenture several months earlier, and now he chose to leave with the British as a wagon driver. On the morning of June 18, Philadelphians arose to find "not one Red Coat to be seen in Town."[54] By that time, Philip Sibbal had decided to desert; perhaps he simply took off his uniform and stayed behind in Philadelphia, where he could melt in with the resident German population.

At the end of June, Jenny became ill with "colic," or abdominal pains. Three of the Drinker children came down with what their mother called "the flux," or intestinal illness. Jenny does not seem to have been as sick; perhaps her sickness was a symptom of something else. After mentioning her illness twice, Elizabeth Drinker is strangely silent about Jenny. Maybe she was preoccupied with her own children's illnesses; she often did not take sick servants very seriously, since they might have pretended to be sick to avoid work. Elizabeth may have had suspicions that Jenny's ailment was the morning sickness of pregnancy. Elizabeth would not have wanted to write of that, in line with her principle of not recording "any thing that might in a future day give pain to any one."[55] There is no further mention of the girl until mid-August, when Elizabeth noted that Jenny was leaving to go to her aunt in Wilmington, "who has wrote for her."[56] Yet Jenny continued to visit Elizabeth Drinker for the next few weeks, until September 7, when "a Negro Woman brought a Letter this Morning for Jane Sibal, formerly Boon; so that Janny [*sic*] is I suppose married to Philip one of the Majors orderly men."[57]

With the British departure, the worst of the servant shortage seemed to be over. The Drinkers hired Molly Lahew to start work the same day Jenny left. Then came "little John Pope," who stayed about sixteen months. "Black Peter" replaced Harry Catter in the stable; when he left a week later, they quickly hired "Black Isaac." Philadelphia's free blacks were able to take advantage of the absence of many white workers who had joined the military on one side or the other, and of the halt to the indentured servant trade from Europe and England. The relief for Elizabeth's servant problem was only temporary. Within a couple of months, she reported that Molly Lahew was misbehaving; Molly went out on a Saturday night and was still missing Sunday night. In December, Betsy Stedman came to live with the Drinkers; she had been a maid for the Drinkers' Quaker neighbors, Abraham and Ann Carlisle, until November 1778, when the Americans executed Abraham as a traitor for working with the British during the occupation. His widow probably could not afford to keep her servants, and so fellow

Quakers like the Drinkers found places for them. Within two days, Elizabeth regretted hiring Betsy Stedman: "Our new Maid has had a visitor all day and has invited hir to lodge with her, without asking leave, times are much changed, and Maids are become mistresses."[58]

Elizabeth's perception was that war and radical politics had given servants new ideas, that the "lower sort" of people now had pretensions of rising above their station in life, actually a perpetual complaint about servants, not new either in America or England. But the Revolution did bring new circumstances, allowing male servants to become soldiers and female servants to escape servitude. The resulting shortage of servants may have given a new sense of strength or independence to the servants who stayed behind. Fewer immigrants came as indentured servants, but well into the nineteenth century printed indenture forms continued to be used for apprenticeships, in which boys learned the mercantile business or a craft such as cabinetmaking and girls learned "the art, trade, and mystery of housewifery."[59] By the 1790s, the Drinkers found a new source of servants, black children bound to them under Pennsylvania's 1780 Gradual Abolition Act, which provided that blacks born after its passage would be free but had to be bound to white families until the age of twenty-eight. Other Quaker families took in American Indian children, who received some education in exchange for their household labor.

Jane Sibbal did become mistress of her own household, in Easton, Pennsylvania, where the American military had maintained its stores during the war. From this site at the Forks of the Delaware River some sixty miles north of Philadelphia, she returned several times in the 1780s and 1790s to visit the Drinkers, usually on her way to Newport, Delaware, "on Busyness for her Husband,"[60] as Elizabeth put it, although in reality Jenny seems to have been a real partner in a family business. The Drinker home provided her with a convenient place to stay on her journey. She usually brought one of her children—first her son Henry and then her daughter Ann—and they stayed in the old nursery where Jenny had once cared for Molly. Unlike many former servants who returned to visit, Jane did not come looking for charity and did not elicit pity. Jane's husband was successful, Elizabeth reported in 1795, adding a bit of ethnic stereotyping: he was "in business at Easttown as a Physician, sells medicine, and makes money fast, German like."[61] In 1795, Jenny's son Henry, who must have been about fourteen, came alone to visit the Drinkers. In 1800, Jenny and Philip moved to Campingtown, just north of the city, where the British barracks had stood in 1778, but they moved back to

Northampton County within a few years. Jenny's last recorded visit to her old mistress was in 1801. Census and tax records show that Philip Sibbal did not own a great deal of land or livestock—one acre and one cow—but he and his wife evidently achieved a modicum of success. Jenny herself does not appear in public records at all. The early census records note only the names of heads of households, with numbers only for the other members of a household. The only public notice of Jenny's existence may be the numeral "1" in the column for "white females 45 and older" living in Philip "Sybolt's" household in Upper Mount Bethel Township, Northampton County, in 1820. Farmer Henry "Sibolt" who lived nearby was probably their son. In nearby Forks Township lived four families with the surname "Seiple," another variant spelling, who may have been related.

Of the other young people Jane had worked with in the Drinker household, George Baker was the most successful. He became an officer in the Continental Army, went into business, married a German woman, and served for ten years as the city treasurer of Philadelphia. His older brother Hilary was mayor of Philadelphia when he died in the yellow fever epidemic of 1798. The German servant, whom Jenny was closest to, Harry Catter, survived his stint as a driver in the war but had fallen on hard times by 1797, when he came to visit the Drinkers on the pretext of picking up his indenture papers. "We gave him some of his Masters old cloaths," Elizabeth wrote, "he wants to borrow, or rather beg, mony to buy Oxen."[62] Nanny Oat disappeared from both the diary and the public record after the Revolution, but Elizabeth continued to have a bad opinion of her family. When Jesse Oat, perhaps Nanny's brother, applied in 1805 to become a member of the Society of Friends, Elizabeth caustically wrote, "If they had no better opinion of the family than I have, they would have nothing to do with them."[63] Quakers looked after one another, and Elizabeth often suspected that poorer people applied for membership as a way of getting easy access to charity. Her animus toward the Oat family seems to have gone beyond her usual suspicions; perhaps behind it lay the unpleasant memory of being separated from her infant son while Sarah Oat took care of him. Ann Kelly's common name makes her impossible to trace for certain in the records; she disappeared from Elizabeth's diary after being threatened with the workhouse. In the 1790s, a Mary Kelly made curtains and bed hangings for Elizabeth and her now-married children, but Elizabeth mentions no relationship to Ann.

Of course, we know much more about the Drinkers' life after the Revolution than we do about any of their servants. Henry Drinker never resumed his mercantile business. Instead, he turned to a variety of moneymaking ventures, including an ironworks, a sawmill, a maple sugar farm, and—most lucrative of all—investment and speculation in western lands. In 1781, when she was forty-six years old, Elizabeth Drinker gave birth to a ninth child, Charles, who was "little more than Skin and Bone" at birth. She hired a succession of wetnurses but they either became sick or were dismissed as "by no means sutted,"[64] and in the end Elizabeth nursed the baby herself, waiting to wean him until he was more than twenty-six months old, later than she had weaned any of her other children. A few months later, she was gratified to note that he was "fat, fresh and hearty," but then he suddenly became ill and the doctor ordered a purging. Twenty minutes afterward, he died, "my dear little Companion over whome, I had almost constantly watchd, from the time of his birth."[65]

Elizabeth lived to see all her surviving children marry well, except for Billy, who was chronically ill and never married. Sally and Nancy both were married in their mid-twenties to established Quaker merchants. Molly, the baby Jenny Boon had cared for, eloped at age twenty-two to marry a young Quaker man. Her father had expressed his disapproval of the match, and Molly was estranged for several months, causing immense distress to her mother. Finally, they were reconciled, and Elizabeth was with her youngest daughter during her first confinement, which ended in a stillbirth. Molly went on to have four children. Of her older sisters, Sally had five children and Nancy, three. Their brother Henry and his wife, Hannah, had fourteen children. In their later years, the Drinkers welcomed a steady stream of grandchildren into their home. Elizabeth Drinker suffered her deepest loss when Sally ("my first born darling") died after a long illness in 1807; she reflected that now "my first, my 3d. my 5th, 7th. and 9th are in their graves."[66] A few months later, in November 1807, Elizabeth Drinker herself was dead at the age of seventy-two. Her husband died two years later, and her sister, in 1815.

All her life, Elizabeth Drinker's family remained among the well-to-do Philadelphia elite, but at times she believed that the Revolution had turned society upside down, transforming servants into masters. In reality, the social upheaval was hardly universal. Most servants—like Ann Oat, Ann Kelly, and Harry Catter—started life poor and probably remained poor most of their lives. Young men like Hilary and George Baker began life more favorably, better educated and able to work as apprentices in Henry Drinker's business rather than as common servants. Few former servants had even such modest success as Jenny Boon, but that success certainly never made her the social equal of her former mistress. Still, she had emerged from servitude and the Revolution as the wife of a fairly successful physician, and Elizabeth Drinker at least thought everything had turned out quite well for her former servant. We can only speculate whether Jenny Boon herself was content with the changes the Revolution had brought.

Notes

1. Elizabeth Drinker, *The Diary of Elizabeth Drinker*, ed. Elaine Forman Crane, 3 vols. (Boston: Northeastern University Press, 1991), 1:232.

2. Diary of Sarah Logan Fisher, printed in Nicholas B. Wainwright, "A Diary of Trifling Occurrences: Philadelphia, 1776–1778," *Pennsylvania Magazine of History and Biography* 82 (1958): 450. Hereafter cited as *PMHB*.

3. Drinker, *Diary*, 1:232.

4. Ibid., 1:235.

5. Ibid., 1:286–87.

6. Ibid., 1:269.

7. Elizabeth Drinker (hereafter, ED) to Henry Drinker (hereafter, HD), July 12, 1771, Drinker Sandwith Papers, Historical Society of Pennsylvania (HSP), Philadelphia. Hereafter cited as Drinker Sandwith Papers.

8. *Pennsylvania Gazette* (Philadelphia), April 1, 1756.

9. Drinker, *Diary*, 3:2086, 2:1192.

10. ED to HD, July 13, 1771, Drinker Sandwith Papers.

11. Diary of Ann Warder, January 15, 1787, HSP, cited in Drinker, *Diary*, 1:xi.

12. "Notes and Queries," *PMHB* 13 (1889): 122.

13. Drinker, *Diary*, 1:5–89 passim.

14. Ibid., 199.

15. Ibid., 207.

16. Ibid., 2:1182.

17. Ibid., 1:321.

18. Ibid., 209.

19. Ibid., 233, 260.

20. *Pennsylvania Gazette*, July 21, 1763.

21. Drinker, *Diary*, 1:204.

22. Ibid., 208.

23. Ibid., 3:1368.

24. Ibid., 1:131.

25. Ibid., 197.

26. Ibid.

27. Ibid., 199.

28. John Drinker, *Observations on the Late Popular Measures* (Philadelphia, 1774), quoted in Steven Rosswurm, *Arms, Country,*

and Class: The Philadelphia Militia and the "Lower Sort" during the American Revolution, 1775–1783 (New Brunswick, NJ: Rutgers University Press, 1987), 42.

29. Drinker, *Diary*, 3:1252.

30. Russell F. Weigley, *Philadelphia: A 300-Year History* (New York: W. W. Norton, 1982), 124.

31. Drinker, *Diary*, 1:225.

32. Ibid., 218.

33. Ibid., 224.

34. Ibid., 233.

35. Ibid., 243.

36. W. C. Ford et al., eds., *Journals of the Continental Congress*, 34 vols. (Washington, DC: U.S. Government Printing Office, 1904–1937), 8:694, quoted in Weigley, *Philadelphia*, 132.

37. HD to ED, January 26, 1778, Drinker Sandwith Papers.

38. ED to HD, December 3, 1777, Drinker Sandwith Papers.

39. Drinker, *Diary*, 1:258.

40. Ibid., 259, 273.

41. Ibid., 260.

42. Ibid., 240–41.

43. Ibid., 266.

44. Ibid., 264.

45. Ibid., 271.

46. Ibid., 272.

47. ED to HD, February 26, 1778, Drinker Sandwith Papers.

48. ED to HD, December 27, 1777, Drinker Sandwith Papers.

49. Drinker, *Diary*, 1:302.

50. ED to HD, November 17, 1777, Drinker Sandwith Papers.

51. Drinker, *Diary*, 1: 259.

52. Ibid., 246–47.

53. Ibid., 306.

54. Ibid., 311.

55. Ibid., 2:1253.

56. Ibid., 1:321.

57. Ibid., 325.

58. Ibid., 337.

59. Indenture between Elizabeth Midcaf and John Rudolph, September 5, 1828, Society Miscellaneous Collection 9c, folder 9, Indentures—Housewifery, HSP.

60. Drinker, *Diary*, 1:440.

61. Ibid., 756.

62. Ibid., 2:903.

63. Ibid., 3:1865.

64. Ibid., 1:391.

65. Ibid., 420.

66. Ibid., 3:2080.

Suggested Readings

The manuscript diary of Elizabeth Drinker and most of her family papers are at the Historical Society of Pennsylvania (HSP) in Philadelphia. Other family papers are in the Quaker Library, Haverford College, Haverford, Pennsylvania. Genealogical information is in the collections of the Genealogical Society of Pennsylvania, at HSP, as well as the *Pennsylvania Genealogical Magazine* and the *Pennsylvania Magazine of History and Biography (PMHB)*, with its cumulative index following volume 75. I have used microfilm censuses, tax lists, wills, deeds, and Orphans' Court records at the Pennsylvania State Archives in Harrisburg, and military records at the David Library of the American Revolution in Washington Crossing, Pennsylvania. The complete diary has been published as *The Diary of Elizabeth Drinker*, ed. Elaine Forman Crane, 3 vols. (Boston: Northeastern University Press, 1991); an abridged edition was published in 1994. Other primary sources are Billy G. Smith, *Life in Early Philadelphia: Documents from the Revolutionary and Early National Periods* (University Park: Pennsylvania State University Press, 1995); and Catherine La Courreye Blecki and Karin A. Wulf, *Milcah Martha Moore's Book: A Commonplace Book from Revolutionary America* (University Park: Pennsylvania State University Press, 1997).

Historians have recently turned their attention to servants and other members of the "lower sort"; for work on Pennsylvania, see Billy G. Smith, *The "Lower Sort": Philadelphia's Laboring People, 1750–1800* (Ithaca, NY: Cornell University Press, 1990); Sharon V. Salinger, *"To Serve Well and Faithfully": Labor and Indentured Servants in Pennsylvania, 1682–1800* (New York: Cambridge University Press, 1987); Steven Rosswurm, *Arms, Country, and Class: The Philadelphia Militia and the "Lower Sort" during the American Revolution, 1775–1783* (New Brunswick, NJ: Rutgers University Press, 1987). For the city, see Russell F. Weigley, *Philadelphia: A 300-Year History* (New York: W. W. Norton, 1982); and Thomas M. Doerflinger, *A Vigorous Spirit of Enterprise: Merchants and Economic Development in Revolutionary Philadelphia* (Chapel Hill: University of North Carolina Press, 1986). On Quakers, see Margaret Hope Bacon, *Mothers of Feminism: The Story of Quaker Women in America* (San Francisco: Harper & Row, 1986); Elizabeth Potts Brown and Susan Mosher Stuard, eds., *Quaker Women over Three Centuries* (New Brunswick, NJ: Rutgers University Press, 1986); and Jack D. Marietta, *The Transformation of American Quakerism, 1748–1783* (Philadelphia: University of Pennsylvania Press, 1984). Pennsylvania women are the focus of Joan M.

Jensen, *Loosening the Bonds: Mid-Atlantic Farm Women, 1750–1850* (New Haven, CT: Yale University Press, 1986), and a special issue on women's history of *PMHB* 107 (1983), no. 1. Loyalists, including Quakers, are the subject of a special issue of *Pennsylvania History* 62 (1995), no. 3.

10

Mary Brant (Konwatsi'tsiaienni Degonwadonti)

"Miss Molly," Feminist Role Model or Mohawk Princess?

Katherine M. J. McKenna

Descended from Mohawk chiefs, Mary Brant (ca. 1736–1796) was a female clan leader among the matrilineal Iroquois, but she also served the British as an intercultural broker and loyalist diplomat. Brant lived as the wife of Sir William Johnson, the British superintendent of Indian Affairs, until his death in 1774. Johnson had urged peace and noninvolvement among the Iroquois; British commanders credited Brant with the continued loyalism of the Iroquois during the Revolution. She assisted refugee loyalists, provided military intelligence, and was rewarded with a handsome British pension at war's end. Was Mary Brant able to use the memory of Johnson to secure Iroquois allegiance to Britain, or did tribal chiefs respond to her identity as a Iroquois matriarch?

Although fearful for the safety of her brother, Joseph Brant, a prominent loyalist warrior, and her two sons, Mary differed from most loyalist women in that her wartime activities were not limited to passive worrying about home and family. Few women expressed political opinions as Brant did. As the title poses it, could she be considered an eighteenth-century feminist? The Iroquois employed her as a diplomatic confidant, even though she had anglicized herself and had even left her daughters in Montreal to receive a genteel education. Mary herself had been educated in English schools and had lived in European-style houses, including her father's and Johnson's. Did British acquaintances emphasize her Indian background or her Englishness? By the end of the Revolution, and as a result of their allegiance to Britain, had Mary and Joseph become more or less attached to European customs? They had abandoned neutrality and joined the British in the hope of choosing the winner and protecting their lands and their way of life, but the American victory ultimately challenged Iroquois land claims south of the Great Lakes.

Katherine M. J. McKenna is the director of the Centre for Women's Studies and Feminist Research at the University of Western Ontario, London, and the author of *A Life of Propriety: Anne Murray Powell and Her Family, 1755–1849* (1994).

The American Revolution could be a dislocating experience for those who were caught up in the front lines of the conflict. For history's designated "losers," the loyalists, it was even more devastating. Many who would have preferred to remain neutral felt forced into the Tory camp for protection against the harassment of patriot committees of safety. Many women married to men suspected of being Tories were left to face looting patriot mobs when their husbands were captured or forced to flee for their lives. For them, the revolutionary conflict could be terrifying and perilous. But, it can be argued, no group lost more as a consequence of siding with the king of England than the mighty Six Nations Iroquois Confederacy. The Six Nations was a political and social union of the Seneca, Oneida, Mohawk, Cayuga, Onondaga, and Tuscarora, dating from as far back as the middle of the fifteenth century. Initially the Six Nations had tried to maintain a stance of neutrality as the white brothers around them feuded. The Great Covenant Chain that bound them in kinship to their English Father, King George III, and which had been constantly reinforced through lavish gifts and hospitality from the English Department of Indian Affairs, proved stronger in the end. The war turned out to be a disaster for the Six Nations, splitting the Confederacy and forcing many into exile on reserves in Canada. At the center of this historic tragedy stands a Mohawk woman, Mary Brant.

Mary Brant, whose name is known to history primarily through the records of white English colonial authorities, remains an enigma for us today. She left behind scarcely any written accounts of her own, so our vision of her thoughts and feelings emerges through the dark glass of second- and thirdhand accounts. Commentators on her life have left a wide variety of images for us to choose from. She is known by two Mohawk names: Konwatsi't-si-aienni (Someone Lends Her a Flower) and Degonwadonti (Two Against One). The first might have been her birth name; the second, after the custom of the Iroquois, was given her as she reached adulthood. The images that the names present, one of delicate femininity, the other of strength in adversity, are in themselves reflective of differing interpretations of her life. She is sometimes seen as a powerful political force in Mohawk society, an Iroquois princess descended from a long line of Mohawk nobility, related to the famous Iroquois chief "King Hendrick," proud, haughty, even at times bloodthirsty. Or she is portrayed as the unmarried "housekeeper" consort to her Lord and Master, the Irishman Sir William Johnson, Baronet, superintendent of Indian Affairs, colonel of the Six Nations, and wealthy landowner. In this role, referred to by European commentators as "Miss Molly," she presided over Johnson's estate and bore him nine children. After his death, according to this version, she stepped into his shoes as his widow and thus, in the eyes of the Indians, adopted his enormous prestige as an influencer of her Mohawk brethren. She was simply following in Sir William's footsteps, without really understanding the implications of the choice to reject the patriot side. Others, in contrast, see her as a devoted loyalist to the crown out of a firm and well-thought-out personal conviction. Mary and her more famous brother, Joseph Brant, are also variously portrayed in the historical record as totally assimilated in white society culturally, and thus suspect to the Mohawks, while at the same time remaining somehow "untamed" and undependable for the whites who were forced by the fortunes of war to rely on their faithfulness.

These inconsistencies reflect not only the scarcity of sources available on Mary's life but also the crude stereotypes of Iroquois culture that dominate much thinking even today. In the eighteenth century, contradictory views were held about Native North Americans. On the one hand, they were viewed as "noble savages" by Enlightenment thinkers such as Jean-Jacques Rousseau. Natives were seen as being uncorrupted by the vices of civilization so evident in the decadent political and cultural climate of Europe. Their nearness to a natural state in the eyes of Europeans meant that their inborn sense of justice was unclouded; their inner voice spoke with a true, clear voice. On the other hand, philosophers such as John Locke and Thomas Hobbes viewed them as lesser-developed beings, living in an uncertain and even hostile "state of nature" without benefit of such civilizing practices as property ownership, and with only the crudest form of self-regulation in government. Even today we can discern these opposing stereotypes. In terms of the historical record, some see the Iroquois Confederacy of the Five (later Six) Nations as an ancient protodemocracy. They argue that it might have even served as a model for the framers of the U.S. Constitution, as well as providing a model of gender equity for nineteenth-century feminists. Others regard the Six Nations as a primitive political structure, adequate for the purpose of containing and channeling Native aggression outward. It could work well only so long as society was relatively simple, but was unable to sustain itself in the face of the complexity of colonial politics and fractured under the pressures of the American revolutionary conflict. The difficulty of analyzing the culture of people who recorded their history in oral traditions and with belts of wampum must be acknowledged. Iroquois society is so different from the dominant culture of today's North America, and so little can be known of its characteristics before white contact, that it is very difficult to prevent white European values from coloring one's interpretation.

Iroquois society is particularly appealing to contemporary feminists, because it appears to offer a model of female political power and autonomy, especially when compared to European and American societies. Historians who once hoped to restore the women of the past with political convictions to the historical record have discovered that only rarely did loyalist or patriot women express their opinions on the momentous political matters of the Revolution. Instead, historians have found women on both sides to be frustratingly indifferent to political rhetoric, irritatingly pathetic in their conventional appeals to male protectors in the face of the armed conflict, and myopically concerned with home and family while great world events swirled around them. The number who, like Mercy Otis Warren and Abigail Adams, had well thought out political analyses and could exhort their powerful husbands, as Adams did, to "remember the ladies" was insignificant in comparison with the generality.

Of course, this censure of the women of the past revealed much more about historians' assumptions than it did about history. By abandoning this critical stance toward these women, we can perhaps understand them on their own terms. Women of eighteenth-century America, although much more involved in the public world than their Victorian descendants were to be, inhabited the domestic sphere to a much greater extent than men did. Their literacy rate was much lower than that of men, for formal education was not deemed essential to their future as wives and mothers. They did not have access to the same public meeting places and the newspapers that shaped many men's opinions of the conflict. They were normally barred from formal participation in public, political activities. The fate of most women was determined by the fortunes of their fathers and husbands. Many of those who were consequently labeled Tories were forced to leave their homes under the attack of patriot mobs, who judged their political loyalty by their husbands' allegiance. Most of them, even those who abhorred the conflict, would have been happy to have remained in their neighborhoods with friends and family close by. Many returned from what they felt as exile to the newly formed American Republic as soon as things settled down after the war, often joined by their husbands. Even among men, a relatively small number had well-articulated political rationalizations of their positions. Often whether men were patriot or loyalist had more to do with circumstance, long-standing community conflicts, and the polarizing effect of the local Revolutionary Committees of Safety.

Mary Brant thus stands in sharp contrast to other women of the revolutionary period. Her intervention was directly responsible for keeping the Iroquois Nation on the side of the British, and she was respected by both American and British colonial authorities. She was an excellent example of what we might call today a "cultural broker," a person who was able to function as an effective communicator between the essentially incompatible European and Six Nations' worldviews. She was not the only woman who was granted such power within Native society. Sarah Cass McGinn, another famous example, had lived among the Iroquois as a child, and was considered one of them. She had sufficient political influence to intercept and cancel a wampum belt containing a message from General Philip Schuyler to the Six Nations warning them to make peace with Congress. She was recognized by the British as a strategic individual in ensuring Iroquois loyalty and often advised at tribal councils. Why were there no women of parallel stature in other communities? Was there something different about Iroquois society?

The status of women in Iroquois society has been a subject of much debate. The consensus that has emerged is that women in the Six Nations were very differently placed from women in white European society. They were not, however, the matriarchal rulers that some would make them. Nor were they equal to men in the liberal feminist sense of equality. Women's political power was not the same as men's power in Iroquois society; rather, it was parallel. Men inhabited the world of the forest, the battle, and the hunt, and women the sphere of the clearing. This division was not at all like the traditional Western restriction of women to the home. Women "owned" all of the aspects of communal life, not in the Western sense of property ownership, but as the acknowledged possessors and leaders of the households. Women lived together with children in the home of the clan matriarch, and men drifted in and out. When a man married, he left the home of his mother and moved into that of his wife. Men contributed the fruits of the hunt—meat and fur. Women cultivated the land and provided the staples that sustained life—the "three sisters," corn, beans, and squash. Men did the heaviest work of clearing the fields and built the homes anew when the tribe moved to fresh land, as the soil was depleted every ten or twenty years.

Although men were the orators and led diplomatic missions, their legitimacy as chiefs was bestowed on them by the head of the council of matrons. Powerful families normally traced their lineage through the female line, not the male, which was logical in a nonpatriarchal society, where one's mother was one's constant parent while fathers came and went. This matrilineal structure is often mistaken for matriarchy. The males led what was essentially a consensual political structure as the chief negotiators, but all members of the tribe, male and female alike, had the ability to veto decisions by ignoring them, and only public acceptance could ensure that the leaders' rulings would be upheld. Men made the decisions in terms of war or peace, but the opinion of women had great influence, and war parties could be vetoed by the ritualistic act of women's refusing to provide provisions for the warpath. When adult male foes were captured in battle, women alone decided whether they were to be killed or adopted as replacements for the men lost from their household, and their decision was inviolable. Old women, in an oral culture in which young and aggressive men often died in battle, were highly revered and even, on occasion, sought out as marriage partners by young men wishing to acquire wisdom. Marriage, although monogamous, was rarely lifelong, and divorce was commonplace. Children always stayed with their mothers. These gender roles were different, but complementary. Each sex had its sphere of power, and in many ways there were separate male and female cultures.

Fundamentally different divisions between men and women existed in white European society. That patriarchal system dictated that men owned all property and were the legal and social masters of their wives and children. Women had no political power, and any influence they exercised was due to the good will of the men in their lives or their good fortune in inheriting a man's property as a single woman and remaining so. A widowed woman without sons who inherited property might also become more influential and autonomous in her community. The widows of Tories would have had most of the family property confiscated in the Revolution, however. Thus it was not surprising that newly homeless loyalist women felt resourceless and confused and resorted to petitioning and begging for male assistance. The situation was very different for the self-sufficient and powerful Iroquois women leaders. Mary Brant's important role in the American Revolution sprang directly from her cultural roots as a Mohawk woman.

Mary Brant's parentage has been the subject of much confusion among her biographers. In true Iroquois fashion, only her mother, Margaret, a Mohawk woman, is definitely known to be her parent. Margaret probably had three husbands, the first two of whom died. At least one of these early husbands was reputed to be a great warrior. Her marriage to Chief Brant took place long after the birth of Mary and her younger brother Joseph, the famous loyalist warrior; in fact, Mary and Joseph may have been only half-siblings. Persistent legends have it that Mary was the granddaughter of the powerful Mohawk chief "King Hendrick," Theyanoguin, who was one of the Iroquois who visited Queen Anne in the early eighteenth century. This connection has never been proven, however. In taking on the Brant name after her mother's last marriage, Mary and Joseph were unusual. Perhaps their mother wished to rescue them from the comparative poverty and obscurity of their roots by associating them with the powerful female line her husband was born into. If so, this plan seems to have worked in the case of Mary, who later rose to a position of leadership among the women of her clan. This may also reflect the Iroquois attitude toward adoption; once adopted, one was not distinguished from those born into the family. Interestingly enough, although Mary was highly respected in Mohawk society, her brother, who was probably valued more by the British, was always seen by the Iroquois as a bit of an overly ambitious upstart.

Little is known about Mary Brant's early life. She was probably born in 1736 at the Mohawk settlement at Canajoharie in the Mohawk Valley, near the present-day town of Little Falls, New York, and was raised in that area. She may have been educated at a Church of England mission school, since she could both read and write with a fine hand. Her English was reputed to be impeccable by the standards of none other than Lady Simcoe, wife of the first governor of Upper Canada. As the daughter of a powerful Mohawk political family, her upbringing was anglicized in a number of ways. She resided in a European-style house that belonged to her father, and, as we have noted, took his name. Living in that household, she would have been privy to the comings and goings of numerous social and diplomatic guests. One of her earliest exposures to political negotiation came as a young woman in the winter of 1754–55, when she accompanied a delegation of twelve Mohawk male leaders to discuss the fraudulent sale of Native lands in the Wyoming Valley with officials at Philadelphia and Albany. In Albany, her exotic good looks were said to have greatly interested a young English captain, whose attraction was not reciprocated by Mary. Her stepfather was said to have been a friend of the powerful Sir William Johnson, and with him, indeed, it was quite a different story.

Sir William was a maverick, a man who found room in the North American wilderness for a freedom of style that he would never have been permitted at home. Born in 1715, the son of landed gentry in County Meath, Ireland, he came to the New World as a young man of twenty-three at the invitation of his uncle, Sir Peter Warren. Sir Peter lived at his luxurious estate on the site of what is now Greenwich Village in New York City, and had recently purchased a tract of thirteen hundred acres on the banks of the Mohawk River. Preferring not to move into this wilderness himself, he invited young William to manage the property and settle some families there. William prospered, presiding over the small empire like a minor potentate. In time he acquired his own land, eventually amassing an estate of some eighty thousand acres of land on the north shore of the Mohawk River. The turning point in William's fortunes from the perspective of the British authorities came in 1755, when during the Seven Years' War he led a detachment of militia against the French, soundly defeating them in the Battle of Lake George. For this, he came to the notice of the king, who gave him £5,000 and made him a baronet. This new-found status did not alter his unconventional style. Although a bachelor, he did not live alone. Since the year following his arrival in 1738, he had lived in a common-law state with the uneducated, indentured German servant Catherine Weisenberg. She had escaped from her master in New York when Johnson encountered her, so he bought her time and moved her into his home as his mistress. He had two daughters and a son by her (in addition to at least two sons by Native women) before her death in 1759. In his will he referred to her as his wife, and there is a story that he married her on her deathbed in order to legitimize their children, but there is no record of this. In any case, Sir William did not enter into a prolonged period of mourning.

Legend has it that Mary Brant first attracted Sir William's eye during a militia muster when a young officer jokingly agreed to her request for a ride. Expecting conventionally ladylike behavior from her, he invited her to jump up, which she did. The startled horse then galloped around the parade ground with Mary hanging on, her dark eyes flashing and long hair streaming behind her. Whether or not this highly romanticized tale is true, Mary and the aging Johnson were somehow brought together, most likely as a consequence of political meetings he would have held with her father. She bore him a child in 1759, probably conceived during Catherine's final illness. The quality of Johnson's attachment to her is revealed in the choice of name for the baby, Peter Warren Johnson, after his powerful benefactor and uncle, a name he had not bestowed on his children with Catherine Weisenberg. Mary moved into Sir William's residence, a blockhouse structure he called Fort Johnson, and four years later, he built an impressive large dwelling, Johnson Hall, where they lived with every possible comfort, surrounded by fine china and Chippendale furniture. Mary and William never married according to the forms of white society, but the Iroquois, who were indifferent to the European marriage ceremony, had no doubt that they were husband and wife. During their years together, until Johnson's death in 1774, Mary gave birth to nine children, eight of whom survived infancy. They were brought up with every available educational and material advantage. Johnson imported a tutor from England for them and sent the eldest son to school at Montreal.

The liaison of Brant and Johnson was a powerful one. Although Mary named her children Johnson, she retained her Mohawk surname, thereby keeping her family's prestige in the Iroquois community. As the wife of a man powerful in both Native and white society, she organized his household, supervised his numerous servants and black slaves, and entertained his many visitors. For the Iroquois, hospitality and gift-giving were important ways that leaders demonstrated and preserved their community position, and, as the dispenser of Johnson's largesse, Mary thereby greatly enhanced her own standing with her people. There are stories that as many as five hundred natives at a time would camp on the Johnson estate, expecting and receiving the bounty of the superintendent of Indian Affairs. White travelers, who also frequently stopped at Johnson Hall, described her as "Miss Molly," a courteous and charming hostess, entertaining in a European fashion, while at the same time retaining her Native dress. She was described as beautiful, fine-featured, and possessed of a quiet dignity, evidence of her reputed noble heritage and status among the Mohawk.

Johnson may not have regarded Mary in the same light as her own people did. He could not have failed to appreciate what his partnership with her did for his reputation among the Six Nations by uniting him with them by blood ties. There is evidence, however, that in European patriarchal style, he resisted her efforts to become more involved in diplomatic negotiations. In her own society, Mary progressively became first a clan mother, then the head of the clan mothers, a position of great power and influence. Her younger brother Joseph was virtually adopted by Sir William, and he too gained stature from the power of both his sister and her husband. William's constant absences on missions of diplomacy related to his position as superintendent of Indian Affairs meant that by default Mary handled many of his other affairs. This role increased as his health gradually deteriorated from the debilitating effects of old war wounds. His health reached a crisis point just as the pressures of his position also became grave. White settlers were increasingly encroaching on Native lands, and there was a real chance of armed conflict. In 1774 a critical meeting of the tribes was held on the Johnson estate. Sir William addressed the conference for two hours under the hot July sun, summoning all his physical resources to persuade the Iroquois to opt for peace. After he concluded, he collapsed into convulsions and shortly afterward died. He was sixty years old, Mary thirty-eight. Iroquois society was plunged into profound mourning for the loss of their friend and ally, their representative of the king in the New World.

After her husband's death, Mary's life changed. Because Johnson, in typical patriarchal European style, had willed his estate to John, his eldest son by Catherine Weisenberg, Mary left Johnson Hall. She returned to live among her people in Canajoharie, where she had her own house and supported herself by trading in rum. In his will, calling her his "housekeeper," Johnson had left her only a plot of land, a female slave, and £200. All the children were provided for, however, and later records of her losses in the Revolution indicate that she left Johnson Hall with a great deal more in movable property. There appear to have been no hard feelings on either Mary's or John Johnson's side at the time of her departure. At Canajoharie, her life was pleasant. She lived in a good house, enjoyed her status among her own people, and prospered in trade.

The Revolutionary War catapulted Mary Brant into greater prominence and simultaneously exiled her from her homeland. Her attachment to the crown through her long association with Johnson, as well as her own knowledge of the political benefits of siding with the British against the encroaching colonists, led her to choose the loyalist side in the conflict. When refugee loyalists hid in the woods, in flight through New York on their way to safety in Canada, Mary fed and assisted them. In August 1777 she dispatched runners to inform her brother Joseph, who was heading a force of Iroquois, that a large body of militia was advancing to attack the rear of the British forces besieging Fort Stanwix. This action resulted in a successful ambush of the patriot militia by loyalist and Iroquois forces. Led by John Johnson, they routed the patriots at Oriskany, which led to a major cleavage in the Six Nations. Many of the Oriska Indians, who were Oneida and had supported the patriot side, suffered in the fight, and they retaliated by attacking Canajoharie. Mary evacuated her home with her family just in time, leaving much valuable property behind. She fled to Cayuga, where the chief took her in.

One of Mary's most critical and famous interventions on behalf of the crown occurred in 1777 at Onondaga, near present-day Syracuse, which was the capital of the Six Nations Confederacy. The tribes were in a state of great crisis. Most of the Six Nations wished to cast their lot with the British king, who gave at least lip service to their traditional rights and was bound to them by the

Great Covenant Chain. In contrast, the colonial settlers thought nothing of stealing Iroquois land. The Six Nations, however, were dispirited over British chances of victory. They had lost many lives and much property on both sides of the recent conflict. At an important council that year about the matter, the leading war chief of the Iroquois Confederacy, the venerable Seneca Chief Sayenqueraghta wavered in his loyalty to the crown, urging a retreat from the conflict. According to Indian Agent Colonel Daniel Claus, Mary "had a pointed conversation with him," publicly criticizing his stand in front of the assembly, "reminding him of the former great Friendship & Attachment which subsisted between him and the late Sir Wm Johnson, whose memory she never mentions but with tears in her eyes, Which affects Indians greatly and to whom, continued she, he so often declared promises to live and die a firm Friend & Ally to the King of England and his Friends." This emotional appeal totally won over the council, who all pledged their continued allegiance. Mary's great prestige on her own account and as the widow of Sir William made her a very influential person. "One word from her," Claus observed, "is more taken notice of" by the Iroquois "than a thousand from any white man without exception."[1]

When, in the summer of 1777, Six Nations refugees began to pour into the military base at Fort Niagara, demanding to be housed, provisioned, and compensated by their British allies, Mary was urged to come there to help keep things in order. Colonel John Butler sent her "repeated & very Pressing & encouraging Messages to come & reside at Niagara." Mohawk etiquette demanded that she not leave hastily the homes of those friends who had welcomed her as their guest, but "at length she brought her leaving there about in such a manner that they could not take it amiss & parted with them in Friendship."[2] At Niagara she was very influential with the Six Nations; as Claus observed, "Mary Brant will outdo fifty Butlers in managing them."[3] The consequence was a great saving to the government, because the only way that a white commanding officer could control the Six Nations was by lavish gift-giving. Still, Mary was expected, as a leading political figure, to provide hospitality on a generous scale. "The Manner she lives here," pointed out Fort Niagara agents of the Montreal trading firm of Taylor and Duffin to Claus, "is pretty expensive to her, puts her to great expence being oblig'd to keep in a manner open house for all those Indians that have any weight in the 6 Natn Confederacy. We have told her we will not see her in want."[4]

In recognition of Brant's expenditures in the service of the crown, Claus sent her a trunkful of goods, and she was given some small sums of money from General Haldimand as well. She was grateful for this. "I am much obliged to you for the care & attention in sending me up those very necessary articles," she wrote to Claus in one of her few surviving letters, "& should be very glad if you have any accounts from New York that you would let me know them. . . . I hope the time is very near when we shall all return to our habitations on the Mohawk River."[5] Mary was anxious for her family to be reunited, and concerned for two of her children who had remained in New York, especially for her son Peter and Mohawk stepson William, both of whom, unknown to her, had died fighting for the British. She had a premonition about their deaths, expressing "great concern at the loss of her two sons being dear to her as being her children a loss to her that she cannot write her thoughts herself . . . were they still alive she thinks one of them might be with her sometimes."[6]

As hundreds of Iroquois poured into Fort Niagara throughout 1777 and 1778, the expense and trouble of providing for them horrified the British authorities. Although the loyalist Butler had urged her to come, the commanding officer, Colonel Mason Bolton, did not appreciate sharing his authority with a Mohawk woman who was used to speaking bluntly and giving forceful political advice. "She wishes to send you a true State of the Disposition of the Six Nations," Taylor and Duffin wrote to Claus, "and she observes plainly it would be useless for her to apply to a certain Gentleman here on account of his own opinion of his own self-sufficiency."[7] Bolton appealed to General Haldimand, who decided to pacify him by sending Mary to Montreal, under the guise of keeping her safe from threatened attack. Only the invitation of such an important personage could have persuaded Mary to leave her aged mother and family at Niagara. "She says," wrote Claus to Haldimand, "her leaving Niagara now is merely owing to your Excellency's kind & friendly Invitation, for it had first seemed very hard for her to leave her old Mother & her Indian relations & friends behind and live in a country where she was an entire stranger in, besides her absence would be regretted by the generality of the Five Nations, she having been their confidant in every Matter of Importance & was consulted thereupon, and prevented many an unbecoming proposal to the Commanding Officer at Niagara."[8] Clearly, Bolton did not recognize these contributions.

Mary did not stay long at Montreal, returning in the fall of 1779. The tide had turned against the Iroquois after the November 1778 battle of Cherry Valley, considered by the patriots to have been a brutal massacre of American settlers. It was led by John Butler's son Walter and joined by many from the Six Nations, including Joseph Brant. Patriot forces retaliated aggressively in the spring and summer of 1779. The Six Nations was broken, and the refugees poured into Niagara. Leaving behind her two youngest daughters to acquire a genteel education among the white community at Montreal, Mary returned to her people. Claus informed Haldimand that:

> Miss Molly, since hearing of the Movements of the Indians, is very desirous of returning among the six Nations, and says that her staying away at this critical Time, may prove very injurious to her character hereafter, being at the head of a society of six Natn Matrons, who have a great deal to say among the Young Men in particular in time of war, and it was with Difficulty she came away only for your Excellency's kind Invitation, tho' not without promise of returning soon, for if she was to forsake them now, they might impute it to fear, and that she foresaw or knew of an impending Danger over the Confederacy which she kept concealed and went out of the way to avoid it, which reflection would be insupportable to her.[9]

Haldimand deferred to her judgement on this. "As to Miss Molly," he wrote in reply to Claus, "if she thinks her presence necessary . . . she must be suffered to depart . . . of course provide for her journey, and give her whatever Presents may be necessary [to give to the Iroquois."][10]

Mary did not return to Niagara. She made it as far as Carleton Island, near present-day Kingston, Ontario, and found that her services were greatly needed there. She wrote Claus complaining that she had had a very "tedeous and disagreeable voyage." Mary was reconciled to staying the winter, but reminded him of the promise, "that I should hear from the Genl. And have his directions of order to be provided at whatever place." She wrote in a conventional style of self-deprecation, "my little services should be wanted which you know I am always ready to do." She did not refrain, however, from giving pointed advice. The commanding officer, Colonel Guy Johnson, had a very poor sense of how to deal with the Iroquois and was later removed from his post. She warned Claus that, "the Indians are a Good deal dissatisfied on Acct. Of the Col.'s hasty temper which I hope he will soon drop. Otherwise it may be Disadvantageous—I need not tell you whatever is promised or told them it ought to be perform'd. Those from Canada," she continued, "are much Dissatisfied on account of his Taking more notice of those that are suspected than them that are known to be Loyal, I tell this only to you that you advise him."[11] It was just this sort of authoritative tone that so annoyed the European male military leaders.

Captain Alexander Frazer at Carleton Island advised Claus in February that he was very happy with Mary, despite her demanding nature. She has, he wrote, "shewed her usual zeal for Gov't by her constant endeavour to maintain the Indians in His Majesty's Interest."[12] Later in March, he reported that "the Chiefs were very careful to keep their people sober and satisfy'd, but their uncommon good behaviour is in a great Measure to be ascribed to Miss Molly Brants influence over them, which is far superior to that of all their Chiefs put together, and she has in the course of this Winter done every thing in Her power to maintain them strongly in the King's Interest." Still, he pointed out that she was "insatiable in her demands for her own family," even though he believed that "her residence here has been a considerable saving to Government, as she check'd the demands of others for presents & provisions."[13]

Perhaps Frazer was not fully aware of the great need Mary would have for provisions to satisfy the demands on her hospitality. It is not easy to understand Frazer's attitude toward Mary Brant. In this he is perhaps typical of the white men who were forced to rely on her because of her great influence among her people. When she left the following spring, of 1780, with Colonel Butler to visit the British headquarters at Quebec, Frazer wrote to Haldimand that her departure was "much against my inclination as I have been informed she is gone to ask Your Excellency for favours & I have no doubt but she will be Unreasonable in her Demands." However, he conceded that, "her family however is numerous, and not easily maintained on the decent footing on which she keeps them." Frazer was worried that Mary might want to move to Niagara, "where she will be a very unwelcome guest to Col. Bolton and most of the other principal people in that quarter, and if she be not humoured in all her demands for herself and her dependents (which are numerous) she may by the violence of her temper be led to create Mischief." Frazer then selflessly offered to keep her at Carleton Island, even offering to build her "some little box of a house . . . as it woud be more comfortable to her family than living in a Barrack Room." Frazer concluded by pointing out that he had, "at my own expence made a tolerable good Garden for her and I have contributed all in my power to have made her situation as comfortable as possible—indeed she seems very well pleased with her treatment, and I have every reason to be satisfy'd with her Conduct through the winter—and as I know herself and her family to be steadily attached to Government I wish them to be attended to."[14] This strange and contradictory letter suggests that Frazer was, in fact, afraid of losing Mary's expertise as a cultural broker between the British and Iroquois worlds at his post. His emphasis on her difficult nature was intended to discourage others from luring her away, and he sweetened the deal with the offer of a house.

Frazer need not have worried. Mary knew that she was needed at Carleton Island and had no plans to return to Niagara. Perhaps she wished to be near her children at school in Montreal. Leaving her son George there with his sisters, she returned, settling across the water at Cataraqui. A small house near the fort was built to accommodate her, and Frazer reported that she "had got into her new house, and Seemed better satisfy'd with her situation than I had ever known her before."[15]

Mary was decidedly not satisfied, however, when she heard of her brother's fight with some of the loyalist forces in a barroom brawl in the spring of 1781. Her concerns about the Iroquois alliance with the crown were brought to the surface by such a seemingly trivial incident. She wrote to Claus:

> It touched me very sore to hear from Niagara how my younger Brother Joseph Brant was used on the 6th of April, by being almost murdered by Col. Johnson's people, what adds to my Grief and Vexation is, that, being scarce returned safe from the Rebel Country, he must be thus treated by those of the King's people who always stay quietly at home, while my brother continuously exposes his life in going against the Enemy, taking prisoners &c as far as in his power.
>
> For which reason I beg you will speedily let His Excellency General Haldimand hear of it, who alone can heal this Breach of peace & Friendship, by his order & reprimand as Commander in Chief.
>
> This usage of my Brother makes me dread the Consequences, as some of the six Nations were Spectators of it, and well remember what Genl Schuyler told them that they would be ill used and despised by the Kings people for their Services, of which they have now a proof. For which reason I entreat His Excellency General Haldimand to use his Authority and settle this Matter, it is hard for me to have an only Brother whom I dearly love to see him thus treated, but what I am most concerned about is that it may affect the Kings Indian Interest.
>
> The whole matter is, that the Officers at Niagara are so haughty & proud, not knowing or considering that the Kings Interest is so nearly connected with that of the Indians. Wherefore I beg you will acquaint His Excellency with this, and let me know his Sentiments.[16]

The incident turned out to be wildly exaggerated and, once the facts were known, it blew over, but the suspicion behind it was real. When the final peace treaty was signed in 1783, the English betrayed the Six Nations by signing away all of their traditional lands south of the Great Lakes. The shock to the Iroquois was profound. They were too dispirited and broken as a consequence of the war, however, to put up much of a protest. They accepted the reservation lands that were given them in Canada, and the British compensated many of them for their documented losses. Mary was rewarded with a pension of £100, the largest granted to any Native person, and had a house built for her in Kingston. Despite her disappointment, when she was asked by American authorities to return after the Revolution due to her influence among her people, she rejected the offer with disdain. When the American emissary, Captain Hendrick Aupaumut, tried to persuade her of his peaceful intentions in 1792, she replied scornfully that if he was truly on a mission of peace, then why were there no women in his party?

We have no other record of Mary's personal feelings about her role in support of the British, but her brother, with whom she was so close, made a revealing statement later in life. He wrote to Thomas Eddy, philosopher and philanthropist: "I was, Sir, born of Indian parents, and lived while a child among those whom you are pleased to call savages; I was afterwards sent to live among the white people, and educated at one of your schools; since which period I have been honored much beyond my deserts . . . and after every exertion to divest myself of prejudice, I am obliged to give my opinion in favor of my own people. . . . In the government you call civilized, the happiness of the people is constantly sacrificed to the splendor of empire."[17]

Mary's own angry response to the perceived insult to her brother echoes this dissatisfaction with the ways of European culture. Her support of the crown had meant the loss of her own personal fortune, and the suffering of her family and her people. Military leaders on both sides sought to use her influence, but tolerated her leadership role with barely repressed resentment.

At Kingston, Mary lived out her days among the white settlers from the Mohawk Valley. Yet she persisted in retaining her native dress, and although she had an excellent command of English, generally refused to speak anything but Mohawk. Her social status in Kingston society was acknowledged and respected. Lady Simcoe, who had commandeered the entire regularly scheduled steamboat traveling from Niagara to Kingston on one occasion in 1794, permitted Mary, who was ill and anxious to get home to Kingston, to travel with her. Mary returned the favor the following year by curing Governor Simcoe of a nasty cough with an Iroquois herbal remedy. Travelers to Kingston spoke of her as a fascinating oddity, occupying a choice pew in St. George's Anglican Church while dressed in buckskin dress and leggings. Her daughters, however, became totally assimilated culturally into the upper reaches of Kingston society, and all married prominent white men. It was at the home of her daughter, Magdalene Ferguson, where Mary lived her last days, dying in April 1796 at the age of sixty.

In Kingston today, Mary Brant is somewhat of a local celebrity. Recently, with the renewed interest in women's history and the renaissance of Native cultural traditions, she has been honored nationally with a commemorative stamp, and the general location of her final resting place was distinguished some years ago with a plaque. Yet, when the local historical society wanted to erect a statue in her honor, there were no images from which it could be modeled. No one knows what Mary looked like. In the end, a Mohawk descendant, a young university student, was used as a model. We do know that Mary is buried somewhere in the graveyard of St. Paul's Anglican Church in downtown Kingston. It is a tranquil spot on a busy street, a very small plot of land, where a few venerable Upper Canadian loyalist families rest. The Reverend John Stuart and his family have a prominent place in the graveyard. The cultivated Philadelphian minister, brought by Sir William Johnson to the Mohawk Valley in 1770, reluctantly fled during the Revolution and gathered his flock around him in the British colony to the north. Mary Brant and he were very likely old friends in their Kingston years. He lies in the churchyard inside an impressive stone enclosure, whose four walls and gated entrance also contain the remains of his wife and descendants. Still, no one knows exactly where Mary Brant lies, no marker appears directly over her grave. Like her living role in white society, she is within the graveyard, but not really of it, and she is certainly not among its leading citizens, despite her accepted noble status in Six Nations society and important political role as a cultural broker for the British. The ambiguity of her role between them—but not of either European or Iroquois society—continues in death as it was in her life.

Notes

1. Colonel Daniel Claus to General Frederick Haldimand, Montreal, August 30, 1779, Haldimand Papers, B114, National Archives of Canada, Ottawa, 63ff. Hereafter cited as Haldimand Papers.

2. Claus to Haldimand, Montreal, August 30, 1779, ibid., B114, 63ff.

3. Claus to Sir John Johnson, Montreal, July 20, 1778, Claus Papers, National Archives of Canada, Ottawa, vol. 25, 17–20. Hereafter cited as Claus Papers.

4. Taylor and Duffin to Claus, Niagara, October 26, 1778, ibid., 42–44.

5. Mary Brant to Claus, Niagara, June 23, 1778, ibid., 2:29.

6. Taylor and Duffin to Claus, Niagara, November 14, 1778, ibid., 25:63–64.

7. Ibid.

8. Claus to Haldimand, Montreal, August 30, 1779, Haldiman Papers, B114, 57–58.

9. Claus to Haldimand, Montreal, September 6, 1779, Haldimand Papers, B114, 70.

10. Haldimand to Claus, Quebec, September 9, 1779, Haldimand Papers, B114, 68.

11. Mary Brant to Claus, Carleton Island, October 5, 1779, Claus Papers, 2:135.

12. Captain Frazer to Claus, Carleton Island, February 23, 1780, ibid.

13. Captain Frazer to Claus, Carleton Island, March 21, 1780, ibid.

14. Frazer to Haldimand, Carleton Island, June 21, 1780, Haldimand Papers, B127, 163.

15. Frazer to Haldimand, Carleton Island, December 13, 1780, ibid.

16. Brant to Claus, undated excerpt, Haldimand Papers, B114, 180–81.

17. As quoted in Jean Johnston, "Molly Brant: Mohawk Matron," *Ontario History* 56 (1964): 124.

Suggested Readings

On Mary Brant's life, see Lois M. Feister and Bonnie Pulis, "Molly Brant: Her Domestic and Political Roles in Eighteenth-Century New York," in *Northeastern Indian Lives, 1632–1816*, ed. Robert S. Grumet (Amherst: University of Massachusetts Press, 1996), 295–320; Earle Thomas, *The Three Faces of Molly Brant* (Kingston, Ontario: Quarry Press, 1996); Joan R. Gunderson, *To Be Useful to the World: Women in Revolutionary America* (New York: Twayne Publishers, 1996); Gretchen Green, "Molly Brant, Catharine Brant and Their Daughters: A Study in Colonial Acculturation," *Ontario History* 81 (1989): 235–50; Barbara Graymont, "Konwatsi'tsiaienni," *Dictionary of Canadian Biography*, vol. 4, 1771–1800 (Toronto: University of Toronto Press, 1988): 416–18; Jean Johnston, "Molly Brant: Mohawk Matron," *Ontario History* 56 (1964): 106–24; and H. Pearson Gundy, "Molly Brant—Loyalist," *Ontario History* 45 (1953): 97–108.

On the status of women in Iroquois society, see W. G. Spittal, ed., *Iroquois Women: An Anthology* (Ohseweken, Ontario: Iroquois Reprints, 1990); Elizabeth Tooker, "Women in Iroquois Society," in *Extending the Rafters: Interdisciplinary Approaches to Iroquoian Studies*, ed. Michael K. Foster et al. (Albany: State University of New York Press, 1984), 109–23; Barbara Graymont, *The Iroquois in the American Revolution* (Syracuse, NY: Syracuse University

Press, 1972); Judith K. Brown, "Economic Position of Women Among the Iroquois," *Ethnohistory* 17 (1970): 151–67; and Martha Champion Randle, "Iroquois Women, Then and Now," Smithsonian Institution, Bureau of American Ethnology, *Bulletin 149* (Washington, DC: Smithsonian Institution, 1951), 167–80. For archival sources that contain correspondence related to Mary's role in the Revolutionary War, see the Haldimand Papers and the Claus Papers at the National Archives of Canada, Ottawa, Ontario.

11

Arthur Lee of Virginia
The Forgotten Revolutionary

John Sainsbury

As a polemicist and a patriot politician in London, Arthur Lee (1740–1792) encouraged imperial support for the revolutionaries' cause. Unlike many subjects in this volume, Lee commented extensively on the Anglo-American disputes by publishing pamphlets and newspaper editorials in England and the colonies. The child of a royal governor, like Eliza Lucas, Lee also grew up on a southern plantation. Lucas and Lee, who were both educated in England, seemed to identify personally with both England and America. In 1765, Lee believed that England was a land of liberty. How then did the American Revolution reshape his political allegiances? The events of the Revolution had not only made Lee an American but also a diplomat to France and a spy for the Continental Congress. As John Sainsbury argues, he became a "professional revolutionary."

Lee's story offers clues to the meaning of freedom and independence for Virginia's slaveholding families. Lee urged that the political condition of the colonies under British rule was another kind of slavery. How then could he argue that slavery as a labor system was most offensive for its effects on white society? Elite families such as the Lees, as well as the impoverished Boones or Prendergasts, were interested in western lands. Given Lee's political connections, was he more successful in securing family land claims than Daniel Boone? Like William Smith, Lee was sometimes accused of self-serving actions and personal contentiousness. Friendship with the Earl of Shelburne, John Wilkes, or Samuel Adams and his rivalry with Benjamin Franklin also influenced his view of British corruption. Given that the Revolution had made Lee a politician as well as a patriot, why was he not more successful in securing a lasting, influential position in the new American government? Why did he not make a suitable Founding Father for voters, or for historians?

An expert in British-American relations during the American Revolution, John Sainsbury teaches at Brock University, St. Catherines, Ontario, and is the author of *Disaffected Patriots: London Supporters of Revolutionary America, 1769–1782* (1987).

Arthur Lee was born on December 21, 1740, the son of Thomas Lee, a socially prominent planter who achieved political eminence as acting governor of the Royal Colony of Virginia. Arthur's early childhood was spent in the elegant environment of Stratford Hall, his family's imposing plantation home in Virginia's Northern Neck. This fertile tidewater region also contained the estates of other leading Virginia families whose fortunes, like that of the Lees, derived from the cultivation of tobacco by African slaves. Privilege and opulence thus surrounded Lee at a tender age, but the uncontending ease and grace of life to which eighteenth-century aristocrats typically aspired would elude him thereafter until the very end of his life. Instead, from early adolescence onward he would lead an existence of almost endless strife and contention. Never one to shy away from controversy, Lee's personality, as well as his abilities, matched the needs of a revolutionary age.

The insecurities, material and emotional, that dogged him can be explained in part by his family circumstances. He had the misfortune of being the youngest of eight children, six of them male, at a time when the inheritance of landed property was generally based on the law of primogeniture. Doubtlessly his energetic and well-connected father would have made generous provision for his intellectually gifted youngest son, but Thomas Lee died in 1750, shortly after the death of his wife Hannah, leaving Arthur's fate in the hands of his eldest brothers, Philip and Thomas. Arthur's relationships with his fraternal guardians were never happy. Although they apparently provided him with adequate funds for his education and a portion of the family inheritance, he remained convinced that they were niggardly and unfair in the disbursement of family money. By way of emotional compensation, he clung for support to the younger siblings, especially Richard Henry (number three in the birth order), who became his chief mentor and who, like Arthur himself, would zealously support the patriot cause during the American Revolution.

Some historians have detected in Lee's family situation an explanation for what they represent as his virtually automatic suspicion of authority or seniority, whether expressed by imperial agents or by senior colleagues within the patriot cause itself, such as Benjamin Franklin. By extension, Lee's reputation, both during his lifetime and posthumously, has suffered from the fact that his actions have invited psychological speculations of a kind that, while often insightful, tend to demean or obscure his genuine achievements. Although, for example, his rivalry with Franklin was fueled by some genuine differences over policy in the tense phase before the outbreak of the American War of Independence, one of Franklin's biographers blames the antagonism on Lee's tendency to be "pathologically suspicious."[1]

Despite the alleged parsimony of the family purse-keepers, Arthur was still provided with the cosmopolitan schooling typical of the Virginia elite. Even before he had reached his eleventh birthday, he was sent across the Atlantic to attend Eton College, a prestigious academy outside London. It was not unusual for upper-class English boys to be sent away to boarding school at a tender age, but the experience must have been especially hard on Arthur, an orphaned youth so far from home. He found some consolation in the classical authors he was coming to revere, and their message of stoicism perhaps inured him to the teasing and bullying that were rife at the institution. Also, perhaps in this alien environment, he began to think of himself as an American, and not merely as a provincial Englishman.

Following a brief visit home in 1760, Lee returned to Britain where, following the advice of the literary lion, Dr. Samuel Johnson, he enrolled as a medical student at the University of Edinburgh. In that Scottish city, he consorted with Johnson's future acolyte, James Boswell; he expressed his displeasure with the women of the town, especially the intellectual ones; and he exhibited squeamishness at a surgical operation—not in itself a disqualification for an eighteenth-century physician—but an early hint that medicine might not be an appropriate career choice. While in Edinburgh, he was also initiated in politics as a student activist. With other expatriates in the so-called Virginia Club, he petitioned the Virginia Council and the House of Burgesses to limit medical licensing in the colony to qualified physicians of the kind that he had every intention of becoming. He also began his career as a pamphleteer, crossing polemical swords with the famed political economist, Adam Smith. In his *Theory of Moral Sentiments*, Smith had castigated American slaveholders for their barbaric treatment of innocent African slaves. Lee shared Smith's opposition to slavery but on very different grounds. Though he denounced the institution as "absolutely repugnant to justice," he was clearly more concerned about its corrupting effects on white society than on its savage exploitation of blacks, and his views on African-American character were depressingly conventional in their racist tone and character.[2] In his later writings, the specter of slavery would be invoked continually, but rarely as it applied to African Americans. Instead, Lee argued, it was the condition that awaited the white colonists unless their liberties were virtuously defended against the illegal encroachments of British imperial power.

Alarm at the tendencies of central government soon became something of a central preoccupation for him. Despite his residence in the Scottish capital, he capitulated fully to the anti-Scottish sentiment that was gripping opposition circles in England. His bête noire was the Earl of Bute, the Scottish courtier and chief minister who had been branded as the enemy of liberty in England and would soon achieve the same invidious status in the eyes of American patriots.

After taking his medical degree in 1765, Lee pondered his future. Should he pursue a career in medicine? And, if so, where? In a letter to Richard Henry, he admitted to feeling homesick, but he also cited his abhorrence of slavery as grounds for moving to England, which he dubbed "the Eden of the world and the land of liberty and independence." (Scotland, by contrast, had become "highly odious and almost detestable" to him.)[3] His hesitations prompted a stinging response from Richard Henry. Using the kind of language that Arthur would himself adopt, he argued that it was colonial Americans themselves who faced the prospect of "Egyptian bondage" at the hands of the mother country. Richard Henry's alarm was in specific response to the passage of the Stamp Act, which sought to impose an internal tax on the colonies. "America . . . has a parent's claim on her decendants," he lectured his brother, and demanded his expeditious return to join the struggle against the latest, and most serious, menace to colonial liberties.[4]

Arthur could scarcely have refused the summons of the brother he so idolized, but before receiving it he had already embarked on a mini-tour of Holland and France. By January 1766 he was back in London, where he attended the parliamentary debate in which the charismatic opposition politician, William Pitt (soon to become the Earl of Chatham), vigorously denounced the Stamp Act. At this time Lee also struck up an acquaintance with Pitt's political lieutenant, the Earl of Shelburne, an enigmatic personality whose apparent dedication to American liberties convinced Lee that the colonists had a powerful ally from within the ranks of the British aristocracy. Shelburne was a member of the Whig nobility, which had dominated British politics for much of the century, but this ruling group was deeply factionalized in the years that followed the accession of George III in 1760. Henceforth, Shelburne, like Pitt, would spend more time in opposition than in government. In London, Lee was cutting a figure in intellectual as well as political circles. Just prior to his departure for Virginia, he was elected a Fellow of the Royal Society, the prestigious organization dedicated to the promotion of scientific enquiry. Fittingly, his sponsor was Benjamin Franklin, America's most eminent scientist; but there was irony here as well, because the two men, while ostensibly allies in the colonial cause, would become bitter personal rivals.

In June 1766, Lee finally returned to Virginia and made a half-hearted effort to establish a medical practice in the colonial capital of Williamsburg. In a more tranquil era, Lee might have continued as a practicing physician, while, perhaps, dabbling in matters of provincial government. In the atmosphere of crisis in the colony, however, it soon became evident that politics not medicine was his true vocation. The Stamp Act had been repealed shortly before his return, but the controversies it stirred did not abate quickly, and at the heart of them was Richard Henry Lee. He had been the main organizer of opposition to the legislation, and his campaign involved an indictment of George Mercer, Virginia's designated stamp distributor. His attack was blunted by the embarrassing revelation that Richard Henry had himself sought the office that he now denounced Mercer for accepting. Conflating family honor with political principle, Arthur entered the fray by continuing the attack on the Mercers and defending his brother's integrity in the columns of the *Virginia Gazette*. He even challenged James Mercer, George's brother, to a duel, although an actual conflict never took place because the antagonists arrived at the dueling venue at different times. Afterward each accused the other of cowardly avoidance of physical combat. A most ungentlemanly confrontation later punctuated the squabble. The Mercers burned Arthur Lee in effigy outside his own door, where James Mercer also reportedly whacked his adversary over the head.

Lee's penchant for controversy continued, even as the passions aroused by the Stamp Act began to die down. As a newly appointed member of the supervisory board of the College of William and Mary, he engaged in a running battle with members of the faculty, who were generally staunch defenders of the Anglican religious establishment and resistant to the wave of opposition to British policy that was sweeping the colony. This dispute portended divisions that would wrack Virginia in the 1770s, but soon Lee was engaged with an issue of broader concern throughout the American colonies: the passage of the Townshend Duties in March 1767, which imposed taxes on a range of items imported by the colonies. Lee reacted quickly, charging Parliament with "changing the mode, but preserving the principle of the Stamp Act."[5] It was not, however, until John Dickinson of Philadelphia published his *Letters from an American Farmer*, attacking the Townshend Act, that colonial opposition caught fire. Lee's self-appointed role was to echo and extend, in a series of letters to the *Virginia Gazette*, Dickinson's carefully crafted polemic. Using the pen name "Monitor," Lee supported Dickinson's attack on the British government's claim that Americans were represented in the House of Commons because each Member of Parliament looked after not merely the interests of his own constituents, but those of the empire as a whole. This constitutional precept was known as "virtual representation," and both authors agreed that it was simply a specious device to obtain taxation without representation.

Lee also endorsed Dickinson's call for greater colonial cooperation—extending to nonimportation agreements—in resisting the duties. And he revived a traditional libertarian call for resisting tendencies to despotism; Americans should seek to obtain a Bill of Rights for the colonies, as their English ancestors had done in the the Glorious Revolution of 1688. His arguments were expressed in a florid style, which pointed to slavery as the inevitable fate of the colonists unless they exhibited the patriotic virtue necessary to preserve their freedom. "Will not our jurisdictions, liberties, and privileges be totally violated?" he wrote. "Shall we not sink into slaves? O liberty! O virtue! O my country."[6] Not everyone on the emerging patriot side was impressed by Lee's efforts. Thomas Jefferson for one thought his message was derivative and his motives self-seeking. But the sheer volume and force of Lee's writings were already marking him out, while he was still in his twenties, as a leading penman of the American Revolution.

Lee was not content, however, to confine his activities to those of polemicist. Even as the newly created Virginia Association was denouncing the Townshend Duties and organizing an embargo on British imports, Lee was traveling northward, intent on creating a coordinated network of opposition to British measures. His reception was sometimes less than enthusiastic, but he did enjoy a cordial welcome from John Dickinson in Philadelphia, where Lee, never shy about offering advice, urged the city's merchants to join a common pact in support of nonimportation.

Lee's travels did not extend to New England, where he would later find many kindred spirits in the political battles ahead. Instead, in the late summer of 1768, he returned abruptly to England, in the company of his brother William, a tobacco merchant. His motives, typically, combined the personal and the political. Rather grandiosely, he envisioned himself as gathering information on the designs of the British government and harmonizing appropriate responses to them throughout the empire. But there was also the pressing question of his professional career. Once in England, after another desultory attempt to establish a medical practice, he concluded that law was a more suitable occupation than medicine. Accordingly, he took up residence in one of London's Inns of Court with the intention of qualifying as an attorney.

Lee would later look back at his sojourn in the imperial metropolis, which lasted through 1776, with nostalgia and pride in his accomplishments. But the passage of time lent enchantment to a period of considerable frustration and thwarted ambition. Certainly his first contact with government did little for his temper. Seeking out the Earl of Hillsborough, the secretary of state for America, Lee pressed the claims of the Mississippi Company (in which his family had a large stake) for an allocation of land in the American interior. He was rebuffed by the minister and continued to meet rejection even after he modified the company's proposals in ways that were more consistent with the British government's restrictive policy on land settlement. What made the rejection even more galling for Lee was that a rival land company, in which Benjamin Franklin was a leading light, appeared to be receiving a more sympathetic reception in government circles. Lee's brush with the government left him convinced that the ministry was corrupt and planted the virus of suspicion in his subsequent dealings with Franklin. It also rendered Lee vulnerable to the charge that his political agenda was driven by self-interest and malice.

Although Lee was losing faith in incumbent politicians, he continued to believe in the ultimate virtue of the British political system. He naively looked forward to the day when the Earl of Shelburne would be returned to high office, from where he would direct a policy of friendship toward the colonies—as well as support for the ambitions of the Mississippi Company. Lee's confidence in his noble friend was reinforced by frequent visits to Shelburne's country estate in Wiltshire. The energetic Lee did not confine his attentions to the Whig aristocracy, however. He also forged a remarkable friendship with John Wilkes, the darling of the London mob, whose bold opposition to government, expressed initially in his publication, *North Briton*, was inflaming politics both inside and outside Parliament. By the late 1760s, he was being celebrated in the American colonies, as well as in Britain, as a staunch friend of liberty. In many respects, Lee's alliance with Wilkes was an odd one. Lee was austere and moralistic, a lifelong bachelor (though not by choice), often awkward in his dealings with women; Wilkes, by contrast, was a flamboyant libertine, whose notoriety was compounded when he was indicted as publisher of an obscene parody entitled *An Essay on Woman*. Yet the friendship between the two men derived from more than political convenience; it was one of genuine warmth and mutual respect. At the time of Lee's return to England, Wilkes was incarcerated in King's Bench Prison as punishment for his allegedly seditious and blasphemous writings. There in comfortable quarters he received visitors—including admiring Americans—in the manner of a potentate rather than a common criminal. He also continued to be a thorn in the side of the government, repeatedly winning election to Parliament as member for the suburban county of Middlesex.

The decision of the House of Commons, in April 1769, to declare Wilkes's most recently defeated opponent the duly elected member for the county provoked a political crisis in England and drew Lee into the volatile world of popular politics in London. Lee was convinced that Wilkes, the Middlesex electors, and the American colonists were jointly victims of government corruption and tyranny and, thus, that their causes would stand or fall together. Accordingly, he busied himself in the nationwide political campaign on behalf of Wilkes. He also became an active member of the Society of the Supporters of the Bill of Rights (the name must surely have appealed to him), an organization, consisting mainly of Wilkes's wealthier backers, which was initially dedicated to relieving the popular hero of his enormous debts. The society soon took on a larger political role, however. Lee envisaged that it would transform the political system by vetting parliamentary candidates and instructing them after election; and he had ambitious plans for coordinating its activities with other dissident groups throughout the empire. His grandiose vision was never realized but, in its role as the inner caucus of the Wilkite movement in London, the society did enjoy some remarkable triumphs, despite defections from its ranks prompted by Wilkes's personal extravagances. In 1773, for example, it organized the election of William Lee and Stephen Sayre (an American friend of the Lees) as sheriffs of the City of London; the election of Wilkes as Lord Mayor would follow in 1774.

Lee placed not only his organizational skills but also his prolific pen at the service of the transatlantic radical opposition. From London, he sent letters to the *Virginia Gazette* exposing the malign intentions of government and continuing to urge the adoption of an American Bill of Rights as the ultimate protection against ministerial tyranny. Adopting the pen name "Junius Americanus" (in conscious emulation of the celebrated "Junius," the anonymous scourge of government), he also bombarded the London press with vitriolic essays. His targets included unpopular government officials in America, whom Lee accused of misrepresenting colonial intentions to the British cabinet. His campaign against Governor Francis Bernard of Massachusetts—written "with a pen dipped in the gall of asps," according to a colleague of the governor—became part of a cause célèbre.[7] It culminated in February 1770 with Bernard ably defending his conduct before the Privy Council, where Lee and his associates were reprobated for bringing "groundless, vexatious, and scandalous" charges against the governor.[8]

Lee's "Junius Americanus" essays, like his other submissions to the London press, were not confined to an English readership. They appeared in the colonial newspapers alongside his other writings, where they constituted a major source of information and opinion about the impending imperial crisis. Of perhaps equal importance in shaping American responses was Lee's correspondence with leading colonial radicals, most notably Samuel Adams of Boston. Although the two men would not meet in person until 1780, their letters had already forged a close personal and political bond between them. Their friendship signified a profound change that the American Revolution entailed for the two men and their respective communities. Before its occurrence, New Englanders and Virginians, though they shared a continent, were worlds apart culturally and politically; now their patriots were finding common cause and, by degrees, a sense of common nationality as well. Perhaps under Adams's influence, Lee began to doubt that the British political system could ever be redeemed. By June 1773, Lee had concluded that George III's "sole wish [is] to be the tyrant of his people."[9] Logically, he could have proceeded from such a judgment toward an advocacy of American independence, but this was a course that Lee followed with reluctance. It is difficult to locate the moment when Lee—who was instinctively more cautious than Adams and more wedded to things British—determined in his own mind that a break with the mother country had become necessary and desirable.

Although, from across the Atlantic, Lee strove for unity among colonial radicals, the small group of American expatriates in London remained deeply factionalized. His relations with Franklin became further embittered when the two men found themselves in competition to succeed Dennys DeBerdt (whose friendship Lee had assiduously cultivated) as agent in London for the Massachusetts Assembly, following DeBerdt's death in April 1770. Traditionally, the colonial agents had operated in a low-key way to represent their respective clients, and they generally eschewed anything that smacked of political controversy on the grounds that the empire consisted of mutually compatible interest groups. This approach was becoming increasingly untenable as political tensions mounted. In this new situation, Lee envisaged reviving the colonial agencies as a system both unified and politically engaged, an integral part of his ambitious scheme to coordinate American responses to government policy. His plans were thwarted, however, when the Massachusetts Assembly chose the more experienced Franklin as its agent, fobbing off his younger rival with the position of Franklin's deputy.

Lee's lack of a formal position in the nexus of empire probably contributed to the bouts of depression that overtook him in the period following the partial repeal of the Townshend Duties in March 1770. He complained periodically that the colonists were sinking into complacency, their virtue corrupted by an unhealthy addiction to material possessions. A swirl of events, beginning in December 1773, changed not only this perception, but the entire climate of imperial relations. In that month, Boston radicals, disguised as Mohawk Indians, dumped cases of East India Company tea—a commodity still subject to taxation—into Boston Harbor. Government reaction to the Boston Tea Party was fast and furious. Its first target was Benjamin Franklin, who on behalf of the Massachusetts Assembly had been complaining bitterly about the alleged corruption of Massachusetts governor Thomas Hutchinson. Lee was in attendance as the Lords of the Privy Council delivered a savage verbal attack on Franklin, lambasting him for securing and publishing Hutchinson's private correspondence. The scene was reminiscent of the Bernard hearings four years before, and Lee quickly recognized its value to the cause of colonial unity. Setting aside his personal hostility to Franklin, he heaped praise on his old rival for his courage in the face of ministerial bullying.

Franklin, now a martyred figure in the eyes of colonial patriots, was obliged to resign the Massachusetts agency in the wake of the affair, leaving Lee in charge. But the Virginian's accession to the position he had long coveted brought him little satisfaction. In the polarized state of imperial relations that followed the Boston Tea Party, colonial agents were deprived of any meaningful role, despite Lee's best efforts. As Parliament debated and passed legislation designed to coerce the colonists into obedience, Lee desperately organized petitions from Americans in London and sought out parliamentarians willing to sponsor them. But their efforts were unavailing in the climate of extreme hostility toward American dissidents that now prevailed in Westminster.

Exhausted by his efforts, and genuinely fearful of legal recriminations from a vengeful government, Lee temporarily withdrew from the hurly-burly of politics. In May 1774 he left for a tour of France, Switzerland, and Italy. He did not entirely neglect the American cause, however. In Paris he composed his most widely read pamphlet, *An Appeal to the Justice and Interests of the People of Great Britain*, a moderate and well-reasoned critique of the British attempt to levy taxes in America. Although this tract certainly enhanced his reputation in the colonies, it had no discernible effect on those it was intended to persuade. Having left France for Switzerland, Lee and his traveling companions attempted to visit the celebrated Voltaire, a pilgrimage that was de rigueur for the self-consciously Enlightened; but on this occasion the usually hospitable Voltaire was unable to receive visitors. In Rome, on the next leg of his journey, Lee received news that brought his continental sojourn to a sudden end. The king had dissolved Parliament and elections had been called. Lee was by now convinced that only a political convulsion in Britain could prevent calamity for the colonists. Seeing in parliamentary elections just such an opportunity, he rushed back to London as fast as wintry conditions in the Alpine passes would allow.

Lee arrived in London at the end of November with the election results already determined. The news was disappointing. Despite some marginal gains by his Wilkite friends, Parliament remained as stubbornly resistant as ever to colonial grievances. Lee was not yet prepared, however, to abandon hope for a political solution to the imperial impasse. He was buoyed up by the first meeting of the Continental Congress in the fall of 1774, and he labored strenuously to encourage Parliament to respond to its overtures. "The proceedings of the Congress meet with universal approbation here, and have operated like an electric shock upon the ministry and their Dependents," he wrote, with excessive optimism, to Richard Henry Lee.[10] With his brother William, he organized merchant petitions in support of the colonists, which he hoped would propel William Pitt (now Lord Chatham) into office at the head of a ministry consisting of the once-disunited factions of parliamentary opposition.

Perhaps in response to prompting from the Lees, the temperamental Lord Chatham did show some welcome signs of wishing to return to the political fray in defense of the empire that he had played such an instrumental role in constructing. In February 1775 he issued a clarion call in the House of Lords for the redress of American grievances on the basis of the Continental Congress's demands, but his eloquence fell largely on deaf ears. The government's response was to announce further coercive measures and declare Massachusetts to be in a state of rebellion. With the parliamentary opposition still confined to the political margins, Lee made a last-ditch attempt to avert the drift to war by mobilizing opinion among London's citizens where pro-American sentiment still ran strongly. On their behalf, he prepared a forceful petition to the king, which condemned his ministers and called for the repeal of all legislation offensive to the colonists. On April 10, 1775, after a procession through the streets of London witnessed by excited and sympathetic crowds, the City Corporation, with Lord Mayor Wilkes at its head, presented the petition to George III.

The king did not look kindly on the petition or its presenters, but in any case the encounter was largely symbolic, because events in the colonies were now taking on a momentum of their own. "There is a silence in the New England provinces, which argues an approaching storm," Lee wrote presciently on April 23.[11] In fact, on April 19, as he danced late into the night as an honored guest at Lord Mayor Wilkes's Easter Ball, the first shots of the American War of Independence had already rung out at Lexington, Massachusetts. As luck would have it, the first accounts of the conflict to cross the Atlantic were placed in Lee's hands, and he was able to use his temporary monopoly of information to effect a significant propaganda coup. While the British government waited impatiently for official news of the first encounter between the redcoats and Massachusetts militiamen, Lee placed luridly biased reports in the newspapers depicting heroic colonial resistance to brutal arbitrary power. Even as the government's own propaganda machine finally swung into action, Lee, through his writings and contact with radical politicians, sought to nurture and extend the antiwar sentiment that existed in the metropolis. Increasingly, however, his efforts were devoted less to the ultimately futile attempt to shift public opinion in England and more to the dangerous task of promoting the success of the armed patriot struggle. Lee was tracing his personal course from resistance to revolution. Ironically, this shift occurred as the Lee brothers were sinking deeper roots into English society. Arthur qualified as a lawyer on May 5, 1775, and spent much of the summer arguing legal briefs; William meanwhile was serving as a London alderman.

By the time that Arthur Lee forwarded Congress's Olive Branch Petition to the British government in September 1775, he was perhaps just going through the motions of seeking reconciliation. In that same month, with John Wilkes acting as intermediary, he began secret meetings with the French playwright Pierre Augustin Caron—better known as Beaumarchais. The two sought ways for forwarding funds from pro-American Englishmen to the colonists. Soon their schemes became more ambitious. Beaumarchais acted as Lee's point of contact with Charles Gravier de Vergennes, the French foreign minister, and the three arranged for large amounts of French money and munitions to be channeled via the French West Indies to the rebellious colonists. This maneuvering was cloak-and-dagger work, and Lee ran a real risk of being arrested for treason even before Congress appointed him as its secret agent in London. The mood of the administration was amply demonstrated in October 1775, when Lee's friend, Stephen Sayre, was arrested for allegedly plotting to seize the Tower of London and overthrow King George III!

Lee's work on behalf of Congress continued through 1776, and at the end of that year he received a new assignment, one suggestive of congressional recognition of his diplomatic abilities and commitment to the patriot cause. Together with Benjamin Franklin and Silas Deane of Connecticut, he was appointed minister plenipotentiary to France, instructed with securing that country's support for American independence, which Congress had declared in July. The decision to leave England and a flourishing legal career was not an easy one for Lee. Writing to Lord Shelburne, he declared his reluctance to "bid adieu, perhaps forever, to a country where from choice I had fixed my fortunes, and to a people whom I most respected and could have loved." But patriotic duty beckoned. "The first object of my life is my country; the first wish of my heart is public liberty. I must see, therefore, the liberties of my country established or perish in the last struggle."[12] Lee had made the final step from active partisan in the colonial cause to professional revolutionary.

Lee enjoyed important successes as a "militia diplomat" in Paris and as a roving commissioner elsewhere in Europe. But the experience was tainted by the rancor that existed between Lee and his fellow commissioners. Lee not only disliked, he also distrusted Franklin and Deane, and the feeling was mutual. Lee complained bitterly that Deane was more interested in lining his own pockets than promoting the interests of the fragile American republic. He even suspected Deane of a traitorous connection with the British. There was, in fact, justice in Lee's charges. While his friend Benjamin Franklin turned a blind eye, Deane used his privileged position to engage in a number of money-grubbing schemes—securing handsome commissions on materials purchased by Congress, speculating in land, even trading with the enemy. Deane's associate, Dr. Edward Bancroft, secretary to the commission, was an out-and-out traitor who routinely supplied the British with the commissioners' secret documents. And modern research has now established that Lee's suspicions about Deane's own loyalties were indeed well grounded.

Lee's complaints about his colleagues in diplomacy found a sympathetic ear among the faction in Congress that grouped around his brothers, Richard Henry and Francis, and his epistolary friend, Samuel Adams. Congress actually recalled Deane in November 1777, upset that, without any authority, he was granting commissions to French officers wishing to serve in America. Yet Lee never achieved satisfactory public vindication in his quarrel with Deane, who proved to be a tenacious and unscrupulous adversary. Most galling for Lee was Deane's partial success in branding Lee himself, the epitome of the virtuous patriot, as a traitor. Deane cunningly exaggerated Lee's attachment to English culture and his well-publicized frustrations with French diplomacy in constructing this entirely false charge. Deane's accusation was assiduously promoted by the enemies of the Lee-Adams faction in Congress, and it was even credited by leading members of the French government. Conrad-Alexandre Gérard, the first French minister to the United States, was in Deane's camp, and until 1782, Foreign Minister Vergennes believed that it was Lee, not Deane, who was the traitor.

Remarkably, perhaps, given the fissures within the American diplomatic mission, it still was able to achieve its ultimate goal. In February 1778, following the victory of American forces at Saratoga, the French signed two treaties with the United States: a Treaty of Amity and Commerce and a Treaty of Alliance. In anticipation of these diplomatic triumphs, Lee, with typical rhetorical excess, wrote to Samuel Adams: "The last ray of British splendor is passing away, and the American sun is emerging in full glory from the clouds which obscured it."[13] Shortly after the treaties were signed, France entered the war against Great Britain. As icing on the diplomatic cake, Lee had earlier embarked on a mission to Spain, a declining but still formidable power. His undertaking was encouraged by his fellow commissioners, who were only too happy to see him depart from Paris. Although he was denied access to the Spanish capital, and the Spanish government balked at supporting American independence, Lee was able to secure generous secret aid for the patriot cause. He was less successful on a similar mission to the Prussian court at Berlin. Back in Paris in time for the signing of the French treaties, Lee even found time for a dalliance with an ardent female admirer, one of the few recorded instances in which he revealed a romantic side to his nature.

The success of the commissioners did nothing to promote reconciliation among them; on the contrary, it provided them with more leisure to indulge in mutual recriminations. By early 1779, Lee was anxious to return to the United States to defend his reputation, but a series of frustrating delays kept him in France until the summer of 1780. Even his return voyage was dogged by controversy. The appointment of the captain of the ship, the frigate *Alliance*, was a matter of dispute between Franklin, who favored naval legend John Paul Jones, and Lee, who had befriended Captain Peter Landais. Eventually, Landais assumed command, but after the *Alliance* put out to sea he provoked a mutiny among the crew and engaged in explosive arguments with Lee himself. The enquiry that followed offered further evidence of Lee's now notorious irascibility and, hence, more ammunition for his political opponents.

Lee disembarked in Boston after an absence of twelve years from what, in the meantime, had become his native country. He received a hero's welcome from the New England radicals, his kindred spirits. Encouraged by Samuel Adams, the Massachusetts Assembly awarded him a tract of land in Maine in appreciation of his prewar services to the state. In the wider national context, Lee's reputation for contentiousness severely constrained his options for a continuing career in public life. In the great affairs that were shaping the new nation, Lee would be more often spectator than participant. Nor would he ever enjoy the status of elder statesman. Much of his energy was consumed in justifying his conduct in Europe. He played no direct role in the preliminary negotiations that were bringing the war to an end, and he watched with alarm as Congress appeared willing to play second fiddle to the French. The fear of the Lee-Adams faction was that France and Britain might cut a deal at the expense of the interests of the the emerging American Republic. Lee did succeed in persuading Congress that it should appoint a single secretary of state for foreign affairs, but his own aspirations for this position were thwarted when that body, by the narrowest of margins, opted for Robert R. Livingston of New York. Lee was able to have a marginal impact on the conduct of diplomacy when, in 1781, he won a seat in Virginia's House of Delegates, which promptly elected him to Congress. There he busied himself with the question of western land settlement, but he also had the satisfaction of witnessing the triumphant conclusion of peace negotiations that confuted his initial pessimism by wringing important concessions from Great Britain.

Lee's diplomatic experience was recognized by the new nation, when he was appointed one of six commissioners charged with securing title to the lands of the Northwest Territories from their Indian inhabitants. The assignment on the frontier provoked some soul searching. It drove out any notions in Lee's mind of settling in the wilderness, while at the same time he seems to have become deeply depressed about his prospects for finding a wife and settling in his native Virginia.

Following his return to Philadelphia, Lee received more sedentary employment as a member of the U.S. Treasury Board. He quickly learned from his latest employment that it was virtually impossible to run a national government without stable revenues derived from taxation. This experience did not push him, however, into the ranks of the so-called federalists, who were seeking to enlarge the powers of the central government. Lee was not a member of the Constitutional Convention that met in Philadelphia in 1787 to forge a new constitution; but as an interested observer, he aligned himself with the antifederalists. Like many of his ilk, Lee was reconciled to the Constitution once assured that it would incorporate a Bill of Rights as a check on the potentially despotic tendencies of central government. The constitutional device he had once fought for as protection against the British government, he now embraced as protection against his own.

Though Lee correctly forecast corrosive party battles between the proponents of states' rights and the federalists, he was sufficiently optimistic about the prospects of the new republic to run in 1788 for election to the newly constituted U.S. House of Representatives. His defeat in that election, followed by a failed attempt to win appointment to the U.S. Supreme Court, marked the definitive end of his political career. After a leisurely tour through Virginia, which included a visit to his childhood home of Stratford, he purchased an estate at Urbanna, on the Rappahannock River. The property was elegant but unpretentious, appropriate to his means. (Lee, after all, was the recipient of only a modest portion of the family fortune, and while he had been reasonably compensated for his years in public service, he was not enriched by them.) The purchase did enable him, though, to fulfill, if only briefly, his long-deferred dream of becoming a gentleman-farmer, the time-honored reward for the virtuous patriot. In a sense, his life had now come full circle. After the years of sound and fury on the public stage, he had returned to the self-contained world of plantation life that he had quit forty years before. His retirement was short but happy. Parted so long from family by the demands of revolution, he took a particular pleasure and pride in acting as a kind of surrogate father to his sister's children, Nancy and Thomas Lee Shippen. He died in December 1792, unlamented and largely forgotten by most of the fellow countrymen whom he had served with such energy. Appropriately it was a New Englander, John Adams, writing thirty years later, who would offer the most fitting tribute: "This man never had justice done him by his country in his lifetime, and I fear he never will have by posterity. His reward cannot be in this world."[14]

Notes

1. Verner W. Crane, *Benjamin Franklin and a Rising People* (Boston, 1954), 135.

2. Arthur Lee, *An Essay in Vindication of the Continental Colonies of America, from a Censure of Mr. Adam Smith, in his Theory of Moral Sentiments, and Some Reflections on Slavery in General* (London, 1764), 39–45.

3. Arthur Lee to Richard Henry Lee, March 20, 1765, in *The Lee Family Papers*, ed. Paul R. Hoffman and John L. Molyneaux, 8 reels microfilm (Charlottesville, VA, 1966), reel 1.

4. Richard Henry Lee to Arthur Lee, July 4, 1765, in *The Letters of Richard Henry Lee*, ed. James Ballagh, 2 vols. (New York, 1911–1914), 1:10–11.

5. Quoted in A. R. Riggs, *The Nine Lives of Arthur Lee* (Williamsburg, VA, 1976), 20.

6. Arthur Lee, *Monitor*, No. 3, in *The Farmer's and Monitor's Letters to the Inhabitants of the British Colonies* (Williamsburg, VA, 1769), 70.

7. Quoted in Riggs, *Nine Lives of Arthur Lee*, 32.

8. A. Matthews, ed., "Letters of Dennys DeBerdt, 1757–1770," *Publications (Transactions) of the Colonial Society of Massachusetts* 13 (1910–11): 410.

9. Lee to Samuel Adams, June 11, 1773, in Richard H. Lee, *Life of Arthur Lee*, 2 vols. (Boston, 1829), 1:232.

10. Quoted in Louis W. Potts, *Arthur Lee: A Virtuous Revolutionary* (Baton Rouge, LA, and London, 1981), 131–32.

11. Arthur Lee to Ralph Izard, April 23, 1775, in Anne Izard Deas, *Correspondence of Mr. Ralph Izard, of South Carolina, from the year 1774 to 1804; with a Short Memoir* (New York, 1844), 70.

12. Lee to Shelburne, December 23, 1776, in *The Revolutionary Diplomatic Correspondence of the United States*, ed. Francis Wharton, 6 vols. (Washington, DC, 1889), 2:239–40.

13. Quoted in Potts, *Arthur Lee*, 188.

14. Quoted in Riggs, *Nine Lives of Arthur Lee*, 82.

Suggested Readings

Arthur Lee was a prolific writer whose correspondence is scattered through a number of archives and libraries, including the libraries of the University of Virginia and Harvard University, and the American Philosophical Society in Philadelphia. Fortunately for the researcher, much of this documentary material has been gathered together in an edited microfilm edition: Paul R. Hoffman and John R. Molyneaux, eds., *The Lee Family Papers*, 8 reels microfilm (Charlottesville, VA, 1966). Those of his pamphlets published in America are available in microform in *Early American Imprints* (Charles Evans Collection). There is also a typical nineteenth-century "life and letters" compilation: Richard H. Lee, *Life of Arthur Lee*, 2 vols. (Boston, 1829). This work contains some useful information but is marred by inaccuracies. More reliable is James Ballagh, ed., *The Letters of Richard Henry Lee*, 2 vols. (New York, 1911–1914). Some important Lee letters also show up in H. A. Cushing, *The Writings of Samuel Adams*, 4 vols. (New York, 1904–1908). Material by or about Lee, especially as it relates to his diplomatic career, is contained in Edmund C. Burnett, *Letters of Members of the Continental Congress*, 8 vols. (Washington, DC,

1921–1936), and Francis Wharton, *The Revolutionary and Diplomatic Correspondence of the United States*, 6 vols. (Washington, DC, 1889).

As John Adams predicted, posterity has not been very kind to Arthur Lee, but he is the subject of a competent modern biography: Louis W. Potts, *Arthur Lee: A Virtuous Revolutionary* (Baton Rouge, LA, and London, 1981). A. R. Riggs, *The Nine Lives of Arthur Lee* (Williamsburg, VA, 1976) is an engaging shorter account. Rhys Isaac, *The Transformation of Virginia, 1740–1790* (Chapel Hill, NC, 1982) is a sophisticated analysis of the political and religious contests in Lee's native province. Lee's involvement with the London radicals can be traced in John Sainsbury, *Disaffected Patriots: London Supporters of Revolutionary America, 1769–1782* (Kingston and Montreal, 1987), and A. R. Riggs, "Arthur Lee, a Radical Virginian in London, 1768–1776," *Virginia Magazine of History and Biography* 78 (July 1970): 268–80. Of the numerous modern works on the diplomacy of the American Revolution, William C. Stinchcombe, *The American Revolution and the French Alliance* (Syracuse, NY, 1969), gives perhaps the fairest account of Lee's contribution.

12

Simon Girty
His War on the Frontier

Phillip W. Hoffman

Frontiersman and Indian interpreter, Simon Girty (1741–1818) had served the Virginia militia and the Continental Congress before he defected to the British in 1778. He had become convinced that American revolutionaries intended to cross the Ohio River and challenge Indian territorial rights. From the age of fifteen, Girty had lived with the Senecas. As a cultural intermediary, he moved easily between white and Indian worlds, but his life story also vividly depicts the lawlessness of the frontier, where liquor flowed, brawls were frequent, and renegade attacks became legendary. How significant was Girty's status as an adopted Seneca to his diplomatic effectiveness? Was his defection to the British consistent with Iroquois diplomacy?

With his brothers and other agents of the British Department of Indian Affairs, Girty participated in frontier raids against the Americans, typically by serving as a spy or warrior in combined Indian-British forces. As Phillip Hoffman notes, Girty attempted to protect a number of prisoners of the Indians, and his motivational speeches encouraged diverse Indian groups to join the British. Did the colonists' image of Girty, the vilified frontiersman, match the reality? Does Girty's understanding of the American Revolution reveal a frontier interpretation about its origins, one that he might have shared with Daniel Boone, Dragging Canoe, or Mary Brant but probably not with residents of colonial seacoast towns, such as Anthony Benezet, William Smith, or Ashley Bowen? Unlike his younger brother, Girty did not choose to live with the Indians at war's end. Did Girty, like Lachlan McGillivray, favor separate spheres for Indians and whites rather than a blending of peoples? Did cultural brokers need to promote the separateness of peoples while serving as ambassadors between them? Leaving his farm, Girty commanded an army of Wyandots in the 1790s, but in the victory of General Anthony Wayne, Girty saw his worst fear come true: the end of Indian independence in the Ohio Valley.

Phillip W. Hoffman is a private scholar who has written articles on Simon Girty and is completing a book-length biography.

The outlawed white man, by Ohio's flood,
Whose vengeance shamed the Indian's thirst for blood;
Whose hellish arts surpassed the redman's far:
Whose hate enkindled many a border war,
Of which each aged grandame hath a tale
At which man's bosom burns and childhood's cheek grows pale.[1]

On the moonless night of March 28, 1778, three men who had a profound influence upon the western and northern Indian nations defected from western Pennsylvania to join the British. Convinced that American intentions toward the Indians no longer coincided with their own, their immediate objective was Goschachgunk (later Coshocton, Ohio), the town seat for the Delawares residing in the Ohio country.

For many years, Alexander McKee had been an officer of the British Department of Indian Affairs and, like Matthew Elliott, he was involved in the fur trade and had married a Shawnee woman. The third man, thirty-seven-year-old Simon Girty, was primarily an interpreter and intermediary to the Six Nations of the Iroquois League, having first served the British Department of Indian Affairs at Fort Pitt for eleven years, then the Virginia militia, then the Continental Congress, and most recently the Continental Army.

Occurring during a critical period of the Revolutionary War, the simultaneous defection of these men was a nightmare for American military leaders and for the rebel colonists who lived along the frontier, for no one was better qualified than Girty, McKee, and Elliott to persuade the still-neutral Indians of the Ohio Valley to pick up a British tomahawk. The defection of McKee and Elliott, long suspected of being loyalists, was no surprise to American authorities. Girty's desertion was another matter.

Famous as a bush fighter and frontiersman with strong Indian connections, Girty had grown up among the Senecas and spoke eleven Indian languages. He was a courageous and accomplished military spy who, thus far, had devoted himself notably to the rebel cause. The preceding fall, while on a mission for General Edward Hand (a Continental Army officer whom Washington had ordered to Fort Pitt to take command of the western war), Girty had been arrested by the Senecas as an American spy. He escaped from them before they could turn him over to British authorities at Niagara. Back at Fort Pitt, he revealed the existence of a new British supply depot he had learned of, which was located at the mouth of the Cuyahoga River. The enemy base was subsequently targeted, and Girty was one of five hundred volunteers who set out in February

1778 to attack it, but who were forced back by inclement weather. The most significant result of the disastrous Cuyahoga expedition was the murder of a few peaceful and innocent Indians, for which the campaign was quickly and derisively dubbed "the Squaw Campaign."

To Girty, General Hand's decisions during the ill-fated expedition signified an ominous change in American Indian policy. When his army had reached the Shenango River, Hand was informed by his scouts that a few Indians were in residence at a small town, some seven miles upstream. Without making any effort to ascertain whether these people were friend or foe, he declared them to be hostile and ordered an attack on the town. As it turned out, the victims were Delawares, members of the only western Indian nation still friendly to the United States. This incident finally convinced Girty that, once they won their independence, the Americans meant to cross the Ohio River and destroy or rout the Indians completely in order to take their lands.

The rebel leaders' objectives were obvious. It was common knowledge to anyone who had long served the British Department of Indian Affairs at Fort Pitt that George Washington, Patrick Henry, and Benjamin Franklin had all been major shareholders of companies that greatly profited from the acquisition, subdivision, and sale of Indian lands to immigrants. The operations of their companies had been abruptly terminated by the King's Proclamation of 1763. Designed to appease the Indians, the proclamation prohibited direct acquisition of Indian lands by private companies or individuals and, by so doing, infuriated the very men who would foment the Revolution and later hold the reins of the rebel government.

The son of a fur trader, Girty was committed to the preservation of a bicultural world with well-defined borders between Indians and whites, a world in which the Indians retained control over their lands and lives, and where, as an interpreter and intermediary, he was of value to both sides. By the spring of 1778, Girty had come to understand that what the rebel leaders were now promising the Indians through intermediaries like himself and what they actually intended for them at war's end were two different things. He had too many Indian friends to go on fighting for the rebels. Sharply aware that his actions were irrevocable, by the night of March 28, 1778, he no longer had any desire to remain a patriot.

The man who became frontier America's most infamous traitor-renegade was the second of four sons born to Simon Girty Sr. and Mary Newton Girty, at their home on the east bank of the Susquehanna River at Paxton, Lancaster County, Pennsylvania.

The elder Girty, indigent, had migrated from Ireland about 1735 and made his way to the frontier where he went to work for a fur trader. He became a popular and successful trader among the Delawares of western Pennsylvania and soon purchased good land, built a house, and courted and married a young English immigrant named Mary Newton.

In 1750, when Simon Jr. was nine years old, his father was mortally wounded in a duel with a man named Samuel Saunders. The killer was subsequently arrested, convicted of manslaughter, and sent to prison. The elder Girty left his family saddled with debt. Three years later his widow was courted by a young man named John Turner, whom she married in 1754. Turner moved his new family to his own property in the Buffalo Valley (present Union County, Pennsylvania), and in 1755, just after the French and Indian War had begun, Mary gave birth to their first child, John Jr. A series of bloody Indian raids took place in the Buffalo Valley and, seeking safety, Turner moved his family to Indian Old Town (present-day Lewistown, Pennsylvania), where he joined the militia and helped to build Fort Granville.

In August 1756 the fort was besieged by French-led Delaware and Shawnee raiders, and the Girty-Turner family members were among those who were captured when it was surrendered. The prisoners were awarded to the Indians, who, loaded with plunder, then marched to the Delaware town of Kittanning, on the Allegheny River. Upon their arrival, Simon's stepfather was pulled aside, stripped naked, and tortured to death. The Kittanning Indians later revealed to a French officer that they had burned Turner because they were convinced that he had murdered their friend, the former trader Simon Girty Sr., in order to possess his wife.

Three weeks later, the Pennsylvania militia destroyed Kittanning and eighteen-year-old Thomas Girty was liberated. However, the other Girty family members remained in Indian hands and were given away when the Delawares abandoned their ruined town. Mary Girty-Turner and her eighteen-month-old infant went to one party of Shawnees, and twelve-year-old James Girty was given to another. Ten-year-old George remained with the Delawares, and fifteen-year-old Simon Jr. was given to a party of western Senecas who took him north to a village located on or near the eastern shore of Lake Erie.

Unlike their peers on the Pennsylvania frontier, where farmer-parents generally hated and feared Indians, the Girty brothers had grown up in the shadow of the fur trade. Their first home had been a place where friendly Indians came and went and were almost always welcomed. From such a background, the three brothers were warmly responsive to the Indians' attempts to resocialize them, and they were quickly adopted.

In replacing a Seneca warrior who had recently been killed, Simon acquired the dead man's identity, familial relationships, and connections. Exhibiting an amazing facility for acquiring new languages, Girty's talent was quickly noticed and nurtured by the Indians who lived in a multilingual environment. During the eight years he lived among them, the Senecas groomed him as an interpreter.

In 1764, following the Pontiac and Guyasuta uprising, the western and northern tribes wished to make peace and to resume trading. The British demanded that the Indians deliver up all their white captives for repatriation. With the names "Simon" and "Jamey" appearing on an English list of returned captives taken in 1756 from Pennsylvania, along with other convincing evidence, it now seems certain that Simon was reunited with his brother James at a British military encampment on the Tuscarawas River on November 14, 1764. Except for young John Turner Jr. (who was to remain in Indian hands until 1765), the Girty family was soon together again on Squirrel Hill, near Fort Pitt.

Twenty-three years of age, Simon was five-feet-nine inches tall, with a thick neck, broad shoulders, and a stocky, muscular body. His eyes were his dominant feature, striking because they were nearly as dark as the jet black hair he wore long and, with his deep tan, he could easily be mistaken for an Indian. He wore Indian clothing in the wilderness, but when in town, he dressed as a businessman. An outspoken, passionate man, his countenance shouted his moods. He had a good sense of humor and earned a reputation as an inveterate prankster. He was a carouser who often spent his evenings going from one tavern to another surrounded by friends. Loyal, accommodating, and forgiving to people he liked, he could become darkly antagonistic, aggressive, and abusive to anyone who angered him. His open friendships with Indians and his frequent defense of their culture got him into a number of brawls.

At Fort Pitt, Deputy Agent for Indian Affairs Lieutenant Alexander McKee, recognizing Girty's unique qualities and linguistic skills, quickly recruited him as an interpreter to the Six Nations. While many of the repatriated white captives of the Indians suffered difficult adjustments, Girty evidently enjoyed his transition. Unlike his younger brothers, James and George, who preferred life among the Indians, or his older brother Thomas, who openly despised them, Girty seemed to delight in visiting one culture and then the other, and had friends everywhere.

In May 1765, McKee put Girty to work interpreting important treaty talks at Fort Pitt. The Indian delegates were pressing the English to resume trade, and their principal spokesman was the noted Seneca chief Guyasuta, who was familiar with Girty and liked him. By the time the talks were concluded, Girty's superb performance as an interpreter and intermediary had been noted by both sides.

Three years later, Girty was present at Fort Stanwix, New York, when, in an attempt to deflect new white immigration to the south and away from their own northern Pennsylvania and New York homelands, the Six Nations of the Iroquois League sold the English large tracts of land situated on the lower Ohio River. These lands were traditional hunting grounds of the Shawnees, Cherokees, and Delawares, who vehemently protested the transaction. By 1774, determined to settle the lands purchased at Fort Stanwix, Virginia went to war against the Shawnees (Dunmore's War). During this conflict, Girty served the cause of Virginia (as well as of the Six Nations) and made a name for himself, first as a spy and messenger and then as a peace emissary. In most of these exploits he was accompanied by a young frontiersman named Simon Kenton, who had become his best friend. The Shawnees gave up the disputed lands, and, in thanks for his service, Governor Lord Dunmore awarded Girty a lieutenant's commission in the Virginia militia, which he soon was forced to surrender when the unit was disbanded at the onset of the American Revolution.

Girty quickly declared himself a patriot. Both English and rebel military leaders recognized that if the western and northern Indian nations allied themselves with one side or the other, their weight would quite likely decide the issue. Accordingly, in the summer of 1775, in order to promote neutrality and to measure British inroads among the western tribes, the government of Virginia sent Captain James Wood to tour the Indian towns of the Ohio country, with Girty as his guide and interpreter. Facing dangerous opposition and severe physical hardships, the two men conducted their daring mission with intelligence and wit; they traversed nearly all the Ohio country and returned to Fort Pitt after more than a month of travel. Wood's subsequent report made it clear that the British were actively engaged in enlisting the Indians as military allies.

America's Indian policy was yet to be decided. George Washington wanted the Indians to serve a combat role, but influential men such as the frontier merchant George Morgan argued strongly for keeping them out of the war. Morgan's faction won, and eventually Congress appointed him commissioner for Indian Affairs, Middle District. His orders were to organize and direct American efforts toward keeping the Indians neutral, and one of the first things he did was recruit Girty as his emissary and agent to the Six Nations. In June 1776, Morgan sent Simon to the Great Council of the Iroquois League, at Onondaga, New York, in a formal attempt to secure a promise of neutrality from the Six Nations. The odds were greatly against Girty's success, for the Mohawks were already raiding for the British, and the Senecas were ready to join them. At Onondaga, he patiently addressed the assembly, carefully putting forward the American peace proposals and their benefits. The quality of Girty's address must have been impressive, since for more than ten years he had listened to and translated the speeches of the greatest orators the Six Nations had been able to send to the British, as well as the words of their English counterparts. Before concluding, the Great Council gave Girty the commitment he had asked for: the Six Nations would remain neutral for the duration of the war. The promise included the Mohawks, whose warriors were to be recalled. It was a triumph for Girty, for Commissioner Morgan, and for the United American States.

Then, just two weeks after his exuberant return to Pittsburgh, Girty's relationship with Morgan exploded, and the commissioner fired him for "ill-behaviour." Years later, writers who were exploiting Girty's notoriety claimed Morgan had fired him for drunken and abusive conduct. What they failed to mention was that, while Morgan was sending Girty and his fellow agents to promise the Indians that the Americans had no postwar designs on their lands, the commissioner himself was investing heavily in the Indiana company. Morgan's interest in the fur trade had steadily diminished, and by the summer of 1776 he appeared to be consumed by land schemes. For the Indians, that transition carried ominous overtones. Fur traders and land speculators were diametrically opposed in their interests. One group required vast tracts of wilderness to produce furs to be harvested cheaply by the Indians, while the other was in the business of displacing Natives to make way for new white settlements. Girty must have realized that the commissioner's duplicity would sooner or later be exposed. Continuing to serve as Morgan's voice to the Indians was no longer in his best interest.

Girty was resilient, and within a few months he accepted the promise of a captain's commission and the command of a company if he could enroll 150 men for a new Virginia regiment of the Continental Army. Much to the chagrin of staff officers who objected to his relationships with Indians and with suspected loyalists such as Alexander McKee, Girty soon achieved his enlistment quota. Instead of being awarded the captaincy he had been promised, he was commissioned a lieutenant, and the command that he had worked for went to another. A few weeks later, when his regiment departed to fight at Charleston, Girty was left behind to serve on detached duty. Outraged, he resigned his commission and went to see General Edward Hand, who hired him to serve as a spy and as his own interpreter and emissary to the Six Nations. Then came the "Squaw Campaign," which, in turn, led to Girty's decision to defect.

The sudden arrival of Girty, McKee, and Elliott at Goschachgunk created an uproar. Although they were still at peace with the United States, the Delawares were reevaluating their status, and advocates for war were fast gaining ground. Girty and his companions explained that they had fled the Americans to serve the king, and they requested that an assembly be called that they could address. Runners were sent to outlying villages.

By design or coincidence, Girty's brother James and his Shawnee wife were also present at Goschachgunk when the fugitives arrived. The younger Girty was transporting a cargo of peace presents consigned to the Shawnees by the Continental Congress. Following a conversation with his brother, James announced that he, too, was quitting the Americans and then he commandeered all the goods left in his care and turned everything over to McKee.

Two nights later, Girty, McKee, and Elliott addressed a large, rapt gathering of Delawares, telling them:

> it was the determination of the American people to kill and destroy the whole Indian race, be they friends or foes, and to possess themselves of their country, and . . . while they were preparing themselves for this purpose, they were also preparing fine-sounding speeches to deceive them, that they might with more safety fall upon and murder them. That now was the time and the only time, for all the nations to rise and turn out to a man against these intruders, and not even suffer them to cross the Ohio, but fall upon them where they should find them, which if not done without delay, their country would be lost to them forever.[2]

Having done their best to incite the Delawares, McKee, Elliott, and James Girty were anxious to be on their way to the Shawnee towns on the Scioto, but—armed with a written recommendation from McKee—Simon left for Detroit to meet with Governor Henry Hamilton to persuade him to let Girty rejoin the British Department of Indian Affairs.

Almost a year earlier, Hamilton had received standing orders to assemble as many Indian warriors as he could and, after providing them with agents (advisers), he was to employ them to terrorize the rebels living on the Virginia and Pennsylvania frontiers.

By the time of Girty's arrival at Detroit, the governor had staffed the Department of Indian Affairs with more than 150 former traders and hunters, men who not only knew how to live among Indians but who also enjoyed it. His agents thoroughly understood the Indians' politics, cultures, and their favored forms of warfare. Although they were seldom placed in battle command over warriors, the agents were well received by the Indian leaders and greatly influenced their choice of military targets.

Despite Girty's prior service to the rebels, Hamilton enlisted him in the department. As "interpreter to McKee," he was to be paid 10 s. a day, the equivalent of a captain's pay. Girty's orders were to live with and gain the confidence of the Indians to whom he was assigned; to ascertain, pass on, and help secure their logistic needs; to advise them regarding military objectives; to accompany them on raids; and to collect as much military intelligence about the enemy as possible. In addition, Girty was instructed that he was to exert every effort to protect American prisoners, particularly noncombatants taken by the warriors, from unnecessary violence.

In mid-June important meetings with representatives from many of the tribes got under way at Detroit, and, aware that the Senecas still regarded Girty as their enemy, Governor Hamilton took special care to introduce him to the assembly, declaring him to be an interpreter who had escaped from the Virginians—someone who had put himself under "the protection of His Majesty, after [having] given satisfactory assurances of his fidelity."[3] Oddly enough, while Hamilton was promoting him to the Indians gathered at Fort Detroit, Girty was simultaneously being declared an American traitor at Lancaster, Pennsylvania, where an $800 bounty was being placed on his head.

Girty was ordered to establish himself among the Mingoes who resided in and around Upper Sandusky. (The Mingoes were a loose collection of Indians from various tribes, the majority of whom were western Senecas who no longer followed the dictates of the Iroquois League.) After settling in at a place called "Solomon's Town," Girty frequently traveled to Detroit, and he was there on the day his brother James arrived from the Shawnee towns for his initial meeting with Governor Hamilton. James was quickly enlisted in the Department of Indian Affairs and assigned to serve the Shawnees. By September both brothers were participating in combat operations against their former countrymen.

In mid-October, Simon, James, and another agent were returning with Shawnee, Wyandot, and Mingo warriors from raids in Pennsylvania and Virginia. Arriving at the Shawnee town of Wapatomica, they were conducted to the large Council House to recount their experiences. A few feet away in the darkened interior, an exhausted, disconsolate American captive sat naked on the ground. His arms were bound behind him and another cord tethered him to a post. Girty was informed that the prisoner had been captured stealing Shawnee horses, and that he had been repeatedly beaten and forced to run several gauntlets. The man's face was badly bruised and swollen and he had been painted black from the waist up, signifying that he had been condemned to death by fire.

Granted permission to interrogate the prisoner, Girty seated himself beside the man and began to question him about troop strength in Kentucky. In a moment, Girty recognized the man's voice and realized the prisoner was his friend Simon Kenton. Horrified, he stood up, drew Kenton to his feet and threw his arms around him telling him to take heart, that he would do everything he could to save him. Then Girty turned to face the Shawnee leaders and to reason with them and plead for his friend's life. After several hours, the issue was decided in Kenton's favor by one vote. He was to be adopted into the tribe. While Kenton was being nursed back to health, Girty bought him new clothes, a horse, saddle, and rifle, and as soon as he was up to it, he led his friend on a tour of the Indian towns. Their trip was cut short by a Shawnee war party that had just returned to Wapatomica, after suffering severe losses while raiding in Kentucky. Hearing that Kenton was still alive, their leader had angrily demanded a new trial. At this one, Girty would not be allowed to speak or intervene on his friend's behalf, and, once again, Kenton was condemned to death by fire. Upper Sandusky was selected as his place of execution, and while the Shawnees marched their now-famous captive northward, forcing him to run more gauntlets and to endure new beatings, Girty hurried ahead, conspiring to save his friend. With considerable help from another Indian agent and from the Mingo chief Logan, Girty's efforts were successful. Minutes before he was to be burned, Kenton was ransomed. Soon afterward, he was marched to Detroit where he was treated by a surgeon, placed on parole, and eventually given work. (Within a year, Kenton had escaped and rejoined American forces in Kentucky.)

Not long afterward, Girty was sent to spy on Fort Pitt, where he trailed a 1,500-man army led by General Edward Hand's replacement, General Lachlan McIntosh. The American troops went downstream along the Ohio River to the mouth of the Beaver, where they built Fort McIntosh. Once the fort was completed, Girty followed McIntosh and his army to a site not far from Goschachgunk, where construction of Fort Laurens began. Just as this fort was completed, the weather turned bitterly cold and McIntosh withdrew, leaving behind a garrison of only 150 men under Girty's old rival, John Gibson, to hold the fort until spring.

Girty returned to Upper Sandusky, made his reports, and in January was back once again in the Fort Laurens area, this time accompanied by eight Mingo warriors. Traveling on snowshoes, Girty and his men were three miles from the fort when they ambushed a mounted sixteen-man supply detail that was on its way back to Fort McIntosh, after having delivered desperately needed clothing, shoes, and food only the day before. Opening fire at close range, Girty and his men killed two soldiers outright, wounded four more, and captured another. The surviving Americans were able to reach Fort Laurens and safety. The soldier whom Girty had captured was carrying a dispatch case full of letters, which neither Simon nor any of his men could read. Girty hurried back to Detroit with his prisoner and the captured documents.

Among the papers Girty had captured were hastily written letters from Gibson to General McIntosh, describing the deplorable state of the defenders at Fort Laurens. In one of them, Gibson mentioned that he had been forewarned that Girty was coming to give him trouble and that he was waiting for him. Although a force of British regulars could not be spared from Detroit to attack the beleaguered American outpost, some 180 Indians, supplemented by Girty, a few Canadians, and 10 volunteers from the King's Eighth Regiment, soon departed from Upper Sandusky to harass Fort Laurens.

The siege began late one afternoon, with the Indians emerging in single file from a dense wood in plain view of the defenders, but well beyond the range of their guns. The warriors then drew out of sight behind a low hill. What the Americans could not see was that, as soon as the warriors got behind the hill, they raced back through the trees to emerge again, repeating the sequence over and over. By sunset the Americans had tallied 870 enemy warriors and were convinced that they were greatly outnumbered. Within a day or two, Girty's presence was duly noted, and Gibson and his men leapt to the mistaken conclusion that it was Girty who had assembled and now commanded the enemy warriors. The siege dragged on until mid-February, by which time the starving defenders were reduced to boiling their moccasins. Finally the Indians, too, ran out of provisions, and simply withdrew. A day later, General McIntosh arrived with a large relief column. Within weeks letters written by McIntosh, Gibson, and others spread word of Girty's deeds, and the mythic Simon Girty was born. Although it had been only a year since his defection and less than six months since he had begun participating in raids with the Indians, Girty was already the most feared and most intensely hated renegade on the American frontier.

In August 1779, Lieutenant George Girty deserted from the U.S. Marines at Kaskaskia, and walked to Detroit to join his brothers. Quickly enlisted in the Department of Indian Affairs, he was assigned to serve the Shawnees at Wapatomica. In October, Simon, his two brothers, and Matthew Elliott were members of a combined raiding party of Wyandots, Shawnees, Mingoes, and Delawares that had been sent out against Kentucky. On the lower Ohio, at the mouth of the Licking River (directly across the river from present-day Cincinnati), they decoyed, ambushed, and destroyed a flotilla of American keelboats that, under the command of Colonel David Rogers, were ferrying war supplies from New Orleans to Fort Pitt. It was a major American defeat. Rogers and forty of his men were killed, and an enormous amount of silver and valuable war matériel fell into British hands. In subsequent rebel accounts, Girty was credited with commanding the hostile Indians and mortally wounding Rogers.

In the spring of 1780 the British readied two thrusts from Detroit: one aimed at the Americans in the Illinois country, the other against Kentucky. The Kentucky campaign, ostensibly commanded by Captain Henry Bird, involved a combined force of several hundred warriors as well as British regulars, Canadian volunteers, and militia. In June, all three Girty brothers were part of this army, which soon overwhelmed Ruddell's and Martin's stations, two small stockaded posts, capturing more than four hundred Americans, men, women, and children. Farms in the area were burned out, hundreds of cattle were gunned down, and the prisoners were made to suffer a long, hungry, forced march all the way to Detroit. Despite British attempts to prevent it, a number of civilians were slain by Indians during the initial actions, and Girty and the other British officers were later accused of provoking the very atrocities they had attempted to curtail.

By early 1781 neither the Americans nor the British had gained the upper hand in the frontier war. Having now become one of the most productive field agents of the British Department of Indian Affairs, Girty was withdrawn from service with the Mingoes and reassigned to the more numerous Wyandots at Upper Sandusky. Sent to spy on George Rogers Clark at his winter quarters at Fort Nelson, near Louisville, Girty and his escorts captured three American militiamen who informed them that Clark had gone to Fort Pitt to help raise an army of three thousand men to lead against Detroit in the coming spring. Girty's intelligence set the British in motion, and they began at once to rally Indians to withstand the expected American thrust. Girty was sent to tour the Indian towns and deliver inspiring speeches. The British cause was helped considerably when Coshocton became the target of a surprise raid by several hundred American volunteers under Colonel Daniel Brodhead.

Clark's attempt to raise men at Fort Pitt failed, and in August the three "Indian Girtys" were part of a British-Indian force that successfully ambushed a large number of Pennsylvania and Virginia volunteers under the command of Colonel Archibald Lochry, who had been sailing down the Ohio River to join Clark. Two nights later, during a victory celebration fueled by captured whiskey, Mohawk war chief Joseph Brant (see Chapter 10 of this volume) boasted that he deserved all the credit for the American defeat. Tiring of his bragging, Girty insulted him. Later that evening, Brant came up to Girty from behind and struck him over the head with a sword. Girty's wound was so deep "the beating of his brain was plainly discernable."[4] A Wyandot medicine man was summoned. Expecting Girty to die, McKee confronted Brant and told him that if Girty expired, he would see to it that Brant was hanged. The Mohawk apologized profusely and blamed his actions on having drunk too much.

Laid up for several weeks, Girty was nursed back to health in a Wyandot village. After his recovery, he carried a large, ragged scar across his forehead and crown, and headaches plagued him for the rest of his life. To mask the scar on his head, he began wearing a scarlet bandana. Then, aware that he was being portrayed as a monster by his former countrymen, he made himself even more conspicuous by winding a crimson sash around his waist, into which he tucked two silver-mounted pistols. The colorful new costume quickly enhanced his notorious image. For the remainder of the war, Girty participated in essentially two types of missions: spy assignments, during which he led a small escort of warriors, or in interpreter-adviser roles in larger actions that involved combined Indian and British forces. Toward the end of the conflict, there is no doubt that Girty's reputation was causing the Americans more damage than his deeds. By 1782 he was being blamed for incidents occurring on the same date but hundreds of miles apart.

The most damning incident of the war for Girty stemmed from his presence at the burning of Colonel William Crawford, who had the misfortune of being captured by Delawares following the battle of Sandusky. Outraged by a previous massacre of ninety-six pacifist, pro-American, Christian Delaware converts (men, women, and children) by American militiamen at the Moravian mission of Gnadenhutten, the traditional Delawares were determined to take their revenge on the unlucky American commander. Following a two-day siege in woods near Upper Sandusky, where they were surrounded by a superior force of Delaware, Shawnee, Wyandot, and Mingo warriors reinforced by British Rangers, Crawford's 500 volunteers had attempted a night breakout, which became a panicked rout. Although most of the Americans eventually made it to safety, Crawford and several others were captured.

Aware of his precarious situation, Crawford asked to meet with Girty, whom he had known for years. Brought to him, he begged Girty to intervene. Unfortunately, Crawford had been taken by angry Delawares with whom Girty had little influence. Confronting the Delaware war chief Captain Pipe, Girty pleaded strongly for Crawford's life, first promising a big ransom from the British at Detroit and then offering his own rifle, horse, money, and everything else he owned. Unmoved, Captain Pipe warned Girty to say nothing more in defense of Crawford, threatening him with death by fire if he persisted.

Wearing the uniform of an English captain, Matthew Elliott was also present at Upper Sandusky, but his attempts to save Crawford were also to no avail, and the man was condemned. The night before he was to be put to death, Girty met with him and suggested a plan of escape which, if successful, would have left Crawford in British hands. Perhaps because he was too physically exhausted to carry out the plan, or perhaps because he believed he could still talk his way out of his predicament, Crawford rejected Girty's scheme.

The next morning, the American commander was stripped, beaten, marched to the place of execution, and then slowly burned to death. One witness, an American woman, later swore she saw Girty depart before Crawford's ordeal began in order to avoid having to witness the cruel spectacle. However, Dr. John Knight, who had been captured along with Crawford, escaped later and reported to American authorities that Girty had done nothing to save Crawford but had enthusiastically participated in his torture. Although Knight's account of Girty's actions differed entirely from the accounts of all the other witnesses (white and Indian) who later gave statements, it was Knight's rendition that was published and broadly circulated in a venom-filled, racist tract in which Girty is portrayed as a bloodthirsty, perverted wretch. The 1782 pamphlet was prefaced by Indian-hating lawyer Hugh Brackinridge, who wrote: "But as they [the Indians] still continue their murders on our frontier, these Narratives may be serviceable to induce our government to take some effectual steps to chastise and suppress them; as from hence they will see that the nature of an Indian is fierce and cruel, and that an extirpation of them would be useful to the world, and honorable to those who can effect it."[5]

For Girty the next major event was the Battle of Blue Licks, during which a large number of foolhardy Kentucky militia were annihilated—including one of Daniel Boone's sons. Occurring in August 1782, Blue Licks was Girty's last combat action of the frontier war and, once again, the Americans mistakenly credited him with having command over all of the enemy forces who fought there. Although he was only an adviser and in command of no one at Blue Licks, Girty apparently did contribute the strategy that lured the Kentuckians into the trap. Not long afterward, when referring to a proposed American expedition to be led against Sandusky by General Irvine, Colonel Arthur Campbell wrote: ". . . it is said he [Irvine] will set out with only 1,200 men. Simon Girty can outnumber him; and flushed with so many victories, to his natural boldness he will be confident."[6] Immediately following the Battle of Blue Licks, a new £1,500 reward was posted in Pennsylvania for Girty's capture or death.

Unknown to Girty, 150 Kentucky volunteers had been hurrying to reinforce their comrades at Blue Licks (arriving a day too late to save them). The officer who commanded the reinforcing company was Captain Simon Kenton. This "close call" may have been the nearest that Girty and Kenton ever came to facing one another over rifle sights.

In retaliation for the American defeat, George Rogers Clark struck back against the Shawnee towns on the Little Miami River in November, but then abruptly was ordered to stand down by General Washington, who was convinced that the British were now curtailing their Indian allies, and that peace was at hand. For Girty and the Indians of the Ohio, the shooting war was over—at least for the moment.

Peace negotiations dragged on for months, and uncertain of the Americans' true intentions, Major Arent De Peyster, British commander at Detroit, sent Girty south in the spring of 1783 to spy on Fort Pitt. On the morning of May 5, near Squirrel Hill (where the "American Girtys" were still living), Simon and an escort of Wyandot warriors took fourteen-year-old John Burkhart captive. Later that day, hearing the roar of big guns from the direction of Fort Pitt, Girty asked young Burkhart why cannons were being fired. "To celebrate the end of the war," the boy answered. Girty hurried back to Detroit, where the end of the conflict was confirmed, and where arrangements were soon made to return the Burkhart boy to his own people. Like many other American captives who had known Girty, Burkhart later remembered him with fondness, saying that he had been gentle and kind to him.

That summer, John Turner Jr. and Thomas Girty went to Canada to renew their relationships with their brothers and to reveal the passing of their mother. Both of the "American Girtys" had suffered because of Simon's notoriety and were thinking of putting down roots in Canada. After a few weeks, however, they returned to Pittsburgh where they lived long and prosperous lives.

With the conclusion of hostilities, Girty was one of the few field agents to remain on the payroll of the British Department of Indian Affairs, and he continued to serve McKee at Upper Sandusky. His new responsibilities included locating and securing the release of American men, women, and children who had been taken by the British and Indians during the war. Sent to find a young woman whose mother had come to the Department of Indian Affairs at Detroit seeking help, Girty located and arranged for the release of seventeen-year-old Catherine Malott, a strikingly beautiful young woman who had been living among the Shawnees since her capture. Apparently, during their journey back to Detroit, the forty-two-year-old Girty fell in love with her. A few months later, in thanks for their services during the war, the Wyandots awarded Girty, Elliott, and other members of the Department of Indian Affairs land located near the mouth of the Detroit River, which deed the British government later approved. Girty built a house on his farm site, and in 1784 he married Catherine Malott at Malden Township, Essex County, Ontario.

Although the British had ostensibly surrendered all their lands south of the Canadian border and east of the Mississippi, the Indians who resided north of the Ohio were determined to prevent American invasion and settlement. In this effort they were strongly supported by the British, who maintained steady trade with them, and who—through agents like Girty, McKee, and Elliott—encouraged their belligerence and provided both political and military support and guidance. Fort Detroit remained in English hands and British Department of Indian Affairs agents continued to operate from stations throughout the Ohio Valley. Spurred on by the English (and the French), the Indians formed alliances and demanded recognition of an Ohio River boundary from the United States.

In 1791 a large American army led by the Northwest Territorial governor, Arthur St. Clair, was sent across the Ohio River to bring the Indians to their knees. The invading Americans were completely destroyed by organized Indian resistance. St. Clair's defeat was the biggest loss ever experienced by an American army, and this time Girty had played a major role in the fighting. The Wyandots had given him complete command of their forces and he had performed brilliantly.

A year later, preceding crucial treaty meetings with U.S. commissioners, several Indian nations met at the Auglaize-Miami portage to draft their demands, and Girty was the only white man allowed to attend these vital strategy sessions. When the talks with the American congressional representatives began, Girty served as the Indians' interpreter, dressed as an Indian and wearing long silver earrings and a feather through the septum of his nose. Indian demands for American recognition of an Ohio River boundary were rejected, and the stage was set for continued conflict.

In 1794, directing a well-trained and well-disciplined American army that he had carefully prepared, General Anthony Wayne crossed the Ohio. He pushed northward, handing the Indians a terrible defeat at Fallen Timbers. Girty was present, along with McKee and Elliott, when, after breaking away from Wayne's forces, fleeing warriors of the allied tribes sought and were refused sanctuary within British-held Fort Miami.

In 1795, Fort Detroit was abandoned by the British. Headquarters for the Department of Indian Affairs was moved to Fort Malden, across the Detroit River not far from Girty's farm. By this time, Girty and his wife had two daughters and a son, and Catherine now delivered their last child, another boy.

After the loss of Detroit, Girty remained on his farm where, as an employee of the Department of Indian Affairs, he frequently entertained and conducted official meetings with tribal representatives. With the passage of time, the effects of his old head wound caused him debilitating headaches and his vision deteriorated. To add to his woes, he broke an ankle that did not heal properly. Dispirited by these turns of events and by his situation, Girty descended into alcoholism. Claiming abuse, his wife left him in 1798, taking their children, Nancy Ann, Sarah, and Prideaux, with her. Only Thomas, their elder son, remained with his father. Grateful for his loyalty, Girty signed over one-half of the Malden farm to him. At the outbreak of the War of 1812, Girty was seventy-one years old, nearly blind, crippled, and too infirm to serve in battle (although he remained on the payroll of the Department of Indian Affairs and continued to serve as an interpreter when called upon). His son Thomas, however, was an early volunteer for that conflict. During one of the first skirmishes of the war he contracted a fatal fever from overexertion in carrying a wounded officer from the battlefield. A grief-stricken Girty buried his favorite son beside the family home.

In September 1813, anticipating the American invasion of Canada, Matthew Elliott warned Girty to flee at once, as enemy troops would surely massacre him if he fell into their hands. Girty joined others from the Department of Indian Affairs who took refuge at a Mohawk village on the Grand River, at Burlington. Surrounded by Indians once again, the old white warrior was well cared for until the war with the United States concluded. Years later, the daughter and son of Simon Kenton confirmed to historian Lyman C. Draper that their father had told them that, only a day or two after the invasion of Canada, he had been able to reach the Girty farm just in time to prevent it from being burned down by angry American troops. Kenton would have been fifty-eight years old by that time.

Blind and feeble, but sober and with his spirit replenished, Girty returned to Malden in 1816 and reconciled with his wife, who moved back home to take care of him. Predeceased by his brothers James and George, Simon Girty succumbed after a brief respiratory illness in February 1818. He was seventy-seven years old. At the end he was closely attended by his family, and troops sent from Fort Malden buried him, with full military honors, beside his son's grave.

It is certain that Girty witnessed atrocities during his war years with the Indians. Yet there is no credible evidence that he ever willingly participated in such events or took any pleasure in viewing them. To his credit, no less than twenty-one Americans, men and women, later attested that while they were captives of the Indians, Girty intervened to save them from torture or death, or to comfort or give them aid.

Exploiting Girty's notoriety, nineteenth-century American writers, such as C. W. Butterfield, U. J. Jones, Edgar Hassler, and Charles McKnight, vilified him to the extreme. Girty's defamation was so potent that many of his descendants were embarrassed by their relationship to him. Even in Canada, official recognition of his service to the Indians and to the British Department of Indian Affairs did not come until July 10, 1995, when the United Empire Loyalists' Association finally honored him with a plaque at his Malden farm site.

When the facts are carefully reviewed, Simon Girty emerges as a man of enormous energy, a nonconformist with strong moral convictions, and someone who put the demonstration of loyalty to family and friends—red or white—above everything else. Despised by eighteenth-, nineteenth-, and even early twentieth-century Americans, he is seen by many today as a hero.

Notes

1. Charles McKnight, *Simon Girty: The White Savage, A Romance of the Border* (Philadelphia, 1880), title page.

2. John Heckewelder, *Narrative of the Missions of the United Brethern* [*sic*] (Philadelphia, 1828; reprint ed., New York: Arno Press, 1971), 171.

3. *Michigan Pioneer and Historical Collections*, 21 vols. (Ann Arbor: Bentley Historical Library, University of Michigan, 1886–1912), 9:443.

4. Lyman C. Draper Manuscripts, State Historical Society of Wisconsin, Madison, microfilm, 20 S 197.

5. Hugh Brackinridge, ed., *Indian Atrocities—Narratives of the Perils and Sufferings of Dr. Knight and John Slover . . . and a letter from H. Brackinridge, on the Rights of the Indians, etc.* (Philadelphia, 1783; reprint ed., Fairfield, WA: Ye Galleon Press, 1983), 5–6.

6. Colonel Arthur Campbell to Colonel William Davies, October 3, 1782, as quoted in Consul Wilshire Butterfield, *History of the Girtys* (Cincinnati, OH, 1890), 199.

Suggested Readings

Abernethy, Thomas P. *Western Lands and the American Revolution*. New York and London: D. Appleton-Century Company, 1937.

Butterfield, Consul Wilshire. *History of the Girtys*. Cincinnati, OH, 1890.

———. *An Historical Account of the Expedition against Sandusky*. Cincinnati, OH, 1873.

———. *Conquest of the Northwest*. Columbus, OH, 1904.

Kenton, Edna. *Simon Kenton*. New York, 1930.

Lyman C. Draper Manuscripts. State Historical Society of Wisconsin, Madison. Microfilm Series B, BB, F, G, S, U, YY.

Wakefield Hassler, Edgar. *Old Westmoreland*. Pittsburgh, PA, 1900.

In addition, the author suggests the following:

Allen, Robert S. *His Majesty's Indian Allies: British Indian Policy in the Defence of Canada, 1774–1815*. Toronto: Dundurn Press, 1992.

Calloway, Colin G. "Simon Girty: Interpreter and Intermediary." In *Being and Becoming Indian: Biographical Studies of North American Frontiers*, ed. James A. Clifton, 38–58. Chicago: Dorsey Press, 1989.

———. *The American Revolution in Indian Country*. New York: Cambridge University Press, 1995.

Graymont, Barbara. *The Iroquois in the American Revolution*. Syracuse, NY: Syracuse University Press, 1972.

Horsman, Reginald. *Matthew Elliott, British Indian Agent*. Detroit: Wayne State University Press, 1964.

Phelps Kellogg, Louise. *Frontier Advance on the Upper Ohio*. Madison: Wisconsin Historical Society, 1916.

———. *Frontier Retreat on the Upper Ohio*. Madison: Wisconsin Historical Society, 1917.

Thaites, R. G., and Louise Phelps Kellogg. *Dunmore's War*. Madison: Wisconsin Historical Society, 1905.

———. *Frontier Defense on the Upper Ohio*. Madison: Wisconsin Historical Society, 1913.

13

Absalom Jones and the African Church of Philadelphia

"To Arise out of the Dust"

Gary B. Nash

Absalom Jones (1746–1818) was not a revolutionary for his wartime activities, but for his role in the creation of the Free African Society, with his colleague Richard Allen, and the African Church of Philadelphia, an organization in which free blacks proclaimed their religious independence from white churches. Unlike fellow Episcopalian William Smith, Jones was a black Episcopal minister who had been born into slavery. After first purchasing his wife's freedom, he later, at the age of thirty-eight, bought his own independence. Given Jones's goal of freedom, why did he and his wife not seek refuge behind British lines during the British occupation of Philadelphia?

Legislators passed a gradual emancipation law for Pennsylvania in 1780, but Gary Nash demonstrates that many potential white benefactors would have preferred free blacks to worship in white churches. Such attitudes, as well as the treatment of African-American parishioners at St. George's, galvanized black goals for religious and cultural independence. Why did the Revolution's spirit of equality not lead Jones to advocate the end of racial separation in the religious sphere? Did the creation of a separate African church represent disillusionment with the rhetoric of the Revolution, or its fulfillment? The original plan lacked a denominational affiliation, but ultimately the majority of black elders favored the Episcopal Church, and, as a committed Methodist, Allen separated from the church. Did peaceful, internal differences between Jones and Allen threaten black unity, or present democratic choices between meaningful alternatives: St. Thomas's Episcopal or Bethel Methodist Church? What was the role of the independent black church in forging an African-American community? Given that white colonial churches were being disestablished in the immediate post-revolutionary era, how can the rising influence of the black church be explained?

An expert on African-American history of the revolutionary era, Gary B. Nash teaches history at the University of California at Los Angeles. He is the author of numerous articles and books, including *The Urban Crucible: The Northern Seaports and the Origins of the*

American Revolution (1979) and *Forging Freedom: The Formation of Philadelphia's Black Community, 1720–1840* (1988).

In an open field outside of Philadelphia on a sultry afternoon in August 1793, about one hundred white construction tradesmen and two of Philadelphia's most important citizens sat down at long tables "under the shade of several large trees" and consumed a bounteous dinner complete with excellent liqueurs and melons for dessert. They were served by a company of Philadelphia's free blacks. Then, after the white Philadelphians arose, about fifty blacks took their places and were waited on at a second sitting of the banquet by "six of the most respectable of the white company." The occasion for this unusual display of racial reciprocity was the raising of the roof for the African Church of Philadelphia, the first free black church in the northern United States. Benjamin Rush, Philadelphia's ebullient doctor, reformer, social activist, and general busybody, toasted, "Peace on earth and good will to men" and "May African churches everywhere soon succeed to African bondage." Describing to his wife the outpouring of emotion on that hot afternoon, he wrote: "Never did I witness such a scene of innocent—nay, more—such virtuous and philanthropic joy. Billy Grey [William Gray] in attempting to express his feelings to us was checked by a flood of tears." After dinner all the blacks converged on John Nicholson and clasped the hand of the city's entrepreneur par excellence, who had lent $2,000 for the building of the church. One old man "addressed him in the following striking language: 'May you live long, sir, and when you die, may you not die eternally.' " Rush rhapsodized, "To me it will be a day to be remembered with pleasure as long as I live."[1]

Another year would pass before the African Church of Philadelphia opened its doors for religious services, but the interracial banquet in August 1793 already foreshadowed two interlocking developments that marked the entire course of black history in the early national period: first, the efforts of former slaves to construct a foundation for freedom and a community-based fortress from which to fight white hostility and oppression through the establishment of independent black churches; and second, their difficult relations with the benevolent portion of the white community whose patronage was essential to the building of black institutions in this era but whose ingrained racial attitudes and desire to maintain social control often led to misperceptions, withdrawal of support, and sometimes opposition.

To understand the birth of the African Church of Philadelphia we must recreate the situation in which the city's free blacks found themselves in the 1780s. On the eve of the Revolution the city's slave population had been declining rapidly as a result of high mortality and low fertility rates, combined with the virtual cessation of slave importations. War further diminished the black population, as many slaves fled with the British when they evacuated the city in the summer of 1778, and many others were sold by their hard-pressed masters, died in the patriot military forces, or simply ran away. By the close of the war only about nine hundred black Philadelphians remained of the fifteen hundred or so who had resided in the city in 1767.

A wartime wave of abolitionist sentiment produced thousands of manumissions that reversed this demographic trend. From Philadelphia's hinterland to the west, from Delaware, Maryland, and Virginia to the south, and from New York, New Jersey, and New England to the north and east came a steady flow of dark-skinned former bondsmen and bondswomen seeking work and the fellowship of other blacks in the premier port city of the North. By 1790 more than 2,100 of them, all but 273 free, lived in the city and its environs. By 1800, in a city where some 63,000 white Philadelphians resided, black numbers had swelled to about 6,400, of whom only 55 remained in bondage.

These gathering black Philadelphians, like former slaves in other parts of the country, had to rethink their relationship to American society in the early years of the Republic. Were they Africans in America who might now return to their homeland? Were they African Americans whose cultural heritage was African but whose future was bound up in creating a separate existence on soil where they had toiled most of their lives? Or were they simply Americans with dark skin, who, in seeking places as free men and women, had to assimilate as quickly as possible into the cultural norms and social institutions of white society? Working out this problem of identity—and choosing strategies for fulfilling the goals they had set—required close attention to the particular locale in which freedmen and freedwomen found themselves or contrived to reach, for the social climate was far from uniform in postrevolutionary America.

Outwardly, Philadelphia beckoned manumitted blacks as a haven from persecution and an arena of opportunity. The center of American Quakerism where the first abolition society in the country had formed, the city was also the location of the state government that in 1780, in the midst of war, had passed the new nation's first gradual abolition act. Philadelphia was also a bustling maritime center that promised employment for migrating African Americans, who rarely possessed the capital to become independent farmers and therefore took to the roads leading to the coastal towns in the postwar years. Philadelphia's drawing power owed something as well to the considerable sympathy among some whites for freed blacks setting out on the road to freedom.

In its internal workings, however, Philadelphia fell far short of the ideal suggested by Rush. The illiterate and often unskilled black men and women who trekked there after the Revolution had to compete for jobs with Irish and German immigrants and did not always find work. Although not disenfranchised by law, free blacks faced some white social pressure to stay away from the polls. Moreover, virtually every institution and social mechanism in the city—religious and secular, economic and social—engaged in discriminatory practices, which flowed like water from the pervasive belief in black inferiority. Against the assumption that blacks were either innately handicapped or had been irreparably degraded by the experience of slavery stood only a minority of white Philadelphians who believed that recently freed slaves could overcome the marks of birth and oppression.

For black immigrants who found their way to Philadelphia after the Revolution, overcoming patterns of behavior peculiar to slavery became a crucial matter. By its nature slavery assumed the superiority of the master class, and even the most benevolent master occupied a power relationship vis-à-vis his slaves that daily reminded them of their lowly condition. Perhaps few American slaves believed they were inferior human beings, but slavery required them to act so. "Governed by fear," as the Pennsylvania Abolition Society put it, they carried into freedom an acute understanding of the tactics of survival, which included an almost instinctive wariness. Moreover, they now had to face the dominant white culture, which was far from ready to treat them as equals and continued to demand complaisant comportment from them. The will to plan rationally, to strive for an independent and dignified existence, to confront racial prejudice, and to work for the future of their children depended upon throwing off the incubus of slavery, an institution that had perpetuated itself by exacting a terrible price for attempts at independent or self-reliant black behavior.

Free blacks also had to confront the contradictory effects of benevolence on their lives. On the one hand, humane Philadelphians, Quakers foremost among them, succored slaves and freedmen and helped them cope with their vulnerability in a racially divided society. On the other, benevolence perpetuated feelings of powerlessness and functioned to maintain white social control.

The positive side of benevolence is seen vividly in the work of Anthony Benezet, the saintly Huguenot immigrant who dedicated so much of his life to the Negro's cause (see Chapter 1 of this volume). Benezet's greatest contribution to black Philadelphians lay in his challenge to the deeply rooted doctrine of black inferiority. He urged his pupils to regard themselves as citizens of the world and argued doggedly, as early as 1762, that the African environment had produced notable cultures and must not be considered as a place of jungle barbarism. He taught his black students that it was the environment of slavery, not an innate condition, that turned Africans in America into degraded and disheartened human beings.

The negative side of benevolence can be seen in the attitudes of many of Benezet's fellow Quakers. The Society of Friends led the way in opposing the slave trade and in manumitting slaves, and its members played a major role in establishing the Pennsylvania Abolition Society in 1775, which had to suspend operations during the war. In 1784, Quakers began visiting black families, quietly urging them to a life of industry and morality and helping those in distress. By the late 1780s the reorganized Pennsylvania Abolition Society was urging slaveowners to free their slaves and exercise stewardship over those who were free—educating them, watching over them, and inculcating in them middle-class values of sobriety, work, morality, and religious faith.

Such services were received among blacks at a cost. "There can be no greater disparity of power," writes historian David Brion Davis, "than that between a man convinced of his own disinterested service and another man who is defined as a helpless object."[2] Even more to the point, Quaker humanitarianism was never based on a deep sense of the "likeness among all persons." Unlike the spartan-living, humble Benezet, most Quakers held themselves apart from other people, white and black. The Society of Friends, in fact, was the only religious group in Philadelphia that refused to accept blacks as members in the 1780s. Theirs was more a "doctrine of stewardship" than a true humanitarianism, and their efforts on behalf of blacks "partook more of condescension than humanitarianism."[3] Thus, Quaker benevolence sometimes perpetuated black dependence, stood in the way of mutual respect between blacks and whites, and hampered autonomous behavior among those emerging from slavery.

Only a few years out of bondage in the 1780s, Philadelphia's free blacks lived in a highly fluid situation, full of possibilities yet also full of difficulties. Included within their gathering ranks were two men who would exert an extraordinary influence on the shaping of Philadelphia's black community, especially in the creation of black churches as the vital center of African-American life. In their backgrounds Absalom Jones and Richard Allen shared much.

Both were born into slavery, Jones in 1746 and Allen in 1760. Both experienced bondage in its rural and urban forms, having been raised partly in Philadelphia and partly in southern Delaware. Both lived under humane white masters and both prevailed upon their owners to allow them to learn to read and write. Both were touched by religion in their formative years, Allen by Methodism and Jones by Anglicanism. Finally, both persuaded their masters to reward faithful service by allowing them to purchase their freedom in the early 1780s.

When their paths crossed in Philadelphia for the first time, probably in 1786, Allen was Jones's junior in years but his senior in religious intensity. About 1778, bearing only the slave name Richard, Allen had been converted to Methodism by itinerant preachers in Delaware. No small part of his awakening may be related to the abolitionist stance of those he heard. For his freedom, in fact, he might have thanked Freeborn Garretson, the silver-tongued circuit rider who had convinced Allen's master that slaveholders at Judgment Day were "weighed in the balance and were found wanting."[4] Shortly thereafter, just before his twentieth birthday, Allen's master, Stokely Sturgis, proposed that Richard and his older brother buy their freedom. Taking a surname to signify his status as a free man, Allen spent the next six years interspersing work as a sawyer and a wagoner with months of riding the Methodist circuits from South Carolina to New York and even into the western Indian country. Traveling with some of the leading early Methodist sojourners, he learned to preach with great effect to black and white audiences alike. By the time he arrived, full of zeal, in the Philadelphia area, probably in February 1786, Allen seems to have completed the crucial psychological "middle passage" by which those who gained freedom in a legal sense procured as well the emotional autonomy that meant they had overcome their dependence upon whites.

No such blinding religious light had filled the mind of Absalom Jones. Born into a prominent merchant-planter family in Sussex County, Delaware, and named simply Absalom, he was taken from the fields into his master's house when he was very young. Removed from the debilitating world of field labor, he gained an opportunity for learning. Absalom later wrote that with pennies given to him from time to time, "I soon bought myself a primer and begged to be taught by any body that I found able and willing to give me the least instruction." Literacy could only have increased the distance between him and those of his age who did not live in the master's house, and hence Absalom became introspective, or "singular," as he termed it.[5] Then, in 1762, his master, Benjamin

Wynkoop, sold Absalom's mother and six siblings, left his Delaware plantation, and moved to Philadelphia, taking the sixteen-year-old slave boy with him. The traumatic breaking up of his family proved to be a turning point in Absalom's life. While bereft of his kin, he had landed in the center of the nascent abolitionist movement in America and in the city where, more than anywhere else in prerevolutionary America, humanitarian reformers had created an atmosphere conducive to education and family formation among slaves. Thus, while he had to work in his master's shop from dawn to dark, Jones prevailed upon Wynkoop in 1766 to allow him to attend a night school for blacks. Soon, Jones was able to write his mother and brothers in his own hand.

In 1770, Absalom married Mary Thomas, the slave of his master's neighbor. Mary and Absalom took vows in St. Peter's Church where the Wynkoop family worshiped. Soon after this, encouraged by the abolitionist sentiment that Quakers and others had spread throughout Philadelphia, he put the tool of literacy to work. After drawing up an appeal for his wife's release, he carried it, with his wife's father at his side, to some of "the principal Friends of this city," asking for their support. "From some we borrowed, and from others we received donations," he later recounted. Thereafter, as war came to Philadelphia, Absalom "made it my business to work until twelve or one o'clock at night, to assist my wife in obtaining a livelihood, and to pay the money that was borrowed to purchase her freedom."[6]

When the British occupied Philadelphia in September 1777, Jones remained at his master's side, resisting the chance to flee with his wife to the British, as did many black Philadelphians. It took Jones years to repay the debt incurred to buy his wife's freedom. But by 1778, Absalom had discharged his obligations and was pleading with his master to allow him to purchase his own freedom. Wynkoop would not consent until October 1, 1784, six years after the first of what Absalom remembered as a series of humble requests. So Jones used his hard-won surplus to purchase a small house and lot in the city.

Probably in 1784, upon gaining his release, Absalom took the surname Jones. It was a common English cognomen, yet one that *he* had chosen and one that could not be mistaken for the Dutch name of his master, whom he had served until he was thirty-eight. But he acted as if he bore his master no grudges. Forbearing, even-tempered, and utterly responsible, he continued to work in Wynkoop's store. More than thirty years later, in an obituary for Jones, it was said that his master, Wynkoop, "always gave him the character of having been a faithful and exemplary servant, remarkable for many good qualities; especially for his being not only of a peaceable demeanour, but for being possessed of the talent of inducing a disposition to it in others."[7]

Allen and Jones met in Philadelphia in 1786 after the Methodist elder in the city sent for Allen to preach to the growing population of blacks and offered him St. George's Church in which to hold meetings—at 5:00 A.M. "Several souls were awakened," Allen remembered years later in relating his life story to his son, "and were earnestly seeking redemption in the blood of Christ." Impressed by the large number of free blacks drifting into the city, and aware that "few of them attended public worship," Allen began supplementing his predawn services at St. George's with daytime meetings on the commons in adjacent Southwark and the Northern Liberties. Soon he had "raised a Society . . . of forty-two members."[8] Among them was Absalom Jones, who had abandoned Anglican services at St. Peter's Church, where his former master still worshiped, in favor of St. George's. Like taking a surname, this was a step in forging a new identity.

Within months of Allen's arrival in Philadelphia, Absalom Jones and two other recently freed slaves, William White and Darius Jennings, had joined the Methodist preacher to discuss forming a separate black religious society. Religion and literacy had helped all these men achieve freedom, so it was natural that, when they looked around them to find the majority of former slaves illiterate and unchurched, they "often communed together upon this painful and important subject in order to form some kind of religious society." Shortly thereafter Allen proposed this "to the most respectable people of color in this city," only to be "met with opposition." Leading white Methodists who heard of the plan objected even more strenuously, using, Allen wrote, "very degrading and insulting language to try to prevent us from going on."[9] Nonetheless, after these deliberations, Jones and Allen decided to organize the Free African Society. Founded in April 1787, it was the first black organization of its kind in America.

Organized in the manner of white benevolent societies, the Free African Society was quasi-religious in character and, beyond that, an organization where the people emerging from the house of bondage could gather strength, develop their own leaders, and explore independent strategies for hammering out a postslavery existence that went beyond formal legal release from thralldom. The society soon began assuming a supervisory role over the moral life of the black community, working to forge a collective black consciousness out of the disparate human material finding its way to Philadelphia. In May 1790 the society attempted to lease the Strangers' Burial Ground in order to turn it into a black cemetery under their control. In the next month the society established "a regular mode of procedure with respect to . . . marriages" and began keeping a book of marriage records. Having assumed quasi-ecclesiastic functions, the society took the final step in September 1790, when a special committee recommended the initiation of formal religious services, which began on January 1, 1791.[10]

Many of the society's enlarged functions bore a decided Quakerly stamp, reflecting the influence of Friends on many of the leading members and the Quakers' early involvement with the Free African Society. However, Richard Allen viewed the Quakerly drift of the Free African Society with concern. He made no objections when the black organization adopted Quaker-like visiting committees in late 1787, or when they instituted the disownment practices of the Friends the next year. But when the society, in 1789, adopted the Quaker practice of beginning meetings with fifteen minutes of silence, Allen led the withdrawal of "a large number" of dissenters whose adherence to Methodism had accustomed them to "an unconstrained outburst of the[ir] feelings in religious worship."[11] Allen came no more to meetings of the African Society but privately began convening some of its members in an attempt to stop the drift of the organization toward the practices of a religious group whose "detachment and introspection were not without value, but . . . did not seem to speak to the immediate needs of black people as Allen saw them."[12]

The adherence of many free blacks to Methodism is not hard to understand. As the first black historian of the African Church of Philadelphia wrote in 1862, the new Methodist preachers "made no pretensions to literary qualifications, and being despised and persecuted as religious enthusiasts, their sympathies naturally turned towards the lowly, who, like themselves, were of small estimate in the sight of worldly greatness."[13] Moreover, Methodism was far more experiential than other denominations, advocating lay preachers and lay societies, simplifying the liturgy of the Book of Common Prayer, and holding meetings in fields and forests or in the city, in sail lofts and homes. Also commending Methodism to former slaves were the well-known antislavery views of its founder, John Wesley, and the Methodist discipline and polity worked out in 1784, which attacked slave trading and slaveholding and barred persons engaged in these practices from holding church offices, as did no other religious group except the Society of Friends.

Perhaps most important, in Philadelphia the passionate preaching of Richard Allen had drawn many blacks to Methodism. Jones and others tried repeatedly to bring Allen back into the bosom of the Free African Society, but when he proved unyielding in his criticisms of their Quakerly innovations, they followed the

Friends' procedure of censuring him "for attempting to sow division among us." When this had no effect, they reluctantly declared in August 1789 that "he has disunited himself from membership with us."[14]

Now the leadership of the Free African Society fell to Absalom Jones. Mild-mannered but persistent, Jones made the crucial connections in the white community that launched plans for building a black church. The ties with the Society of Friends were wearing thin by the summer of 1791, because many Quakers objected to the Sunday psalm singing by blacks in the Quaker schoolhouse. But Jones, perhaps understanding the limits of the Quaker connection, had been forging new patronage lines to one of Philadelphia's most influential citizens—the widely connected, opinionated Benjamin Rush. Over the next four years it was Rush who became the Anthony Benezet of the 1790s so far as Philadelphia's free blacks were concerned. As a young physician before the Revolution, Rush had written a passionate antislavery pamphlet at the urging of Anthony Benezet. By 1787, Rush was thoroughly converted to the free blacks' cause, becoming one of the Abolition Society's most active members and writing a friend in Boston that "I love even the name of Africa, and never see a Negro slave or freeman without emotions which I seldom feel in the same degree towards my unfortunate fellow creatures of a fairer complexion."[15]

By 1791, Jones and a small group of emerging black activists had fixed their sights on building a community, or "union," black church. It was to be formed, as Rush said, from "the scattered and unconnected [black] appendages of most of the religious societies in the city" and from an even larger number of blacks "ignorant and unknown to any religious society."[16] Lacking denominational affiliation, it would not be tied to creeds or ordinances governing most white churches. Its goal was black unity in Christian fellowship, and beyond that a concern for the general welfare of the city's blacks. Jones and his group, in fact, proposed to build a black school first and then a church, though the two enterprises were hardly separable in their minds. Their formula was to become the classic one for the black church as it would emerge in the United States, "a pattern of religious commitment that has a double focus—the free and autonomous worship of God in the way Black people want to worship him, and the unity and social welfare of the Black community."[17]

Aided by Rush, Jones and his cohorts drew up a plan for a separate black church. Attempting to cast their appeal broadly, they adopted articles of association and a plan of church government "so general as to embrace all, and yet so orthodox in cardinal points as offend none."[18] The church was to be named the African Church of Philadelphia, and it was under this title, devoid of denominational reference, that the work of raising subscriptions went forward for the next three years. Jones and his group drew Richard Allen back into the fold, and eight leaders were selected to act as the "representatives" of the African Church. In a ringing broadside appeal for support, they argued that a black church would gather hundreds of those who worshiped in none of the white churches of the city, because "men were more influenced [by] their moral equals than by their superiors . . . and more easily governed by persons chosen by themselves for that purpose, than by persons who are placed over them by accidental circumstances."[19]

This democratic argument was accompanied by another that indicated the ideology of racial separation that Jones was hammering out. "Africans and their descendants" needed their own church because of the "attraction and relationship" among those bound together by "a nearly equal and general deficiency of education, by total ignorance, or only humble attainments in religion," and by the color line drawn by custom. All of this argued for the "necessity and propriety of separate and exclusive means, and opportunities of worshiping God, of instructing their youth, and of taking care of their poor."[20] Such a decisive step toward black self-assertiveness signified the pivotal role in the life of emancipated slaves that the black church would assume in an era when the centrality to community life of the white churches, disestablished and fragmented by the Revolution, was diminishing. Black religion would be, as one historian has explained, "the one impregnable corner of the world where consolation, solidarity and mutual aid could be found and from which the master and the bossman—at least in the North—could be effectively barred."[21]

Having enunciated the concept of a racially separate, nondenominational, and socially oriented church, Jones and the seven other trustees began the work of financing its construction. Rush's suggestions for circulating a broadside appeal with subscription papers—a tried and true method of raising money in Philadelphia—had been received by the black leaders, he wrote, "with a joy which transported one of them to take me by the hand as a brother."[22] When the work of circulating the subscription papers began in the fall of 1791, Rush tried to stay in the background, convinced that "the work will prosper the better for my keeping myself out of sight." But he was hardly capable of self-effacement, and word of his role in the plans soon circulated through the city. William White, rector of Christ Church and recently appointed bishop of the Episcopal Church in Pennsylvania, accosted Rush in the streets and "expressed his disapprobation to the proposed

African church," because "it originated in pride." Leading Quakers also conveyed their displeasure to Absalom Jones, and the Methodists threatened to disown any black Methodist who participated in the undertaking.[23] Paternalistic Philadelphians discovered that helping their black brothers proved more satisfactory than seeing them help themselves.

Such disapproval from Episcopalians, Quakers, and Methodists, some of whom had been active in the Abolition Society, drove home the lesson that even whites who claimed to have befriended free blacks were unwilling to see them move beyond white control. An early historian of black Methodism, reflecting in 1867 on the final separation of Richard Allen from the white Methodist Church, dwelt on precisely this point. "The giant crime committed by the Founders of the African Methodist Episcopal Church," wrote Benjamin Tanner, "was that they dared to organize a Church of men, men to think for themselves, men to talk for themselves, men to act for themselves: A Church of men who support from their own substance, however scanty, the ministration of the Word which they receive; men who spurn to have their churches built for them, and their pastors supported from the coffers of some charitable organization; men who prefer to live by the sweat of their own brow and be free."[24]

The opposition of white leaders partially undermined the appeal for building funds. Some modest contributions were garnered, including donations from George Washington and Thomas Jefferson. Rush himself contributed £25. But after six months, with money only trickling in, Jones and Allen decided to take to the streets themselves. Believing "that if we put our trust in the Lord, he would stand by us," Allen recounted, "we went out with our subscription paper and met with great success," collecting $360 on the first day.[25]

Thereafter the going got harder and much of the early optimism began to fade. The initial subscriptions proved sufficient, however, to buy two adjacent lots on Fifth Street, only a block from the Statehouse, for $450. But most blacks had only small amounts to contribute from their meager resources, and most whites seemed to have snapped their pocketbooks shut at the thought of an autonomous black church. White church leaders, who had initially responded to the idea of a separate black church as a piece of arrogance on the part of a people so recently released from slavery, now began calculating the effect on their own churches. "The old and established [religious] societies," Rush confided to a friend, "look shy at them, each having lost some of its members by the new association." Still, Rush did not waver in his conviction that "the poor blacks will succeed in forming themselves into a distinct independent church."[26]

Whatever their difficulties, the resolve of black Philadelphians to form a separate church was strengthened in the fall of 1792 in one of the most dramatic confrontations in early American church history. A number of black leaders were still attending services at St. George's Methodist Church, where the congregation had outgrown the seating capacity. When the elders decided to expand their house of worship, black Philadelphians contributed money and labor to the effort. Then, on the first Sunday after the renovations were completed, the elders informed the black worshipers who filed into the service that they must sit in a segregated section of the newly built gallery. Allen later recounted:

> We expected to take the seats over the ones we formerly occupied below, not knowing any better. We took those seats; meeting had begun, and they were nearly done singing, and just as we got to the seats, the Elder said, "Let us pray." We had not been long upon our knees before I heard considerable scuffling and loud talking. I raised my head up and saw one of the trustees, H—— M——, having hold of the Rev. Absalom Jones, pulling him off his knees, and saying, "You must get up, you must not kneel here." Mr. Jones replied, "Wait until the prayer is over, and I will get up, and trouble you no more." With that he [H. M.] beckoned to one of the trustees, Mr. L——S——, to come to his assistance. He came and went to William White [a black worshiper] to pull him up. By this time prayer was over, and we all went out of the church in a body, and they were no more plagued by us in the church.[27]

The St. George's incident confirmed what many blacks must have suspected—that there would be no truly biracial Christian community in the white churches of the city. Allen recalled that after the incident the black leaders renewed their determination "to worship God under our own vine and fig tree" and "were filled with fresh vigor to get a house erected to worship God in."[28]

By late 1792, with money coming in very slowly for construction of the African Church, the black leaders faced the prospect that they could not raise sufficient funds to build a church on the lots they had purchased. To their rescue came the unlikeliest of figures—the Welsh immigrant John Nicholson, who had blazed meteorically onto the Philadelphia scene after the war as state comptroller and high-flying speculator in western lands and revolutionary loan certificates. Not wholly accepted in polite Philadelphia circles, and uninvolved in the work of the Abolition Society, Nicholson provided what none of the established Philadelphia elite would offer—a large loan to begin construction. "Humanity, charity, and patriotism never united their claims in a petition with more force than in the present instance," Rush wrote to Nicholson in a letter hand-carried by William Gray and Absalom Jones. "You *will* not—you *cannot*" refuse their request "for the sake of Religion & Christianity and as this is the first Institution of the kind. . . ."[29]

It took two months more to execute the mortgage and another month to draw up building contracts. Finally, in March 1793, with reports of continued black rebellion in the French West Indies filtering into Philadelphia, the city's free blacks and some of their white benefactors gathered to see earth turned for the church. Writing a quarter of a century later, Allen remembered the day vividly: "As I was the first proposer of the African Church, I put the first spade into the ground to dig the cellar for the same. This was the first African church or meeting house to be erected in the United States of America."[30]

Before the two-story brick building could be completed, its humble founders had to endure additional difficulties. Like most visionaries, Jones and his cohorts had planned expansively, designing a brick church capacious enough to seat eight hundred. The cost estimates for the building ran to $3,560. Even with the $1,000 loan from Nicholson, more money had to be raised. Another kind of black movement for independence paradoxically undermined this attempt. With hundreds of French planters fleeing the Afro-French rebellion in Saint Domingue and streaming into Philadelphia with French-speaking slaves at their sides, many white city dwellers reneged on their pledges to the African Church in order to help the destitute white slaveholders now taking refuge in their city. Philadelphia's free blacks learned that even the most sympathetic white men placed the distress of white slaveowners, even those from outside the United States, ahead of the aspirations of those who had been slaves.

Nicholson again came to the rescue, lending another $1,000 in mid-August. Ten days later the black leaders staged the roof-raising banquet on the edge of the city. But even as glasses were raised in toasts, ill fortune struck again, this time delaying the completion of the church for nearly a year. It came in the form of the worst epidemic of yellow fever in the history of North America. The first victims succumbed late in July 1793; by late August the fever had reached epidemic proportions. With twenty Philadelphians dying daily of the putrid fever, shopkeepers began closing their doors, and all who could afford it commandeered horses, wagons, and carriages to carry their families out of the city. Hardest hit were the laboring poor. Living in crowded alleys and courts where the fever spread fastest, they were too poor to flee, sometimes too poor even to pay for a doctor.

By early September, the social fabric of the city was torn in pieces. Soon, with more than one hundred people dying every day, the work of tending the sick and burying the dead exceeded the capacity of the doctors and city authorities, because most nurses, carters, and gravediggers, who regarded the disease as contagious, refused to go near the sick, dying, and dead. Husbands fled wives of many years who were in the throes of death, parents abandoned sick children, masters thrust servants into the streets. Mathew Carey, the main chronicler of the catastrophe, wrote that "less concern was felt for the loss of a parent, a husband, a wife or an only child than, on other occasions, would have been caused by the death of a servant, or even a favorite lap-dog." Hundreds perished for lack of treatment, "without a human being to hand them a drink of water, to administer medicines, or to perform any charitable office for them."[31] By mid-October the poor were starving, and the dead lay everywhere in the streets, while thousands of those who could afford to had moved to the countryside.

Into this calamitous breach stepped Philadelphia's free blacks. Benjamin Rush, who played generalissimo of the relief forces, implored Richard Allen in early September to lead his people forward as nurses, gravediggers, and drivers of the death carts. Assuring Allen that the malignant fever "passes by persons of your color," he suggested that this God-bestowed exemption from the disease laid blacks "under an obligation to offer your services to attend the sick."[32]

The Free African Society met on September 5, 1793, to consider Rush's request. Much of what had transpired in the last six years might have inclined them to spurn the requests for aid—the humiliating incident at St. George's the year before, the opposition to establishing their own church, and most recently the readiness of those who had signed their subscription lists to beg off in order to aid slaveowning French planters, who arrived with their chattel property in tow and then attempted, though unsuccessfully, to overturn the state law requiring manumission of any slave brought into the state by an owner establishing residence. But much had also transpired that argued for aiding the white community's desperate plight—the encouragement they had received in planning their church, the considerable aid of the Abolition Society, and the personal solicitation of Rush, their closest adviser.

A pamphlet written by Absalom Jones and Richard Allen after the epidemic indicates that they saw this as a God-sent opportunity to prove their courage and worth and to show that they could drive anger and bitterness from their hearts. Perhaps they could dissolve white racism by demonstrating that in their capabilities, civic virtue, and Christian humanitarianism they were not inferior, but in fact superior, to those who regarded former slaves as a degraded, hopelessly backward people. The "God who knows the hearts of all men, and the propensity of a slave to hate his oppressor," they wrote, "hath strictly forbidden it in his chosen people." Philadelphia's black Christians would act as the Good Samaritan, the despised man who aided a fellow human in desperate need when all the respected men of the community turned their heads away. They would succor those who despised and opposed them, because "the meek and humble Jesus, the great pattern of humanity, and every other virtue that can adorn and dignify men, hath commanded [us] to love our enemies, to do good to them that hate and despitefully use us."[33]

On September 6, 1793, Jones and Allen offered their services to the mayor, who immediately placed notices in the newspapers notifying citizens that they could apply to Jones or Allen for aid. "The African Society, intended for the relief of destitute Negroes," wrote the best authority on the epidemic, "suddenly assumed the most onerous, the most disgusting burdens of demoralized whites." They nursed the sick, carried away the dead, dug graves, and transported the afflicted to an emergency lazaretto set up outside the city. Jones, Allen, and William Gray, under instructions from Rush, acted as auxiliary doctors, bleeding patients and administering purges. By September 7, wrote Rush, Jones and Gray were "furnish[ing] nurses to most of my patients."[34] Before the epidemic ran its course, Rush's untutored black assistants had bled more than eight hundred patients, making notes on each case for Rush as they worked through the day. At night they drove the death carts to the cemeteries.

Within two weeks, Rush's assertion that Negroes were immune to the infectious fever had proven a ghastly error. Seventy Philadelphians were dying each day, and now blacks were numerous among them. "The Negroes are everywhere submitting to the disorder," Rush wrote on September 26, "and Richard Allen who had led their van is very ill."[35] In the first weeks of October, mortality raged through the half-abandoned city like a brushfire. On October 11 alone, 119 died. Still convinced "that it was our duty to do all the good we could to our suffering fellow mortals," Jones, Allen, and the other blacks carried out their gruesome tasks.[36] By the end of the month nearly 12,000 whites, along with the national and state governments, had fled the city, and nearly 4,000 persons, including about 240 blacks, had succumbed to the fever. Not until early November did the epidemic pass.

Work on the African Church, suspended for nearly three months during the yellow fever crisis, resumed in December 1793. It took further fundraising and another six months to complete the building. In soliciting support in the white community the black leaders may have expected to draw on the credit they had accumulated through their heroic efforts during the terrible days of autumn. But even this altruism had to be defended, for Mathew Carey, the Irish immigrant publisher in the city, publicly vilified the free blacks for opportunistically charging exorbitant fees to nurse the sick and remove the dead. Carey's pamphlet, *A Short Account of the Malignant Fever*, was itself a lesson in deriving profit from mass misery. Selling briskly, it went through four editions between November 14 and December 20. Carey provided a narrative account of the terrifying epidemic and appended lists of the dead. But the city's saviors in Carey's account were the rising merchant, Stephen Girard, and other whites who organized an emergency hospital just outside the city, where they selflessly tended the sick and dying. For the black Philadelphians who drove the death carts, buried the dead, and nursed the sick in the back streets and alleys, Carey had few good words.

Carey's *Short Account* drew a shocked response from Jones and Allen. They did not deny that some opportunistic persons "in low circumstances," both white and black, charged extravagant prices to nurse or remove the infected. This behavior was to be expected, "especially under the loathsomeness of many of the sick, when nature shuddered at the thoughts of the infection, and the task was aggravated by lunacy, and being left much alone" with the sick. But Philadelphians should consider such stories, they argued, alongside those of the many blacks who asked no recompense at all, content to take whatever the patient thought proper to give. One old black woman, when asked her fee, answered, "A dinner, master, on a cold winter's day." Caesar Cranchell, a founding member of the African Society, swore he would not "sell my life for money," even though he should die, which he did in the process of tending sick whites. Jones, Allen, Gray, and most other blacks had remained in the city throughout the biological terror, while nearly twenty thousand whites, including Carey, had fled. Assured that they were immune from the disease, black Philadelphians had remained in the city, only to learn otherwise; before cold weather ended the scourge, nearly one-tenth of the black population had died, as great a proportion as among whites. "Was not this in a great degree the effect of the services of the unjustly vilified black people?" asked Jones and Allen.[37]

As workmen completed the African Church, Philadelphia's blacks gathered to make a momentous decision about denominational affiliation. A "large majority" of the black elders and deacons favored uniting with the Episcopal (formerly Anglican) Church, with only Jones and Allen opting for the Methodists. The majority view is understandable for several reasons. The local Methodist church had insulted Philadelphia's blacks just a few years before, and the presiding white elder remained opposed to a separate black church and, recounted Allen, "would neither be for us nor have anything to do with us."[38] Moreover, Methodism, while an evangelical and popular movement, operated under an autocratic ecclesiastical structure whereby its congregants had no voice in the pastoral affairs of their church or in the church's annual conferences.

The Episcopal Church, on the other hand, had much to commend it to Philadelphia's free blacks. It was theologically flexible and tinged with evangelicalism since before the Revolution, and its authority structure was more fluid than that of the Methodists. Many black Philadelphians, both slaves and free persons, had married, worshiped, and christened their children in the city's three Episcopal churches. Furthermore, their two closest white supporters were Episcopalians—Benjamin Rush, who had converted from Presbyterianism in 1787, and Joseph Pilmore, the former Methodist who, after returning to Philadelphia as an Episcopal priest, had ministered to the Free African Society's religious meetings.

Steadfast in his conviction that "there was no religious sect or denomination that would suit the capacity of the colored people as well as the Methodist," Allen quietly withdrew again. He could not accept the invitation to be the minister of the church. "I informed them," he wrote later, "that I could not be anything else but a Methodist, as I was born and awakened under them, and I could go no further with them, for I was a Methodist, and would leave them in peace and love."[39]

With Allen declining to lead them, the deacons and elders turned to Absalom Jones. He lacked Allen's exhortatory gifts, but his balance, tenacity, education, and dignified leadership qualities all commended him. His "devotion to the sick and dying" during the terrible days of the yellow fever epidemic had also earned him affection in the black community. "Administering to the bodily as well as the spiritual wants to many poor sufferers, and soothing the last moments of many departing souls among his people," it was later written, "he became greatly endeared to the colored race."[40]

With Jones leading them, the elders and deacons of the African Church of Philadelphia began to formalize the union with the Episcopal Church in July 1794. The black Philadelphians agreed to "commit all the ecclesiastical affairs of our church to the government of the Protestant Episcopal Church of North America," while at the same time securing internal control of their church—and church property—through a constitution that gave them and their successors "the power of choosing our minister and assistant minister," provided that members were to be admitted only by the minister and church wardens, and specified that the officers of the church—the vestrymen and deacon—were to be chosen by ballot from among members of at least twelve months' standing. Finally, only "men of color, who were Africans, or the descendants of the African race," could elect or be elected into any church office except that of minister and assistant minister. With the help of Benjamin Rush, they had contrived a formula for maintaining black control of the church, while allowing for the absence of trained blacks to fill the ministry. They had "declared a conformity to our Church in Doctrine, Discipline, and Worship," wrote Bishop William White, but simultaneously they had gained the promise of ordination of their leader, Absalom Jones, while preserving the all-important rights of self-government.[41]

On July 17, 1794, the African Church of Philadelphia opened its doors for worship. The published account of the dedication ceremony indicates that most of the white ministerial opposition had melted. "The venerable Clergy of almost every denomination, and a number of other very respectable citizens were present," a witness related. James Abercrombie, assistant minister of Christ Church, officiated, and Samuel Magaw, rector of St. Paul's Church, gave the sermon from the text: "Ethiopia shall soon stretch out her hands unto God" (Psalms 68:31). The discourse was from Isaiah: "The people that walked in darkness have seen a great light"—the same epigraph that was etched in marble above the church doors (Isaiah 9:2).[42] But we may imagine that the worshipers, those who were black and those who were white, derived different meanings from this epigraph.

Magaw's sermon stressed the need for gratitude and subservience on the part of the blacks who crowded the church. They or their fathers, he preached, had come from the heathenish lands of Senegal, Gambia, Benin, Angola, and Congo, and that burden of birth had been increased by the dismal effects of slavery, which "sinks the mind, no less than the body, . . . destroys all principle; corrupts the feelings; prevents man from either discerning, or choosing aright in anything." Having providentially been brought from "a land of Pagan darkness, to a land of Gospel light," these former slaves must now maintain their gratitude to the white Christians who freed them and donated or lent money to build the church. As for their brethren still in slavery, they should pray—but not take action. He emphasized the need for black passivity and moderation in all things and warned them to suppress the pride that was on the rise among them. Instead, they should cultivate "an obliging, friendly, meek conversation." Their church, Magaw counseled, in a perfect display of white paternalism, owed its existence to the benevolent action of whites. That it had been born in strife and discrimination and had arisen only when free blacks defied the opposition of white churchmen received no mention.

How did black Philadelphians receive Magaw's message? It must have confirmed among many of them the wisdom of forming a black church, not only to worship God in their own way but as a means of proving themselves and thus achieving equality and real freedom. By setting alongside Magaw's advice the thoughts of Jones and Allen, published a few months before, we can better comprehend the social and psychological struggle of free blacks: "You try what you can to prevent our rising from the state of barbarism you represent us to be in," wrote Jones and Allen in their reply to Mathew Carey, "but we can tell you from a degree of experience, that a black man, although reduced to the most abject state human nature is capable of, short of real madness, can think, reflect, and feel injuries, although it may not be with the same degree of keen resentment and revenge, that you who have been and are our great oppressors, would manifest if reduced to the pitiable condition of a slave." This hot indictment of white oppression and denigration of blacks was followed by an insistence on the capabilities of Africans and their descendants, which echoed Benezet's views. "We believe, if you would try the experiment of taking a few black children, and cultivate their minds with the same care, and let them have the same prospect in view, as to living in the world, as you would wish for your own children, you would find them upon the trial, they were not inferior in mental endowments."[43]

One month later, Absalom Jones preached the alternative black interpretation of the words from Isaiah—"the people that walked in darkness have seen a great light." The "darkness" through which they had walked was not the land of their birth but slavery. And the "great light" they had now seen was the light of freedom as well as the light of Christianity. In recording the "Causes and Motives" for establishing the African Church, written just a month after the church opened, Jones again expressed the rising tide of black determination to find strategies that would promote strength, security, and a decent existence. They had learned, Jones wrote, "to arise out of the dust and shake ourselves, and throw off that servile fear, that the habit of oppression and bondage trained us up in." In what seems to be a direct reference to the charges of Bishop White about black "pride," Jones continued that they wished "to avoid all appearance of evil, by self-conceitedness, or any intent to promote or establish any new human device among us"; hence they had decided to "resign and conform ourselves" to the Protestant Episcopal Church of North America.[44] Nonetheless, this was to be an autonomous black church, as their constitution spelled out.

Although he did not mention it, Jones might have added that the black "pride" and determination to create their own institutions drew much sustenance from the day-to-day accomplishments of Philadelphia's blacks during the decade that followed the Revolution. Through their ability to establish families and residences, by their demonstrated capacity to sustain themselves as free laborers and artisans, and in their success at conducting themselves morally, soberly, and civilly, they must have proved to themselves the groundless and racist character of the prevalent white view that former slaves were a permanently corrupted people.

This is not to argue that the transition from slavery to freedom was without its hazards. Philadelphia in the 1790s was full of struggling black sojourners, many with limited skills, who arrived by water and land from every direction. Hundreds of them at first could not establish independent black households, many had to bind out their children, and only a minority rose above a pinched and precarious existence. But their general ability to fashion a respectable life for themselves, giving credence to the arguments of Benezet, helped to galvanize leaders and convince them of their capability to establish separate churches.

As black Philadelphians completed St. Thomas's African Episcopal Church and formalized its affiliation with the Protestant Episcopal Church, Richard Allen continued to pursue his vision of black Methodism. Successful as a carter, trader, and master of chimney sweeps, he used his own money to purchase a blacksmith shop and haul it to a site he had bought at Sixth and Lombard Streets. Renovated as a humble house of worship, it opened its doors for a dedication service led by Bishop Francis Asbury on June 29, 1794. The Reverend John Dickens, the white Methodist elder recently assigned to Philadelphia, prayed "that it might be a 'Bethel' to the gathering of thousands of souls."[45] This marked the birth of "Mother Bethel," the first congregation of what became, in 1816, the independent African Methodist Episcopal Church.

Although the sources have allowed us to follow primarily the efforts of black leaders to point the way forward by organizing separate churches, it is important to measure the response of the mass of ordinary former slaves to the establishment of St. Thomas's and Bethel because that can tell us, if only imperfectly, about an emerging black consciousness in Philadelphia. All of the available sources indicate an extraordinary response by Philadelphia's free blacks to the establishment of separate churches where they might worship, organize themselves, and develop their own leadership apart from white supervision.

In 1794, in the year they were founded, St. Thomas's and Bethel recorded 146 and 108 members respectively; one year later they had increased their membership to 427 and 121. Besides no fewer than 548 registered members in the two churches, "a floating congregation of at least a hundred or more persons" attended St. Thomas's, according to the church's first historian, and a number of others must have done so at Bethel.[46] The proportion of black adults who joined the two churches must have been about 40 percent of the 1,500 who lived in the city. This level of church participation was probably higher than that among whites in general and perhaps twice as high as among whites of the laboring classes. These figures are all the more impressive in view of the fact that about half of the city's free blacks were living in the households of whites, many as indentured servants, and therefore were less than fully free to act autonomously, while hundreds of others were French-speaking blacks recently manumitted by their Saint Domingue refugee masters or newly arrived migrants, often destitute and old, from the South.

The independent black church movement led by Absalom Jones and Richard Allen was the first major expression of racial strength and the most important instrument for furthering the social and psychological liberation of recently freed slaves. Bishop White had been correct, though in ways he knew not, when he reacted in anger in 1791 to news that free blacks were planning their own church, charging that their plan "originated in pride." That "pride" was really a growing feeling of strength and a conviction that black identity, self-sufficiency, self-determination, and the search for freedom and equality could best be nurtured in the early years of the Republic through independent black churches.

Absalom Jones tended his flock at St. Thomas's for a quarter-century, until he died in 1818 at seventy-one years of age. He guided his parishioners through a period of intensifying white racism, helped them take January 1 as their national holiday (because in 1808 it marked the end of the legal slave trade), and led them in building schools, mutual aid organizations, and literary societies. Though unnoticed in the history books from which young Americans learn about their founding period, Jones accomplished more in a lifetime than all but a handful of white Americans to make the revolutionary credo a reality. While struggling against congealing white racism, men like Jones became, in a peculiar way, the conscience of the nation. It was they, along with a small number of white reformers, who emerged in the early nineteenth century to demand of the Constitution, as one historian puts it, "more than its slave-holding creators dared to dream, wrestling it toward an integrity that the [Founding] Fathers would not give it."[47]

Notes

1. Benjamin Rush to Julia Rush, August 22, 1793, *Letters of Benjamin Rush*, ed. L. H. Butterfield, 2 vols. (Princeton, NJ, 1951), 2:639.

2. David Brion Davis, *The Problem of Slavery in the Age of Revolution, 1770–1823* (Ithaca, NY, 1975), 254.

3. Sydney V. James, *A People among People: Quaker Benevolence in Eighteenth-Century America* (Cambridge, MA, 1963), 316–19.

4. *The Life Experience and Gospel Labors of the Rt. Rev. Richard Allen, To Which is Annexed The Rise and Progress of the African Methodist Episcopal Church in the United States of America* (Nashville, TN, 1960), 17.

5. "Sketch of Jones," in William Douglass, *Annals of the First African Church in the United States of America, now styled the African Episcopal Church of St. Thomas* (Philadelphia, 1862), 118–21.

6. Ibid.

7. *American Daily Advertiser* (Philadelphia), February 19, 1818.

8. *Autobiography of Richard Allen*, in R. R. Wright Jr., *Bishops of the African Methodist Church* (Nashville, TN, 1963), 53–54.

9. Ibid., 54. The quotation about "often communed together" is from the preamble to the constitution of the Free African Society, in Douglass, *Annals*, 15.

10. Douglass, *Annals*, 18–41, where extracts of the Free African Society's minutes, no longer extant, are recorded.

11. Ibid., 18–23.

12. Carol V. R. George, *Segregated Sabbaths: Richard Allen and the Rise of Independent Black Churches, 1760–1845* (New York, 1973), 57.

13. Douglass, *Annals*, 9.

14. Ibid., 24.

15. Rush to Jeremy Belknap, August 18, 1788, *Letters of Rush*, 1:482.

16. *Extract of a Letter from Dr. Benjamin Rush, of Philadelphia, to Granville Sharp* (London, 1792), 6–7.

17. Gayraud S. Wilmore, *Black Religion and Black Radicalism: An Interpretation of the Religious History of the Afro-American People* (Garden City, NY, 1972), 114.

18. *Extract of a Letter from Rush*, 4.

19. "Address of the Representatives of the African Church," in ibid., 6–7.

20. Ibid.

21. Wilmore, *Black Religion and Black Radicalism*, 106.

22. Rush to Julia Rush, July 16, 1791, *Letters of Rush*, 1:599–600.

23. George W. Corner, ed., *The Autobiography of Benjamin Rush* (Princeton, NJ, 1948), 202.

24. Benjamin T. Tanner, *An Apology for African Methodism* (Baltimore, 1867), 16.

25. *Autobiography of Allen*, 55.

26. Rush to Jeremy Belknap, June 21, 1792, *Letters of Rush*, 1:620.

27. *Autobiography of Allen*, 55.

28. Ibid.

29. Rush to John Nicholson, November 28, 1792, *Letters of Rush*, 1:624.

30. *Autobiography of Allen*, 57.

31. Mathew Carey, *A Short Account of the Malignant Fever* (Philadelphia, 1794), 23.

32. Rush to Richard Allen, [September 1793], Mss. Correspondence of Rush, Library Company of Philadelphia, 38:32.

33. Absalom Jones and Richard Allen, *A Narrative of the Proceedings of the Black People, During the late Awful Calamity in Philadelphia, in the year 1793* . . . (Philadelphia, 1794), 24–25.

34. J. H. Powell, *Bring Out Your Dead: The Great Plague of Yellow Fever in Philadelphia in 1793* (Philadelphia, 1949), 96–98; Rush to ———, September 7, 1793, *Letters of Rush*, 2:654.

35. Rush to Julia Rush, September 13, 25, 1793, *Letters of Rush*, 2:663, 683–84.

36. Jones and Allen, *Narrative of the Black People*, 15–16; *Minutes of the proceedings of the Committee* . . . (Philadelphia, 1794), 204.

37. Jones and Allen, *Narrative of the Black People*, 7–16.

38. *Autobiography of Allen*, 57–58.

39. Ibid., 58–59.

40. George F. Bragg, *Richard Allen and Absalom Jones* (Baltimore, 1915), unpaginated.

41. The constitution is in Douglass, *Annals*, 96–99. White's statement is quoted in Edgar L. Pennington, "The Work of the Bray Associates in Pennsylvania," *Pennsylvania Magazine of History and Biography* 58 (1934): 22.

42. Samuel Magaw, *A Discourse Delivered July 17th 1794, in the African Church of Philadelphia, on the occasion of opening the said Church and holding public worship in it for the first time* (Philadelphia, 1794), reprinted in Douglass, *Annals*, 58–81.

43. Jones and Allen, *Narrative of the Black People*, 23–24.

44. Absalom Jones, "Causes and Motives for Establishing St. Thomas's African Church of Philadelphia," in Douglass, *Annals*, 93–95.

45. *Autobiography of Allen*, 59.

46. Douglass, *Annals*, 110.

47. Vincent Harding, "Wrestling toward the Dawn: The Afro-American Freedom Movement and the Changing Constitution," *Journal of American History* 74 (1987): 719.

Suggested Readings

Recapturing the life of African Americans in the revolutionary era takes patience and resourcefulness because the printed record is very thin. Jones himself wrote only a few pages about his life, published in the first history of Jones's church by a later minister, William Douglass. Only in a short newspaper notice of his death in 1818—hardly a proper obituary—can one find details about his career. Jones wrote and delivered many sermons from the pulpit, but only a few of them were published. His most distinct footprints, in written form, are in *A Narrative of the Proceedings of the Black People, During the late Awful Calamity in Philadelphia, in the year 1793* . . . (Philadelphia, 1794).

Jones can be brought from the shadows only by reconstructing the city in which he spent most of his life and reconstructing the life of African Americans in Philadelphia through the records of the Pennsylvania Abolition Society, newspapers, city directories, municipal records, deed books, and the like. The fullest treatment of black Philadelphia in the era of Absalom Jones is Gary B. Nash, *Forging Freedom: The Formation of Philadelphia's Black Community, 1720–1840* (Cambridge, MA, 1988). Also important is Billy G. Smith, *The "Lower Sort": Philadelphia's Laboring People, 1750–1800* (Ithaca, NY, 1990);

and Carol V. R. George, *Segregated Sabbaths: Richard Allen and the Rise of Independent Black Churches, 1760–1845* (New York, 1973). For a broader view of African Americans in the American Revolution, see Benjamin Quarles, *The Negro in the American Revolution* (Chapel Hill, 1996 [1961]).

14

Baroness Friederike von Riedesel
"Mrs. General"

Michelle Leung

As the wife of a Hessian general who fought with the British, Baroness Friederike von Riedesel (1746–1808) provides an outsider's perspective on the American Revolution. Her travels in England, Canada, and the rebelling American colonies allowed for extensive social commentary in her eyewitness journal. Like other women who traveled with the British or the Continental Army, Friederike was a camp follower, yet her elite rank as the wife of a general meant that she did not experience camp life thoroughly. In a house with officers' families or in her own rented quarters, Friederike never really knew economic hardship.

The Baroness experienced many of the realities of warfare as she tended injured soldiers, consoled recent widows, worried about her husband, and criticized British commanders. Her husband's military choices clearly shaped community definitions of the Riedesels as loyalists, but to whom was Friederike loyal? As Michelle Leung's detailed account reveals, the Baroness clearly recognized that as a prisoner of war, she was treated more as a guest than a captive. Their social status insulated Friederike and her children and even allowed high-ranking American revolutionaries to befriend them. As captives of the Continental Congress, how might Friederike and her husband, Friedrich, have interpreted their situation differently? Might captivity have ensured familial security for the Baroness, but entailed professional defeat and personal depression for her husband? How did their situation differ from that of Elizabeth and Henry Drinker? Eventually, Friedrich was sent to British-held New York as part of a prisoner exchange, stationed at Long Island, and then sent to Canada. Their North American sojourn had so profoundly influenced the Riedesels that they named one daughter America and another Canada. Yet, like the Pinckneys or the Lees, the Riedesels also felt their allegiances to their European homeland deeply. Friederike appeared most content to return to Wolfenbuttel. The adventure of war had never complemented her primary interest in family stability.

Michelle Leung is a historian at the University of Toronto. Her research focuses on the loyalists of northern New York.

German Baroness Friederike von Riedesel began a remarkable journey on May 11, 1776. She was going to America. Her decision to undertake this trip was an extraordinary one, because her destination was a foreign country in a state of civil war. Like thousands of women who had crossed the Atlantic Ocean since European settlement began in the sixteenth century, she was motivated by a desire to reunite her family. Her husband, Major General Friedrich von Riedesel, was a general in the Hessian army of Duke Karl I of Brunswick, the prince of an independent state in western Germany, whose military assistance was hired by King George III. The Hessians' reputation as excellent soldiers and their alliance with Great Britain during the Seven Years' War convinced the king that he could end the war quickly by renting these troops. As a mercenary, the General stood to gain financially from this opportunity if the Americans were defeated. Friederike, on the other hand, would have argued that it was love, honor, and duty that compelled her to follow him into a battle zone.

The memoir she wrote of this North American tour is much more than an eighteenth-century travelogue. It is at once a love story, a firsthand account of General John Burgoyne's failed invasion of New York, and a social commentary on eighteenth-century fashion, morals, and cultural practices. Undertaken and completed between 1795 and 1799, over a decade after the end of the Revolution, the published story of her tour omitted certain details either through forgetfulness or selective editing. In spite of its flaws, her insight into the lives of soldiers' families reveals a great deal about the role of army camp followers, a role that has long been obscured by the notion that the battlefield was no place for women and children. As a foreign aristocrat and the wife of a high-ranking officer, she was acquainted with prominent figures of the Revolution. Her experiences tell quite a different story from the one in most history books.

Friederike Charlotte Luise von Massow was born in 1746 to a Prussian general and his wife. The details of her youth are obscure, but as a daughter of a general in the service of Frederick the Great of Prussia in northern Germany, she was exposed at an early age to the demands that families of professional soldiers faced. During the Seven Years' War, General von Massow moved his family to Minden, a town on the Weser River, where the English and German troops had defeated the French in 1759. It was here that the fifteen-year-old Friederike met her future husband; he was one of many officers who visited the von Massow home. They married in 1762, when Friederike was sixteen and Friedrich was twenty-four years of age. The marriage had been arranged by their families, but bride and groom expressed deep affection for each other in the letters they wrote. Although Friedrich was heir to the Riedesel ancestral home at Lauterbach, he was dependent on his captain's salary to support a wife. After the wedding, he returned to service in Wolfenbuttel while Friederike went home to her parents. Periodic separations were common, given the groom's occupation, but they ended when their first child was born in 1766. Their son Christian died shortly after his first birthday. In 1771 their daughter Philippina died at eleven months. These tragedies weighed heavily on the Riedesels and would subsequently influence the Baroness's decision to join her husband overseas.

Their fortunes had improved considerably when war broke out in the American colonies. They had purchased a home in Wolfenbuttel sometime in early 1776. Two daughters, Augusta and Friederike, born in 1771 and 1774, had survived infancy, and the Baroness was pregnant again. Not wanting to endure a lengthy separation from Friedrich, she persuaded her husband to allow her and the children to join him. He agreed since it was common for women to accompany the troops, but imposed two conditions for their safety. The Baroness could not leave Wolfenbuttel until the baby had been delivered (then known as "a confinement"), and a woman of quality must accompany them. While she reluctantly accepted these terms for the sake of the children, her mother had other ideas. Upon hearing of her intentions, Mrs. von Massow begged and then ordered her daughter to remain in Germany, but Friederike maintained her resolve. She reminded her mother that not only was it a wife's duty to follow her husband, but that she and the children also longed to be with the General.

However admirable her intentions were, Friederike remained anxious about the journey. Lurid stories of savage cannibals and Americans who ate horses and cats filled her head. Moreover, she knew no English. At other times, she worried about the enormous responsibilities that lay ahead. Women of her rank rarely traveled abroad without a reputable male companion to manage their affairs and protect them. The Riedesels agreed that the family's old and trusted servant, Rockel, would travel with her and the children and serve some of those functions, but Friederike would have to ensure that everyone arrived safely and within budget. As the Baroness waited for the birth of her child, Friedrich's frequent letters brought news and comfort to his wife and children. His last letter before sailing overseas, dated the day the troops left Wolfenbuttel, on February 22, 1776, announced that he had been promoted to major general, and he lovingly called her "Mrs. General." In later correspondence, he sent advice detailing budgets to cover the costs of travel from their home to Calais, France, where they must hire a boat to take them to England, and the preparations Friederike must make when she arrived there. He told her to write Secretary of State for the Colonies Lord George Germain and seek his assistance in arranging overseas transportation. The General even found her a traveling companion, Hannah Foy, the wife of Captain Edward Foy, an English artillery officer they had met in Minden. On April 4, one month after the birth of their daughter Caroline, her husband sent instructions that they must not leave until they received his first letters from America. What Friederike did not know was that he had begun to have doubts about the trip she was to undertake.

Whatever reservations Mrs. General entertained, she had overcome them by May 14, 1776. The Baroness, her three daughters, Rockel, and two women servants boarded their carriage and began their journey to England. Her first impressions of their trip were discouraging. The family's carriage, a mark of their aristocratic rank, made them easy prey for swindlers. Innkeepers charged exorbitant prices or tried to take advantage of their naïveté. Worries that highwaymen might rob them also preoccupied the Baroness. While passing through a forest one evening, the corpse of a man who had been hanged from a tree came through their carriage window. With the exception of these events, she recalled many years later, the two-week trip to Calais was generally a happy one. From Calais, a packet boat took them to Dover, and she reported that the ship was so well kept that her fears about sea travel disappeared.

The group arrived in London on June 1, but it was only a short-lived moment of relief for the Baroness. In Calais she had been persuaded by a French innkeeper to hire for their protection a man who claimed he was a gentleman. Her landlord in London revealed that they had been duped after he mistook the whole traveling party for scoundrels because of their association with this well-known rogue. She later discovered that the family's hired protector was a confidence man. Although the situation was rectified, it was not the last humiliation Friederike would suffer in England. While strolling with her children in St. James's Park, she and the girls were ridiculed. They had been mistaken for French women because their clothes were too elegant and she had had the audacity to carry a fan while wearing a hat. A very style-conscious woman, Friederike took the girls to the park again the next day, thinking that she had mastered the English fashion, and was mocked again. English children did not wear ribbons or hats shaped like the ones her daughters wore. The Baroness promptly removed the ribbons and then exchanged insults with her tormentors.

Anxious to begin plans for the transatlantic voyage, Friederike went to meet Hannah Foy in Bristol, as General von Riedesel had instructed. When they arrived on June 11, a crowd formed to gawk at their carriage and its occupants. The crowd's curiosity upset Rockel, who began to call out insults in his broken English. The onlookers responded in kind, and Rockel knocked down one of the crowd; the others attacked him. Had it not been for a local magistrate who rescued them, Friederike was certain the incident would have ended in disaster. The experience led the Baroness, in tears, to despair over her ignorance of the English language and customs. She was unable to ask for necessities. After six weeks in Bristol, she had learned enough English to carry on a simple conversation and understand the newspapers, which carried reports of the war. As much as she prided herself on her great accomplishment, it was still a lonely and miserable time for her children and the servants.

The main source of the Riedesel family's unhappiness in Bristol was the delays that kept them from the General. Mrs. Foy was reluctant to leave until she received news from her officer-husband in Canada. When a letter finally arrived in late summer, Friederike began to prepare for the voyage. Lord Germain helped to arrange their passage on a packet. As their September departure approached, and the ship was ready to sail, the Baroness learned that it was very risky to make the crossing in hurricane season. Even if the family should reach Canada on this sailing, their separation from the General still would continue until the Saint Lawrence River thawed in spring. On September 19 the Baroness wrote a long letter to Friedrich, knowing that it was the last news he would have from his family before spring, when ships could cross the Atlantic again more safely.

The Baroness and her family, resigned to staying the winter in London, were taken in by a Captain Young and his wife. The captain had served as an adjutant under the Duke of Brunswick and knew General Riedesel. The Youngs invited the family to stay with them in London so that the Baroness could save on expenses. Depressed at her separation from the General and not wanting to waste money, Friederike declined her hostess's frequent invitations to accompany her on social outings and stayed behind with the children. This behavior alienated Mrs. Young.

What Friederike understood about the war in the American colonies at this time was only how it impacted on her chances of a reunion with her husband. From the newspapers, she knew that General William Howe's army had taken control of New York City in late autumn 1776, and if her husband was among the Hessian troops there, a passage to New York from London could easily be arranged. If they arrived in Quebec and the General was in New York, it would be impossible for either of them to get through enemy lines. Those matters she could understand, but the politics of the rebellion escaped her. Although her husband fought with the British, the Baroness certainly never considered herself a loyalist. She did express loyalty to England's king, which must have been a product of Germany's close ties with England during her lifetime. While American contemporaries would have thought of her as a loyalist, her journal never expressed any interest in the philosophical and political issues of the Revolution.

The highlight of the Baroness's winter in London was a visit to the royal palace on New Year's Day, 1777. Although Friederike was an aristocrat, she was unfamiliar with the court customs of King George and Queen Charlotte of England. Years later she recalled how she blushed when the king kissed her. She remembered both monarchs fondly for their kind words about General Riedesel and their concern for her and the children.

The Baroness and her party finally boarded a ship for North America on April 15, 1777. Lord Germain had advised her that General Riedesel had remained in Canada. Their fleet, consisting of thirty-two vessels, including two warships, set sail on April 18. She had invited Mrs. Foy as she knew this gesture would please her husband. Within the first week, in unusually rough seas, seasickness afflicted all the passengers. Friederike kept herself busy caring for the girls because the servants were too sick to tend to them. The Baroness formed friendships with the ships' officers and their families, but Mrs. Foy's entourage became a source of annoyance. Mrs. Foy's sister, who accompanied them on the voyage, behaved erratically the entire trip. The Foys' maid, Mademoiselle Nancy, pilfered the captain's wine and was too friendly with the sailors. Friederike was particularly upset that the sergeant of the troops often spent Saturday nights with Nancy near the Baroness's quarters. In part to avoid witnessing these dalliances, Friederike shared her meals with the ships' officers and their families.

After eight weeks at sea, the Baroness had her first glimpse of Quebec. Upon hearing of the fleet's arrival, ships in the harbor fired welcoming cannons. But the Baroness's arrival was marred by disappointment. Expecting to meet her husband, she received news instead that the General and his troops had left to join the British army under General John Burgoyne's command. On June 11, Governor and Lady Carleton were the first to welcome the Baroness and her family to Quebec.

Friederike's impressions of Quebec were mixed. From afar, she thought it presented a fine view, but up close the city seemed ugly. She disliked its steep streets, walking on which she likened to mountain climbing. Having managed to conform to English fashion, the Baroness now found she did not fit in with the wives of other Brunswick officers in Canada. Friederike reported their surprise at seeing her dressed in the English style. These women still wore traditional waistcoats, short wraps, and round caps that covered their ears. She also discerned the social distinctions in the attire of Canadian women. Ordinary women wore long scarlet-colored coats, petticoats, long-sleeved jackets, and big hoods that covered the whole head and face. An aristocratic woman in Canadian society wore a coat made of silk and a dormeuse, a long cap with large colored bows, to distinguish herself from the ordinary habitants.

Before the Riedesels could have their long-awaited reunion, several more obstacles stood in the way. From Quebec, Friederike, her children, and the servants began their journey late on June 11 to the town of Trois Rivières, about seventy-five miles southwest of Quebec on the Saint Lawrence River, where the German troops had wintered. The General had advised them to go there because it was a more economical place to live than Quebec or Montreal and she would find many of their countrymen in the town. He wrote that a fully furnished house with a garden awaited her. Through stormy weather, they went by boat, *calèche* (a sled with wheels), and canoe. When they arrived, Abbé Saint-Onge, the grand vicar at Trois Rivières, welcomed the group and offered the use of his *calèche* so they could meet the General at Chambly, yet another eighty-five miles south of Trois Rivières. Finally, on June 15 the Riedesel family was reunited. In his own journal, the General expressed amazement that his children had already forgotten their mother tongue and spoke only English. Two days later, General Riedesel had to return to his troops and continue his southward march toward the Americans' stronghold at Fort Ticonderoga.

Friederike regarded her husband's decision to send them back to Trois Rivières as a great disappointment. Perhaps he anticipated that the war would soon be over. The British forces had swept southward along Lake George with ease and expected support from local Tories when they reached the Hudson Valley. It therefore made great sense for Riedesel to spare his wife and daughters any further dislocation. He promised to send for them as soon as it was safe for women to accompany the army.

In the meantime, Friederike devoted herself to caring for the children, needlework, and reading. She complained that mail service was slow and that, when she did receive letters from Friedrich, the news was often old. The grand vicar and his cousin, Miss Cabenac, were frequent visitors. Later, Friederike learned that Miss Cabenac was not the vicar's cousin but his mistress and that this practice was common among gentlemen of Saint-Onge's station in Canada. The Baroness was not shocked by this custom since European military officers often kept mistresses. In her journal, she remembered the grand vicar and Miss Cabenac as cheerful and pleasant people. On her outings into the town and countryside, the Baroness observed that the habitants were friendly people and boasted that they had a good standard of living. On occasion, she visited and enjoyed the company of the Ursuline nuns at Trois Rivières.

In August the General sent his aide, Captain Samuel Willoe, to fetch the Riedesel family. Traveling by boat, they had to stop at nightfall and set up camp on an island. The party formed makeshift beds using boat cushions and their coats. Friederike noticed that Captain Willoe seemed uneasy during the night and had ordered the soldiers to build fires around their camp. The next morning she inquired as to the reason for these precautions and discovered that they had spent the night on Isle aux Sonnettes (Rattlesnake Island). Captain Willoe had only learned of this fact after nightfall when it was too dangerous to continue their trip. They quickly packed up and left. After the day's journey, the party spent the night on board. They finally arrived at Fort Edward on August 14. After a short reunion, the General left again. He returned after the Battle of Bennington, which the Baroness described as an unfortunate affair because not only had the Americans won, but more than two hundred soldiers had been killed and another six hundred loyalists had been taken prisoner. News arrived shortly afterward that the Americans had cut off routes to Canada. Had the Baroness and the girls left Trois Rivières any later, they might have faced a much longer separation from their husband and father.

In spite of the British army's losses, Friederike was very happy to be living within the English and German camps. As a general's wife, she shared a house with other officers and their wives. One room housed the Riedesels while their maids slept in the hall. Meals prepared by the General's cook were eaten outside or in the barn. In the evenings, she would get the children ready for bed while the adults played cards. Whether there were any other children besides the Riedesel girls in that house is uncertain, although there were more than two thousand women and children in the camps. The majority of these women were not of high rank like the Baroness, but farmers' wives who had followed the army for protection. They performed useful tasks such as washing clothes and cooking for their soldier husbands. There were also some prostitutes among these camp followers.

When the army began to march again on September 11, General Burgoyne gave permission to Friederike and the other officers' wives to follow. Although Friedrich worried about his wife's safety, he was glad to see her every day. In her memoir, the Baroness recalled that spirits were high in the camps and that General Burgoyne felt confident of victory. She was distressed, however, that the wives of English officers were so familiar with the army's plans and talked so openly about them. She wondered on many occasions whether such open talk had allowed the Americans to gain prior knowledge of British plans.

Whatever hardships Mrs. General had faced on her journey so far, none had prepared her for what was to come. On September 19 she witnessed her first battle. Twenty-four miles north of the city of Albany, New York, American general Horatio Gates had established a camp near Freeman's Farm to halt the British. Since General Burgoyne's plan was to capture Albany, he ordered an attack on the American position. Three columns advanced on the Americans, but they took an early offensive and drove Burgoyne's center column back. Half of his eleven hundred men were killed or wounded. Had it not been for the intervention of Generals Riedesel and Phillips and their troops, the British could not have held their position. While the fighting went on, dying and injured men were brought to the house where the family was living; Captain Young's nephew, who later succumbed to gangrene, was among them. The Baroness remembered hearing him groan his last breath through the house's thin walls. When the army left Freeman's Farm, she observed how beautiful—and deserted—the countryside appeared. The locals had fled to the safety of the American army.

As camp followers, Friederike and the children remained an hour's distance from the army, but she visited her husband every day and ate her meals with him. Eventually, she and the girls moved into a log cabin so that they could be closer to his camp. Although she was glad to be with her husband and his troops, she knew he was losing sleep over the British forces' lack of progress. Every day the General and his men made brief attacks that seemed to have no effect on the enemy.

The Baroness later recalled that the British position weakened on October 7, 1777. She remembered that the General and his men left on a reconnaissance mission amid great commotion. Thinking that this was another short attack, she remained calm until several Native Americans under her husband's command told her they were headed to battle. For the rest of the day, she heard nothing but gunfire. General Simon Fraser, mortally wounded in the stomach, was brought to her house, which before long was full of injured men. When Friedrich returned in the evening, he confided to his wife that things were going badly and that she must be prepared to leave at any moment.

Their terror continued into the next day. General Fraser died in the morning, but his body remained in open view. Throughout the day, other wounded officers arrived at their home, and the bombardment began anew. At six o'clock, she attended a funeral for Fraser hastily arranged by Burgoyne. Afterward, their retreat began. Friederike, the children, and their maids got into their *calèches* and left the camp. After they arrived in Saratoga, wet and cold from the rain, they lay down on straw and slept.

In her own assessment of the retreat, the Baroness found General Burgoyne's behavior disgraceful. While his troops waited for orders to continue their withdrawal, the Baroness later claimed, General Burgoyne had neglected his duties by spending the night drinking champagne and making merry with his mistress, the wife of a commissary. When the Americans caught up with Burgoyne's army the next afternoon, General Riedesel told his wife and children to take refuge in a nearby house. For six days, women, children, and the wounded remained there in the cellar. Friederike was unable to sleep the first night. Her childrens' sobs, a foul smell, and fear kept her awake. By morning she found enough courage to undertake the task of cleaning and organizing this refuge. They slept on straw and subsisted on food brought to them by General Riedesel's cook and on wine, as water was scarce. Of this experience, the Baroness later recounted that she had been more dead than alive from worry about the General: she was the only officer's wife in this refuge whose husband had not been wounded or killed.

Greatly outnumbered by the enemy, Burgoyne went to negotiate with the Americans. During these talks, hostilities ceased, and Friederike was relieved that her husband was able to sleep. Rockel had confided to her that Friedrich despaired at the thought they would all be taken prisoners. On October 15, Burgoyne called a council of war to announce the Americans' terms, whereby the British and German troops were to go to Boston to be transported back to England. Two days later, the capitulation went into effect.

When Friederike and the children entered the American camp, they were truly surprised. The Americans did not show any disdain toward them. Instead, they bowed to the Baroness and expressed pity for the hardships she and the children endured. General Philip Schuyler greeted the Riedesel women and took them to General Gates's tent. Friederike recorded her astonishment in finding the American and British generals on such good terms with one another. She noted that these men even ate together at General Gates's table that very night. Sensing that the Baroness would be uncomfortable in such exclusively male company, Schuyler invited her and the children to dine in his tent.

This meeting marked the beginning of a warm relationship between the Riedesel and Schuyler families. General Schuyler offered his house to the Riedesels while arrangements for their journey to Boston were finalized. Friederike later remarked that the Schuyler family had shown remarkable generosity to them despite their British affiliation and despite the damage that General Burgoyne's army had inflicted on the family's properties.

Not all Americans demonstrated such kindness. The Baroness expressed dismay that, although they had a guard of ten to twenty Americans, their belongings were stolen on their second night in Albany. They relied on gifts from friends to replace some things, but it was a shortage of available goods rather than poverty that frustrated Friederike. In her memoirs, she recalled that it took almost three years to replace all the articles they had lost.

Life in Massachusetts, even as hostages of the Continental Congress, was relatively pleasant for the Riedesels. They lived in a farmer's attic for the first three weeks and then moved into a house in Cambridge that was once owned by a loyalist. The Baroness was very happy in their Cambridge dwelling, which had its own garden and orchard. The General, on the other hand, suffered from depression over his captivity. Working in the garden was the only pastime that lifted his mood.

It was during their stay in Cambridge that Friederike began to understand how polarized American society had become. She went to Boston several times to see the Schuylers' daughter, Angelica, known to the Baroness as "Mrs. Carter," but the General was not permitted to enter the city. On these visits she discovered the beauty of the city, but found it full of enthusiastic patriots and wicked people, especially the women, who gave her dirty looks and spat when she passed. Friederike also recalled families whose loyalties were divided between the king and the republicans. These experiences led her to reflect on how terrible it was to be caught in a civil war. Although the Baroness never gave any indication that the family felt unsafe, a ball she gave to celebrate her husband's birthday nearly ended in disaster. At the end of the evening, guests drank a toast to the king's health and sang "God Save the King." The commotion and noise had attracted a large crowd of Americans who thought the Riedesels were planning a counterrevolt. Luckily, no action was taken against them.

Because the Continental Congress refused to ratify the terms of the surrender at Saratoga, the General and his men remained in the colonies. As winter approached in November 1778, the Riedesels were ordered to Virginia. They had a chance meeting with the Marquis de Lafayette at New Hartford and dined with him. The Baroness was surprised to hear Lafayette speak so kindly of England and the king, but she lacked the courage to ask why he was in arms against them. They parted, and the Riedesels, their children, and the troops continued their long trek to Virginia. Although the Baroness did not remember how long they traveled each day, she did recall that the General twice gave his troops a week to rest and reassemble. Everywhere along their journey they relied on the kindness of strangers, many of whom refused to offer anything but ill will. Sometimes they subsisted on bread, coffee, tea, and sugar.

The Baroness and her party arrived in Colle, Virginia, in February 1779. The General and his troops had gone ahead to make preparations and had rented the home of Italian horticulturist Philip Mazzei. Lack of food remained a problem for the rest of the winter because of the thousands of British and German troops at Charlottesville. Conditions had improved by spring. Friedrich had a larger house and garden built to accommodate his family and food was plentiful again. Their only complaints were the extreme heat and wind they suffered in summer and their yearning to return to Wolfenbuttel.

When among friends in their new home, including Thomas Jefferson and several relatives of George Washington, Friederike indulged in music and sometimes in singing and dancing. Generally, however, she found the Virginians' disposition peculiar; their behavior went to such extremes, singing and dancing one moment, silent and still the next. The Baroness also remarked in her journal that she had heard stories of their immorality, including incest and wife swapping, although she never had any evidence to support these tales.

Virginian slavery also left a negative impression on the Baroness. She thought that most plantation owners treated their slaves badly by letting them walk about naked until they were fifteen or sixteen years old. She observed that the overseers overworked and underfed their fieldhands. House slaves could be recognized instantly because they were well dressed and fed. Friederike claimed that slaves regarded having children as a misfortune, since the children must suffer their parents' fate as slaves. Nevertheless, she did not make any connection between American claims for independence and the conditions of slavery she observed.

During their stay in Virginia, the General suffered a severe case of sunstroke, which, the Baroness wrote, was her greatest grief while living in America. He collapsed in their garden and had to be carried home. The regiment's surgeon bled him and recommended a visit to the local spa at Frederick's Springs, which only worsened his condition. Not only did his headaches continue, but he remained depressed and became increasingly irritable. Friederike remembered that a Virginian had come to call simply because he was curious to see some Germans. Although this impertinence amused the Baroness, it caused her husband to break down at the thought of how their circumstances had reduced them. Years later, she still regretted this episode and worried about what would have happened to her and the children if the General had died then.

During their stay at Frederick's Springs, the General received orders to go to New York. The Americans intended to exchange him and General William Phillips for officers held hostage by the British. This practice of prisoner exchange was common during the Revolution, especially among officers, but soldiers' families were also held hostage by both sides until an exchange could be made. Although the Baroness was happy about this decision, she later reflected that whenever they became comfortable, they had to move again. In August 1779 the Baroness and her daughters left for New York, while the General returned to Colle to make arrangements for the maintenance of his troops. They stopped in Maryland and stayed at the plantation of a loyalist, Mrs. Mary Darnall Carroll. They then proceeded to York, Pennsylvania, to meet the General, stayed at Bethlehem for two days, and moved on to Elizabeth, New Jersey, where they received General Washington's orders to return, because Congress had not approved the exchange. Friederike, who was pregnant again and had suffered much discomfort on the trip, now despaired at the thought of going back. Their party returned to Bethlehem to wait until plans for the exchange were finalized. At the end of November, they were allowed to enter New York on parole.

Life in British-held New York was very pleasant again for the Riedesels. Governor William Tryon hosted the family, and the Baroness fondly remembered him as a man of great kindness. Among her other acquaintances were General Lord Charles Cornwallis, General Henry Clinton, and the ill-fated Major John André, who was later hanged as a spy for his role in Benedict Arnold's defection. General Clinton even offered his country home to the Riedesels and arranged to have the children inoculated against smallpox since there was an epidemic in the city. They gladly accepted both. When the family returned, they were pleased to find that Governor Tryon had furnished their house.

To cheer the Baroness, General Phillips gave a ball to honor the queen's birthday on January 24, 1780. Friederike was chosen to represent Queen Charlotte as Queen of the Ball. By all contemporary accounts, it was a spectacular occasion. On the day of the party, a salute was fired from Fort George at noon, followed by another at one o'clock from the king's ships in the harbor. An elaborate ceremony at Governor Tryon's home welcomed the Baroness as the guest of honor. The governor then presented the local society ladies to Friederike. At six o'clock, she was escorted by Governor Tryon and General James Pattison to the ball. Dancing went on until midnight, then dinner was served. The Baroness sat under a canopy and drank the first toast. Local newspapers reported that it was the most elegant ball ever given in North America.

Although the Riedesels lived well in New York, the family still experienced hard times with the town under wartime siege and shortages. The cost of food was very high, and even when they had money, products were not always available. They suffered from extreme cold during the winter; sometimes it was so cold that the Baroness kept the children in bed. Tickets for rationed wood went unsatisfied. Still, they were more fortunate than the poor who burned lard to keep warm. At times the General bartered items his family could spare to obtain goods they needed.

As Friederike's confinement approached, she and her husband chose the name Americus for their child, believing they would have a son. On March 7, they had a daughter and named her America. Shortly after the christening, everyone in the Riedesel household fell ill. Augusta and Caroline suffered from asthma, and little America became gravely ill. A cholera epidemic swept through New York affecting twenty people in their household, including the General. Friederike nursed them constantly, fearing that they would die. Each day at least fifty to sixty people died from the disease in New York City. Since many of the servants also became ill, she had to take over the household duties. Whether the Baroness remained healthy during this episode is uncertain, although her husband did express concern for her health in his memoirs. By the end of summer, everyone had recovered.

In the autumn of 1780 the General was finally exchanged. General Clinton appointed him a lieutenant general in his army, thereby entitling him to receive English pay, for which the family was grateful. The General was stationed at Long Island, but because his quarters were not heated, the family remained in New York. He became gravely ill over the winter, and doctors informed the Baroness that the General's poor health would never improve as long as they lived in such a damp climate. To raise his spirits, the Baroness and the girls moved to Long Island in the spring. With their house so close to the East River, the Baroness often worried that Americans would abduct her husband and spent many sleepless nights listening for signs of danger.

In May 1781, Clinton decided that General Riedesel should return to Canada and take command of the Hessian troops stationed there. Not wishing to abuse the kindness of the English, Friederike returned all the furniture that Governor Tryon had given them except for one bed. The Baroness later regretted this gesture, because the Americans, who gained control of New York later, burned all these furnishings, and little furniture was to be had in Quebec. The Riedesels were also sorry they had not purchased the freedom of an African-American family who had served them well in New York. British policy recognized only loyalists' ownership of slaves, and promised freedom to those who escaped from their rebel masters or were confiscated by the British. Just before they departed in July 1781, the master of this slave family, who was formerly a patriot but now claimed to support the British, brought an order to reclaim his property. The General tried to buy the servants' freedom, but the Baroness claimed the scoundrel's price was exorbitant.

From New York harbor, a small ship took the family to Halifax, Nova Scotia. Friederike wrote her mother that everyone was comfortable, but in reality, their ship narrowly escaped several accidents. Lieutenant Governor Andrew Hamond welcomed the family and invited them to lunch. Friederike recorded that the seafood was especially good and that lobsters, rarely caught in the region before the Revolution, were now found in abundance. Locals joked that the lobsters had left the mainland because they were good royalists. After the General retrieved a mattress into which his wife had sewn the Brunswick regimental flags for protection, the family headed for Quebec.

The General's new post in Canada was a mixed blessing for the Riedesels. After their arrival in September, Governor General Frederick Haldimand kept General Riedesel busy at his new post in Sorel. After such a long period of inactivity in the American colonies, Haldimand's confidence in Friedrich's abilities boosted his spirits. The cooler climate seemed to improve his health, too. Governor Haldimand even purchased a house for the Riedesels so they could live together in comfort. For a while the Baroness was happily caught up in establishing their new household. There were plenty of rooms for the family, their servants, and entertaining. The Riedesels never suffered shortages of food or wood as they had in New York, because Sorel was not under constant siege from the Americans. The cold winters made it possible to store large quantities of food in the attic, and a huge stove with pipes that ran to the ceiling heated the rest of the house.

Friederike, nevertheless, found life difficult at Sorel when winter came. They lived outside the town, so she felt isolated. Other than her children and the servants, she had no female companions. Many of the Brunswick soldiers had brought their wives to Sorel, but there is no indication that the Baroness was a part of their social circle. All the visitors the Riedesels entertained in their home were men. Although she had been warned in Quebec that Governor Haldimand was a difficult man who was not to be trusted, they became good friends. He tried to lighten her spirits by inviting the family to join him in Quebec and Montreal.

As the General had many Native Americans under his command, the Baroness took up her many opportunities to observe and meet them. She found them hospitable and jovial people—not the savages of her imagination. She also corrected her earlier opinion that the Natives who had abandoned the British at Saratoga were cowards, and now she believed that they had run away to avoid being captured and killed by the Americans. Friederike noted that she met Joseph Brant, the Mohawk chief (see Chapter 10 of this volume) whom Haldimand held in high esteem. Dressed in either military or Indian clothing, Brant impressed her as a clever and gentle man with good manners.

The arrival of spring in Canada cheered Friederike, and she was pregnant again. The General had a large piece of land behind their house plowed for a garden and planted with more than one thousand fruit trees. The family kept cows, fowl, and hogs, and Friederike made her own butter. She noted that although her husband's men thought Canada was a promised land, they still longed for Germany.

In the fall of 1782 the General went to Isle aux Noix to supervise the construction of a fort. She described this as a very lonely time, although he came home every three or four weeks. Correspondence from her mother may have contributed to these feelings. A letter, over a year old when Friederike received it, brought news that her mother had remarried after several years of widowhood. Although Friederike was upset by this announcement, she was more alarmed to learn that her mother had written her every month for the last two years but only three of those letters had reached her. The birth of another daughter, christened Canada because of the Riedesels' fondness for their current home, was followed by tragedy, as the child survived only five months. Governor Haldimand invited the family to his new home in Quebec, hoping that a change of scene would ease their sorrow. While the Riedesels were in Quebec, the General learned that his father had died. Friederike reflected that now they all longed to go home. Public knowledge that a preliminary peace treaty ending the war had been signed was widespread since spring. The return of the Hessian troops to Germany was imminent. During their summer stay at the governor's house, Haldimand informed them that they were to leave for Europe. They returned to Sorel to make preparations.

For Mrs. General, their arrival in England was the start of a great homecoming. She found the month-long crossing, deemed fast for its day, rough and slow. While the General and his aides went to London, his wife and children visited old acquaintances in Portsmouth and London. During their short stay in London, they were reunited with friends and had another audience with the royal family. While the General discussed American affairs with the king, Friederike had tea and cakes with the queen and the princesses. The Baroness was pleased to hear that the queen had inquired after her and recounted her many adventures for the group. Although the monarchs invited them to return to the palace, they could not accept because their fleet was ready to take the troops back to Germany. They arrived there at the end of September 1783. While the General waited for the rest of his troops to arrive, the family went home to Wolfenbuttel. A week later the Baroness had the great joy of seeing her husband and his troops march through Wolfenbuttel as their friends and family watched. The homecoming was followed by a dinner at court in Brunswick on the next day. Mrs. General was home at last.

Suggested Readings

This essay is based mostly on the memoirs of Baroness and General von Riedesel. *Baroness von Riedesel and the American Revolution: Journal and Correspondence of a Tour of Duty, 1776–1783*, trans. Marvin L. Brown Jr. (Chapel Hill, NC, 1965), is the most recent version and contains many of the couple's letters. See also Max von Eelking, *Memoirs, and Letters and Journals of Major General Riedesel during his Residence in America*, trans. William L. Stone, 2 vols. (Albany, 1868). Other correspondence can be found in the Riedesel Papers held at the McCord Library, McGill University, Montreal, and the Haldimand Papers at the National Archives of Canada, Ottawa.

There are very few works on women camp followers in the American Revolution. The best known, Walter Hart Blumental, *Women Camp Followers of the American Revolution* (Philadelphia, 1952), is outdated and presents a very unflattering view of women who followed the British camps. More recent and scholarly treatments can be found in: Linda K. Kerber, *Women of the Republic: Intellect and Ideology in Revolutionary America* (Chapel Hill, NC,

1980); Janice Potter-MacKinnon, *While the Women Only Wept: Loyalist Refugee Women in Eastern Ontario* (Montreal and Kingston, 1993); and Holly A. Mayer, *Belonging to the Army: Camp Followers and Community during the American Revolution* (Columbia, SC, 1996).

15

Judith Sargent Murray
The American Revolution and the Rights of Women

Sheila Skemp

As a famous essayist, Judith Sargent Murray (1751–1820) of Gloucester, Massachusetts, used her pen to comment on the rights of women. The daughter of a wealthy merchant, Judith became keenly aware of the limitations that society placed upon women, even those of her social position. In arguing that women were the intellectual equals of men and valuable contributors to the new Republic, especially as republican mothers, Murray urged that women's private actions had public consequences. Like Eliza Lucas Pinckney, Murray also emphasized the importance of virtue in the character of male family members and in the patriot conduct of the war. Her wartime experiences demonstrated women's vulnerability, but also their opportunities for expanding their roles. How unique and influential were Murray's opinions, and what might have prompted Judith to write under pseudonyms? Could women of a lower social position, such as Jane Boon, have shared Murray's egalitarian vision? Given her interest in women's rights, why did she not advocate political rights for women?

As an author and an advocate of women's rights, Judith Sargent Murray was not a typical New England woman of her era. Her concern with being a good Christian woman was more typical, although her choice of Universalism was somewhat unconventional. As Sheila Skemp reminds us, the Revolution's legacies for women were mixed, for it both reinforced and challenged traditional gender values. Simultaneously, it intertwined public and private concerns. Was it hypocritical for American patriots to want political independence and equality from England, but a continuation of dependent relationships within the family? Although a member of a patriot family, Murray seemed to commiserate with her uncle, a loyalist driven from Gloucester. Did such attitudes reflect a personal lack of interest in politics or a commitment to other nonpolitical concerns? Was Murray more or less interested in politics than Baroness von Riedesel, Eliza Lucas Pinckney, or Elizabeth Drinker?

Sheila Skemp teaches colonial American history at the University of Mississippi. She is the author of *William Franklin: Son of a Patriot, Servant of a King* (1990) and *Judith Sargent Murray: A Brief Biography with Documents* (1998).

In the fall of 1779, four large men-of-war sailed into the harbor at Gloucester, Massachusetts. Alarms rang out, guns discharged, and frantic inhabitants clogged the streets. As women and children fled their homes, men raced to the fort to protect the town from imminent invasion. Judith Sargent Stevens was alone. She knew that her merchant husband John was somewhere on the high seas, trying desperately to wring a profit from a trade that was always precarious, and especially so in time of war. Left to her own resources, Judith ran desperately to a friend's dwelling some two miles away. She hoped to get someone to help her salvage at least some of her belongings before the king's men landed on Gloucester's shores and began plundering the possessions of unprotected civilians. As she raced through a dark and abandoned wood, she "trembled in the dread of insult," knowing that women who wandered into the countryside without male protection seemed almost to invite unwanted attention. American ruffians were as likely to harass them as were British sailors. Judith's worst fears seemed about to be realized when some "uncivilized barbarians" appeared before her, reviling her "in language the most brutal" and threatening to "lay violent hands upon [her] person." Fortunately, they "confined their abuse to words," and she arrived at her friend's house shaken but unmolested.[1] When the two returned to the Stevens residence, they were relieved to discover that the "enemy" ships that had so frightened Gloucester's inhabitants had in fact been American vessels. The British threat to property and person had never existed.

Although her fright had been triggered by a false alarm, Judith Stevens was not comforted. Like most American women, she had heard stories of the depredations on both humans and property that were the trademark of an "inhuman enemy," and she could not rest easy so long as the possibility of attack remained.[2] At war's end she witnessed the consequences of British hostilities firsthand, when she took a trip through Connecticut and viewed the ruins of New England towns that had not been so fortunate as her native home. In Groton sixty-two women had become widows during a single hour of fighting. In New Haven, British soldiers had even destroyed the featherbeds—850 in all—in what Judith saw as a gratuitous attack on innocent American civilians. Such destruction did nothing to support the British war effort, but it cost New Haven's women dearly, as they struggled to put their homes back together again after the attack. In a war in which the boundaries between the "war front" and the "home front" were vague and always permeable, no one was really safe.

Years later, when she was a published author and had witnessed the production of two of her plays in Boston's Federal Street Theater, Judith Sargent Murray (earlier Judith Stevens) could laugh at her fright. Indeed, by the 1790s, she was able to view her entire wartime experience as positive, providing her, as it did, with the language she would use to insist that women should enjoy the benefits of a war fought in the name of liberty, equality, and independence. More than Mercy Otis Warren, even more than Abigail Adams, Murray was at the center of the national discussion concerning the proper role of women in the years after the American Revolution. She was more consistent than any of her contemporaries in her determination to apply the language of the Revolution to women's experience, to claim that women, like men, had a natural right to "life, liberty, and the pursuit of happiness." Her poetry, her essays, and her three-volume "miscellany," *The Gleaner* (1798), were all intended to prove—implicitly or explicitly—that women were the intellectual equals of men.

Judith Sargent Murray's early life gave little indication that she would become one of America's earliest proponents of equality for women. She was born in Gloucester, Massachusetts, on May 1, 1751, the eldest of eight children, four of whom lived to adulthood. Both her mother and father came from a long line of prosperous Gloucester merchants who had left England for America in the seventeenth century. Her grandfather, Epes Sargent, had been among Gloucester's wealthiest and most cosmopolitan early inhabitants. Her father Winthrop and her uncles Epes and Daniel were all prominent citizens of a town whose most important inhabitants drew their living from the sea. Judith always enjoyed a quiet sense of her family's superiority in a society where lineage and wealth mattered a great deal. Not surprisingly, upon the death of her first husband, John Stevens, in 1787, Judith reverted to her maiden name. When she married again the following year, this time to the Reverend John Murray, she refused to relinquish it. She was fond of the name "Sargent," she explained, and she insisted upon signing all her correspondence as Judith Sargent Murray.[3] Indeed, Murray's character was shaped as much by the sense of entitlement she enjoyed as a consequence of her inherited social position as it was by the changes wrought by the American Revolution.

Even as a child, however, Murray discovered that the automatic respect she expected for her family name was undercut by the limitations she confronted as a woman. When she was just two years old, her brother Winthrop was born. Winthrop enjoyed the best education his parents could buy. He attended Boston Latin School and graduated from Harvard in 1771. While Judith learned to read and write and gained a superficial knowledge of French, her parents steadfastly opposed her pleas for further formal education, especially for lessons in the classics. She was, she claimed with pardonable hyperbole, "a wild and untutored child of nature."[4]

If she resented her poor educational background, young Judith Sargent hardly saw this as a reason to become a rebel or to condemn her society publicly for its unfair treatment of women. When she thought about her future at all, she imagined a conventional life for herself. She would be a good Christian—which in eighteenth-century Gloucester meant that she would embrace the beliefs of her Puritan ancestors—a respectable wife and mother, and an ordinary woman of her class and era. In 1769 she married her first husband, John Stevens, a Gloucester merchant, who, despite his family's recent financial reversals, promised to provide for his bride in the manner that she no doubt expected. John's poor business sense meant that the couple lived more precariously than either would have liked. Still, Judith's father was always there, willing to help his hapless son-in-law, until the commercial depression that devastated Gloucester's merchant community during, and especially after, the American Revolution made it impossible for him to continue to do so.

Neither her husband's financial difficulties nor the coming of the American Revolution were the first events that disrupted the normal rhythms of Judith Stevens's life. That disruption came in 1774, with the appearance in town of English émigré John Murray, an itinerant minister who proclaimed the doctrine of "Universalism" in his travels up and down the New England coast. The Sargents, Stevenses, and some of their friends had already been introduced to the writing of Murray's mentor, English minister James Relly (ca. 1722–1778), and when they heard that one of Relly's most able and charismatic disciples was preaching nearby, they begged him to visit Gloucester.

Judith was transformed by John Murray's first sermon. He "enlarged my views," she said, "expanded my ideas, dissipated my doubts."[5] More than that, Universalism helped her attack the views of those who established a gendered link between body and essence. The Universalist faith placed special emphasis on the spiritual nature of humanity, insisting that from the beginning of creation all humans had been united spiritually with Christ, that the subsequent acquisition of a body in no way altered the spiritual essence of humanity. The body, they said, was merely a shell, a temporary house for the soul. The eternal and genderless soul mobilized and controlled the body. Moreover, the spiritual unity of all humans implied the basic equality of men and women. God's benevolence, Judith Sargent Murray always insisted, knew "no bounds," for all people, of whatever "sect, age, country or even sex," were part of "one grand, vast, collected family of human nature."[6] The implications of such a perspective were profound. If spirit was the defining characteristic of all humans, then women and men were not only equal, they were—in those areas that truly mattered—identical.

Judith Stevens was not the only member of Gloucester's First Parish Church to be moved by John Murray's eloquence. In 1778 sixty-one individuals, including Judith and John Stevens, formed America's first Universalist church and designated John Murray as their minister. Murray continued his itinerant ministry, but whenever he was in Gloucester, he boarded with the Stevenses.

If her religious views gave Judith Sargent Murray an ideological basis that she could use to attack notions of gender inequality to her own satisfaction, the language of the American Revolution was more acceptable, and more accessible to her readers than was the language of Universalism. The war itself helped create a hospitable climate for a challenge to traditional views of gender identity. In practical terms, as women were mobilized in various ways to support the war effort, old social roles broke down, at least temporarily, causing men and women alike to question notions of women as weak and irrational, to blur gender distinctions, to intermingle traditional gender roles, and in some cases even to claim that women enjoyed some status as citizens of the Republic. In theoretical terms, revolutionary rhetoric, with its emphasis on universal, "natural" rights, its attack on patriarchal government, and its celebration of the virtues of independence and equality also led many denizens of the new nation to question older constructs of gender and to call for a new paradigm upon which to build relationships between men and women. When patriots decried the world of the English fathers as warlike, violent, and disorderly, contrasting it with the New World where an abundant and fertile landscape invited everyone to live in peace, equality, and harmony, they were surely privileging traits conventionally viewed as feminine. Liberty, in the art and literature of the period, appeared as a lady, after all, and Columbia, the designation by which many people referred to America, was a woman.

The experience of women in the American Revolution provides ample proof of the Janus-faced nature of war. This conflict was declared, fought, and won by men at a time when women's political role was virtually nonexistent. Moreover, women won neither political nor economic equality at war's end. If American men rejected a hierarchical system of government in favor of one based on republican principles, they remained comfortable with a political order that celebrated independence and equality, even while they remained wedded to notions of dependence and deference in their own families. The very fact that men did the bulk of the fighting, while women remained at home, reconfirmed the notion that helpless women needed men to protect them. Ironically, as Judith Stevens had surely realized on the night she thought that a British invasion of Gloucester was imminent, whenever men left home to serve their country and to protect its liberties, they left their own families more alone, less protected than ever. Judith never referred to her own fears of enemy capture with pride. Her wartime experience accentuated her sense of vulnerability, not her confidence in her own ability. Still, the American Revolution set the stage for a possible transformation in America's history. It was an event that threatened to stand traditional values on their head. A war fought in the name of equality and universal human rights, a war that challenged social hierarchy and ascribed status, and demanded essential rights for all its inhabitants, surely should have had some relevance to women.

Indeed, as Judith Stevens's experience indicates, historians have probably created a false dichotomy when they have discussed the Revolution's meaning for American women. At one and the same time, the war both reinforced *and* challenged traditional gender definitions. The Revolution reminded women that there were spaces that they could not enter, but it also provided them with the opportunity to criticize male public behavior from their own gendered perspective. If it did not give most of them a sense of their own right or ability to enter the public sphere, it nevertheless gave elite white women like Judith a sense of entitlement. It enabled them to privilege their own values over the masculine notions of republican virtue—bravery, public-spiritedness, and martial honor—that so dominated public discourse in their day. For Stevens, the Revolution was a defining moment, as it enabled her to begin questioning the legal, social, and economic systems within which she had clearly prospered for so long.

Like most members of her family, Judith was a patriot. Her parents supported the American war effort. Her favorite brother, Winthrop, was a Continental officer. Her husband joined the Gloucester Committee of Safety, a local organization designed to protect the town from enemy attack as well as from the machinations of crown sympathizers. Even native Englishman John Murray, Judith's future husband, did his part in a war waged against his own countrymen by serving briefly as a chaplain for the First Rhode Island Regiment until ill health made it impossible for him to continue his duties. Still, if she supported independence, Stevens viewed the Revolution with mixed feelings, and she often wished that the "unnatural contest" between England and America could have been avoided altogether.[7] When she wrote of the war to her brother Winthrop, she reminded him that "the contending parties are the offspring of some happy brother and sister like you or me," and she regretted the tears of parents who wept to see their children destroying one another.[8] Her laments were not mere rhetoric. Her beloved uncle, Epes Sargent, was a loyalist, and she had watched with dismay as a "gothic mob" drove him and his family from Gloucester, forcing them "to wander in a state of exile far from their peaceful home."[9] The longer hostilities lasted, the more convinced Judith became that her initial reservations were justified. Viewing the war from the sidelines and analyzing its consequences from an increasingly alienated perspective, she began to understand how gendered notions of politics and war worked to define her identity and to limit her possibilities. At war's end, she used the rhetoric of the Revolution for her own purposes, challenging old notions of gender differences and insisting that women, like men, should be allowed to soar to the "loftiest heights."[10]

Although most women did not risk their lives on the battlefield, they had their own burdens to bear, their own sacrifices to make in the name of independence. Women's sacrifices, however, were largely unsung, and few women expected recognition—much less a reward—for their efforts. While no enemy soldier ever threatened her person, Judith Stevens—like virtually all American women—did not escape the effects of war. Even her ordinary domestic duties became more difficult during wartime. As the value of Continental currency declined and scarce supplies drove up the price of necessary goods, she spent many a "wearisome day" going from shop to shop in the "vain hope" of purchasing the barest necessities.[11] The precarious state of her husband's finances made her economic position especially onerous. Mercantile activity was always risky, but war magnified the normal perils of trade. Although John Stevens enjoyed brief success as a privateer, he suffered heavy losses at war's end, and Judith had good reason to blame his eventual bankruptcy on the disruptions of the commercial depression that devastated Gloucester in the wake of the American Revolution.

Women suffered emotionally as well as materially during the war. Life in Judith's native Gloucester changed dramatically with the coming of hostilities—and not for the better. The "frequent alarms, drum beating, bells ringing," the "warlike preparations," and the sight of men bearing "instruments of death" served as constant reminders that these were, indeed, "barbarous times."[12] More than once, moreover, rumors of imminent enemy attack forced her and her mother to flee Gloucester for the relative safety of the Massachusetts interior.

Most of all, she missed her brother Winthrop, whose absence left a "mournful void" in her life.[13] Her worries about his safety were unending. Even her dreams were haunted by images of his death. Whenever she heard an account of a battle that left the countryside "purple with human gore," she was convinced that Winthrop was among the dead.[14] In December 1780 she traveled to a crowded inn in Medfield, Massachusetts, to attend to her wounded brother before watching him return to the front.

Indeed, even in the beginning, Judith Stevens worried about the potential consequences of the war. While she was devoted to the cause of independence, she deplored the means her countrymen used to attain it. She despised the intolerance of those Americans who refused to countenance even the mildest dissent from the patriot establishment, confiscating the property of men like her uncle Epes, who wished only to be left alone to support his family. She worried that the conduct of the war itself would render military men coarse, vulgar, and inhumane. As she saw it, her duty to her country demanded that she monitor the activities of those who fought in her country's name, and, if necessary, that she advocate a change in the conduct of the war itself. She wanted American soldiers to adhere to the moral and religious values that women in particular held dear. Significantly, in her position as a self-proclaimed—if private—critic of the war, she was able to turn her "inferior" womanly status into a virtue. As an outsider, a spectator, as someone who had no direct stake in defending her country's military strategy, she was in a better position than her brother to perceive the moral weaknesses that characterized—indeed, permeated—the American war effort.

Judith Stevens insisted that soldiers should maintain a strict adherence to the highest moral principles, and she despised—no doubt because she did not understand—the compromises that public men, especially military men, made in the world of politics and war. Her letters, essays, and poetry became increasingly preoccupied with images of "death and carnage."[15] When she imagined the "laurel wreath" that her brother might one day wear, she began to envision it "steep'd in blood."[16] War, she knew, meant not only glory, but the "slaughter" of untold numbers of individuals who shared "kindred blood, from kindred veins."[17] Innocent civilians were as likely to be destroyed by the savagery of the battlefield as were professional soldiers. Even those women and children who never faced an enemy's bayonet were victims of war. Every American victory created "desolate widows," "destitute orphans," "bereaved friends," and "aged parent[s]" who would forever mourn the loss of their loved ones.[18]

War did more than kill and maim innocent soldiers and civilians on both sides. Much worse, and in the end much more threatening to American virtue, was the way it coarsened and corrupted the spirit of those who emerged from the battlefield physically unscathed. Thus, Judith Stevens was even more concerned about the moral well-being of her brother than she was about his physical safety. In the beginning she had been proud of Winthrop's decision to join Washington's army, even as she imagined that his decision to serve the patriot cause would redound to his own benefit. She assumed, as Winthrop himself did, that his valor on the battlefield would earn him much-deserved recognition, honor, and "pecuniary advantages" in the postwar world.[19] His "career of glory" would also make him a better person.[20] It would refine his judgment; his formal training in the classics at Harvard would be supplemented by a new understanding of the ways of the "real" world. The war, she assured Winthrop, will "ripen your knowledge beyond your years."[21] Most important, his exploits would earn him the admiration and gratitude of all Americans.

If military life gave Winthrop Sargent a chance to improve his character and to advance his own prospects, war also threatened to destroy the moral and religious characters of its participants. Camp life was rough and vulgar. Soldiers and officers cursed, drank, and failed to keep the sabbath. War led normally upright men to cut corners, to dissimulate, to play the game of war unfairly. America was so focused on the need for victory that its officers countenanced any means that promised to achieve their end. Stevens was particularly outraged in 1779, when she read accounts of an American naval victory off the coast of Massachusetts. Rumor had it that the Americans had won the battle only because they had employed deceptive practices. They had sailed their vessel under the colors of the enemy, luring "brave English sailors" into a deadly trap. Judith viewed such a ploy as inexcusable, as she mourned her country's inability "in these degenerate times" to live up to the standards set up by the heroes of ancient Greece. "I sigh," she mourned, "for the superior heroism of those ancient times, and I regret that I was not born in the days of other years." She continued, "deceit is deemed a virtue," and he "who can most successfully dissemble is the most renowned."[22] If her criticisms of American duplicity reveal Judith's naive understanding of Greek history, they also reflect the moralistic flavor of her views of the war.

In some ways even worse was the way American soldiers and officers treated one another. Winthrop himself was a proud and demanding officer who always insisted upon strict compliance with military discipline and was quick to punish those who failed to meet his exacting standards. His sister, however, pled the case of "those unhappy beings doomed to suffer the severity of military discipline." How, she wondered, could men claim to fight for liberty while asking their own soldiers to surrender one of the "dearest prerogatives of nature"? While she acknowledged that by commenting on military matters she had "wandered from [her] sphere," Judith was convinced that anyone, even a woman, could see that harsh punishments often transgressed the bounds of morality. "Surely," she protested, "strict justice must recoil, when the poor impotent being is led forth to a punishment, sometimes insupportable for the crimes which his superior commits with impunity."[23]

The Revolutionary War forced Judith Stevens to acknowledge what she had once only vaguely recognized or understood: a wide gap divided the active male world from the passive and protected female sphere. While individual women may have served briefly as their husband's surrogates, or may even have picked up a musket to defend themselves from enemy soldiers, the war remained largely the theater of male privilege and male responsibility. The patriot movement was built at least in part upon the foundations of civic republicanism, which assumed that the fate of any nation was largely determined by the virtue of its inhabitants, even as it described virtue in traditionally masculine terms. It was the "manly" attributes of physical strength, bravery, military heroism, independent and uncorrupted patriotism, and the willingness to sacrifice one's life for the good of the country that defined virtue and guaranteed its possessors the right to full citizenship. Cowardice, idleness, luxury, and dependence—all attributes traditionally associated with women—were the polar opposites of republican virtue. In a world that defined virtue in public, active, and militaristic terms, where the surest route to recognition and honor was through war, women were clearly not viewed as political—or even as significant—beings.

It is true that Americans had placed a high value on republican virtue before 1775, but the war served to underscore its significance. Judith Sargent Murray's lifelong rebellion against the privileges that traditional republican ideology accorded men began with the American Revolution, as she struggled to secure some public recognition for women's talents and women's values. She did so in two, somewhat conflicting, ways.

In 1775, when the fighting began, Judith Stevens's critique of the war led her to assert the worth of traditionally defined feminine attributes. "Our sex," she wrote, "is form'd for tenderness and love," and she proclaimed her pride in "taking rank with the softer sex."[24] If Stevens was tacitly willing to concede that men and women were different in some essential ways, she was even more determined later to blur what she saw as the artificial line that divided the male from the female world. As early as 1778 she began to argue that women were as rational, as public-spirited, as politically "interested" as men. She repeated this refrain for the rest of her life. "Am I not," she asked her brother, "interested, as a sister, in whatever can affect you, and am I not likewise most essentially interested as a daughter of Columbia? Yes, indeed, I am truly interested, for in the fate of my Country, in the Virtue of her Legislature, my most important wishes are involved."[25] If women were "interested" in politics, they were also capable of exercising rational political judgments. Indeed, Stevens thought that women would be found "deficient" if they allowed their country to sink into a pit of corruption rather than to lift a finger in the defense of public morality. What, after all, was politics "but a capability of distinguishing that which will probably advance the real interest of a Community. . . . Ought a female to become odious, or even to be subjected to censure, merely because she happens to understand what would best conduce to the prosperity of her Country?" If politics, like war, was fundamentally a moral issue, who was more qualified than women to judge the merits of any public issue? In a world where many people were beginning to argue that women were more moral, more pious, more likely to act benevolently than men, the answer to Judith's rhetorical question was clear. Moreover, if women were human, if they suffered the effects of their country's losses just as men did, if they were "equally concerned with men in the public weal," then they clearly had a right, even a duty, to influence their own government.[26]

Judith Stevens insisted that women possessed the "manly" qualities of intelligence, rationality, and public-spiritedness—qualities that equipped them to exercise political judgment. She also believed that they had the ability to enter the field of battle if their services were required. Throughout the war, she heard stories of women who had successfully defended themselves from enemy attack. When she began writing *The Gleaner*, she expanded upon the lessons she had learned during the war, eagerly pointing out that both ancient and modern history provided numerous examples to prove that women were physically and emotionally capable of donning a suit of armor and slaying the enemy in a righteous cause. "Courage is by no means *exclusively* a masculine virtue," she insisted, as she cited countless instances of women who fought with "undaunted courage" and "heroic firmness."[27]

Even as Judith argued that women had the ability to enter the male world of politics and war, she also believed that men—

with some effort—could learn to cultivate in themselves the values and moral characteristics that women possessed almost naturally. She refused to believe that the "tender passions" were incompatible with military endeavors. "The brave are always humane," she insisted, and the truly virtuous soldier exhibited "every gentler Virtue" and "the finer feeling of benevolence."[28] Surely, she argued, compassion "is not altogether confined to the female bosom."[29] Soldiers could be beneficient, tender, and humane without becoming cowards or risking their chances for glory. The ideal soldier was merciful to his enemies, able to "nobly rise above all personal enmity, and receive him who combated in the field as the friend of [his] youth." He was ever sympathetic, and always rushed to the aid of any suffering soldier, no matter what uniform he wore or what breach of discipline he may have committed.[30]

Judith Stevens's attempts to feminize the war effort, even as she argued that women had the right to reap the fruits of an American victory, were unsuccessful. When she expressed her views on political or military affairs, even John Murray, who admired her talent as a writer and encouraged her to publish her poems, treated her views with paternalistic amusement, warning that she was in danger of becoming a "female politician," an unnatural species he suggestively characterized as an "amphibious animal."[31] Moreover, she began to worry that even her beloved brother could not withstand the corrupting influences of military life, and with growing intensity she urged him to return to civilian life. Martial glory, she began to think, was a mere chimera. "Tell me," she demanded, "is it not true, that there are times when the *post* of *honour* is a *private station*?" Was it not "high time" for the true patriot to "seek an asylum from publick ingratitude, to hasten to that retirement which awaits him in the bosom of his friends? to books and all those contemplations which may free him for better days and more effectual exertions?" John Adams, she pointed out, never took up his sword in defense of his country. Yet his patriotism was undeniable, and his contributions to the American cause were of the highest order. Why, she wondered, was the willingness to sacrifice one's life for one's country deemed the best proof of patriotism, when it was possible to serve the country in so many other, even more virtuous, ways?[32]

In her attempt to draw a sharp and increasingly invidious contrast between war and peace, battlefield and the home front, public and private virtue, Judith Stevens was not simply reflecting the values of many American soldiers who, like George Washington, looked forward to retiring from public life at war's end. She was, at least in part, trying to feminize the male culture that the war represented. She wanted, in the words of historian Ruth Bloch, to "universalize what [her society] deemed essentially feminine traits."[33] Moreover, even before the war ended she had begun to move toward a new definition of virtue, a definition that emphasized private qualities over public honor.

The more she saw of war, the more critical of its ramifications Stevens became. Society always mocked those who stayed at home because of their "womanish fear," but she often thought that it was the soldier's values that were misplaced.[34] While she was quick to praise worthy military leaders, she invariably insisted that the true hero took up his sword with the greatest reluctance, and that like a venerable Cincinnatus, he "gladly put off the robes of power" at war's end.[35] A soldier, she argued, could best measure his virtue by the extent to which he detested the duties that his country thrust upon him. More and more, she began to paint verbal pictures of her brother at war's end, when he was no longer clad in "steel and armed with the instruments of death," and she longed for the time when the "military youth" would once again take up the life of the "humane Philosopher, and the gentle shepherd."[36]

In many ways, Judith Stevens's views were no different from those of a host of women who were troubled by wartime immorality, who insisted that soldiers and officers alike should be faithful to the Christian precepts upon which their own moral foundations were built. Many women believed that they were morally superior by virtue of their status as civilians. Virtually all of them longed for the day when their countrymen could lay down their arms, when they no longer had to worry about the death of loved ones, or to endure the loneliness and anxiety that characterized their waking hours. When most of these women looked forward to the end of hostilities, they hoped simply to turn back the clock, to return to their old routines, to forget that the war had ever occurred.

Judith Stevens had a different and more ambitious vision of the postwar world. As she listened to the rhetoric of American patriots, as she contemplated the sacrifices that she and other women had made for the cause of liberty, she began to hope that a new and independent America would usher in an enlightened age that would recognize women's native abilities, acknowledge their contributions to the public weal, and accord them an opportunity to cultivate and use their talents in ways that had been unimaginable under British rule. Her wartime experiences forced her to question the fundamental limits she faced as a woman because of the arbitrary customs that her society accepted without question. She was willing to scrounge for scarce food and supplies and to endure the absence of loved ones. She was only too glad to rush to a crowded and drafty inn to nurse her wounded brother back to health. She could not tolerate, however, the way her countrymen ignored her own contributions to the war effort, even while they showered praises upon the men who risked their lives on the battlefield. While Winthrop was "actively engaged in struggling for the sacred rights of Mankind," she remained in a "confined situation," as her life was "encircled by one Eternal sameness."[37] So long as the war continued, the differences separating men and women would be tremendous; male sacrifices on the battlefield would be privileged, and only men would be able to earn the gratitude of their compatriots. If men paid a price for their role in helping America achieve its independence, they could expect a hero's welcome at war's end. Women, too, made their sacrifices for their country, but they expected no recognition, much less a reward, for the services they rendered.

"From conspicuous rewards of merit," Judith Murray later observed, "the female world, seem injudiciously excluded. To man the road of preferment is thrown open—glory crowns the military hero." Women, on the other hand, enjoyed nothing but "*secondary* or *reflected* fame." She longed for the construction of a new government that would reward that virtue, which was "natal in the female bosom," and she was convinced that everyone—not just women—would ultimately benefit from such a wise and magnanimous policy.[38] In ancient Rome, she pointed out, the Senate honored the economic sacrifices women made for their country. If frugality and simplicity were hallmarks of republican virtue, then American women, acting as prudent housewives, were surely doing their part to preserve the moral foundations of the fledgling nation. Yet in America, she said, women seldom won public praise for their private sacrifices.

Judith Sargent Murray believed that women had much to offer the infant Republic. But so long as society valued the "masculine virtues" of bravery, independence, and public-spiritedness, men's military exploits would continue to garner the admiration of most Americans, while the quiet and ordinary work that women did every day would pass unnoticed. Even worse, if Americans believed that women had contributed nothing of importance to the war effort, then no one would imagine that they deserved political or economic benefits at war's end. Only when the country returned to peaceful pursuits would women have a chance to prove their worth. When intellectual pursuits became more important than military prowess and physical strength, when private morality was recognized as providing the foundations for public virtue, then, and only then, would the line between male and female become less impenetrable. Only then would softer virtues prevail—in the bosoms of men as well as of women.

Only at war's end did Judith Stevens begin to hope that the values women held dear would at last gain the ascendency. Reason would return, she thought, and with it the life of the mind—where the examples of ancient and modern history, as well as the precepts of Universalism, provided evidence to prove that women and men were equal—would resume its rightful place. The arts and sciences would be celebrated. Poetry would be as instrumental as military exploits in defining the character of the new nation. Historians would document and celebrate the triumphs of America's soldiers on the battlefield, so that future generations would appreciate and imitate the sacrifices that had been made in their names. Like her republican counterpart, Mercy Otis Warren, Murray believed that if men's efforts to win American liberty had been essential, it was up to women to write about those efforts, to keep them alive, and thus to define and preserve the moral values upon which the new nation was based. America would become venerated, not for its military might, but for the virtue of its citizens and the superiority of its literature. "Writers of every Class"—and presumably of both sexes—she predicted, would "wield the pen." "Imagination would mark the historic page," and talented women would have a chance to assume a rightful place as honored members of their society.[39]

With the coming of peace, Judith found that, at least initially, she had little time to utilize her talents on the public stage. These were eventful years for Judith Stevens, filled with uncertainty and heartache. Her husband's fortunes plummeted—in large measure due to the postwar depression that devastated Gloucester's fishing industry. In 1787, Stevens died alone on the Dutch island of Saint Eustatius, where he had gone to escape his creditors and to recoup his financial losses. Less than two years later, Judith married the Reverend John Murray.

Her second marriage, based, she said, on a judicious combination of "mutual esteem, mutual friendship, mutual confidence," was by all accounts a happy one.[40] The Stevenses had been childless. Consequently, Judith was overjoyed in January of 1789 to discover that she was pregnant, and devastated when her son George was stillborn. The birth, two years later, of Julia Maria helped her recover from her loss, and she took on the role of motherhood with a spirit that sometimes bordered on the fanatical.

Despite the energy she invested in her duties as wife and mother, Murray found that her marriage gave her both the time and the confidence to begin writing for publication at a relatively steady pace. John Murray had always praised her ability and had persuaded her to publish her Universalist "Catechism" in 1782.

After that, she submitted an occasional piece to the *Massachusetts Magazine*, writing under the pen name, "Constantia." Her "Desultory thoughts upon the utility of encouraging a degree of self-complacency, especially in female bosoms," appeared in the *Gentleman and Lady's Town and Country Magazine* in 1784. By 1792 she was sending her essays to the *Massachusetts Magazine* on a monthly basis. Her more political essays, in which she sang the praises of George Washington, John Adams, and the Federalist party, and demanded equal education for women appeared under the pseudonym, "The Gleaner." She continued to write as "Constantia," when she commented on less controversial topics—honesty, industry, and piety, for instance—in what she called her "Repository" essays.

In 1793 the Murrays moved to Boston, where John served as a minister to the city's small but devout Universalist congregation. There, Judith wrote two plays, *The Medium* (1795) and *The Traveller Returned* (1796), both of which were performed at Boston's newly created Federal Street Theater. Disappointed by the tepid critical and popular response to her efforts, she returned to writing poetry and essays. Her most famous work, *The Gleaner*, a compendium that included essays, poetry, the novel-like story of "Margaretta," and her two plays, was published in 1798.

Judith Sargent Murray used her talents as a poet, essayist, and playwright to win fame for herself and, she claimed, to guide the new nation—especially its young people—along the path of rectitude. Above all, she used her influence to demand more rights for women. She insisted that women were the intellectual equals of men, that custom and lack of opportunity, not innate ignorance, explained women's apparent deficiencies. She called upon young women to "*reverence themselves*," to put "independence . . . within their grasp," so that they could take control of their own lives rather than rely on husbands, brothers, or the charity of complete strangers to support them.[41] Her emphasis on the importance of economic independence for women had profound implications for a society that linked independence to political rights.

Judith Sargent Murray was never a nineteenth-century suffragist. Like virtually all eighteenth-century women, she exhibited no interest in attaining the vote for women. While she conceived of a time when America might produce a "female Washington," she did not make office holding for women a priority.[42] Still, she defended women's right to enter the political arena. Often she simply claimed that wives and mothers played a significant public role whenever they used their influence to educate their husbands and sons in the ways of virtue and good citizenship. Intelligent and moral women, she thought, could use their skills and their naturally empathetic characters to provide the basis for an orderly and virtuous society. In this sense, their contributions to the nation's welfare were at least as important as the services of soldiers or politicians. The morals of America's children, and thus of America's future, were in their hands.

Murray was never content merely to exercise her influence indirectly. She always reserved the right to express her views in public and to write authoritatively on every subject, not just on "women's issues." Simply by publishing her own writing, she was joining those women on both sides of the Atlantic who challenged traditional gender definitions and crossed customary gender boundaries. Writing was an act of assertion. To write for publication was to enter the once-forbidden public arena, probing and even attempting to renegotiate the boundaries that divided the male from the female world. Physically, she might remain in her home, in the private sphere. Yet by participating in the vigorous public dialogue that dominated the nation's intellectual and political life, she was implicitly claiming some rights of citizenship for herself. Writing provided a way, as Murray put it, "to travel from one quarter of the globe to another" while remaining "stationary."[43] It allowed women to exert a direct influence on public affairs without relying on their husbands or sons to speak for them. The decision to publish was not only to seek fame, but to seek power as well.

By the beginning of the nineteenth century, Judith Sargent Murray had become convinced that she would never realize her dream of personal fame, nor would women in her own age achieve the potential that the American Revolution had once seemed to promise. Murray managed to earn a small profit from *The Gleaner*, enabling her to pay off the mortgage on the family's Boston home. Still, although she gained readers throughout the United States, and even sent a few copies to England, she was never able to sell all of the thousand copies of the volumes that she had ordered. Moreover, her effort received decidedly mixed reviews. President John Adams, to whom *The Gleaner* was dedicated, praised her essays, as did her friends and relatives. Supporters of the Republican party, as well as many people who distrusted anything emanating from the pen of a Universalist, attacked them.

Murray published very little after *The Gleaner* appeared, as the needs of her family grew more and more demanding. She served as a substitute mother for five of her brother Winthrop's children and stepchildren, who lived with the Murrays at various times to take advantage of Boston's superior schools. In 1801, John suffered a stroke; eight years later, he was totally debilitated by a second seizure, forcing Judith to spend much of her time at her husband's bedside. With his death in 1815, Judith Sargent Murray and her daughter made plans to leave Boston for the Mississippi Territory. Julia Maria had married Mississippi planter Adam Bingaman in 1811, immediately after Bingaman's graduation from Harvard. In 1816, Judith, Julia Maria, and Julia Maria's daughter Charlotte began their southward journey. Judith Sargent Murray lived with her daughter and son-in-law until her death in 1820.

It is impossible to know whether Murray would have published more of her work after 1798 if her own life had not been so busy and unsettled. By the end of the century, Americans seemed to be less interested in challenging the traditional orthodoxies than they had been in the Republic's first, more heady days, and women throughout the United States were finding that their declarations of equality were falling on increasingly unreceptive ears. In Murray's New England, the French Revolution had dampened enthusiasm for reform or even innovation, and she often found that she had to defend her own views from those who had begun to see support for women's equality as tainted with subversion. Still, while she only occasionally expressed her views in public after the appearance of *The Gleaner*, Murray never abandoned her belief in women's intellectual equality, nor did she cease to hope that women would be taught to "*reverence themselves*."

Notes

1. Judith Stevens to John Murray, September 6, 1779, Judith Sargent Murray, Letterbook, 1:227, 229, Mississippi Archives, Jackson, Mississippi. Hereafter cited as Letterbook.

2. Judith Stevens to John Murray, September 6, 1779, ibid., 1:228.

3. Judith Sargent Murray to Winthrop Sargent, May 17, 1780, ibid., 2:283.

4. Judith Sargent Murray to Winthrop Sargent, November 28, 1784, ibid., 1:196.

5. Judith Stevens to John Murray, November 14, 1774, ibid., 1:13.

6. Judith Sargent Murray, *The Gleaner: A Miscellaneous Production in Three Volumes* (Boston: L. Thomas and E. T. Andrews, 1798), 1:159.

7. Judith Stevens to John Murray, October 1, 1775, Letterbook, 1:25.

8. Judith Stevens to Winthrop Sargent Jr., October 28, 1781, ibid., 1:358.

9. Judith Sargent Murray, "Reflections during a fine Morning upon existing circumstances," 1775, Repository, 18, 20, Mississippi Archives, Jackson, Mississippi. Hereafter cited as Repository.

10. Judith Sargent Murray to Mr. Redding of Falmouth, England, May 7, 1808, Letterbook, 11:208.

11. Judith Stevens to Winthrop Sargent, September 8, 1779, Letterbook, 1:232.

12. Judith Stevens to Judith Sargent, November [?], 1778, ibid., 26; Judith Stevens to John Murray, June 17, 1775, ibid., 19; Judith Stevens to John Murray, June 28, 17[82], Letterbook, 2:37.

13. Judith Stevens to Winthrop Sargent, May 15, 1781, ibid., 42.

14. Judith Stevens to Winthrop Sargent, November [?], 1777, Letterbook, 1:78.

15. Judith Stevens to John Murray, November 30, 1780, ibid., 298.

16. Murray, "Vanity," Poetry, 4:43, Mississippi Archives, Jackson, Mississippi. Hereafter cited as Poetry.

17. Murray, "On the ill-fated Penobscot Expedition," ibid., 1:192.

18. Judith Stevens to John Murray, September 16, 1779, Letterbook, 1:234.

19. Judith Stevens to Winthrop Sargent, April 5, 1779, ibid., 174.

20. Judith Stevens to Winthrop Sargent, April 5, 1779, ibid.

21. Judith Stevens to Winthrop Sargent, July 3, 1778, ibid., 122.

22. Judith Stevens to John Murray, September 16, 1779, ibid., 234, 235.

23. Judith Stevens to Winthrop Sargent, July 20, August 25, 1779, ibid., 342, 346.

24. Murray, "Sentiments," Poetry, 1:136; Murray, "A Party of Pleasure," Repository, 361.

25. Judith Sargent Murray to Winthrop Sargent, January 28, 1796, Letterbook, 9:533.

26. Judith Sargent Murray to Mrs. H——— of York, November 25, 1800, Letterbook, 11:227–29.

27. Murray, *The Gleaner*, 3:192, 193.

28. Judith Stevens to Winthrop Sargent, February 25, 1778, Letterbook, 1:90.

29. Judith Stevens to Winthrop Sargent, August 25, 1781, ibid., 346.

30. Judith Stevens to John Murray, October 8, 1779, October 1, 1776, ibid., 237.

31. Judith Stevens to John Murray, August 31, 1778, ibid., 151.

32. Judith Stevens to Winthrop Sargent, August 25, 1781, ibid., 346; Judith Sargent Murray to Winthrop and Judith Sargent, October 12, 1788, Letterbook, 2:350.

33. Ruth Bloch, "Untangling the Roots of Modern Sex Roles: A Survey of Four Centuries of Change," *Signs* 4 (1978): 250.

34. Judith Stevens to Winthrop Sargent, May 17, 1780, Letterbook, 1:218.

35. Murray, "The Traveller Returned," in *The Gleaner*, 3:136.

36. Judith Stevens to Winthrop Sargent, May 17, 1780, Letterbook, 1:218.

37. Judith Stevens to Winthrop Sargent, February 25, 1778, December 1, 1779, April 5, 1780, ibid., 88, 262, 271.

38. Murray, *The Gleaner*, 2:217.

39. Murray, "On reading the institution of the Cincinnati," January 28, 1784, Poetry, 3:182.

40. Murray, *The Gleaner*, 1:136.

41. Ibid., 168.

42. Judith Sargent Murray to Mr. Redding, May 7, 1801, Letterbook, 11:288.

43. Judith Sargent Murray to Mr. Holderness of Wexford, Ireland, August 11, 1798, ibid., 10:265.

Suggested Readings

Baym, Nina. *American Women Writers and the Work of History, 1790–1860*. New Brunswick, NJ: Rutgers University Press, 1995.

Bloch, Ruth H. "The Gendered Meanings of Virtue in Revolutionary America." *Signs* 13 (Fall 1987): 37–59.

Crane, Elaine F. "Dependence in the Era of Independence: The Role of Women in a Republican Society." In *The American Revolution: Its Character and Limits*, ed. Jack Greene, 253–75. New York: New York University Press, 1987.

Field, Vena Bernadette. *Constantia: A Study of the Life and Works of Judith Sargent Murray, 1751–1820*. Orono: University Press of Maine, 1931.

Gunderson, Joan R. "Independence, Citizenship, and the American Revolution." *Signs* 13 (Fall 1987): 59–77.

Kerber, Linda K. *Women of the Republic: Intellect and Ideology in Revolutionary America*. Chapel Hill: University of North Carolina Press, 1980.

Norton, Mary Beth. *Liberty's Daughters: The Revolutionary Experience of American Women, 1750–1800*. Boston: Little, Brown, 1980.

Skemp, Sheila L. *Judith Sargent Murray: A Short Biography with Documents*. Boston: Bedford Press, 1998.

Ulrich, Laurel Thatcher. " 'Daughters of Liberty': Religious Women in Revolutionary New England." In *Women in the Age of the American Revolution*, ed. Ronald Hoffman and Peter J. Albert, 211–43. Charlottesville: University Press of Virginia, 1989.

Wilson, Joan Hoff. "The Illusion of Change: Women and the American Revolution." In *The American Revolution: Explorations in the History of American Radicalism*, ed. Alfred F. Young, 383–446. DeKalb: University of Northern Illinois Press, 1976.

Students who would like to read Judith Sargent Murray in her own words may consult Judith Sargent Murray, *The Gleaner*

(Schenectady, NY: Union College Press, 1992). Her Letterbooks, which include twenty-five hundred letters written between 1765 and 1816, as well as many unpublished poems and essays, are available at the Mississippi Archives in Jackson, Mississippi. Microfilm copies of the Letterbooks may be purchased from the archives.

16

Phillis Wheatley

Speaking Liberty to the "Modern Egyptians"

David Grimsted

Like Judith Sargent Murray, Phillis Wheatley (ca. 1754–1784) gained notoriety as a New England author. In her short life, this African-American slave became a Christian, an internationally known poet, and a free woman. Unlike Absalom Jones, who declared his independence by picking his own surname, Phillis Wheatley's derived from the name of the slave ship that brought her to America and the surname of her owners, John and Susanna Wheatley of Boston. As an adolescent, Phillis found that revolutionary themes of liberty and slavery suggested to her an affinity between the colonists and African-American slaves. The printing of her poems, supported by evangelical and antislavery advocates, could prove that slaves might be sensitive and refined geniuses. Why was Thomas Jefferson not among Wheatley's admirers?

Wheatley frequently used poetic double meanings to suggest that the political struggles for independence from British tyranny carried an antislavery message for those willing to acknowledge it. Members of one Virginia family may have been inspired by her poems to free large numbers of their slaves, thereby revealing the practical power of poetry. Uninterested in African colonization, Wheatley identified herself not as an African, but as a Christian and an American. Did Phillis have a different view of race relations and Christianity from Absalom Jones? Did their experiences as slaves and as free blacks account for differing opinions on racial and religious integration versus segregation? Freed in 1774, after the publication of her poetry in London, Wheatley attained that personal independence that had eluded her since her capture in Africa, and in 1778 she married a free black, John Peters. Did she find greater success as the treasured possession of Susanna Wheatley, or as Mrs. Peters? As David Grimsted reveals, her poverty, regular pregnancies, and poor health provided their own kind of bondage and an untimely demise.

David Grimsted teaches at the University of Maryland, College Park. He is the author of numerous publications, including an essay on Phillis Wheatley in Ronald Hoffman and Peter Albert, eds., *Women in the Age of the American Revolution* (1989).

She was sold off a slave ship from Africa in 1761 when she was seven or eight years old. At least her new Boston owners decided that their purchase, clothed only in a scrap of old carpet, was about that age since she was losing her baby teeth. Less than twenty-five years later she died with her last surviving infant, and both were buried in an unknown and probably unmarked grave. Such events were typical enough of the lives of the thousands of African slaves who were brought and bought into the mainland English colonies. Their lives, like their graves, provide little evidence either of their sorrows, both those ordained by a system of bondage and those that came from life's chances, or of their resilient dreams and joys.

There was nothing typical, however, about Phillis Wheatley's life between her sale as a frightened child on a Boston wharf and her death as an enfeebled young mother. Only six years after her arrival in this strange world, she had learned a new language, accepted a new faith, and developed ties of love and support that allowed her to write:

> 'Twas mercy brought me from my Pagan land,
> Taught my benighted soul to understand
> That there's a God, that there's a Saviour too;

It was a simple statement that the writer felt Africa a world well lost for the faith that she had found, but the conclusion of the poem was not a criticism of her native land, but of the America that had come to be her home:

> Some view our sable race with scornful eye,
> "Their colour is a diabolic die."
> Remember, *Christians*, *Negros*, black as *Cain*,
> May be refin'd, and join th'angelic train.[1]

The slave girl, barely in her teens, was already using poetry to lecture gently her fellow Christians on the vicious folly of confusing darkness of skin with that of sin. So quietly and orthodoxly did she argue the absolute difference between a "benighted soul" and a bedarkened complexion that no one would care or dare to object to what she said.

The slave had already become a Christian, a poet, and a subtle racial strategist in the language she loved. She was soon to gain considerable communal respect and support, and then an international reputation as a published poet, a celebrity, and an exemplar of the abilities of her race. Her poems were to remain a prime proof of the equality of racial ability for opponents of slavery and racism long after her death, and an object of necessary scorn for those who developed racist theories of a "diabolic die" in order to justify oppressing blacks, slave and free.

Her name well suggested the tensions between racism and equality, slavery and liberty, human exploitation and potential that shaped her life, writings, and significance. *Phillis* was the name of the slave ship that brought her from Africa, and Wheatley the name of those who first owned, and soon loved and nurtured, the gifted girl. John Wheatley, a well-off merchant tailor, bought her for his wife, Susanna, who wanted a personal servant as she aged. Susanna chose the small, solemn, frightened child cut off from the world left behind and baffled by the strange speech, sights, culture, religion, and people who looked at her so sharply in the slave mart anchored in Boston Harbor. The seven-year-old would grow to embrace all these things, in part because they, in unprecedented ways, came to embrace the talents and intelligence she possessed. Perhaps the sensitive girl even then saw that the woman who fixed her attention on her did so, not with the entrepreneurial eye that prevailed among these respectable purchasers, but with humane sympathy. Certainly, mutual need and support were to turn to love quickly as the lives of the frail white woman and the small black child intertwined.

Phillis, in her new home, met the teenaged Wheatley children, Mary and Nathaniel, and the several blacks who composed the domestic staff in the Wheatleys' comfortable home. She soon felt the affectionate warmth her sensitive intelligence evoked from the family. Susanna was surprised to see Phillis copying letters from a book, and Mary Wheatley, ten years older than the slave, became her enthusiastic teacher. Her precocious pupil learned to read and write English almost as quickly as she learned to speak it. The family took pride in Phillis's quick mind and gentle ways, and that broad intellectual encouragement that sustained her literary career began.

Susanna taught Phillis something else that was to become equally important to the black girl and to her poetry: Christianity. Susanna was part of a remarkable group of evangelical women in England and America who supported revivals and religious outreach. Most had some ties to the great revivalist, George Whitefield, and many of them showed a special enthusiasm and support for the spiritual-intellectual well-being of society's "outsiders": the poor, Native Americans, and slaves. These women were in no sense social radicals, but their lives as women sharpened their sense of the quality and equality of all humans before God and made them the group most ready to question their age's social hierarchies, including those of race, to promote pure faith. Phillis came to share their intense belief, and it was they who provided the crucial encouragement for her writing and publication. Their ministerial friends seconded their enthusiasm and probably provided most of the books of poetry, theology, and classical mythology that Phillis read as she shaped her mind and talent.

The poet clearly learned, too, from events outside her home and church. Her first years in America were the first years of resistance to British policies that were to lead to the struggle for independence. When the slave ship *Phillis* anchored in Boston, the British were on the verge of their victory over the French in the Great War for Empire. The defeat of this common enemy of Britain and its colonies undercut a central cause of mutual need and cooperation. Britain was now anxious both to recoup some of the costs of this expensive war and to take tighter rein over the colonies. The colonists were reluctant to pay more in taxes or limitations when the "protection" Britain talked about was so clearly a pretense for taking more money and control from them.

Nowhere was the conflict leading to war so intense as in Boston. From the family home, the Wheatleys could have seen the events that became known as the Boston Massacre. They lived within blocks of the Stamp Act violence and the Boston Tea Party, and Phillis wrote poems on each of these events. What is surprising is how comfortable this young enslaved woman was writing on political themes, a rare American poet who turned her pen to support the Revolution. Perhaps no other woman poet, before or since, wrote so often on contemporary politics as did Wheatley, supposedly barred by age, sex, race, and servitude from concern with those things at the time so securely the province of mature and well-off men.

The political situation especially interested Wheatley because the American rhetoric against Britain had personal application to her enslavement. Wheatley had learned to be evocative about this connection even in elegies, poems written to honor those who had recently died, by talking about death as a tyrant and by referring to its brutal power and iron chains. But the American vocabulary of liberty and slavery, when used by a poet who steadily reminded readers that she was black, had implications for her "peculiar" situation. Wheatley said not only what patriots wanted to hear but also applied the clichés' implications where slaveholders did not wish to follow. In "America" (1768) Wheatley laid out her political poetics clearly. The poem is an amusing picture of irritable Mother Britannia overtaxing her American child and making "the Best of Infants" cry. This idea was introduced with a personal note:

> Thy Power, O Liberty, makes strong the weak
> And (wond'rous instinct) Ethiopians speak.
> Sometimes by Simile, a victory's won. . . .[2]

No one during the Revolution insisted more influentially on the simile between American and black liberty than this Ethiopian who steadily pointed her pen at the "iron chain" of excessive power.

Despite affection and encouragement, Phillis Wheatley's position was uneasy as well as unusual. She was treated "as a daughter" by Susanna, but the Wheatleys had other slaves, who were not maltreated but kept in their place. There are some telling anecdotes in the account of Wheatley descendant Margaretta Matilda Odell, which has provided most of what is known of Phillis's private life. Written on the basis of family oral tradition more than fifty years after Phillis Wheatley died, this account seems careful and honest, despite some omissions tied to the "long memory" involved. Odell tells of Susanna Wheatley calling one slave a "varlet" for letting "my Phillis" sit outside on the carriage next to him when he drove the girl home from a dinner.[3] Odell also reports that Phillis was often invited to parties in Boston's best homes, but she usually asked to dine at a separate table so that no one might be offended by eating with a black. Phillis's tact in living in some sense a double life, as a part of and apart from white society, is apparent in the subtle way Wheatley quietly inserted her racial and slave identity while asserting her broader human and religious interests. None of her poems centers on the issues of slavery and race, but she regularly mentioned her identity, and almost always used imagery and color-coded messages that reminded her audiences of racial realities while creating minimal wariness in her white readers.

Wheatley's poetry was subtly intelligent and venturous, but had some limitations as well. These had less to do with her age, sex, race, or servitude than with the thin New England poetic tradition in which she worked, which largely celebrated particular people, especially in death elegies, or particular occasions. Her first published poem was stimulated by hearing two sailors tell John Wheatley of their close escape from a storm. The bulk of her poetry fell into this socially respected but very limited genre: on the comings and goings of people, hurricanes, or diseases, and especially on deaths. Of her fifty-four known extant poems, eighteen are elegies or condolences on the recently deceased, and thirteen commemorate events in particular people's lives. Twelve elaborate ideas on such things as imagination, recollection, providence, atheism, or Harvard, and three retell classical and biblical stories or passages. Eight of these poems (including two elegies) center on political personages, events, or controversies. While Wheatley often inserted passages about her race, her muse, her situation, and her feelings, only two poems center on her own experiences, including her last poem, a self-elegy. Writing good poems in a society where poetry was less an artistic calling than an aspect of communal service was not easy.

Wheatley's elegies are her most conventional poems, although many of them, especially those to ministers who supported her aspirations such as Samuel Sewall, Samuel Cooper, and John Moorhead, have lines of some incisive feeling. If one thinks of them as personal gestures of support to mentors, friends, and acquaintances at moments of loss, they take on dignity. Wheatley also managed to bring much variety to poems where the situation required the repetition of a few sentiments: of sadness, the need for acceptance, and the hope of heaven. In a poem written to console a pregnant friend, Lucy Marshall, on her husband's death, Wheatley wrote:

> The babe unborn in the dark womb is tos't
> And seems in anguish for its father lost.[4]

The connecting of "lost" here to both embryo and dead father movingly joins the two dark wombs that bound life. Wheatley's honesty of belief and feeling gave dignity and a modicum of emotion to handling a poetic role whose functions she well understood:

> Now sorrow is incumbent on thy heart,
> Permit the muse a cordial to impart.[5]

There were limitations, too, in Wheatley's poetic model. On occasion, Wheatley wrote in quatrains, but the bulk of her verse is in the pattern of Alexander Pope's iambic pentameter couplets, with their regular rhythms and the sometimes loveless couplings of their rhymes. Such processional regularity contributes to a quality both formal and formulaic in much of her writing, as do her classical references. Pope's influence is probably at work again here, along with Wheatley's yearning for the higher formal education denied women. Perhaps Wheatley's most feminist poem was one chiding Harvard students for insufficiently taking advantage of the educational opportunities denied her and other women. John Wheatley reported in 1773 that Phillis was an eager student of Latin, the tongue that at that time separated the educated boys from the girls. Doubtless these learned allusions meant much to Wheatley and her female support circle. Lacking the strikingly original images or rhythms associated with Shakespearean or

Romantic beauty, her poetry brings a supple and intelligent vitality, under conventional garb, to her faith, her friendships, her country's politics, and her personal commitments in support of liberty in all forms.

People were right to see Wheatley's accomplishments as almost incredible in one so situated. Wheatley wrote her first letter just four years after her arrival in America; she was probably fourteen when she commemorated the Boston Massacre in verse, sixteen when she gained some international reputation with her elegy on revivalist George Whitefield, and only nineteen when her book of poems was published in London. Two years later her poetry had been praised by leading British critics and by such diverse figures as Benjamin Rush, George Washington, Voltaire, and black essayist Ignatius Sancho. In Virginia a tutor read her poems and their reviews to his young pupil, Bob Carter, both of them excited at what a slave had created; the boy's family was later to free more slaves than any other in the United States. Never had twelve years of exposure to English been turned to such account, and seldom had literature been so integrated with such major political questions. A French visitor to America called her, in 1779, "one of the strangest creatures in the country and perhaps in the whole world."[6] Wheatley was, as she chose to call herself in one of her subscription proposals, a "*rara avis in terra*," or one of earth's rare birds.[7] She had learned at least some Latin.

She was a caged bird, and would have never sung to the world had not the Wheatleys, some ministers, and a circle of evangelical women worked to bring her poetry to the world's attention. Susanna Wheatley was at the center of a sisterhood of evangelical acquaintances who were Phillis's main support network. Wheatley's first published poem appeared in the Rhode Island *Newport Mercury*, introduced with a squib probably written by Susanna Wheatley or Sarah Osborn. Osborn had integrated blacks into her school in the early 1760s, about the time she became the center of a major revival. For almost five years, until her health deteriorated, she conducted religious meetings every evening but Saturday that attracted hundreds of people to her home each week. The largest group was that for blacks, doubtless including Wheatley's closest black friend and correspondent, Obour Tanner.

Wheatley's most frequently published poem broadened this circle of support. The fame of George Whitefield ensured that Wheatley's elegy on the revivalist was widely printed, separately and with other tributes, on both sides of the Atlantic. The dedication of the poem to the "Great Countess" made sense; the Countess of Huntingdon had long been a chief supporter of Whitefield and other evangelical efforts in England and abroad. It was also a sensibly calculated tactic to gain the countess's patronage, though perhaps that had been secured even earlier. Whitefield had stayed with the Wheatleys on his last American visit, and Susanna Wheatley had corresponded with him about their shared evangelical interests. At any rate, Phillis sent the poem to the countess with a deferential note that noted her race. The countess read it with delight over both its religious sentiments and the race of the poet.

The countess's support was to prove central to the publication of Wheatley's book of poetry in London. In late 1770, Phillis had sent the elegy to the countess, who then asked to see other poems. They were sent to an evangelical printer, Archibald Bell, who read them to the countess. She listened with rapture, exclaiming, " 'Is not this or that very fine? Do read another,' and then expressed herself she found her heart knit to her."[8] The knitting of this woman's heart to evangelical women's support of Wheatley's poetry assured a prestigious London printing under prominent auspices.

About this time, in February of 1772, a "proposal" to publish Wheatley's poems appeared in Boston. This request for subscribers was a common eighteenth-century mode of eliciting money and readying public interest for works to be published. Word soon came from England of press interest there, with printer Archibald Bell making, during that year, "repeated" requests for a testimony of authenticity to squelch doubts about the slave woman's authorship. In November 1772, John Wheatley sent a statement to Bell. Susanna wrote this, as well as the testimonial of authenticity that Bell had requested, signed by twenty-eight prominent Bostonians of the day, including Governor Thomas Hutchinson, the lieutenant governor, John Hancock, James Bowdoin, and seven leading ministers. The scholar who has added most to knowledge about Wheatley's life recently, William H. Robinson, has argued that racial prejudice in Boston caused the proposal to "fail" there. The number and prominence of Wheatley's Boston supporters, and how closely the London plans followed the Boston proposal, make it more likely that the chance of a prestigious London publication supplanted the original project.

Scholar Henry Louis Gates has offered a fanciful account of one of the events surrounding publication. He claims that the twenty-eight Bostonian signers who were gathered in 1772 to grill Phillis on the authenticity of her poems asked her to discuss Greek mythology, conjugate Latin verbs, and recite poetic passages before finding Wheatley's responses "more than sufficient." It is an amusing story but one for which there exists neither evidence nor probability. His "curious anecdote" of "one of the oddest oral examinations on record" neglects how well known Phillis's skill was in religious and social Boston.[9] The gentlemen attesting authenticity mention no meeting, and say that not "we" but some of "the best judges," presumably clergymen, had examined Wheatley and were sure of her capability and honesty.[10] The testimonial wording was often identical to that in the earlier Boston proposals. Susanna wrote both, and either John or one of the supportive clergy circulated the statement to the other well-known men, who were happy to attest to the truth of what both common opinion and respected acquaintances asserted.

Bell was sent what he and Phillis's supporters knew would matter: a document making it hard for doubters or detractors to have or raise suspicions about the slave woman's authorship. In addition, Susanna arranged the printing of stories about the people testing Phillis by asking her to write on particular topics. Supposedly "On Recollection" and the poem in praise of the Earl of Dartmouth were written in triumphant response to such tests. Susanna's tactics worked. No one ever publicly doubted the author's authenticity except Thomas Jefferson, and he very obliquely, when he attacked her poetry as part of one of the first "suggestions" that blacks were an inherently inferior species of human being.[11]

Such care in handling public opinion occurred because Susanna, Phillis, and their circle had a social agenda. Earlier publicity had referred to the poet's race, but in 1772 and after her slave status was stressed. The poems would now show the world the potential of those people most denied any chance for self-development: slaves. The Boston proposals said that the poems were written by a "Negro girl, from the strength of her own genius, it being just a few years since she came to this town, an uncultivated Barbarian from Africa," and concluded by calling Wheatley "a very uncommon genius at present a slave." John Wheatley's testimonial to Phillis's intellect was endorsed "by her Master, who bought her and with whom she now lives." The twenty-eight Bostonians' statement included the proposal's wording about the author's coming from Africa, but sharpened the slavery link: she "has ever since been and now is, under the Disadvantage of serving as a Slave in a Family in Town."[12]

It is clear that the Wheatleys wanted no credit for the advantages that had been Phillis's slave lot in order to make a social point. The antislavery movement was just beginning in the 1770s. When Phillis Wheatley went to England prior to publication of the poems, the two men who introduced her to London society were Granville Sharp and John Thornton, both with ties to the countess and both antislavery leaders as the movement commenced. In the colonies, the leading non-Quaker figure was the Reverend Samuel Hopkins, handpicked by the now-bedridden Sarah Osborn and her "sorority" to head Newport's First Congregational Church and to carry on her religious and racial work. To talk only of the "disadvantages" Phillis had faced was to underline the human potential that the gross exploitation of slavery commonly crushed. Clearly Phillis and Susanna Wheatley and the other evangelicals who supported them understood well by this time that the poems were a means of attacking slavery. Yet the thrust was subtle enough to attract readers not tied to that cause for almost a decade before defenders of slavery, led by Thomas Jefferson, felt the need to attack a document that so deeply questioned their developing theories of racial inferiority. Wheatley's poems advertised that slaves could think, feel, write, and create as sensitively as their exploiters.

The substantial changes between the contents of the book proposed to Boston in early 1772 and the one printed in London a year and one-half later show both the political acumen of the Wheatley circle and how fertile—and how freed—was Phillis's talent under the encouragement of pending publication. Twelve of the poems in the Boston proposal were omitted from the London collection, many of them because their pro-colonial sentiments would offend an English audience. Praise of American heroes was now unsuitable, as were images of an irritable Mother Britannia overtaxing America. Yet Wheatley had learned how much she could say safely if she spoke quietly, and the pro-American passages in poems such as those in praise of Whitefield and Dartmouth remained intact. No better example exists of Wheatley's poetic politics than the ode "To the King's Most Excellent Majesty." It begins:

> Your subjects hope, dread sire—
> The crown upon your brows may flourish long,
> And that your arm may in your God be strong!

This sounds respectfully conventional enough so that one does not notice too strongly that the poet then singles out that

> . . . of thy favors past
> The meanest peasants most admire the last.*

Her asterisk referred one to the bottom of the page, where one learned that George's last best action was "the Repeal of the Stamp Act." A bit more sonorous praise leads to the final lines:

> Great God, direct, and guard him from on high
> And from his head let ev'ry evil fly!
> And may each clime with equal gladness see
> A monarch's smiles can set his subjects free![13]

The stately proprieties were just enough to let people hear but not quite grasp that this Boston slave girl was telling her king that she hoped God would help him get rid of his evil ideas and make all glad by cheerfully letting his subjects free themselves. She was, as one Boston admirer said, "an artful jade."[14]

Wheatley's art and her politics were clearest in the book's second political poem. Wheatley's ode to the politician credited with repealing the Stamp Act, the Earl of Dartmouth, possibly written in response to one of her "tests," was certainly central in the campaign to ready a broad audience for her work. Phillis sent it to the earl in late 1772 with an ingratiating letter, and Susanna had it published after Phillis went to England in June 1773, with the story about its being written as a test of Phillis's poetic facility. The poem begins with an image of Freedom rising like the sun on New England since Dartmouth removed all but England's "silken reins." This first section concludes by telling America:

> No longer shall thou dread the iron chain,
> Which wanton *Tyranny* with lawless hand
> Had made, and with it meant t'enslave the land.

After this concentration of the imagery—iron chain, wanton Tyranny, enslavement—that Wheatley had long used to tie the evils of black bondage to her personal and political themes, the poet stated her antislavery argument directly. The earl might wonder, she wrote, about the source of her "love of Freedom" and "wishes for the common good." The simple answer was that, "young in life," she had been "snatch'd" from Africa, the tragedy of which she put in its primary emotive terms: the "excruciating" grief of the parent and the steeliness of heart "by no misery moved" of those who made money through the suffering of hapless parents and babes "belov'd":

> Such, such my case. And can I then but pray
> Others may never feel tyrannic sway?

This brief and unarguable indictment of slavery's cruelty leads to a final section asking that Dartmouth continue to "sooth the griefs" of America and thus earn both worldly honor and Godly favor.[15] That America's griefs included those of its slaves again goes without saying. Wheatley simply set the personal antislavery plea here in the center of her poem, book, and works and let its pervasive meaning reverberate with those willing to hear.

The Earl of Dartmouth poem was one of the twenty-two published in London that was unmentioned in the Boston proposals, most of them written in about a year's time. These poems, which include the best Wheatley wrote, suggest Wheatley's poetic range when she was freed from being a commemorator of special occasions. Two new poems praised African artistic achievement, one directed to slave painter Scipio Moorhead, a Boston acquaintance of Wheatley, and the other, which opened the book, connecting her own art to that of Terence "of Africa's sable race," a Roman slave who, like her, wrote his plays wholly within the "western" canon.[16] New also was Wheatley's only retelling of a classical myth, that of Niobe with its theme of the dangers of powerful pride. In the bloodiness of this poem, and in that of the two Biblical passages Wheatley made into poems, one glimpses the black anger beneath Wheatley's neoclassic surface. Her account of the Goliath story bloodily celebrated the victory of the mocked over those deemed all-powerful, while her paraphrase of verses from Isaiah has Christ bestride a battlefield filled with "the dying and the dead":

> Compres'd in wrath the swelling wine-press groan'd,
> It bled, and pour'd the gushing purple round.[17]

The passage was to be pressed to similar service by Julia Ward Howe, author of the great Civil War anthem, "The Battle Hymn of the Republic," some four score and nine years later, because the United States was unwilling to listen to Wheatley's, and its own, reflections on the deadly fruits of gross tyranny.

Seven of the new poems were philosophic ones, in which Wheatley expressed most movingly her sense of the limitations she labored under and in which she found the richest material metaphors for her racial egalitarianism. Some of these references are fairly casual, as when she slips into "On Recollection" lines about how fearful memory is to "the race/who scorn her warnings and despise her grace." "On Imagination" is one of Wheatley's most potently personal poems. It tells how poetic "fancy" breaks frozen "iron bands," allowing waters to "murmur o'er the sands." The images thus tied to her creativity are bright and refreshing, but it is fancy alone that gives her such freedom. The poem closes bleakly with Wheatley announcing the frosty victory of her New England home:

> *Winter* austere forbids me to aspire,
> And northern tempests damp the rising fire;
> They chill the tides of *Fancy's* flowing sea,
> Cease then, my song, cease the unequal lay.[18]

The rare rough rhythm of the last line and the way "flowing sea" freezes into the doubly hissing "cease" point to the double sense of the closing words: the lay or song unequal to her dreams within the very unequal lay of her social position.

In her hymns to morning and evening and in her thoughts on Providence, Wheatley developed her richest natural corollaries to her racial argument. She put it most simply in these short paired hymns. The first praises Aurora for bringing the light and its attendant beauties, but the sun, "the illustrious king of day," also wilts with his heat. The second remarks on the even brighter colors of sunset, and then the coming of dusk, so that all should be

> Fill'd with the praise of him who gives the light,
> And draws the sable curtains of the night.[19]

These poems argue gracefully that good adheres neither to light nor dark, to the white nor the sable, but to their wholesome interplay. This basic idea Wheatley expanded in her most sophisticated poem, "Thoughts on the Works of Providence." Wheatley took her sun image and tied it to the need for balance in human and spiritual life, emphasizing the mutuality of warmth and shade, day and night, strength and gentleness, black and white. It is a poem "to praise the monarch of the earth and skies," the sun and the Son. It contains many of her most moving images, such as the sun slumbering at sunset in the ocean's arms or God revealed in the Newtonian universe's "vast machine." The "God who whirls surrounding spheres" establishes the sun as a "peerless monarch," but a limited one:

> That *Wisdom*, which attends *Jehovah's* ways,
> Shines most conspicuous in the solar rays:
> Without them, destitute of heat and light,
> This world would be the reign of endless night:
> In their excess how would our race complain
> Abhorring life! how hate its length'ned chain!

The ideal here is Newtonian balance, specifically tied to enough but not too much sun. But the poem has emphasized that the sun is the source of power, a monarch, so that the imagery of the last two lines is also political and, most strongly, racial. In "length'ned chain" Wheatley found the perfect metaphor for her condition: well treated certainly, even loved and admired, but bound and, because of that, on the verge of abhorring life.

There follows Wheatley's closest paraphrase-commentary on Alexander Pope, in which God fends off threatening Chaos, not by creating Newton, but by Himself, saying, "Let there be light." This is joined to a praise of Night, now pictured as a time of freedom, where Fancy reigns in dreams "on pleasure now, and now on vengeance bent." In this passage, where Wheatley evoked the subconscious, pleasure and vengeance are joined as the objects of darkest dreams, ones that she saw as linked to the restoration of waking balance, reason, and "improv'd" functioning. God's mercy both allows and restrains the dreamed expression of black anger:

> When want and woes might be our righteous lot,
> Our God forgetting, by our God forgot!

After this, Wheatley's most tautly aphoristic line, the poet concludes with a dialogue between Reason and Love, in which the two embrace, but not before they affirm the supremacy of Love, which "every creature's wants supplies" to "nourish all" equally.[20]

Some of the new poems accompanied Phillis when she, together with the Wheatleys' son, sailed for London in the late spring of 1773. The journey was ostensibly made to restore Wheatley's health, but it was also intended to promote her book. Her sponsors saw that she met prominent people who would create interest in the writings of this unusual poet. On Wheatley's departure, Susanna sent out press copy, illustrated with poems, to both British and American publications. Archibald Bell did the same in London and posted in his shop window the letter of authenticity that Boston's leaders had signed.

Wheatley also may have carried to London her only known portrait, which became the frontispiece for her book, an engraving of the painting that Susanna Wheatley commissioned of her much-loved slave, probably done by another talented slave, Scipio Moorhead. Owned by the Reverend John Moorhead, who had baptized Phillis, Scipio was trained in art by Mrs. Moorhead, a friend of Susanna and herself a painter. Scipio Moorhead's portrait of Phillis Wheatley was carefully constructed to underline the antislavery message of the book. It presented an attractive young black woman, simply but fashionably dressed, seated at a table with book, ink stand, and paper. With quill pen in hand and a finger gently indenting her cheek, the poet looks into the distance at her thoughts. The image underlined slaves' human potential: sensitive, cultivated, thoughtful, and literary.

Susanna saw to it that the most prominent American in London, Benjamin Franklin, paid Phillis a visit, and the Lord Mayor received her, presenting her with a copy of *Paradise Lost*, while Granville Sharp and John Thornton, early British antislavery advocates, introduced her to London society. Phillis would have visited the Countess of Huntingdon in Wales, had an audience with George III, and watched her book through the press had not Susanna's worsening health called her back to Boston. Upon her return, Wheatley was manumitted. She later gave conflicting stories about why and when. In one letter Phillis said she was freed at Susanna's dying request, and in another, at the urging of British friends. No public announcement was made, and the timing suggests antislavery strategy. Freedom was bestowed just after publication so the poems could be presented honestly as the work of a slave.

A large shipment of copies of her book, from which she was to derive the profit, followed Wheatley to Boston. Phillis urged friends and ministerial supporters to help sell the volumes; her letters to them show a nice integration of religious piety and economic acumen. Somewhat later, reviews arrived from London, where the book was noticed widely and favorably in leading literary journals. These must have been happy months for Wheatley, despite the shadow of Susanna's long illness and death in the early spring of 1774. Captain John Paul Jones wrote a poem to "the Celebrated Phillis the African Favorite" of the muses. Phillis conducted a poetic flirtation with a lieutenant in the British navy, who urged the world to

> Behold with reverence, and with joy adore,
> The lovely daughter of the Afric shore.

Such praise, along with a picture of Africa as Eden, triggered Wheatley's only light-hearted poem in response. She mildly laughed at the officer's comparison of her to Milton and Newton, but was pleased to toy with the idea of Africa as Eden:

> Charm'd with thy painting, how my bosom burns!
> And pleasing Gambia on my soul returns.

She also returned praise for praise, calling her admirer "the muse's darling, and the prince of song."[21]

The sense of increased independence is also clear in letters Wheatley wrote at this time. One was a reply to a letter of Samson Occom, a minister and Mohegan Indian who preceded Phillis as a protégé of the Wheatleys and the Countess of Huntingdon. Occom had traveled in England in 1766 under the countess's auspices, and collected £11,000 for Indian missionary work. Missionary Eleazar Wheelock by this time had wearied of the hard work of converting Indians and was determined to devote the money Occom gathered to setting up a school for whites, Dartmouth College. The whites so trained, Wheelock pretended, would then convert Indians. Wheelock worked tirelessly to discredit or drive Occom into the wilderness. Only the support of the Wheatleys and of John Thornton offered Occom some protection and help.

Occom, with good reason somewhat embittered toward white ministers, wrote Phillis Wheatley a letter attacking men of faith who talked of freedom in Christ, but showed no concern about human slavery. Wheatley responded in a vein of subtle sophistication that put the message of her poetry in clear-cut prose. She thought "highly reasonable what you offer in Vindication" of blacks' "natural Rights" and the "glorious dispensation of civil and religious Liberty, which are so inseparably united." Israel detested Egyptian slavery, she concluded,

> for in every human Breast, God has implanted a Principle, which we call Love of Freedom; it is impatient of Oppression, and pants for Deliverance; and by the Leave of our Modern Egyptians I will assert, that the same Principle lives in us. God grant Deliverance in his own way and Time, and get him honor upon all those whose Avarice impels them to countenance and help forward the Calamities of their Fellow Creatures. This I desire not for their Hurt, but to convince them of the strange Absurdity of their Conduct whose Words and Actions are so diametrically opposite. How well the Cry for Liberty, and the reverse Disposition for the Exercise of oppressive Power over others agree—I humbly think it does not require the Penetration of a Philosopher to determine.[22]

In contrast to Occom's accusatory anger, Wheatley's discussion of slavery here as always was cool and said little more than what most Americans could accept. She simply stuck almost every Christian's and patriot's favorite clichés to the one institution to which they were disinclined to apply their sacred and self-evident truths. Wheatley was the first literary African American to apply the tactics of Ralph Ellison's wise old black in his novel, *The Invisible Man* (1947). Wheatley steadily worked to "overcome 'em with the yeses" by tying the injustices that American whites meted out to blacks to "principles they themselves had dreamed out of the chaos and darkness of the feudal past, and which they had violated and compromised to the point of absurdity even in their own corrupt minds."[23]

A second letter of 1774 revealed Wheatley's strong-minded sense of who she was. When Samson Occum and Samuel Hopkins suggested that Wheatley should perhaps become a missionary to Africa, she gave firm but polite excuses. When kindly and bluff John Thornton suggested she consider marrying some black missionary going off to Christianize Africa, she gently but devastatingly demolished the idea. She began by mocking the notion that marriages were made for evangelical reasons: "I believe they are either of them good enough if not too good for me, or they would not be fit for Missionaries; but why do you, hon'd sir, wish those poor men so much trouble as to carry me on so long a voyage?" She continued by making clear the muddleheadedness of the whole colonization assumption that blacks belonged in Africa, by inverting the prejudices that partly fueled that "solution": "Upon my arrival, how like a Barbarian shou'd I look to the Natives; I can promise that my tongue shall be quiet for a strong reason indeed, being an utter stranger to the language of Anamaboe." Wheatley had no intention of being a cultural barbarian all over again. Wheatley knew who she was, a Christian and an American, and was not about to let others define her life by their ideas of what "Africans" should do. She wryly concluded with her final assertion of self-determination, "I am unacquainted with those Missionaries in Person."[24]

After 1774, accelerating resistance to the British turned Wheatley's pen back to politics in several poems in praise of American patriots, most notably George Washington. In 1775 she sent her poetic tribute to him, and he responded by inviting her to visit him. He probably appreciated her description of him as "first in peace and honors" and as "fam'd for thy valour, and for thy virtues more." And perhaps he did not consider Wheatley's usual insertion of phrases tying the slave's cause to the American, when she threatened anyone "who dares disgrace/ the land of freedom's heaven-defended race," or who too late repented of their "thirst of boundless power."[25] Washington treated "Miss Phillis" civilly, praised her poem, and probably sent it to the *Virginia Gazette*, which published it.

Of these poems the most significant was her elegy to General David Wooster. Wooster had been a correspondent of Wheatley's, and with his wife, Mary, one of the promoters of her book. Wheatley attested to Wooster's antislavery credentials by having him offer in his dying words his hope that Americans would always live "virtuous, brave and free." Yet how could Americans presume God's blessing

> While yet (O deed Ungenerous!) they disgrace
> And hold in bondage Afric's blameless race?
> Let Virtue reign—and Thou accord our prayers
> Be victory our's, and generous freedom theirs.[26]

The year 1778 was to prove a hard one for many Americans. For Phillis Wheatley these dislocations of war were complicated by a change in her personal situation. That year both John Wheatley and Mary Wheatley Lathrop died, and Phillis married a handsome and talented free black of many trades, John Peters. There is no evidence as to how Wheatley felt about her husband or the marriage that in six years produced three children, all of whom died in infancy. The evidence is clear only that these were Phillis's hardest years, a time of poverty, struggle, and illness. Peters had some education and had worked in Boston as a lawyer and shopkeeper. Some accounts mentioned his abilities; others judged him proud and irresponsible, qualities of blacks often joined in the era's white mind. All that is known is that he and Phillis became impoverished and stayed that way until her death. At times Phillis lived apart from him, dependent again on the charity of Wheatley relatives. After Phillis died, Peters left Boston with her literary remains, some of which fell into the hands of Julia Rush, another member of Susanna's evangelical circle.

Wheatley's poetry in these hard years provided little financial support. Twice Wheatley unsuccessfully solicited subscriptions for a publication: in October 1779, a year after her marriage and in the middle of the Revolutionary War, and in September 1784, a few months after the war's end and before her death. The timing could not have been worse: money was scarce, and the future uncertain. Also, the Wheatley deaths and the marriage to Peters probably frazzled the bonds with Wheatley's former circle of support. Peters seems to have shared none of Phillis's religious commitments, which may have made it more difficult for her to maintain her evangelical connections. Whatever Wheatley's tensions as a respected slave girl and then an admired free black woman in white society, her comfortable life there ill prepared her for the hard times that befell her as Mrs. Peters. There is a terrible bondage in poverty, frequent pregnancies, and ill health.

The five years after 1774 were productive ones for Wheatley; the 1779 proposals listed the titles of thirty-three new poems, only six of which are known to survive. Most of them were in the familiar Wheatley canon—elegies, occasional lines, poems in praise of patriots, or centered on classical or philosophic musings. Only two titles, "Ocean" and "Niagara," hint at some movement toward nature description and Romanticism. No Wheatley poems are extant from the years between 1779 and 1784. Perhaps they have been lost; perhaps the burdens of impoverishment and childbearing and child-burying clogged the poet's heart and pen. In 1784, however, Wheatley published two poems individually as small pamphlets. They are typical Wheatley works, one elegiac and one patriotic, that suggest no flagging of the poet's skill. There is a personal insert in her elegy to the Reverend Samuel Cooper:

> The hapless Muse, her loss in Cooper mourns,
> And as she sits, she writes, and weeps, by turns;[27]

The touching tone here and the picture given of the feeble black woman at the bedside of the dying "friend sincere" who had encouraged her poetry suggest Wheatley's broader losses during the war. In no other poem did Wheatley weep.

"Liberty and Peace" once again exulted in American victory and renewed peace with Britain and the world. The poem is about the coming of freedom "array'd with claims divine," and again her audience was not forced to notice its subtle ties to her race's freedom, though Wheatley's injunctions were clear enough:

> Perish that Thirst of boundless Power, that drew
> On *Albion's* Head the Curse to Tyrants due.
> But thou appeas'd submit to Heaven's decree,
> That bids a Realm of Freedom rival thee![28]

There is no better example than this of Wheatley's poetics of double meaning. The crime was "thirst for boundless power," and now England must accept divine judgment that the United States rival England as a nation free and equal, that also must now itself become truly a "Realm of Freedom."

Wheatley's final poem was an elegy to herself, probably written shortly before her death. "An Elegy on Leaving" describes a regretful move from a rural spot to a noisy city, but the natural Arcadia soon becomes the place where "first my bosom felt poetic flame." Now those times of joy and creativity are gone forever, but the last lines Wheatley wrote were not despairing:

> But come, sweet Hope, from thy divine retreat,
> Come to my breast, and chase my cares away,
> Bring calm Content to gild my gloomy seat,
> And cheer my bosom with her heav'nly ray.[29]

Wheatley's "On Leaving" offered her few religious assurances, but she had good reason to hope and to be content. She had written and lived with integrity in trying times and difficult circumstances. She had accomplished much: the first American black to publish a book; the first black American woman to gain some international reputation as a poet; the first black American woman to publish antislavery comment.

After Wheatley died, her political importance grew. British and American antislavery leaders used her poems as proof of black ability and, hence, the monstrosity of slavery. There was a sort of praise, too, even in the disparagement of people such as Thomas Jefferson who began to develop a scientific "racism" to excuse that slavery their principles decried and their comforts demanded. Jefferson wrote the year after Wheatley died, in the only book he published, *Notes on the State of Virginia*: "Religion indeed has produced a Phillis Whately [*sic*]; but it could not produce a poet. The compositions published under her name are below the dignity of criticism. The heroes of the Dunciad are to her, as Hercules to the author of that poem."[30] Jefferson here, with snide nastiness, tied Alexander Pope's physical handicaps to Wheatley's aesthetic deformity, in poems Jefferson implied she did not really write. The Virginian spelled her name wrong, showing his lack of familiarity with her work, but he knew whom he had to discredit if people were to accept his extended "suggestion" that blacks were an innately inferior species of being. Later eighteenth-century antiracists attacked Jefferson and praised Wheatley, perhaps faintly but pungently enough: there was no evidence of any Southern planter or, for that matter, any white American, capable of writing such good poetry.

Over the years, Wheatley's poetic testimony went marching on, mocked by racists, sometimes black as well as white, but offering an example, an inspiration, a hope to those disliking the color line as a divider of humans. Wheatley's poems have been published in at least twenty editions since 1773, with many of them reprinted several times. She has never been forgotten, and within the last twenty years there has been accelerating appreciation of her, not as a great poet but as a remarkably intelligent one, highly original in her poetic strategies to plead the cause of her faith, her nation, and her race.

Wheatley died in "sweet Hope" of the better world her poetry had promised to so many friends and acquaintances. She probably also hoped that freedom for her race was coming, although antislavery advances in the United States were to slow during her last years and then stop shortly after she died. She did her life's work well, a remarkable woman with some remarkable friends, about whom it could be said as Wheatley wrote of another:

> Still live thy merits, where thy name is known,
> As the sweet Rose, its blooming beauty gone,
> Retains its fragrance with a long perfume.[31]

Notes

1. "On Being Brought from Africa to America," *The Collected Works of Phillis Wheatley*, ed. John Shields (New York: Oxford University Press, 1988), 18.

2. "America" (1768), ibid., 134.

3. Margaretta Matilda Odell, "Memoir," in *Memoir and Poems of Phillis Wheatley, A Native African and a Slave* . . . (Boston: Isaac Knapp, 1838), 15–16.

4. "On the Death of Dr. Samuel Marshall" (1771), *Collected Works*, 87.

5. "To a Clergyman on the Death of His Lady," ibid., 55.

6. Eugene P. Chase, ed., *Our Revolutionary Forefathers: The Letters of François, Marquis de Barbé-Marbois . . . , 1779–85* (New York: Duffield, 1929), 85.

7. "Proposals" (1779), *Collected Works*, 192.

8. Susanna Wheatley, quoting a letter in which Captain Robert Calif quoted the countess, to Samson Occom, March 29, 1773, in *Historical Magazine* 2 (1858): 178–79.

9. "Foreword: In Her Own Write," *Collected Works*, vii–viii.

10. "To the Public" (1773), ibid., 7.

11. Thomas Jefferson, *Notes on the State of Virginia* (1785; reprint ed., New York: Harper Torchbooks, 1964), 135. Jefferson, in his only book, criticized slavery strongly, stressing its vicious influence on white character, but also suggested that it must continue unless an impossibly elaborate plan for the removal of all blacks freed were adopted. He also strongly "suggested" that blacks were a separate and inherently inferior species in a passage full of extreme racist stereotypes.

12. "Proposals for Printing by Subscription" (1772); John Wheatley Letter (1772); "To the Public" (1773), *Collected Works*, 188, 6, 7.

13. "To the King's Most Excellent Majesty" (1778), ibid., 17.

14. John Andrews to William Barrell, January 28, 1774, Andrews-Eliot Papers, Massachusetts Historical Society, Boston. Andrews's several letters about Wheatley, and other references in Boston correspondence, suggest her local fame at this time.

15. "To the Right Honorable William, Earl of Dartmouth, His Majesty's Principal Secretary of State for North America, etc.," *Collected Works*, 73–75.

16. "To Maecenas," ibid., 11.

17. "Isaiah lxiii, 1–8," ibid., 60–61.

18. "On Recollection" and "On Imagination," ibid., 63, 66–69.

19. "An Hymn to the Morning" and "An Hymn to the Evening," ibid., 56–59.

20. "Thoughts on the Works of Providence," ibid., 43–50.

21. John Paul Jones to Hector McNeill, no date; facsimile in Sidney Kaplan, *The Black Presence in the American Revolution* (Washington, DC: National Portrait Gallery, 1973), 161.

22. Phillis Wheatley to Samson Occom, February 11, 1774, *Collected Works*, 176–77.

23. Ralph Ellison, *Invisible Man* (New York: Random House, 1947), 13, 438.

24. Phillis Wheatley to John Thornton, October 30, 1774, *Collected Works*, 184.

25. "To His Excellency George Washington" (1775), ibid., 145–46.

26. "On the Death of General Wooster" (1778), ibid., 149–50.

27. "An Elegy Sacred to the Memory of That Great Divine, the Reverend and Learned Dr. Samuel Cooper" (1784), ibid., 153.

28. "Liberty and Peace" (1784), ibid., 155.

29. "An Elegy on Leaving—" (1784), ibid., 157.
30. Jefferson, *Notes on the State of Virginia*, 135.
31. "Elegy to Cooper," *Collected Works*, 153.

Suggested Readings

The best and most complete edition of Wheatley's writings is that recently edited by John Shields, *The Collected Works of Phillis Wheatley* (New York: Oxford University Press, 1988), which includes Shields's interpretive appreciation. In recent years, Mukhtar Ali Isani and Robert Nuncio have discovered "lost" poems of Wheatley (included in the Shields volume), giving hope that more writings may be found. William H. Robinson has done much to uncover new information about the poet's life, in *Phillis Wheatley and Her Writings* (New York: Garland, 1984), and has edited a good collection of opinion on Wheatley, ranging from eighteenth-century comments to recent scholarly articles, *Critical Essays on Phillis Wheatley* (Boston: G. K. Hall, 1982). There is no satisfactory biography; the fictional work, intended for young people, of Shirley Graham DuBois, *The Story of Phillis Wheatley* (New York: J. Messner, 1949), has long called attention to her life. There are much biographical data in Merle A. Richmond, *Bid the Vassal Soar: Interpretive Essays on the Life of Phillis Wheatley and George Moses Horton* (Washington, DC: Howard University Press, 1974); the book also offers an introduction to the negative criticism of Wheatley from a black perspective, on the grounds that her work is insufficiently racial. Russell J. Reising, *Loose Ends: Closure and Crisis in the American Social Text* (Durham, NC: Duke University Press, 1996), suggests the recent, more positive literary evaluation of Wheatley, treating her comfortably along with such figures as Emily Dickinson, Herman Melville, and Henry James. The fullest treatment of Wheatley's evangelical sisterhood of support and of her key role in early controversies over antislavery and racism is David Grimsted, "Anglo-American Racism and Phillis Wheatley's 'Sable Veil,' 'Lengthen'd Chain,' and 'Knitted Heart,' " in *Women in the Age of the American Revolution*, ed. Ronald Hoffman and Peter Albert (Charlottesville: University Press of Virginia, 1989), 338–444.

17

Benjamin Gilbert and Jacob Nagle

Soldiers of the American Revolution

John Shy

The Revolutionary War marked a coming of age for the new nation and for Benjamin Gilbert (1755–1828) of Massachusetts and Jacob Nagle (1762–1841) of Pennsylvania, who both served in the American military. For two ordinary men, Gilbert and Nagle left extraordinarily rich written accounts of their lives. Youths when the Revolution began, they both served in local regiments, and yet military service and travel broadened their worldview. While Gilbert provides an eyewitness account of camp life in the Continental Army, Nagle's adventures included captivity as a prisoner of war. How did Gilbert's perspective on the battle of Saratoga differ from Friederike von Riedesel's? As Judith Sargent Murray wondered, was military discipline inconsistent with American values of liberty? Given the experiences of Gilbert and Nagle, were Eliza Lucas Pinckney and Murray justified in worrying about soldiers' temptations to immorality?

Gilbert achieved officer rank and reenlisted, while Nagle became a patriot privateer and later a member of the Royal Navy. In calling Gilbert a success and Nagle a failure, what is being measured? What role did chance, or family connections, play in their contrasting fates? How did Nagle's seafaring experiences compare with those of Ashley Bowen? At war's end, Gilbert left the army, married, and became a farmer in western New York and later a New York legislator. As a professional sailor, Nagle traveled to more distant and exotic places, including Australia. Both Gilbert and Nagle died as Revolutionary War heroes, even though Nagle had served much longer in the Royal Navy than in the patriot cause. As John Shy concludes, each character represents a different type of American: Gilbert, the middle-class western farmer; and Nagle, the supreme individualist.

John Shy, an expert in the military history of the American Revolution, is the author of numerous books and articles, including *Toward Lexington: The Role of the British Army in the Coming of the American Revolution* (1965) and *A People Numerous and Armed: Reflections on the Military Struggle for American Independence* (1990). He has long taught at the University of Michigan.

Wars are fought by the very young. However and wherever wars start, invariably men—and now women—barely out of their childhood do the actual fighting and most of the dying. The War for American Independence, 1775–1783, was no exception. American political leaders, many in their forties, had mobilized opposition to British taxation and other measures that most Americans felt violated a long-standing limitation of the power of British government to rule the colonies. When this political opposition led to violence and then to open warfare in 1775, men of that same older generation, such as George Washington (age forty-three in 1775), became the generals and colonels commanding the rebel armies. Younger men, in their thirties or late twenties, were the captains who led companies of fifty or one hundred men into battle. But after the first few months of fighting around Boston, where men of every age turned out to serve briefly, the hard, dirty work of fighting for independence fell mostly on thousands of mere boys.

Eight years later, when American independence was finally won, those boys were men, hardened and changed by their experience of war. When we think of the impact of the American Revolutionary War, we usually recall the stirring words of the 1776 Declaration of Independence—"all men are created equal"—with its definition of the American cause as "life, liberty, and the pursuit of happiness." But for thousands of very young men, and a few women who disguised themselves as men, the true impact of the Revolution was in the specific way it sent their lives spinning quickly into a new orbit, with the final destination out of their control.

The experiences of two ordinary young men, Benjamin Gilbert and Jacob Nagle, both still in their teens when war erupted in 1775, allow us to see in detail how the American Revolution changed, profoundly but very differently, two lives. Both men survived the war, dying in their seventies to public praise as heroes of the American Revolution. Each, for his own personal reasons, created a careful written record of his life, accounts that have survived down to our own time and given us a rare chance to trace and assess the impact of the Revolutionary War on two ordinary yet very different lives.

Benjamin Gilbert, still in his teens, went to war the day it began in April 1775. When early on a spring morning British regular soldiers and Massachusetts militiamen opened fire on one another at Lexington, not far from Boston, Benjamin was living in the town of Brookfield, about fifty miles west of the action. But Benjamin was already a soldier in Brookfield's "minute" company—a militia unit of about fifty local men who had been training for just such an emergency and were ready to march when the news came that fighting had broken out. Within a few hours after the first reports of Lexington reached towns like Brookfield, minute companies like Gilbert's from all over Massachusetts were on the road to Boston. Brookfield's company was too far away (a good two-day march) to see any action in this first battle of what would be known as the War of American Independence, but Gilbert and his comrades joined thousands of others who surrounded the port town of Boston, where British troops had retreated after two days of bloody fighting along the road to Lexington and the nearby town of Concord, which had been their original objective.

From these first days of the war, Benjamin Gilbert *may* have kept a written record of his military experience. We say "*may*," because personal records for this early period of his military service have never been found. But we do have his diary, beginning New Year's Day 1778, that continues into the postwar years, as well as letters written by Gilbert that he copied either on blank pages in the diary or into a separate notebook. Diary-keeping as a way of tracking one's moral behavior and religious condition was an old New England custom. Many diaries kept by New England common soldiers in the colonial and Revolutionary wars have come down to us, and obviously young Benjamin Gilbert was a diary-keeping Yankee. So it seems reasonable to think that he kept a record from the very beginning, a record that has been lost. But we can roughly reconstruct what happened to him in the early years of the war from army records, and also from his own pension application, submitted to the federal government long after the war. Only in 1778, his third year at war, can we begin to learn about his life in rich detail.

Jacob Nagle, Gilbert's even younger counterpart from Pennsylvania, probably kept no such day-to-day records, although we cannot be sure. What Nagle left us was a very detailed memoir of his life, written when he was an old man. Memories often become blurry and distorted as the years pass, and so there is good reason to ask why we should trust the memory of old Jacob Nagle on events of his teens and twenties. The answer is in the details he recorded of his service in the American army, and later as a prisoner of war and at sea. These details can be checked against official records, and in virtually every case they match exactly. There is no way Nagle could have invented the stories in his memoir, because the details were buried in records that were not available to him at the time. Either he had a wonderfully clear memory, or his final, handwritten memoir (which was found among his possessions after his death) was based on other personal records, perhaps diaries like those kept by Gilbert or letters that have not survived. All we have from Jacob Nagle is the memoir, but it is at least as rich in personal insight as the diaries and letters of Benjamin Gilbert.

Gilbert, at age nineteen, was in the war first. Why? What motivated him? His deeper motives remain a mystery, but we can feel certain that his family and community figured significantly in sending him off to war. Brookfield, Massachusetts, was a fairly typical New England country town, first settled a century before the American Revolution on land cleared by previous Indian settlers. In 1675, Indians returned to Brookfield and waged one of the bloodiest wars in all American history, "King Philip's War." Brookfield, out on the frontier of English settlement, was destroyed and its site abandoned for a decade.

When Brookfield began to be resettled in the 1680s, many of the new settlers came from the older coastal town of Ipswich, and the English family name of Gilbert was prominent among them. Brookfield was not a prosperous town; most of the houses, even after the Revolution, were poorly built and unpainted. But like other towns, Brookfield taxed itself to build a meetinghouse and hire a Congregational minister, and by 1750 even to pay a "School Dame" to teach its children. Young Benjamin Gilbert attended the town school while his father and grandfather were serving in the colonial wars against the French that ended with a complete British victory in 1763. The inhabitants of Brookfield were proud to be British, but they were even more devoted to the British traditions of liberty and self-government. New British policies toward the American colonies after 1763 seemed to threaten those traditions, and though the center of agitation, protest, and resistance was Boston, Brookfield solidly supported Boston in the political battle that turned into war by 1775. Surely young Benjamin Gilbert felt the influences of his own town.

Daniel Gilbert, Benjamin's father, a veteran of the failed military campaign of 1757 to save Fort William Henry, familiar to those who have read the book or seen the film *The Last of the Mohicans*, was an officer in the Worcester County militia and also a "selectman," one of the town's elected board of managers. Despite these military and political offices, Daniel was no more than a well-off farmer, because most of the Gilbert family wealth had been inherited by Daniel's older brother Joseph. Benjamin's uncle was listed in town records as a merchant, whose sons—Benjamin's cousins—attended Yale and Dartmouth while Benjamin would make his way through life on what he had learned from the "School Dame." The family's military tradition may have been a reason for his joining Brookfield's "minute company" when it was formed in 1774 and marching to war in 1775. Desire for adventure is also normal in a young man, and maybe the New England army swarming around

Boston looked to an ambitious boy like both Adventure and Opportunity.

Within days at Boston, Benjamin had enlisted in the company commanded by a Brookfield neighbor, Captain Peter Harwood, part of the regiment commanded by Colonel Ebenezer Learned. Learned's regiment was stationed at Roxbury on the far right of the American line ringing the British garrison of Boston, so when the British attacked in June at the left end of the American line at Bunker Hill, Learned's men came under fire but were not in the American line of battle, which the British finally overran after suffering enormous casualties. Although Benjamin could not possibly have reached Lexington in time for the April battle, and almost surely was not in the heavy fighting at Bunker Hill in June, his son would engrave on his father's tombstone "Lexington" and "Bunker Hill." Benjamin Gilbert would not be the first, or the last, veteran to claim to have taken part in a battle he just missed, but the third battle name on the tombstone—"Saratoga"—would be fully earned.

In March 1776 the British navy evacuated the Boston garrison, which had failed to break the American siege. Learned's Massachusetts regiment, now renamed the Third Continental, under the general command of George Washington, who had been chosen by the Congress in Philadelphia to lead the American military effort, moved with the main army to New York, the likeliest point for the next British attack. Against superior British seapower, the port of New York was essentially indefensible, but Congress and Washington, faced with a shaky American union that was still struggling to declare independence from British rule, felt compelled to make their best effort. Gilbert and the Third Continentals escaped being caught in one of the worst defeats in American military history, at Brooklyn Heights on Long Island in August, but they saw plenty of combat. In July, British warships had sailed up the Hudson, past Manhattan Island, firing at the American artillery guarding the bank. Several British shots hit the camp of Gilbert's regiment, one flying between the legs of two of his comrades, but no one was hurt.

Far more serious was Benjamin's first real battle in October, when the Third, as part of a Massachusetts brigade of about eight hundred men commanded by John Glover of Marblehead, at Pelham Bay in the Bronx, stopped a much larger British landing force trying to cut off the retreating American army. Mission accomplished, Glover's exhausted brigade marched northwest to safety and rest, leaving six dead comrades; Gilbert's new regimental commander, William Shepard, was hit in the throat by a British bullet but survived.

The little battle of Pelham Bay, one of few successful American actions in the 1776 New York campaign, was unlike anything Gilbert had experienced before. Armed with not very accurate smooth-bore, single-shot muskets that required almost a minute to reload, Gilbert and his few hundred inexperienced comrades had faced at close quarters in an open field thousands of well-trained British infantry, bayonets fixed, moving in to kill them. Little imagination is needed to realize how he must have felt. As Washington's defeated and disintegrating army straggled across New Jersey to reach the Delaware River, Gilbert stayed with Glover's brigade east of the Hudson River, part of a larger force left by Washington to guard against any British move northward, toward New England. In late November, hard-pressed and desperate for reinforcements, Washington ordered these eastern troops to join him as quickly as possible on the west bank of the Delaware.

At about the time of the traditional New England Thanksgiving in 1776, Benjamin Gilbert and his comrades were loading into boats at Peekskill, New York, and crossing the mighty Hudson River. Winter was coming, and British officers noted that the Americans they had killed or captured wore only light clothing and sometimes lacked even shoes, stockings, and blankets. As Gilbert clambered out of the boat and onto the Jersey shore, hoisting his pack and musket for the long, hilly trek to the Delaware, he was in a foreign country. Brookfield and Boston were home, but this—New York and New Jersey—was a strange land. He could not have guessed that for much of the next seven years this foreign country, the lower Hudson Valley, would become his backyard, and he would come to know it very well—a new "home."

In his application for a federal pension, submitted when he was sixty-two, Benjamin Gilbert mentioned no battles, but said that he had served the "whole" campaign of 1776, so we may assume that he was a member of Glover's brigade on Christmas night when it crossed the ice-strewn Delaware, marched nine miles down the river road in a snowstorm to Trenton, where it surprised and killed or captured almost a thousand German regulars, hired by Britain to reinforce its army in America. This small but spectacular American victory was won at just the moment when many observers thought the American rebellion had collapsed. But we cannot assume that Gilbert was present a week later, in early January 1777, when Washington won another small but politically crucial victory at Princeton, just ten miles away, because no surviving record for the regiment tells us who stayed and who left when their enlistments expired. Gilbert, like his comrades in Boston, had enlisted the previous January for exactly one year, and that year was up December 31, 1776. All the New Englanders, beaten, tired, and ill prepared for winter, wanted to go home, and many did so. Some had left before the victory at Trenton, convinced that travel time should be part of their enlisted service. Washington had begged them to stay and to reenlist for a longer term. Some stayed but very few reenlisted in Washington's army. Even John Glover, a gallant brigade commander, went home after Trenton, and his own regiment—the Fourteenth Continentals—went with him. Benjamin Gilbert may have done the same, as was his undoubted right.

Once back home, he did not pick up the plow and resume the life of a Yankee farmboy, secure in the belief that he had done his share of fighting and suffering and that some other sturdy American lad would take his place. Instead, in January 1777 he rejoined the army, this time enlisting for three years, under two family friends—Captain Daniel Shays and Colonel Rufus Putnam. Happy to recruit a seasoned combat veteran of twenty-two, they made him a sergeant in the Fifth Massachusetts Regiment, in which he would serve until the end of the war. By late spring, Putnam's men were marching, not southward to join Washington, but westward to stop a British invasion from Canada. The plan for 1777, adopted in London, to crush the American rebellion, called for the British army in New York to engage Washington in decisive battle, while another army, moving directly south from Montreal, drove a stake into the heart of the American cause. It was this army from Canada that Gilbert would face.

Fort Ticonderoga had fallen to the British advance before Gilbert and the Fifth Massachusetts Regiment joined the retreating American army in July. He was just one of thousands of soldiers coming from New England to reinforce the failing effort to stop the Canadian invasion. At the final major battle fought near Saratoga, on October 7, Colonel Putnam's regiment helped stop the British attack and then captured a supporting redoubt manned by German regulars. Several days later men from the Fifth Massachusetts were part of the force that cut off the last line of British retreat. British surrender at Saratoga brought France openly into the war as an American ally, ensuring that Britain would never be able to defeat the colonial rebels.

Benjamin Gilbert must have done well at Saratoga because he was promoted soon after to sergeant major, or top sergeant in Shays's company. Very likely he had been one of forty volunteers at Saratoga under Captain Nathan Goodale, who had captured the boats in which the British had hoped to get away, because later Gilbert was transferred to Goodale's company. From the end of 1777, we have the full, personal record of Gilbert's service to the end of the war, and of his life afterward.

While Benjamin Gilbert was helping to win the battle of Saratoga, Jacob Nagle was getting a taste of war in his home state of Pennsylvania. Like Benjamin Gilbert, Jacob lived in a small town, Reading, about fifty miles inland from a major seaport, in his case, Philadelphia. His father was a militia officer, a veteran of the last colonial war, and a local political officeholder; and like Benjamin Gilbert, Jacob had younger sisters but no brothers. Jacob's father, George, recruited a company of riflemen when the news of Lexington arrived in Reading, Pennsylvania, and he led them to Boston in 1775. The town of Reading, settled heavily by German immigrants like the Nagles in the decades before 1775, was not so outspoken in its opposition to British policies as Brookfield, Massachusetts, but, with the outbreak of war, there seemed little question as to which side the town would support. George Nagle was a blacksmith, and also the sheriff of Berks County, but in January 1776 he was appointed major of the Fifth Pennsylvania Regiment. Major Nagle took his fourteen-year-old son Jacob with him to Philadelphia, where the boy saw life in the barracks. Though sixteen was usually the minimum age for military service, some big boys lied about their age, and some officers, like Major Nagle, enlisted underage sons to serve as personal orderlies or "waiters." Enrolled as a soldier in Captain Gibbs Jones's company of Colonel Thomas Proctor's artillery regiment, Jacob became part of Washington's army in 1777, facing the invasion of his homeland by a British army that had landed in Maryland at the head of Chesapeake Bay.

Benjamin Gilbert was marching to Saratoga when young Jacob Nagle experienced defeat at Brandywine Creek, where Delaware abuts Pennsylvania. It was along the Brandywine that Washington planned to stop the British advance on the American capital at Philadelphia. The battle of the Brandywine is not one of the glorious moments in American military history. As had happened a year earlier on Long Island, Washington was badly out-generaled. But as Jacob later wrote, he could "not pretend to give a discription of the action, only where I was myself."[1] Most of the British army moved well out of sight up the Brandywine Valley to outflank the American line, but young Nagle and his comrades thought that they and their cannons were facing the main enemy attack. Jacob had eaten almost nothing for three days, and the battle opened for him when a British cannonball shot away the kettle cooking what he expected to be a "glorious" breakfast. Infantry moved back and forth across the meadowland in front of his position, and when he rested from the day's heat in the shade of a wagon, another British shot knocked off a wagon wheel. British infantry charged the position held by his father's regiment, to his right, and he saw a red-coated British officer leading the charge simply disappear in a blast from one of Captain Jones's brass cannons. He never forgot his horror when he saw soldiers hastily burying an American officer whom, for a few moments in the confusion of battle, Nagle mistook for his own father.

Soon they heard that British troops were coming down the roads behind them, and the order came to withdraw. His company abandoned their cannon when, with all the horses dead, they could not be pulled across the swampy ground. As the retreat became a rout, Jacob remembered seeing a beautiful white horse, handsomely appointed and running free, but he was too frightened by enemy fire to try to catch it. Faint from thirst, he was saved by an older comrade who pushed through fugitives crowded around a well to bring Jacob a canteen of water. A steady cold rain during the next days made the long retreat of the beaten army miserable, but Colonel Proctor gave Jacob a spare horse to ride until, "driping wet and shivering with cold," he was invited into an ammunition wagon to get warm and dry.[2] At Yellow Springs, about twenty-five miles from Philadelphia, the army encamped, and Jacob was given a "furlow" to go home to Reading. There he learned that his mother had been caring for a wounded American soldier, about his own age, who had finally died of three bullet wounds. Although he returned to army duty for a few weeks in 1777, seeing the encampment at Valley Forge, and for a few more weeks in spring 1778, Jacob Nagle had had enough of the army. Underage and the only son of a senior officer, he easily got his discharge.

In 1778, at the midpoint of the War for American Independence, the lives of our two young Americans sharply diverged. Benjamin Gilbert, a seasoned combat veteran of twenty-three, committed himself to army life. Jacob Nagle, barely sixteen, went home and stayed there for a few years. Gilbert would serve in the army to the very end of the war, in late 1783, and then build a new life, fairly prosperous and eminently respectable, far from his Brookfield home, out on the New York frontier. Jacob Nagle chose very differently. As he reached manhood, he too left home, making another contribution to the American cause, but then drifted through the turmoil of war into a long career of incredible adventure, never finding stability or security, never seeking respectability, and never avoiding trouble. It is tempting to say that Jacob Nagle, unlike Benjamin Gilbert, was a failure, ruined by the fortunes of war. But perhaps it is wiser to tell their stories, and let the reader judge.

After Saratoga, Gilbert's regiment moved down the Hudson Valley to West Point, where a massive rocky outcropping forces the river to make a sharp bend, thereby providing a natural defensive position for the American army about fifty miles north of Manhattan Island, the British headquarters. For almost six years, West Point and vicinity would be Gilbert's home base. Later travelers admired the great natural beauty of the spot, where wooded mountains plunge sharply into the river, and a plateau stretching to the point of land offers a breathtaking view up the valley. But all the beauty was lost on Gilbert. Seeing it for the first time with the eyes of a farmer, he wrote in his diary that it was "a Rough Desolate place."[3] Much later, in 1782, striving to put his impressions into elaborate language that he had picked up from reading popular eighteenth-century literature, he described West Point to his younger stepbrother back in Brookfield:

> Stationed in a concavity between two Stupendious Spercial Hills where Nature has excluded it from her most beautiful part. No Magnificent landscapes to feast my eyes nor Verdant groves to ravish my sences, or purling streams, nor mumering rivelets to cool or refresh me. . . . If I indulge my eyes to wander abroad with hopes of beholding some beautifull objects I at once perceive my hopes Blasted. Instead of beholding spacious planes, Vegetable Fields, or beautified parks, I observe one continued series of convexative Rock and prominent Clifts.[4]

Even allowing for shaky spelling and dubious word choice, we may guess that Gilbert wrote this letter when he was drunk. Elated by a recent promotion to lieutenant and participation the previous fall in the decisive Yorktown campaign that had virtually ended all British hope for victory over the rebellious Americans, Gilbert had just returned from a furlough spent at home in Brookfield. His diary records a round of visits, parties, and more than a little drinking. Other evidence strongly indicates that, during his furlough, he had also made a sexual conquest of Patience, the daughter of Colonel James Converse, one of the most prominent men in Worcester County and commander of the county militia regiment. So the letter to his stepbrother was written after enjoying a hero's welcome back home, and a few days after his depressing return to the grimy reality of military routine. No longer the boy who had gone to war as a fifer with the Brookfield minutemen in 1775, he was a fully formed man, nearing his twenty-seventh birthday, when he wrote this pompous, silly, and probably drunken description of where he had spent most of the past four years.

Skipping ahead four years, from 1778 to 1782, may seem unfair to the story, but Benjamin Gilbert's life at war after 1777 was not—with a few exceptions—very exciting or as dangerous as it had been in 1776 and 1777. With the British army fortified on and around Manhattan, Washington deployed most of his army at least a long day's march northward, in the hills of New Jersey and near the Hudson highlands, with West Point as the central point. Here Sergeant, later Lieutenant, Gilbert did his duty and made his own life as pleasant as possible. The two armies warily watched one another, patrolling, raiding, and skirmishing across the no-man's land that separated them, making plans that usually fell through, and waiting for a chance to end the war in one decisive blow. Gilbert served in some of the American detachments that roamed down into Westchester County, hoping to ambush the enemy and trying to avoid being ambushed. He was never wounded or captured on these expeditions, although once he almost broke a leg returning to camp drunk at night, after visiting a nearby farmhouse. The rest of his time he spent training new recruits, doing army paperwork, repairing and cleaning his clothing, attending to his own bodily needs—including an occasional bath—and otherwise finding ways to pass the time. Reading, picking berries in season, playing cards and ball games, talking, and writing letters were among the ways he recorded in his diary—itself a way to fight the boredom of army life. But his most frequently noted pastimes were hunting women and drinking.

Jacob Nagle's father, colonel of the Tenth Pennsylvania Regiment in 1777, left the army in an obscure scandal and then moved his family to Philadelphia after the British gave up the city in 1778. There he later opened a waterfront tavern catering to sailors, and Jacob decided to go to sea. He offers no explanation in his memoir, but a reasonable guess is that, by then eighteen and with his memory of what happened on the Brandywine still fresh, he was strongly disinclined to be dragged back into the army. Perhaps the remembered unpleasantness of military service on land repelled him as much as the risk of being killed. Listening to the sailors' salty talk at his father's tavern also may have been a factor. It is clear from the record that he was physically strong and did not lack courage, but the sea must have looked, as it has for many other young men, the more attractive wartime alternative. And so, early in 1780 (when Benjamin Gilbert was home on leave, being promoted to officer rank, and signing up for another three years in the army), Jacob Nagle joined the tiny American navy by signing on the USS *Saratoga*, then being built in Philadelphia. When launching of the *Saratoga* was delayed, young Nagle impatiently turned to another line of sea service—privateering.

Privateers were privately owned and managed warships that contributed to the war effort by attacking British supply and merchant ships, with their crews paid in shares of whatever they captured. Many observers considered privateering as little more than legalized piracy as well as a drain on the youthful pool of manpower badly needed by the army. Nevertheless, the appeal of privateering to young men hoping to improve themselves even while fighting for American independence was irresistible, and it proved very popular as the war dragged on. For Nagle, it was the most important decision of his life.

His first ship, the sixteen-gun brig *Fair American*, sailed down Delaware Bay in May 1780, and Nagle quickly learned that the lower bay was swarming with armed enemies—not British warships, but American loyalist privateers, Tory bandits preying on every ship slower and weaker than their own. Nagle confronted suddenly what Gilbert had learned more gradually while roaming the dangerous roads of Westchester County, New York: about one American in five was bitterly opposed to the Revolution, and many of them were ready to take up arms to resist it. Nagle's ship survived the perils of Tory predators, and, out in the Atlantic, soon took numerous prizes: British merchant ships, laden with wine, dry goods, and crockery, to be sent back up the dangerous bay to Philadelphia for condemnation and sale. For sailors like Nagle, it was far more profitable than service in the army, as well as far more exciting and dangerous. Brutal and dishonest ships' officers, quite unlike the paternalistic Colonel Proctor and Captain Jones whom Nagle had known as a young artillery soldier, were frequently encountered, as were thuggish shipmates. But Nagle, almost fully grown though not a big man, was athletic, unafraid to fight when necessary, and able to take care of himself. After a few voyages he was an experienced sailor.

He could not, however, control the fortunes of war. On a voyage in late 1781 to the West Indies, his ship was captured by a British warship, and Nagle was imprisoned on the island of St. Christopher. The battle of Yorktown, just weeks earlier, had virtually decided the outcome of the American war on the mainland, but the British and French navies were still waging an all-out struggle for defense of their extremely valuable West Indian islands. A French attack on St. Christopher "liberated" Nagle, but confusion over his true identity led to his re-imprisonment. When the French and British agreed to an exchange of prisoners, Nagle was included as a "British" sailor. At the end of the war in 1783, while Gilbert was agonizing at West Point over what to do with himself when peace broke out, Jacob Nagle found himself serving on a British man-of-war, sailing "home" to Britain.

We left Lieutenant Benjamin Gilbert near the end of the war, still in the army, drinking too much, and chasing women. However we may judge what had become a distinct pattern of behavior, we can see, nevertheless, how extended service in the Revolutionary War had affected his life. Soldiers with little to keep them occupied are likely to find their own ways of releasing energy and relieving boredom. The war in Gilbert's sector during the years after Saratoga was not especially active, yet Washington did not dare move or reduce his force up the Hudson. Gilbert was part of that essential force, keeping the British garrison in New York more or less pinned down, but he was also a normal young man. Months of inactivity, broken only by occasional alarms (usually false) and one brief but dramatic journey (to Virginia and the entrapment of a British army at Yorktown in the fall of 1781), could not be a healthy situation for any young man. In the diary and letters there is more than a hint that he had adjusted well to military life, perhaps even grown attached to it, enjoying the comradeship of his fellow sergeants and officers, and in the process had become a fairly good soldier. On the other hand, he had known little except the army during his few years as an adult. And as chances offered, he fell into the behavior so typical of soldiers through the ages, drinking too much, too often, and literally grabbing any available woman. The details are clear enough in the diary; the wonder is that no one later destroyed the evidence and that it has come down to us with only a few places showing where someone had tried to erase a name or initials.

At Yorktown, where Washington swiftly brought his troops from New York with a French force marching from its base in Rhode Island, while a French fleet drove the British navy out of Chesapeake Bay, the British had lost the war, surrendering a field army just as they had four years earlier at Saratoga. Lieutenant Benjamin Gilbert, according to his 1828 obituary, had "commanded a platoon in the detachment led by the late Gen[eral Alexander] Hamilton at the storming of the redoubt at Yorktown."[5] Gilbert failed to mention this heroic act in his letters or diary, so perhaps it seemed more important to him that "the Ladies [of Virginia] are exceeding Amouris . . . and amongst the Vulgar any man that is given to concupcience [that is, lust] may have his fill. The Ladies are Exceeding fond of the Northern Gentlemen, Especially those of the Army."[6] Though he may have been simply teasing an absent friend and fellow officer in a letter, the comment also suggests his state of mind in the seventh year of his military service.

Standard histories of the Revolution stress the physical hardships of the Continental Army, unpaid, badly clothed and housed, ill-fed, neglected both by Congress and the states, which were supposed to look after their own regiments. Gilbert's diary and letters record the ups and downs of life in the Continental Army. Almost never in Gilbert's record was there a question of freezing, starving, or sheer survival. Instead, extreme discomfort and neglect led to low morale, desertion, and even mutiny. A breakdown of discipline was the greatest threat to the army, but the great danger to the individual, greater even than enemy fire, was illness. Wet, cold, tired, unclean, sleeping badly, and malnourished, soldiers were prey to colds and a host of more serious ailments. Medical science was rudimentary and often worse than no treatment at all; in any case, the medical service of the Continental Army was grossly inadequate.

Benjamin Gilbert, a strong, healthy young man, suffered several bouts of debilitating illness during the war. The worst one occurred in winter 1778–79, when he had been disabled, but luckily was sheltered and cared for by the Hoyt family in Danbury, Connecticut, a major American supply base to which his regiment had marched in September. His symptoms—described in detail—included mouth sores, periodic vomiting, and general weakness, and suggest a serious vitamin deficiency, made worse by his fairly heavy drinking. He had remained an invalid for almost six months. His father had traveled more than a hundred miles from Brookfield to visit him, probably afraid that his son was dying. The following September he was laid up again for more than a week, but then he had injured himself stumbling back to camp in the dark in the wake of an all-night drunk. At the end of the war, in June 1783, desperately worried over what he would do to survive after leaving the army, he told his father, "my [physical] constitution is so far spent, that I am not able to earn the one half per Month or day that I was before the war."[7]

At one time, Gilbert talked of settling in Vermont after the war, and later he hoped to buy land near Albany, New York, that was to be sold after having been confiscated from its American loyalist owners. But a clause in the peace treaty, signed in 1783, forbade any further confiscation of Tory property, and all Gilbert knew when he finally left the army was that he would never live in Brookfield again. In September 1782, Lieutenant Benjamin Gilbert received a letter from his hometown accusing him of fathering the child that Patience Converse was then carrying. His first response, a letter to Colonel James Converse, Patience's father and a close family friend, was apologetic, even admitting that "the misfortunes that have befel your Daughter and myself are Just punishments for our unwarrantable practises."[8] But very soon after he was backing away and denying his responsibility, and in a letter to his father he even accused a friend, Isaac Cutler, of being the true father. He later brushed off a demand from Colonel Converse to return immediately to Brookfield, apparently to marry Patience, on the grounds that he could not leave the army "without relinquishing every Idea of Honour (which I hold much dearer than life)."[9]

Finally in November 1783, after leaving the army for good, he settled his dispute with Patience Converse and her father. With a

Worcester County warrant out for his arrest, he called on Colonel Converse and agreed to pay £30 (roughly $150, but at least ten times that today), and in return he received a written "acquittal," or receipt. There the affair ended. He had spent his last year in the army drinking more than ever and becoming a regular customer at "Wyoma," a brothel near the army's main encampment at New Windsor, just north of West Point.

Gilbert had detoured on his journey back to Brookfield, stopping at Danbury to call on the Hoyts, the family that had cared for him during his long illness five years earlier. He was on his best behavior and stayed two months. Perhaps he was putting off as long as possible the unpleasant but inevitable interview with the irate Colonel Converse. He obviously enjoyed his first postwar autumn in western Connecticut, and he also resumed an acquaintance with the family of the Hoyts' neighbor, Captain John Cornwall, whose wife and mother had taken a hand in Gilbert's nursing years before, and with whose son Francis he had played checkers to pass the time. Probably because he had been too ill to misbehave, Gilbert had made a favorable impression on the Hoyts and the Cornwalls, and they welcomed his return. There Gilbert found a wife. Mary, the daughter of Captain John Cornwall, was only fourteen in 1778, but she was a young woman when Gilbert returned. At dinners, dances, and afternoon teas, Mary Cornwall and Benjamin Gilbert fell in love.

First, Benjamin had to go home and deal with the Converse problem. He did so by December. Then, in March 1784 he traveled, not south to Danbury, but westward from Brookfield, calling on his old comrades, Captain Daniel Shays, who two years later would lead the farmers' rebellion bearing his name, and Colonel Rufus Putnam, who spent a few days teaching Gilbert the rudiments of surveying. Leaving Putnam, he traveled to Albany and the Mohawk River, where he looked first for a job and then for a farm. South of the Mohawk, toward Otsego Lake, Gilbert found what he was looking for. In the Cherry Valley, best known for a terrible Indian raid during the Revolutionary War, Gilbert took a job teaching school and bought a farm. After establishing himself and saving a little money, he journeyed back to Brookfield to see his "Dada," then on to Danbury, where he and Mary Cornwall were married.[10]

Their first years were not easy. Farm work was very hard for both of them, their crops did not always do well, and livestock suffered from prowling bears and wolves, which, as Benjamin reported to her father, frightened Mary. Not only did both fathers help the young couple with money, tools, affection, and advice, but Benjamin acquired a valuable patron. William Cooper, the father of the novelist James Fenimore Cooper, was the founding father of

Otsego County and its seat at Cooperstown and the unofficial king of the whole region, which included Cherry Valley. In time, Benjamin became a political henchman of William Cooper and, through his patronage, a local official, county sheriff, and several terms a New York legislator, running as a Federalist in the hotly contested politics of western New York. While maintaining contact with his old friend, the rebel Daniel Shays, Gilbert climbed to the conservative side of the political fence. Mary bore eleven children, they attended the Baptist Church, and Benjamin became a pillar of the local Freemasons, which he had joined while in the army. When he died in 1828, the *Cherry-Valley Gazette* lamented the passing of a hero of the American Revolution.

Jacob Nagle's postwar life, compared to Gilbert's, was far more eventful and exciting. After being paid off for his wartime service at the British naval base of Plymouth in April 1783, Nagle did not seek the first ship "home" to Philadelphia, though there were many such ships there, as British merchants rushed to be the first back in the American market. Instead he elected to see the great city of London, and while his money lasted, he enjoyed the sights and pleasures offered by London to men of the seafaring class. A few months later, with his money gone, he rejoined the Royal Navy. Jacob Nagle had become, or was fast becoming, a professional sailor.

The sailor's life took him on the flagship of the legendary First Fleet to Australia in 1787, when the new colony was being settled. Later he served in the wars of the French Revolution and under the Mediterranean command of the greatest of all British naval heroes, Horatio Nelson, in 1796–97. During the Napoleonic Wars, Nagle would serve in the merchant marine.

Returning to England in 1795, he "took a liking to a daughter of Mr. Pitmuns," a boatwright whose three sons he had known previously, "a lively hansome girl in my eye, and maried hur."[11] They had children, how many is unknown, although he seldom saw his wife until he brought the family to Lisbon, where he was stationed, in 1802. A yellow fever epidemic swept Lisbon soon after, and within six weeks Nagle was, in his own words, "left alone."[12] Almost immediately he sold his goods in Lisbon and took ship as a cabin passenger to Norfolk, Virginia, and then to Philadelphia. Nothing except the sequence of his narrative connects the two events—the death of his wife and children and his journey home to the United States—but the emotional connection is obvious. Nowhere else in his memoir did he mention his wife and children. In Philadelphia he found that his parents had died, but that his three sisters and many cousins were still living. To see his uncle he traveled to Reading, his birthplace, and there he received a small legacy left to him by his Grandfather Nagle. In a four-month sojourn in rural

Pennsylvania and Maryland, he saw almost all of his family as well as many old friends, but what those meetings meant to him he leaves us to guess. In November he signed on a ship carrying American corn to Spain and Portugal.

Jacob Nagle had done everything sailors have done throughout time: been drunk, mugged, robbed, cheated, beaten up, imprisoned, press-ganged, flogged with a cat-o'-nine-tails, and almost killed by a cannonball. He had known whores and other easy young women, fought often with his fists and other handy weapons, deserted, and, in 1797 on a British warship cruising off Toulon in the Mediterranean, engaged in a mutiny for which the crew was luckily forgiven. He had escaped hanging and serious injury. Although there is no bragging in his memoir, he was clearly an exceptionally able seaman. Early in his seafaring career, his literacy, brains, and toughness won him promotion to boatswain, but he declined to serve. Later, he virtually commanded the HMS *Netley*, a sloop of war, serving as quartermaster to a capable but inexperienced commander. Nagle was officer material, but clearly he had no interest in holding power and exercising responsibility. He was a free spirit, and determined to remain that way. That he had never lost his national identity is also clear. When in 1808 he led fellow crewmen in demanding their pay from a stingy Scottish shipowner, the owner greeted Nagle with the words: "Well, Mr. American, how do you do?"[13]

A voyage under armed convoy to China in 1806 escaped the French privateers infesting the Indian Ocean, but not a Southeast Asian disease called "the white flux." Nagle escaped again when almost all his shipmates went down with the disease, but on his next voyage, to Nova Scotia, his luck ran out. Working in a ship's boat, when no one would volunteer to join him to free a dangerously fouled anchor cable in heavy, freezing seas off the coast of Cape Breton, he suffered a severe chill—"hypothermia" is the modern medical term—and he may never have fully recovered. He was forty-six, and even his powerful body and spirit were wearing out.

He made other voyages, especially to Latin America, but on one of them, in 1812, his health gave way, and he was left in a British hospital in Rio de Janeiro. Whether by design or not, it was a good time for an American to lie low while his two countries fought the War of 1812. After leaving the hospital, he worked a variety of shore-based jobs, tending bar, keeping books, and skippering a pleasure boat. An abortive attempt to leave Rio landed him, alone and sick, confused and unable to speak Portuguese, at the small Brazilian town of Porto Seguro, where for one of the few times in his memoir he tells us how he felt. He sat down on some logs and began

> to reflect, in my illness, though I had traveled a good many years through the four quarters of the globe, been a prisoner twice, cast a way three times, and the ship foundering under me, two days and a night in an open boat on the wide ocion without anything to eat or water to norish us, and numbers of times in want of water or victuals, at other times in action, and men slain a long side of me, and with all, at this minute it apeared to me that I was in greater distress and missery than I had ever been in any country during my life. I fell on my nees, and never did I pray with a sincerer hart than I did at that presentime.[14]

A kindly black woman, wife of the master of a local fishing boat, fed him and gave him shelter, and he appears to have taken up fishing thereafter. Although he soon made contact with the American consul up the coast at Bahia, he stayed in Brazil until 1821, when he signed on a ship sailing for Norfolk, Virginia. He crossed the Atlantic a few more times, but after another stay in the hospital, in New York in 1824, he took ship for Baltimore, and there unpacked his seabag for the last time, at the age of sixty-two.

The last sixteen years of his life were spent trekking between eastern Pennsylvania and Maryland, and northern Ohio, seeking shelter with whatever family member would take him for a while and finding work at whatever menial or clerical job would make him a little money. In an age when the hundreds of miles between Hagerstown, Maryland, or Philadelphia at one end and Canton or Perrysburg, Ohio, at the other are easily passed in a day's drive on high-speed highways, Nagle's forlorn walks on the rutted, dusty, or muddy roads across that corrugated landscape through heat, rain, sleet, and snow, across creeks with no bridges and toward a night's destination that was never sure at the start of each day, seem poignant beyond words. People along the way were often kind to him, as the black lady in Porto Seguro had been, but once, walking from the national capital to Baltimore, he observed of Jacksonian America: "I must say this of the country, they have no respet or humanity for a person in poverty."[15] An old man, worn out, lonely, and unwanted, but unbroken in spirit, he never quit and rarely complained even as he must have felt the end coming in his final port at Canton, Ohio. When he died seven months after the last entry in his memoir, in early 1841 at age seventy-nine, he left virtually nothing, except the memories of people who had known this remarkable old bird, and a unique and marvelous record of his life. Although he had served only a short time in the American Revolution and much longer in the Royal Navy, both the *Stark County Democrat* (Canton) and the *Advertiser and Journal* of Cincinnati noted his passing under the same headline: "ANOTHER REVO-

LUTIONARY SOLDIER GONE!" But if old Nagle was greeted by his Maker, perhaps the better words were those spoken by the Scottish shipowner to him in 1808: "Well, Mr. American, how do you do?"

Looking back at these two young lives amid war and revolution, we readily see the great role played by what appears to be chance: service in the army, on land, kept Benjamin Gilbert physically tied to the territorial United States, while service at sea turned young Jacob Nagle into a lifelong vagabond, rootless, wandering, far more at the mercy of chance than Gilbert ever was. But there was more than chance working in their lives: Gilbert, on the verge of making a mess of his personal life in the last few years of the war, pulled himself together, married well, stopped drinking heavily and trying to seduce every young woman he met, took advantage of the opportunities offered by peace and American independence, worked hard, raised a family, was elected to public office, and died in an aura of respectability. Nagle, by contrast, given chances to return to his family and the United States after the war, never showed much interest in doing so until the death of his wife and children in 1802; he was just as likely to sign on another ship going in the other direction.

As we try to probe these two lives more deeply, we notice an important difference in the role played by their families. Gilbert's letters to his father Daniel, back in Brookfield, are frequent, respectful, and affectionate. More than once, he asked his father for help with clothing, money, or other matters. In the Patience Converse scandal, his father stood by him, and Lieutenant Gilbert's reports of the war and the army, though not free of complaint, are crafted to get his father's approval. He does not talk to his father about women and drinking, and it is clear that he cares deeply about his father's opinion. Ultimately, he shaped his own life on that of his father—farmer, militia officer, elected official, respected member of his community. Benjamin's mother had died in childbirth, in 1772, and we know little of her, or of his two stepmothers, but he wrote from the army to his young sisters, extolling the virtue of chastity and warning them against men who would steal it from them. Obviously, family mattered to him.

Family also mattered to Jacob Nagle. He remembered being on a French schooner at Martinique in 1782 (aged twenty) "walking the deck till 2 or 3 in the morning, crying and fretting for the loss of my parents, never being so long from home before, when 14 or 16 shells would be flying in the air at one time."[16] He also remembered that in 1780, returning home from his first privateering voyage, his mother at first did not recognize him, and his father had been away, out trying to warn him about the press-gang looking for sailors. Later, his mother nursed him through a fever that she thought would be fatal. To his father's reputation there clung something unsavory; he was perhaps not the best of role models. By the end of the war and during the long years after, he had lost touch with his parents and does not mention missing them or wanting to see them (his father died in 1789, his mother in 1793) or his sisters. Only when he retired from seafaring penniless and in poor health did he seek out family, a sister, a cousin, a nephew—anyone who would take in an old, broken-down, slightly disreputable sailor. He never gave up, but from his memoir comes a sense that, unlike Gilbert, family had ceased to be a focal point for his life and that he was, perhaps as much by choice as by chance, something like a seagoing version of that great figure of later American folklore—the lonesome cowboy.

In Gilbert it is easy to see how, coming through war and out of revolution, he typified the thousands of Americans who seized opportunity, moved westward, and pursued happiness to become the middle-class backbone of American democracy. But in Jacob Nagle, we see something radically different yet equally American—the brave, battered survivor, the supreme individualist for whom life is an endless challenge, the whole world is "home," and "family" is the human race.

Notes

1. *The Nagle Journal: A Diary of the Life of Jacob Nagle, Sailor, From the Year 1775 to 1841*, ed. John C. Dann (New York, 1988), 10.

2. Ibid., 10.

3. The first section of Gilbert's diary, 1778–1782, has been published as *A Citizen-Soldier in the American Revolution: The Diary of Benjamin Gilbert in Massachusetts and New York*, ed. Rebecca D. Symmes (Cooperstown, NY, 1980), 29. Hereafter cited as *Gilbert Diary*.

4. Gilbert letter to Aaron Kimball, April 30, 1782, *Winding Down: The Revolutionary War Letters of Lieutenant Benjamin Gilbert of Massachusetts, 1780–1783*, ed. John Shy (Ann Arbor, MI, 1989), 56. Hereafter cited as *Gilbert Letters*.

5. *Cherry-Valley [New York] Gazette*, January 29, 1828.

6. Gilbert to Lieutenant Park Holland [August 1781], *Gilbert Letters*, 47.

7. Gilbert to his father [ca. June 6, 1783], ibid., 107.

8. Gilbert to Colonel Converse [September 30, 1782], ibid., 69.

9. Gilbert to Colonel Converse, March 24, 1783, ibid., 91. By that date, her pregnancy had passed its term. There is no mention in the record of actual childbirth.

10. He uses the affectionate term in a letter to Daniel Shays, September 26, 1785, *Gilbert Diary*, 77–78.
11. *Nagle Journal*, 186.
12. Ibid., 248.
13. Ibid., 278.
14. Ibid., 312–13.
15. Ibid., 333.
16. Ibid., 53.

Suggested Readings

Nothing is better than the published primary evidence for the lives of these two men. Gilbert's exists in two slim volumes. His diary from 1778 to early 1782, plus a few letters between 1785 and 1788, is available in *A Citizen-Soldier in the American Revolution: The Diary of Benjamin Gilbert in Massachusetts and New York*, edited by Rebecca D. Symmes (Cooperstown, NY, 1980). His letterbook for 1780–1783 is published in *Winding Down: The Revolutionary War Letters of Lieutenant Benjamin Gilbert of Massachusetts, 1780–1783*, edited by John Shy (Ann Arbor, MI, 1989). The second part of his diary, for 1782–1786, was discovered not many years ago and is now in the New York State Historical Association at Cooperstown, New York. It has never been published, but was used by permission in the publication of the letterbook. Some of Gilbert's political correspondence from 1793 to 1797 is in the Paul F. Cooper Jr. Archives, Hartwick College, Oneonta, New York, and was used by permission in writing this chapter. All we have for Jacob Nagle appears in one published volume, *The Nagle Journal: A Diary of the Life of Jacob Nagle, Sailor, From the Year 1775 to 1841*, edited by John C. Dann (New York, 1988). The editorial introductions and commentary as well as the illustrations in each of these three published volumes add a great deal to our understanding of Gilbert and Nagle.

For the Revolutionary War and the men who fought it, two very different books provide interesting background and comparisons: Charles Royster, *A Revolutionary People at War: The Continental Army and American Character, 1775–1783* (Chapel Hill, NC, 1979), and John C. Dann, ed., *The Revolution Remembered: Eyewitness Accounts of the War of Independence* (Chicago, 1980). Both Gilbert and Nagle applied for federal pensions long after the war, and the latter book offers a careful selection from the thousands of pension applications submitted by revolutionary veterans that are now in the National Archives.

Marcus B. Rediker, *Between the Devil and the Deep Blue Sea: Merchant Seamen, Pirates, and the Anglo-American Maritime World, 1700–1750* (New York, 1987), is a stimulating and much-discussed account of the sailor's world just before Nagle joined it. On the British navy when Nagle belonged to it, there is G. J. Marcus, *The Age of Nelson: The Royal Navy, 1793–1815* (New York, 1971); and on naval life, there is Dudley Pope, *Life in Nelson's Navy* (Annapolis, MD, 1981). Christopher Lloyd, *The British Seaman, 1200–1860: A Social Survey* (London, 1968), is a readable survey of the sailor's way of life. On privateering in the American Revolution, a valuable chapter by W. Minchinton and D. Starkey is found in *Ships, Seafaring and Society: Essays in Maritime History*, edited by Timothy J. Runyan (Detroit, 1987).

Robert A. Gross, *The Minutemen and Their World* (New York, 1976), is a highly readable, prize-winning account of the impact of the Revolutionary War on a New England town, Concord, Massachusetts, not unlike Gilbert's Brookfield, while a Pulitzer Prize-winning exploration of the upstate New York world in which Gilbert spent his postwar life is Alan Taylor, *William Cooper's Town: Power and Persuasion on the Frontier of the Early American Republic* (New York, 1995).

Index